THE REPUBLIC
OF PLATO

TO

F. C. C.

in gratitude for many hours
patiently given to the amendment of
this version
by one whose sense of good English
is a never-failing guide

THE REPUBLIC
OF PLATO

TRANSLATED WITH INTRODUCTION AND NOTES BY

FRANCIS MACDONALD CORNFORD
Litt.D., F.B.A.
Fellow of Trinity College, Cambridge

OXFORD UNIVERSITY PRESS
LONDON   OXFORD   NEW YORK

First published by Oxford University Press, London, 1941
First issued as an Oxford University Press paperback, 1945
printing, last digit: 80 79 78
Printed in the United States of America

PREFACE

THIS version aims at conveying to the English reader as much as possible of the thought of the *Republic* in the most convenient and least misleading form. I have, accordingly, taken certain liberties, which it is reasonable to suppose that Plato would have sanctioned in an edition prepared for the modern press. The traditional division into ten 'books,' i.e. papyrus rolls, has been discarded, as an accidental expedient of ancient book-production, having little more to do with the structure of the argument than the division of every Victorian novel into three volumes had to do with the structure of the stories. The dialogue falls naturally into six main parts, and these I have subdivided, where minor breaks occur, into forty chapters. The notes prefixed to the chapters are designed to hold the thread of the argument and to explain matters which Plato could take for granted as within the common knowledge of his readers. The sole purpose is to bring out what Plato meant, not to attack or defend his opinions. These are better left to the judgement of the reader. For sympathetic and more detailed interpretation, the best guide known to me is R. L. Nettleship's *Lectures on the Republic of Plato.* Professor Ernest Barker's *Greek Political Theory* (1918) reviews all Plato's works and the speculations of his predecessors in this field. In *Plato To-day* Mr. R. H. S. Crossman has made a lively and provocative experiment in confronting Plato with the political problems of the present day.

Some authors can be translated almost word for word. The reader may fairly claim to be told why this method cannot do justice to the matter and the manner of Plato's discourse. In brief, the answer is that in many places the effect in English is misleading, or tedious, or grotesque and silly, or pompous and verbose. Since no scholar would apply most of these epithets to the original, there must be something wrong with the current practice of translators.

Many key-words, such as 'music,' 'gymnastic,' 'virtue,' 'philosophy,' have shifted their meaning or acquired false associations for English ears. One who opened Jowett's version at random and lighted on the statement (at 549 B) that the best guardian for a man's 'virtue' is 'philosophy tempered with music,' might run away with the idea that, in order to avoid irregular relations with women, he had better play the violin in the intervals of studying metaphysics. There may be some truth in this; but only after reading widely in other parts of the book would he discover that it was not quite what Plato meant by describing *logos,* combined with *musiké,* as the only sure safeguard of *areté.*

The unfortunate effect of a too literal translation may be illustrated by some extracts from the Loeb edition:

'This then,' said I, 'if haply you now understand, is what you must say I then meant, by the statement that of all things that are such as to be of something those that are just themselves only are of things just themselves only, but things of a certain kind are of things of a certain kind' (438 D, vol. i, p. 393).

With the help of the context and some explanatory notes, the reader, it is true, will gather that the sense of this dark saying is as follows:

'This, then, if you understand me now, is what I meant by saying that, of two correlative terms, the one is qualified if, and only if, the other is so.'

But if he is more concerned to follow Plato's argument than to relish the simplicities of Greek idiom, he may prefer the paraphrase. Here is another passage:

'In heaven's name!' said I, 'suppose someone had questioned him thus: "Tell me, Simonides, the art that renders what that is due and befitting to what is called the art of medicine?" What do you take it would have been his answer?' 'Obviously,' he said, 'the art that renders to bodies drugs, foods, and drinks.' 'And the art that renders to what things what that is due and befitting is called the culinary art?' 'Seasoning to meats.' 'Good. In the same way tell me the art that renders what to whom would be denominated justice.' 'If we are to follow the previous examples, Socrates, it is that which renders benefits and harms to friends and enemies' (332 c, vol. i, p. 25).

Here, even if the double question—'renders what to what'—were reduced to normal English, the repetitions would still sound pedantic and clumsy; and the reader, as he toiled along, might well wonder why Plato has been upheld, in every age, as a master of elegant prose.[1]

It is a curious fact that in parts of the dialogue where the thought is most difficult—notably in chapter xxiv (the Line)—it is packed into the smallest number of words, so that some expansion is required. But in the main bulk of the work the style is (as the ancients said) 'copious'; and, since often a single Greek word can only be represented by two or three in English, the literal translator may easily find that the number of words he has used exceeds Plato's by 20 or 25 per cent. I have tried, by various means, to keep down this version to nearly the same length as the text. Only a few passages, chiefly in the earlier books, have been omitted altogether, for reasons given in the notes. Much more space has been saved by leaving out many of the formal expressions of assent interjected by Glaucon and Adeimantus, and thus allowing Socrates to advance one step in his argument in a single connected speech. This liberty has been taken sparingly in the first Part, where the company join in a genuine conversation; but, from the moment when the two brothers have opened their case against Justice in chapter v and Socrates begins his reply, the dialogue is in substance a continuous discourse, to which Glaucon and Adeimantus contribute very little. The convention of question and answer becomes formal and frequently tedious. Plato himself came near to abandoning it in his latest work, the Laws, where the Athenian lectures for pages together without interruption. I have not hesitated to spare the reader time and effort by omissions which the following passage (421 c, p. 112 of this version) may serve to illustrate:

'I wonder whether you will agree on another point closely connected with that and concerned with the craftsmen. Is it not true that they also are spoilt and turned into bad workmen by wealth and poverty alike?

[1] It is fair to add that I have constantly consulted the Loeb translation as a valuable clue to the construction of the Greek.

How so?

In this way. When a potter grows rich, will he go on with his trade? Does he not become idle and careless, and consequently a worse potter? And equally, if he is too poor to provide himself with tools and other things he needs for his craft, his work will be worse, and he will not make such good craftsmen of his sons and apprentices. So work and workmen suffer from both causes, poverty and riches as well.'

Here there are 117 words for 121 in the Greek. Davies and Vaughan require 155,[1] as follows:

I wonder whether you will think the proposition that is sister to the last satisfactory also.

What may that be? [2]

Consider whether the other craftsmen are similarly injured and spoiled by *these agencies.*

What agencies do you mean? [2]

Wealth, *I said,* and poverty.

How so?

Thus: Do you think that a potter after he has grown rich will care to attend to his trade any longer?

Certainly not.

But he will become *more* idle and careless *than he was before?* [3]

Yes, much more.

Then *does he not become* a worse potter?

Yes, a much worse potter too.

On the other hand, if he is prevented by poverty from providing himself with tools or any other requisite of his trade, he will produce inferior articles and his sons and apprentices will not be taught their trade so well.

Inevitably.

Then both these conditions, riches and poverty, deteriorate the productions of the artisans, and the artisans themselves.

If the reader finds this version easier to follow and feels himself defrauded by the omission of the words in italics, let him betake

---

[1] Jowett uses 150 words; Dr. Lindsay, 151; Shorey (Loeb edition), 157.

[2] It is a very frequent idiom in Greek dialogue, to ask a man what he is going to say before he has had time to say it. The effect is unnatural in English and sometimes ludicrous.

[3] Unlike the English here, the Greek does not suggest that the potter was idle and careless before he became rich.

himself to Davies and Vaughan.[4] Their scholarship was considerably more exact than Jowett's. Henry Jackson told me that once, when a passage from the *Republic* was set in the Fellowship Examination at Trinity College, Cambridge, he had marked the versions of Jowett and of Davies and Vaughan by the same standard as those of the candidates. The two former Fellows of Trinity came out at the top, the late Master of Balliol at the bottom. It must be remembered, however, that Jackson himself was a Fellow of Trinity.

In quality, Plato's style rises and sinks with his theme, ranging from the tone of ordinary conversation to an almost lyrical eloquence. I have tried to reflect these modulations, while keeping to a language with some claim to be normal English, not too obviously of any particular date, and such as a cultivated person may read without discomfort.

The translation has been made from Burnet's text. It seemed unnecessary to give reasons for departing, here and there, from his readings or punctuation.

The Introduction tells the story of Plato's life, so far as possible in his own words, down to the time when he wrote the *Republic*. Here, as elsewhere, I have held it to be the translator's business to let the author speak for himself and to put the reader in a position to exercise his own judgement according to the light that is in him.

F. M. C.

---

[4] Or, better, to Dr. Lindsay (Everyman's Library), who follows the text as closely and writes in a simpler style.

CONTENTS

xi

INTRODUCTION

PLATO, son of Ariston and Perictione, was born in 428/7 B.C. and died, at the age of eighty or eighty-one, in 348/7. Both parents came of distinguished families. His elder brothers, Glaucon and Adeimantus, appear as young men in the *Republic*. In his youth Plato became closely attached to Socrates, who by that time was wholly engaged in the mission to his fellow citizens described in the *Apology*.[1] Socrates was the one man in Athens who, in those distracting days of war and revolution, stood aloof from active life to inquire, with anyone who cared to talk with him, what men should live for. Under this influence Plato's thought, from first to last, was chiefly bent on the question how society could be reshaped so that man might realize the best that is in him. This is, above all, the theme of his central work, the *Republic*.

All Plato's childhood and youth were spent under the shadow of the Peloponnesian War. The death of Pericles in 429 had marked the close of the golden age (as it must have seemed in retrospect) of fully developed democracy under the personal guidance of a disinterested statesman. Born in the year of the revolution at Corcyra and the revolt of Mitylene, Plato, as a child of twelve, had seen the Athenian fleet set sail on the disastrous expedition against Syracuse, and he was twenty-three when Athens capitulated and lost her empire to Sparta. The steps by which this empire had grown out of a defensive league of maritime states, formed after the repulse of the Persian invader at Salamis (480), are traced in the first book of Thucydides. The rule of Periclean democracy over subjects who had once been allies had not been oppressive; but the Athenians themselves, as represented by their envoys at Sparta on the eve of the war, can find no better excuse than the plea that empire was forced upon them by the three most powerful motives, ambition, fear, and interest.

[1] See Sir R. Livingstone's *Portrait of Socrates* in this series and F. M. Cornford, *Before and after Socrates*, Cambridge, 1932.

'We are not the first who have aspired to rule; the world has ever held that the weaker must be kept down by the stronger. And we think that we are worthy of power; and there was a time when you thought so too; but now when you mean expediency you talk about justice. Did justice ever deter anyone from taking by force whatever he could? Men who indulge the natural ambition of empire deserve credit if they are in any degree more careful of justice than they need be. How moderate we arc would speedily appear if others took our place.' [1]

The same philosophy of imperialism is even more frankly expressed by the Athenian representatives in the dialogue with the Melians which Thucydides prefixed to his story of Athens' aggression against Syracuse. It is also the philosophy of Thrasymachus in the first Part of the *Republic*.

The Peloponnesian War was, to a greater extent than Thucydides seems to have realized, a struggle between the business interests of Athens and Corinth for commercial supremacy in the West: all wars, Plato remarked, are made for the sake of getting money. And, as at other times in the world's history, the same all-powerful motive was inflaming, within the several states, the ever-present conflict between oligarch and democrat or, in simpler terms, between rich and poor—the conflict which it was one of Plato's chief aims to extinguish.[2] Thucydides, in his famous reflections on the massacre of the oligarchs at Corcyra in 427, observes that 'in peace and prosperity both states and individuals are actuated by higher motives, because they do not fall under the dominion of imperious necessities; but war, which takes away the comfortable provision of daily life, is a hard master, and tends to assimilate men's characters to their conditions' (iii. 82, Jowett). He notes how the motives of party-strife, greed, and ambition were masked by specious names, 'the one party professing to uphold the constitutional equality of the many, the other the wisdom of an aristocracy, while they made the public interests, to which in name they were devoted, in reality their prize.' Both parties went

[1] Thucydides i. 76 (Jowett), written perhaps when Sparta had taken the place of Athens and set up a much worse tyranny over the subject cities.
[2] See chap. xxx.

to extremes of violence and treachery. At Athens the revolutions which occurred during the war were comparatively peaceful. Some of Plato's relations on his mother's side were active in the oligarchic reaction against the misconduct of the war by the democratic leaders. A letter written near the end of his long life recalls his state of mind when his friends were trying to enlist a recruit whose gifts of character and intellect were so remarkable.

'When I was young, I had the same experience that comes to so many: I thought that, as soon as I should be my own master, I should enter public life. This intention was favoured by certain circumstances in the political situation at Athens. The existing constitution was generally condemned, and a revolution took place.[1] . . . Some of the leaders were relatives and friends of mine, and they at once invited me to co-operate, as if this were the natural course for me to take. No wonder that, young as I was, I imagined they would bring the state under their management from an iniquitous to a right way of life. Accordingly I watched closely to see what they would do. It was not long before I saw these men make the former constitution seem like a paradise. In particular they tried to send Socrates, my friend, then advanced in years—a man whom I should not hesitate to call the most righteous man then living—with other persons, to arrest one of the citizens by violence for execution.[2] Their purpose, no doubt, was to implicate Socrates, with or without his will, in their proceedings. He refused, preferring to face any danger rather than be a party to their infamous deeds. Seeing all this and other things as bad, I was disgusted and drew back from the evils of the time.

'Not long afterwards the Thirty fell and the whole constitution was changed.[3] Once more I was attracted, though less eagerly, towards taking an active part in politics. In these unquiet times much was still going on that might move one to disgust, and it was no wonder that, during the revolutionary changes, some took savage vengeance upon

[1] The oligarchic revolution of 404 B.C. when Plato was 23, too young to hold office under Cleisthenes' law. A body known as the Thirty seized supreme power. Among the leaders were Plato's uncle Charmides and his cousin Critias.

[2] Plato's *Apology* 32 c gives a fuller account of this attempt to make Socrates an accomplice in the arrest of Leon of Salamis.

[3] The Thirty, after about a year and a half of power, were superseded by the exiled democrats in 403 B.C. A prominent man in the restored democracy was Anytus, the chief accuser of Socrates on the charge of 'not believing in the gods of Athens and demoralizing the young men. Socrates was executed in 399.

their enemies; but on the whole the returning exiles showed great moderation. Unfortunately, however, some of the men in power brought my friend Socrates to trial on an abominable charge, the very last that could be made against Socrates—the charge of impiety. He was condemned and put to death—he who had refused to share the infamy of arresting one of the accusers' own friends when they themselves were in exile and misfortune.

'When I considered these things and the men who were directing public affairs, and made a closer study, as I grew older, of law and custom, the harder it seemed to me to govern a state rightly. Without friends and trustworthy associates it was impossible to act; and these could not readily be found among my acquaintance, now that Athens was no longer ruled by the manners and institutions of our forefathers; and to make new associates was by no means easy. At the same time the whole fabric of law and custom was going from bad to worse at an alarming rate. The result was that I, who had at first been full of eagerness for a public career, when I saw all this happening and everything going to pieces, fell at last into bewilderment. I did not cease to think in what way this situation might be amended and in particular the whole organization of the state; but I was all the while waiting for the right opportunity for action.'

This passage reveals much of Plato's character. Neither he nor his friends had yet seen that his extraordinary gifts were not those of a man of action, who knows that, if he is to get anything done, he must put up with associates who are not to his liking, lay aside ideal aspirations, and stoop to opportunism and compromise. He is already dreaming of the perfect society, and capable of imagining that the 'Thirty Tyrants,' of all men, might effect a moral reformation. It is not surprising that an occasion which he would consider 'the right opportunity for action' never presented itself. He stood between two powerful forces, pulling opposite ways: the importunities of his political friends, appealing to his natural ambition, and the influence of Socrates, deepened by the recent impression of his trial and death. Among the promising young men pictured in the early dialogues as conversing with Socrates, one figure is missing, the most important of all, Plato himself. But perhaps his position may be illustrated from a dialogue in which Alcibiades, on the threshold of public life, is convinced that he will not be fit to advise his country until he has attained self-knowledge, or the knowledge of good and evil.[1] Socrates' moral discovery had opened a gulf at Plato's feet. His conception of the meaning and end of life was revolutionary and far-reaching in its implications. And he had died sooner than yield an inch to men who asked no more of him than that he should hold his tongue. If his companions had been disposed to treat some of his conversation as paradox and to discount his humour and irony, here was the indisputable proof that he meant what he said. The whole bearing of what he meant on the exigencies of practical life would need some thinking out. After his death, a few of his closest friends, including Plato, withdrew to Megara, resolved to defend his memory and to continue his work. Plato chose to do this by writing imaginary conversations, showing how very far Socrates had been from 'demoralizing the young men.' The scenes were laid in Plato's childhood, or in some cases before his birth. This method enabled him to formulate the essentials of Socrates' philosophy, without obtruding himself or departing from his master's practice of asking questions and criticizing the answers. The outward serenity of these pictures of a past generation completely masks the personal searchings of heart revealed in the letter above quoted. But the reflection whose results are distilled in this exquisite form may have been undertaken partly to clear Plato's own mind, before coming to a decision on the problem whether it was possible, without a degrading surrender, to serve Athens as an active statesman, even if the opportunity should come.

The calm surface is broken in the *Gorgias,* written probably just about the time of Plato's first visit to Sicily, when he was forty (388/7). Between the lines we can read here his final answer to the friends who had sought to draw him into politics. The rival claims of the contemplative and the active life are represented by the contrast between philosophy and rhetoric. Rhetoric is the art of the public speaker, the 'orator,' who in a democracy exercised his power by persuading the Assembly, a mass meeting of irresponsible individuals, to approve his measures. Also, under constant threat of

---

[1] Plato(?), *Alcibiades* I. Compare the allusion to Alcibiades on p. 202 below.

impeachment by his enemies, his political existence might depend on being able to defend himself in a court of law. Reduced to its simplest terms, rhetoric means the art of persuading a crowd that a certain course of action is the right one to take, or a certain person has the right on his side. But where is the assurance that the persuasive orator knows what is right, what ends are worth achieving by public policy, or what are the means to individual happiness? Philosophy, to Socrates and Plato, meant precisely the pursuit of that wisdom which can assess the true value of all the things we desire. So the discussion broadens into a survey of the whole field of public life. Gorgias' hot-headed pupil, Polus, claims that the orator wields the despot's power to do whatever he likes. Socrates replies that unlimited power without the knowledge of good and evil is at the best unenviable, and that the tyrant who uses it to exterminate his enemies and rivals is the most miserable of men—a theme to be further developed in the *Republic* (chap. xxxiii). It is better to suffer wrong than to do it; better to be chastised for wrong-doing than to escape punishment by the arts of the forensic orator.

Polus cannot challenge these paradoxes, because he has not renounced conventional morality. So at this point Callicles breaks in. He is not, so far as we know, an historical person; he is the man of the world, whose view of life is to be set in contrast with the philosopher's, represented by Socrates. The universal character of this confrontation is marked where Socrates begs Callicles to be serious:

'There is no question which a man of any sense could take more seriously than this which we are now discussing: what course of life one ought to follow—whether it is to be those manly activities, as you call them, in which you urge me to take part, speaking in the Assembly and engaging in public business like you and your friends, or this life of mine, spent in the pursuit of wisdom' (500 c).

Callicles opens his case with a vigorous profession of the faith which underlies the 'manly activities' of the politician. It is substantially the doctrine of Thrasymachus, a eulogy of 'injustice.' To get more than one's equal share of the world's advantages is the natural right of the strong man. It is conventionally called 'unjust'; but conventions are made by the multitude of the inferior, who praise equality, the watchword of democracy, because they cannot get the lion's share for themselves. Callicles appeals to the example of the lower animals and to the unmitigated selfishness which at all times governs international relations. In private life he believes himself to be a whole-hearted hedonist.

The discussion which follows is marked by a bitterness of tone rarely found elsewhere in the dialogues. The explanation may be sought in the conflict which had distracted Plato's own mind. The voice of his political friends is to be heard in the speech where Callicles contrasts the two lives of public activity and philosophic study. After asserting the strong man's right to burst the bonds of convention, he continues:

'That, then, is the truth, as you will find out if you will have done with philosophy and turn to things of more importance. Philosophy, you know, Socrates, is well enough if it is taken up with moderation at the proper age; but to spend too long a time over it spoils a man for life.[1] He may have quite good natural gifts, but if he goes on with such study too late in life, it must end in his missing all that experience which a man of good position ought to possess, if he is to make his mark. Such people know nothing about the institutions of their country, nothing of the language of ordinary social relations, public or private, nothing of the pleasures and ambitions of common humanity; in a word, they prove to be completely ignorant of the ways of the world. So, as soon as they make an appearance in any public transaction or business of their own, they become ridiculous, just as, I dare say, men of affairs cut a ludicrous figure in these arguments of yours. The fact is, as Euripides says, that

"a man shows best
Where he outshines himself; to climb that height
He'll spend in labour more than half his days."

He fights shy of the points where he shows at a disadvantage and gives them a bad name, while he cries up his strong points out of loyalty to himself, hoping in that way to be singing his own praises.

[1] Cf. Adeimantus' objection at *Rep.* 487 B (p. 194).

'But, no doubt, the best course is to have something of both. Just for purposes of education it is a good thing to take up philosophy; there is no disgrace in it for a young lad; but when a man who is getting on in years still sticks to it, the thing becomes ridiculous. I feel towards philosophers, Socrates, much as I do towards people who lisp and behave like children. When I see a child who is still young enough to talk in that way naturally, lisping at his play, I like it, as a charming trait of gentle breeding, which suits his age; whereas, when I hear a small child speaking distinctly, it offends my ear and seems to me only fit for a slave. But when you find a grown man lisping and behaving childishly, the effect is contemptible; you want to beat him for being so unmanly. Now that is how I feel towards philosophers. I like to see a young lad at such studies; they seem suitable and are evidence of good breeding; if he neglected them, I should set him down as a low-born fellow, who would never have the spirit to play an honourable part in the world. But when I see an older man unable to get away from his philosophising, then, Socrates, I begin to think that there is a man who needs a good beating. For, as I was saying, such a person, however gifted, is bound to lose his manly qualities, if he keeps away from the centres of public resort—the market-place, as the poet says, where famous men are made—and creeps away to spend the rest of his life whispering with three or four youngsters in a corner, and never makes his voice heard on any matter worthy of a free man's utterance.'

The choice between philosophy and a political career was not one that a younger man could possibly have put before the Socrates we know from the dialogues, at any time in the last twenty years of his life, when he was wholly occupied with his mission. It is noteworthy that no dramatic date can be fixed for the conversation in the *Gorgias,* and even the scene is left unspecified. This vagueness is intentional. When Plato wishes to make us feel as if we were living again at some fifth-century time and place, he does so; notably in the *Laches,* the *Protagoras,* or the *Symposium*. But in the *Gorgias* the impression is deliberately blurred by anachronisms,[1] with the result that transparent allusions to Socrates' trial and

---

[1] The death of Pericles (429 B.C.) is described as recent. Nicias is spoken of in terms which could not have been used after the Sicilian expedition (415-413). Yet Archelaus has become tyrant of Macedon (414/413), and Euripides' *Antiope* (about 408) is quoted.

death do not seem out of place. The problem is Plato's own. Callicles is the devil's advocate, standing for those men of the world who had tried to enlist him, and also for the impulse in Plato himself which had tempted him to yield. Even now the trouble was not laid to rest by his refusal. Some twenty years later (367), when he was invited to Sicily a second time, he was tormented by the fear of being taken for a mere dreamer, if he should decline the opportunity, however unpromising, of carrying his ideas into practice.[1] His conclusion, when he wrote the *Gorgias,* was that to enter politics without sacrificing the ideals he had learnt from Socrates would be to court Socrates' fate and to incur a useless martyrdom. This is indicated where Socrates, after claiming to be the one man in Athens who understands true statesmanship, adds that if he were called before a tribunal, he would have no more chance of acquittal than a doctor arraigned before a jury of children by a pastry-cook. In the letter already quoted (*Ep.* vii. 331 D), among some general reflections on the giving of political advice, Plato defines the prudent man's attitude towards his own country. He should express his disapproval, unless he thinks that no one will listen or it will cost him his life. He must not use revolutionary violence; if that is the only expedient, he should refrain from action and pray for the best both for himself and for his country. All these passages find an echo in the *Republic,* where the philosopher, in his enforced inaction, is compared to the traveller taking shelter under a wall from a driving storm of dust and hail, 'content if he can keep his hands clean from iniquity while this life lasts, and when the end comes take his departure, with good hopes, in serenity and peace' (496 D, p. 204).

Callicles quotes from Euripides' *Antiope* a passage where Zethus urges his twin brother Amphion, who had 'built the walls of Thebes with ravishing sounds of his melodious lute,' to abandon his art and take to the active life. It is significant that this contrast should occur in a play written towards the close of the war. In the sixth century the wise man had been a man of affairs, like Solon

[1] *Ep.* vii. 327-8.

the lawgiver and others of the Seven Sages. The death of Pericles at the beginning of the Peloponnesian War had marked the moment when the men of thought and the men of action began to take different paths, destined to diverge more and more widely until the Stoic sage renounced his local allegiance to become a citizen of the universe. Pericles had been the last philosophic statesman. His loftiness of spirit, as Socrates remarks in the *Phaedrus,* was due to his converse with Anaxagoras, whose speculations gave Pericles an insight and a breadth of view which he carried into his practical work as leader of the democratic Assembly. Under the stress of war, men of thought, like Thucydides and Euripides, went into exile, voluntary or enforced. Socrates just fulfilled his civic duties, but kept clear of politics. The task of winning the war was left to business men like Cleon, or ambitious egoists like Alcibiades. To Plato, this drifting apart of the men of thought and the men of action was a disastrous calamity, indeed the root of the social evils of his time. His problem, as presented in the *Gorgias,* was not to be solved merely by dropping out of public life to become absorbed in abstract speculation. Philosophy meant to him what it had meant to his master. The Socratic philosophy, analysed and formulated in the early dialogues, was not the study of nature or logic or metaphysics; it was the pursuit of wisdom, and to achieve wisdom would be to achieve human perfection, well-being, happiness. This again meant not merely 'caring for one's own soul' as an isolated individual, saving himself and leaving society to its fate. Human excellence, as Plato and Aristotle after him always maintained, is the excellence of an essentially social creature, a citizen. To produce this experience and consequent well-being is the true end of the 'Royal Art' of statesmanship. Hence the life of philosophy and the life of the active statesman ought not to be, as they appeared to Callicles, alternative careers, but a single life in which all the highest powers of man would find full expression. Society could be saved only by reuniting the two elements which had been drifting apart. This is the theoretical or perfect solution, which Plato says he had formulated before his first visit to Sicily. The long passage above quoted from the seventh Letter continues as follows:

'At last I perceived that the constitution of all existing states is bad and their institutions all but past remedy without a combination of radical measures and fortunate circumstance; and I was driven to affirm, in praise of true philosophy, that only from the standpoint of such philosophy was it possible to take a correct view of public and private right, and that accordingly the human race would never see the end of trouble until true lovers of wisdom should come to hold political power, or the holders of political power should, by some divine appointment, become true lovers of wisdom.

'It was in this mind that I first went to Sicily and Italy.'

So, towards his fortieth year, Plato arrived at the paradox which was to be explained and defended in the central part of the *Republic*. The bitter tone of the *Gorgias* suggests that he then saw no way of carrying this theoretical solution into practice. The path to power in democratic Athens was definitely closed. But the first visit to the court of Dionysius I at Syracuse opened up the prospect of intervening, directly or indirectly, in the affairs of a state under a different type of constitution, which might conceivably be reformed from above. If the multitude can hardly be won over to Socratic principles, the conversion of a despot, in full control of a city-state, might lead to a reformation remotely comparable to Calvin's theocracy at Geneva. Socrates alludes to this prospect where he says (*Rep.* 502 A, p. 210):

'No one will dispute that kings and hereditary rulers might have sons with a philosophic nature, and these might conceivably escape corruption. . . . One would be enough to effect all this reform that now seems so incredible, if he had subjects disposed to obey; for it is surely not impossible that they should consent to carry out our laws and customs when laid down by a ruler.'

Dionysius I was a self-made and entirely unscrupulous despot, who, after coming to terms with the Carthaginian invaders of Sicily, had established his personal rule at Syracuse, enslaved or devastated the neighbouring Greek cities, and was now trying to add lower Italy to his dominions. His career has probably contributed several traits to the portrait of the despot in chapter xxxii. In the seventh Letter Plato says nothing of his intercourse with

Dionysius, but only of the friendship he formed with the despot's brother-in-law, Dion, whom he came to regard with passionate attachment as an ideal disciple.

'I became acquainted with Dion,. then a young man, and without knowing it began to work for the future overthrow of a despotism, by telling him what I thought was best for mankind and advising him to act upon it. Dion, with his ready understanding, was quick to grasp the arguments I put before him. He listened with keener attention than any young man I have ever met with; and he determined to live for the future a different life from that of the Greeks in Italy and Sicily, preferring virtue to pleasure and luxury. So he continued until the death of Dionysius (twenty years later, 368 B.C.), earning thereby the dislike of those who led the usual life of a despot's court' (*Ep.* vii. 327 A).

Plato tells us no more of what happened on this first visit. Plutarch, in his Life of Dion, repeats anecdotes of doubtful authenticity. Dion is said to have persuaded Dionysius to hear Plato discourse on the theme that despots least of all men possess the qualities of true manhood and that the life of justice is alone happy. It is certain, at any rate, that Plato's friends soon found it necessary to arrange for his departure. It may be true that, on the prompting of Dionysius, Pollis, a Spartan emissary who sailed on the same ship, landed Plato on Aegina, which was then at war with Athens; that he was sold as a slave and redeemed by Anniceris of Cyrene; and that the purchase-money, refunded by Plato's friends, was used to buy the land on which the Academy was founded.

The Academy was, for the remaining half of his long life, the centre of Plato's interest and his means of indirectly influencing the course of politics. It was primarily a school of philosophic statesmen, which was to attract from foreign states young men whose position and prospects were more fortunate than those of Plato's own youth, and to train them for the exercise of the Royal Art. Some of its features were modelled on the Pythagorean communities, which had been dispersed in the second half of the previous century, but had found a rallying-point at Tarentum. This city presided over a confederacy of Greek colonies in South Italy, and was itself under the personal ascendancy of the Pythagorean Archytas, who, being also a notable mathematician, was a successful example of the philosophic ruler in a moderate democracy. The *Republic* (600 A, p. 330) mentions Pythagoras as having surrounded himself with a band of intimate disciples, who loved him for the inspiration of his society and handed down a 'way of life' distinguishing them from the rest of the world. If Plato could never hope to rule Athens, he could aspire, as president of the first university, to animate with his ideals the future rulers of other states. At the same time he would continue to write Socratic dialogues, setting forth his own development of the Socratic philosophy in a form which would reach the educated public throughout the Greek world and attract pupils to the Academy.

The School owed its name to the grove of a hero Academus (or Hecademus) in the garden where it was built. The legal ownership was probably vested in the School as a corporate cult-society, presided over by the Muses and their leader Apollo, who had their altar and regular offerings. The students must have contributed to the cost of maintenance. A wider circle was admitted to Plato's lectures; but in the actual teaching the conversational method of Socrates was, so far as possible, perpetuated. Some already accredited teachers, like Eudoxus of Cnidos, joined the society. Aristotle came at the age of seventeen and remained till Plato's death twenty years later.

Among the chief dialogues which may, with some probability, be assigned to the two decades following the foundation of the Academy are the *Meno, Phaedo, Symposium, Republic, Phaedrus*. These works reveal clearly, for the first time, the characteristically Platonic philosophy, whose twin pillars are the belief in a world of intelligible Forms or 'Ideas' existing independently of the things we see and touch, and the belief in an immortal soul existing in separation from the body, both before birth and after death. It is the philosophy of a spirit which turns away from this mortal region to set its hopes on things beyond the reach of time and change. Within the *Republic* itself, the more completely Plato discloses all that is meant by the pursuit of wisdom, the farther recedes the prospect that the evils of human life will ever be cured by the enthronement of reason in any possible form of society. There is no facile optimism in the programme here laid down for the philosophic statesmen to be trained at the Academy, no compromise between existing conditions and those enduring and unquestionable principles on which reform must be based, if reform is to produce a stable and harmonious order. And when the outline of the perfect society has been traced, the doubt is confessed, whether the perfection of any human institutions can withstand the disintegrating touch of time. The Muses themselves pronounce the doom of the ideal state before it has even seen the light: 'Hard as it may be for a state so framed to be shaken, yet, since all that comes into being must decay, even a fabric like this will not endure for ever, but will suffer dissolution' (546 A, p. 269).

These words preface an account of the decline of society and of the individual soul, as if it were written in man's fate that every attempt to scale the heavens should be followed by a descent into hell. The lowest depth to which the state can fall is despotism; and in the soul of the despotic man, whom the Greeks called 'tyrant,' the three most powerful motives, ambition, fear, and greed, have finally triumphed over reason and humanity. The startling resemblance between the portrait of this character in chapter xxxii and some of the present rulers of mankind warns us that Thrasymachus' doctrine, professing as it does to lay bare the real truth about human nature in politics, is still very much alive.

Socrates' arguments with Thrasymachus in the first Part may strike the reader as scholastic and abstract in form and too remote from our modern habits of thought. They are, no doubt, of a kind that Socrates would use in dealing with the professionally clever disputants known as Sophists. His two young friends refuse to accept them as conclusive. At the beginning of Part II they reopen Thrasymachus' case with an earnestness which calls for a more profound analysis and defence of justice. The reply fills the remainder of the *Republic*. It rests ultimately on the conviction that materialistic egoism misconceives that good 'which every soul pursues as the end of all her actions, dimly divining its existence, but perplexed and unable to grasp its nature with the same clearness and assurance as in dealing with other things, and so missing whatever value those other things might have' (505 E, p. 216). To possess this good would be happiness; to know it would be wisdom; to seek the knowledge of it is what Plato means by philosophy. If it is true that this knowledge can be gained only by highly gifted natures after a long course of intellectual discipline and practical experience, then it is hard to deny the central paradox of the *Republic,* that the human race will never see the end of troubles until political power is entrusted to the lover of wisdom; who has learnt what makes life worth living and who will 'despise all existing honours as mean and worthless, caring only for the right and the honours to be gained from that, and above all for justice as the one indispensable thing in whose service and maintenance he will reorganize his own state' (540 D, p. 262).

In such terms the author of the earliest Utopia in European literature confronts the modern reader with the ultimate problem of politics: How can the state be so ordered as to place effective control in the hands of men who understand that you cannot make either an individual or a society happy by making them richer or more powerful than their neighbours? So long as knowledge is valued as the means to power, and power as the means to wealth, the helm of the ship will be grasped by the ambitious man, whose Bible is Machiavelli's *Prince,* or by the man of business, whose Bible is his profit and loss account. It is Plato's merit to have seen that this problem looms up, in every age, behind all the superficial arguments of political expediency. Every reader will find something to disagree with in Plato's solution, even when transposed into terms appropriate to modern conditions; but if he will seriously ask himself why he disagrees and what alternative he can propose, the effort will help him to clear his own mind. Plato's purpose will then be achieved, at least in part; for he never forgot the lesson of Socrates, that wisdom begins when a man finds out that he does not know what he thinks he knows.

PART I (Book I)

SOME CURRENT VIEWS OF JUSTICE

THE main question to be answered in the *Republic* is: What does Justice mean, and how can it be realized in human society? The Greek word for 'just' has as many senses as the English 'right.' It can mean: observant of custom or of duty, righteous; fair, honest; legally right, lawful; what is due to or from a person, deserts, rights; what one ought to do. Thus it covers the whole field of the individual's conduct in so far as it affects others—all that they have a 'right' to expect from him or he has a right to expect from them, whatever is right as opposed to wrong. A proverbial saying declared that justice is the sum of all virtue.

The demand for a definition of Justice seems to imply that there is some conception in which all these applications of the word meet like lines converging to a common centre; or, in more concrete terms, that there is some principle whereby human life might be so organized that there would exist a just society composed of just men. The justice of the society would secure that each member of it should perform his duties and enjoy his rights. As a quality residing in each individual, justice would mean that his personal life—or as a Greek would say, his soul—was correspondingly ordered with respect to the rights and duties of each part of his nature.

A society so composed and organized would be ideal, in the sense that it would offer a standard of perfection by which all existing societies might be measured and appraised according to the degrees in which they fell short of it. Any proposed reform, moreover, might be judged by its tendency to bring us nearer to, or farther from, this goal. The *Republic* is the first systematic attempt ever made to describe this ideal, not as a baseless dream, but as a possible framework within which man's nature, with its unalterable claims, might find well-being and happiness. Without some such goal in view, statecraft must be either blind and aimless or directed (as it commonly is) to false and worthless ends.

If a man of sceptical and inquiring mind were to ask, in any mixed company of intelligent people, for a definition of 'right' or 'justice,' the answers produced would be likely to be superficial and to cover only some part of the field. They might also reveal fundamental differences of conviction about what Socrates calls the most important of all questions: how we ought to live. In the first Part of the *Republic* Socrates opens up the whole range of inquiry by eliciting some typical views of the nature of justice and criticizing them as either inadequate or false. The criticism naturally reveals some glimpses of the principles which will guide the construction that is to follow.

CHAPTER I (I. 327–331 D)

CEPHALUS: JUSTICE AS HONESTY IN WORD AND DEED

The whole imaginary conversation is narrated by Socrates to an unspecified audience. The company who will take part in it assemble at the house of Cephalus, a retired manufacturer living at the Piraeus, the harbour town about five miles from Athens. It includes, besides Plato's elder brothers, Glaucon and Adeimantus, Cephalus' sons, Polemarchus, Lysias, well known as a writer of speeches, and Euthydemus; Thrasymachus of Chàlcedon, a noted teacher of rhetoric, who may have formulated the definition of justice as 'the interest of the stronger,' though hardly any evidence about his opinions exists outside the Republic; *and a number of Socrates' young friends. The occasion is the festival of Bendis, a goddess whose cult had been imported from Thrace. Cephalus embodies the wisdom of a long life honourably spent in business. He is well-to-do, but values money as a means to that peace of mind which comes of honesty and the ability to render to gods and men their due. This is what he understands by 'right' conduct or justice.*

SOCRATES. I walked down to the Piraeus yesterday with Glaucon, the son of Ariston, to make my prayers to the goddess. As this was the first celebration of her festival, I wished also to see how the ceremony would be conducted. The Thracians, I thought, made as

fine a show in the procession as our own people, though they did
well enough. The prayers and the spectacle were over, and we were
leaving to go back to the city, when from some way off Polemarchus, the son of Cephalus, caught sight of us starting homewards
and sent his slave running to ask us to wait for him. The boy
caught my garment from behind and gave me the message.

I turned round and asked where his master was.

There, he answered; coming up behind. Please wait.

Very well, said Glaucon; we will.

A minute later Polemarchus joined us, with Glaucon's brother,
Adeimantus, and Niceratus, the son of Nicias, and some others
who must have been at the procession.

Socrates, said Polemarchus, I do believe you are starting back to
town and leaving us.

You have guessed right, I answered.

Well, he said, you see what a large party we are?

I do.

Unless you are more than a match for us, then, you must stay
here.

Isn't there another alternative? said I; we might convince you
that you must let us go.

How will you convince us, if we refuse to listen?

We cannot, said Glaucon.

Well, we shall refuse; make up your minds to that.

Here Adeimantus interposed: Don't you even know that in the
evening there is going to be a torch-race on horseback in honour of
the goddess?

On horseback! I exclaimed; that is something new. How will
they do it? Are the riders going to race with torches and hand
them on to one another?

Just so, said Polemarchus. Besides, there will be a festival lasting
all night, which will be worth seeing. We will go out after dinner
and look on. We shall find plenty of young men there and we can
have a talk. So please stay, and don't disappoint us.

It looks as if we had better stay, said Glaucon.

Well, said I, if you think so, we will.

Accordingly, we went home with Polemarchus; and there we

found his brothers, Lysias and Euthydemus, as well as Thrasymachus of Chalcedon, Charmantides of Paeania, and Cleitophon, the
son of Aristonymus. Polemarchus' father, Cephalus, was at home
too. I had not seen him for some time, and it struck me that he
had aged a good deal. He was sitting in a cushioned chair, wearing
a garland, as he had just been conducting a sacrifice in the court-
yard. There were some chairs standing round, and we sat down beside him.

As soon as he saw me, Cephalus greeted me. You don't often
come down to the Piraeus to visit us, Socrates, he said. But you
ought to. If I still had the strength to walk to town easily, you
would not have to come here; we would come to you. But, as
things are, you really ought to come here oftener. I find, I can assure you, that in proportion as bodily pleasures lose their savour,
my appetite for the things of the mind grows keener and I enjoy
discussing them more than ever. So you must not disappoint me.
Treat us like old friends, and come here often to have a talk with
these young men.

To tell the truth, Cephalus, I answered, I enjoy talking with very
old people. They have gone before us on a road by which we too
may have to travel, and I think we do well to learn from them
what it is like, easy or difficult, rough or smooth. And now that
you have reached an age when your foot, as the poets say, is on the
threshold, I should like to hear what report you can give and
whether you find it a painful time of life.

I will tell you by all means what it seems like to me, Socrates.
Some of us old men often meet, true to the old saying that people
of the same age like to be together. Most of our company are very
sorry for themselves, looking back with regret to the pleasures of
their young days, all the delights connected with love affairs and
merry-making. They are vexed at being deprived of what seems
to them so important; life was good in those days, they think, and
now they have no life at all. Some complain that their families
have no respect for their years, and make that a reason for harping
on all the miseries old age has brought. But to my mind, Socrates,
they are laying the blame on the wrong shoulders. If the fault
were in old age, so far as that goes, I and all who have ever reached

my time of life would have the same experience; but in point of fact, I have met many who felt quite differently. For instance, I remember someone asking Sophocles, the poet, whether he was still capable of enjoying a woman. 'Don't talk in that way,' he answered; 'I am only too glad to be free of all that; it is like escaping from bondage to a raging madman.' I thought that a good answer at the time, and I still think so; for certainly a great peace comes when age sets us free from passions of that sort. When they weaken and relax their hold, most certainly it means, as Sophocles said, a release from servitude to many forms of madness. All these troubles, Socrates, including the complaints about not being respected, have only one cause; and that is not old age, but a man's character. If you have a contented mind at peace with itself, age is no intolerable burden; without that, Socrates, age and youth will be equally painful.

I was charmed with these words and wanted him to go on talking; so I tried to draw him out. I fancy, Cephalus, said I, most people will not accept that account; they imagine that it is not character that makes your burden light, but your wealth. The rich, they say, have many consolations.

That is true, he replied; they do not believe me; and there is something in their suggestion, though not so much as they suppose. When a man from Seriphus [1] taunted Themistocles and told him that his fame was due not to himself but to his country, Themistocles made a good retort: 'Certainly, if I had been born a Seriphian, I should not be famous; but no more would you, if you had been born at Athens.' And so one might say to men who are not rich and feel old age burdensome: If it is true that a good man will not find it easy to bear old age and poverty combined, no more will riches ever make a bad man contented and cheerful.

And was your wealth, Cephalus, mostly inherited or have you made your own fortune?

Made my fortune, Socrates? As a man of business I stand somewhere between my grandfather and my father. My grandfather, who was my namesake, inherited about as much property as I have

[1] An insignificant island, among the Cyclades.

now and more than doubled it; whereas my father Lysanias reduced it below its present level. I shall be content if I can leave
these sons of mine not less than I inherited, and perhaps a little
more.

I asked, said I, because you strike me as not caring overmuch
about money; and that is generally so with men who have not
made their own fortune. Those who have are twice as fond of
their possessions as other people. They have the same affection for
the money they have earned that poets have for their poems, or
fathers for their children: they not merely find it useful, as we
all do, but it means much to them as being of their own creation.
That makes them disagreeable company; they have not a good
word for anything but riches.

That is quite true.

It is indeed, I said; but one more question: what do you take
to be the greatest advantage you have got from being wealthy?

One that perhaps not many people would take my word for. I
can tell you, Socrates, that, when the prospect of dying is near at
hand, a man begins to feel some alarm about things that never
troubled him before. He may have laughed at those stories they
tell of another world and of punishments there for wrongdoing
in this life; but now the soul is tormented by a doubt whether
they may not be true. Maybe from the weakness of old age, or perhaps because, now that he is nearer to what lies beyond, he begins
to get some glimpse of it himself—at any rate he is beset with
fear and misgiving; he begins thinking over the past: is there
anyone he has wronged? If he finds that his life has been full of
wrongdoing, he starts up from his sleep in terror like a child, and
his life is haunted by dark forebodings; whereas, if his conscience
is clear, that 'sweet Hope' that Pindar speaks of is always with
him to tend his age. Indeed, Socrates, there is great charm in those
lines describing the man who has led a life of righteousness:

> Hope is his sweet companion, she who guides
> Man's wandering purpose, warms his heart
> And nurses tenderly his age.

That is admirably expressed, admirably. Now in this, as I believe, lies the chief value of wealth, not for everyone, perhaps, but for the right-thinking man. It can do much to save us from going to that other world in fear of having cheated or deceived anyone even unintentionally or of being in debt to some god for sacrifice or to some man for money. Wealth has many other uses, of course; but, taking one with another, I should regard this as the best use that can be made of it by a man of sense.

You put your case admirably, Cephalus, said I. But take this matter of doing right: can we say that it really consists in nothing more nor less than telling the truth and paying back anything we may have received? Are not these very actions sometimes right and sometimes wrong? Suppose, for example, a friend who had lent us a weapon were to go mad and then ask for it back, surely anyone would say we ought not to return it. It would not be 'right' to do so; nor yet to tell the truth without reserve to a madman.

No, it would not.

Right conduct, then, cannot be defined as telling the truth and restoring anything we have been trusted with.

Yes, it can, Polemarchus broke in, at least if we are to believe Simonides.

Well, well, said Cephalus, I will bequeath the argument to you. It is time for me to attend to the sacrifice.

Your part, then, said Polemarchus, will fall to me as your heir.

By all means, said Cephalus with a smile; and with that he left us, to see to the sacrifice.

CHAPTER II (I. 331 E–336 A)

POLEMARCHUS: JUSTICE AS HELPING FRIENDS AND HARMING ENEMIES

Criticism now begins. No doubt it is generally right or just to tell the truth and pay one's debts; but no list of external actions such as these can tell us what is meant by justice, the name of the quality they have in common. Also what is superficially the same action, e.g. repayment of a loan, may completely change its character when we take into account the antecedents and consequences which form its wider context.

Polemarchus can only meet this objection by citing a maxim borrowed from a famous poet. In Greece, where there was no sacred book like the Bible, the poets were regarded as inspired authorities on religion and morals; but Socrates, when he questioned them, found them unable to give any rational account of their teaching (Apology, 22 B). Polemarchus, too, has never thought out the implications of defining justice as 'giving every man his due.' What is it that is due, and to whom?

Socrates' first object is to bring home to Polemarchus the vagueness of his ideas by leading him on to an absurd conclusion. In approaching a very large and obscure question, the first step is to convince one who thinks he can answer it with a compact formula that he knows much less than he imagines and cannot even understand his own formula.

Plato often, as here, compares the practice of morality to the useful (not the fine) arts or crafts: medicine, navigation, shoemaking. He even speaks of an 'art of justice.' He adopted Socrates' belief that there should be an art of living, analogous to the craftsman's knowledge and consequent ability to achieve a purposed end. A builder, building a house, knows what he is setting out to do and how to do it; he can account for all his actions as contributing to his end. This knowledge and ability constitute the craft embodied in the builder and his special excellence or 'virtue' (areté), qua builder. Similarly a man can live well only if he knows clearly what is the end of life, what things are of real value, and how they are to be attained. This knowledge is the moral virtue of man, qua man, and constitutes the art of living. If a man imagines that the end of life is to gain wealth or power, which are valueless in themselves, all his actions will be misdirected. This doctrine is fundamental in the Republic. It leads to the central thesis that society must be ruled by men who have learnt, by long and severe train-

Harm = no 'justice' ?

*ing, not only the true end of human life, but the meaning of good-
ness in all its forms.*

THEN, said I, if you are to inherit this discussion, tell me, what is
this saying of Simonides about right conduct which you approve?

That it is just to render every man his due. That seems to me a
fair statement.

It is certainly hard to question the inspired wisdom of a poet
like Simonides; but what this saying means you may know, Polemarchus, but I do not. Obviously it does not mean what we were
speaking of just now—returning something we have been entrusted
with to the owner even when he has gone out of his mind. And yet
surely it is his due, if he asks for it back?

Yes.

But it is out of the question to give it back when he has gone
mad?

True.

Simonides, then, must have meant something different from that
when he said it was just to render a man his due.

Certainly he did; his idea was that, as between friends, what one
owes to another is to do him good, not harm.

I see, said I; to repay money entrusted to one is not to render
what is due, if the two parties are friends and the repayment proves
harmful to the lender. That is what you say Simonides meant?

Yes, certainly.

And what about enemies? Are we to render whatever is their
due to them?

Yes certainly, what really is due to them; which means, I suppose, what is appropriate to an enemy—some sort of injury.

It seems, then, that Simonides was using words with a hidden
meaning, as poets will. He really meant to define justice as rendering to everyone what is appropriate to him; only he called that his
'due.'

Well, why not?

But look here, said I. Suppose we could question Simonides about
the art of medicine—whether a physician can be described as ren-

dering to some object what is due or appropriate to it; how do
you think he would answer?

That the physician administers the appropriate diet or remedies
to the body.

And the art of cookery—can that be described in the same way?

Yes; the cook gives the appropriate seasoning to his dishes.

Good. And the practice of justice?

If we are to follow those analogies, Socrates, justice would be
rendering services or injuries to friends or enemies.

So Simonides means by justice doing good to friends and harm
to enemies?

I think so.

And in matters of health who would be the most competent to
treat friends and enemies in that way?

A physician.

And on a voyage, as regards the dangers of the sea?

A ship's captain.

In what sphere of action, then, will the just man be the most
competent to do good or harm?

In war, I should imagine; when he is fighting on the side of
his friends and against his enemies.

I see. But when we are well and staying on shore, the doctor
and the ship's captain are of no use to us.

True.

Is it also true that the just man is useless when we are not at
war?

I should not say that.

So justice has its uses in peace-time too?

Yes.

Like farming, which is useful for producing crops, or shoemaking, which is useful for providing us with shoes. Can you tell me
for what purposes justice is useful or profitable in time of peace?

For matters of business, Socrates.

In a partnership, you mean?

Yes.

But if we are playing draughts, or laying bricks, or making

music, will the just man be as good and helpful a partner as an expert draught-player, or a builder, or a musician?

No.

Then in what kind of partnership will he be more helpful?

Where money is involved, I suppose.

Except, perhaps, Polemarchus, when we are putting our money to some use. If we are buying or selling a horse, a judge of horses would be a better partner; or if we are dealing in ships, a ship-wright or a sea-captain.

I suppose so.

Well, when will the just man be specially useful in handling our money?

When we want to deposit it for safe-keeping.

When the money is to lie idle, in fact?

Yes.

So justice begins to be useful only when our money is out of use?

Perhaps so.

And in the same way, I suppose, if a pruning-knife is to be used, or a shield, or a lyre, then a vine-dresser, or a soldier, or a musician will be of service; but justice is helpful only when these things are to be kept safe. In fact justice is never of any use in using things; it becomes useful when they are useless.

That seems to follow.

If that is so, my friend, justice can hardly be a thing of much value. And here is another point. In boxing or fighting of any sort skill in dealing blows goes with skill in keeping them off; and the same doctor that can keep us from disease would also be clever at producing it by stealth; or again, a general will be good at keeping his army safe, if he can also cheat the enemy and steal his plans and dispositions. So a man who is expert in keeping things will always make an expert thief.

Apparently.

The just man, then, being good at keeping money safe, will also be good at stealing it.

That seems to be the conclusion, at any rate.

So the just man turns out to be a kind of thief. You must have learnt that from Homer, who showed his predilection for Odysseus' grandfather Autolycus by remarking that he surpassed all men in cheating and perjury. Justice, according to you and Homer and Simonides, turns out to be a form of skill in cheating, provided it be to help a friend or harm an enemy. That was what you meant?

Good God, no, he protested; but I have forgotten now what I did mean. All the same, I do still believe that justice consists in helping one's friends and harming one's enemies.

[*The argument now becomes more serious. Polemarchus, though puzzled, clings to the belief that it must be right to help friends and harm enemies. This was a traditional maxim of Greek morality, never doubted till Socrates denied it: no one had ever said that we ought to do good, or even refrain from doing harm, to them that hate us. Socrates' denial rests on his principle, later adopted by the Stoics, that the only thing that is good in itself is the goodness, virtue, well-being of the human soul. The only way really to injure a man is to make him a worse man. This cannot be the function of justice.*]

Which do you mean by a man's friends and enemies—those whom he believes to be good honest people and the reverse, or those who really are, though they may not seem so?

Naturally, his loves and hates depend on what he believes.

But don't people often mistake an honest man for a rogue, or a rogue for an honest man; in which case they regard good people as enemies and bad people as friends?

No doubt.

But all the same, it will then be right for them to help the rogue and to injure the good man?

Apparently.

And yet a good man is one who is not given to doing wrong.

True.

According to your account, then, it is right to ill-treat a man who does no wrong.

No, no, Socrates; that can't be sound doctrine.

It must be the wrongdoers, then, that it is right to injure, and the honest that are to be helped.

That sounds better.

Then, Polemarchus, the conclusion will be that for a bad judge of character it will often be right to injure his friends, when they really are rogues, and to help his enemies, when they really are honest men—the exact opposite of what we took Simonides to mean.

That certainly does follow, he said. We must shift our ground. Perhaps our definition of friend and enemy was wrong.

What definition, Polemarchus?

We said a friend was one whom we believe to be an honest man.

And how are we to define him now?

As one who really is honest as well as seeming so. If he merely seems so, he will be only a seeming friend. And the same will apply to enemies.

On this showing, then, it is the good people that will be our friends, the wicked our enemies.

Yes.

You would have us, in fact, add something to our original definition of justice: it will not mean merely doing good to friends and harm to enemies, but doing good to friends who are good, and harm to enemies who are wicked.

Yes, I think that is all right.

Can it really be a just man's business to harm any human being?

Certainly; it is right for him to harm bad men who are his enemies.

But does not harming a horse or a dog mean making it a worse horse or dog, so that each will be a less perfect creature in its own special way?

Yes.

Isn't that also true of human beings—that to harm them means making them worse men by the standard of human excellence?

Yes.

And is not justice a peculiarly human excellence?

Undoubtedly.

To harm a man, then, must mean making him less just.

I suppose so.

But a musician or a riding-master cannot be exercising his special skill, if he makes his pupils unmusical or bad riders.

No.

Whereas the just man is to exercise his justice by making men unjust? Or, in more general terms, the good are to make men bad by exercising their virtue? Can that be so?

No, it cannot.

It can no more be the function of goodness to do harm than of heat to cool or of drought to produce moisture. So if the just man is good, the business of harming people, whether friends or not, must belong to his opposite, the unjust.

I think that is perfectly true, Socrates.

So it was not a wise saying that justice is giving every man his due, if that means that harm is due from the just man to his enemies, as well as help to his friends. That is not true; because we have found that it is never right to harm anyone.

I agree.

Then you and I will make common cause against anyone who attributes that doctrine to Simonides or to any of the old canonical sages, like Bias or Pittacus.

Yes, he said, I am prepared to support you.

Do you know, I think that account of justice, as helping friends and harming enemies, must be due to some despot, so rich and powerful that he thought he could do as he liked—someone like Periander, or Perdiccas, or Xerxes, or Ismenias of Thebes.

That is extremely probable.

Very good, said I; and now that we have disposed of that definition of justice, can anyone suggest another?

CHAPTER III (I. 336 B-347 E)

THRASYMACHUS: JUSTICE AS THE INTEREST OF THE STRONGER

Socrates has opposed to the popular conception of justice one of his own deepest convictions. Polemarchus' ready acceptance of this

provokes a violent protest from Thrasymachus, who represents the
doctrine that might is right in an extreme form. He holds that
justice or right is nothing but the name given by the men actually
holding power in any state to any actions they enjoin by law upon
their subjects; and that all their laws are framed to promote their
own personal or class interests. 'Just' accordingly means what is for
the interest of the stronger, ruling party. Right and wrong have no
other meaning at all. This is not a theory of social contract: it is
not suggested that the subject has ever made a bargain with the
ruler, sacrificing some of his liberty to gain the benefits of a social
order. The ruler imposes his 'rights' by sheer force. The perfect ex-
ample of such a ruler is the despot (the Greek 'tyrant'), whose po-
sition Thrasymachus regards as supremely enviable. He is precisely
the man who has the will and the power to 'do good to himself and
his friends and to harm his enemies.'

The discussion begins by clearing up the ambiguities of Thrasy-
machus' formula. The word translated 'stronger' commonly means
also 'superior' or 'better'; but 'better' has no moral sense for
Thrasymachus, who does not recognize the existence of morality.
The superiority of the stronger lies in the skill and determination
which enable them to seize and hold power. 'Interest,' again, means
the personal satisfaction and aggrandizement of the ruling indi-
viduals.

ALL this time Thrasymachus had been trying more than once to
break in upon our conversation; but his neighbours had restrained
him, wishing to hear the argument to the end. In the pause after
my last words he could keep quiet no longer; but gathering himself up like a wild beast he sprang at us as if he would tear us in
pieces. Polemarchus and I were frightened out of our wits, when
he burst out to the whole company:

What is the matter with you two, Socrates? Why do you go on
in this imbecile way, politely deferring to each other's nonsense?
If you really want to know what justice means, stop asking questions and scoring off the answers you get. You know very well it is
easier to ask questions than to answer them. Answer yourself, and
tell us what you think justice means. I won't have you telling us

it is the same as what is obligatory or useful or advantageous or profitable or expedient; I want a clear and precise statement; I won't put up with that sort of verbiage.

I was amazed by this onslaught and looked at him in terror. If I had not seen this wolf before he saw me, I really believe I should have been struck dumb;[1] but fortunately I had looked at him earlier, when he was beginning to get exasperated with our argument; so I was able to reply, though rather tremulously:

Don't be hard on us, Thrasymachus. If Polemarchus and I have gone astray in our search, you may be quite sure the mistake was not intentional. If we had been looking for a piece of gold, we should never have deliberately allowed politeness to spoil our chance of finding it; and now when we are looking for justice, a thing much more precious than gold, you cannot imagine we should defer to each other in that foolish way and not do our best to bring it to light. You must believe we are in earnest, my friend; but I am afraid the task is beyond our powers, and we might expect a man of your ability to pity us instead of being so severe.

Thrasymachus replied with a burst of sardonic laughter.

Good Lord, he said; Socrates at his old trick of shamming ignorance! I knew it; I told the others you would refuse to commit yourself and do anything sooner than answer a question.

Yes, Thrasymachus, I replied; because you are clever enough to know that if you asked someone what are the factors of the number twelve, and at the same time warned him: 'Look here, you are not to tell me that 12 is twice 6, or 3 times 4, or 6 times 2, or 4 times 3; I won't put up with any such nonsense'—you must surely see that no one would answer a question put like that. He would say: 'What do you mean, Thrasymachus? Am I forbidden to give any of these answers, even if one happens to be right? Do you want me to give a wrong one?' What would you say to that?

Humph! said he. As if that were a fair analogy!

I don't see why it is not, said I; but in any case, do you suppose our barring a certain answer would prevent the man from giving it, if he thought it was the truth?

[1] A popular superstition, that if a wolf sees you first, you become dumb.

Do you mean that you are going to give me one of those answers I barred?

I should not be surprised, if it seemed to me true, on reflection.

And what if I give you another definition of justice, better than any of those? What penalty are you prepared to pay?[1]

The penalty deserved by ignorance, which must surely be to receive instruction from the wise. So I would suggest that as a suitable punishment.

I like your notion of a penalty! he said; but you must pay the costs as well.

I will, when I have any money.

That will be all right, said Glaucon; we will all subscribe for Socrates. So let us have your definition, Thrasymachus.

Oh yes, he said; so that Socrates may play the old game of questioning and refuting someone else, instead of giving an answer himself!

But really, I protested, what can you expect from a man who does not know the answer or profess to know it, and, besides that, has been forbidden by no mean authority to put forward any notions he may have? Surely the definition should naturally come from you, who say you do know the answer and can tell it us. Please do not disappoint us. I should take it as a kindness, and I hope you will not be chary of giving Glaucon and the rest of us the advantage of your instruction.

Glaucon and the others added their entreaties to mine. Thrasymachus was evidently longing to win credit, for he was sure he had an admirable answer ready, though he made a show of insisting that I should be the one to reply. In the end he gave way and exclaimed:

So this is what Socrates' wisdom comes to! He refuses to teach, and goes about learning from others without offering so much as thanks in return.

I do learn from others, Thrasymachus; that is quite true; but

[1] In certain lawsuits the defendant, if found guilty, was allowed to propose a penalty alternative to that demanded by the prosecution. The judges then decided which should be inflicted. The 'costs' here means the fee which the sophist, unlike Socrates, expected from his pupils.

you are wrong to call me ungrateful. I give in return all I can—praise; for I have no money. And how ready I am to applaud any idea that seems to me sound, you will see in a moment, when you have stated your own; for I am sure that will be sound.

Listen then, Thrasymachus began. What I say is that 'just' or 'right' means nothing but what is to the interest of the stronger party. Well, where is your applause? You don't mean to give it me.

I will, as soon as I understand, I said. I don't see yet what you mean by right being the interest of the stronger party. For instance, Polydamas, the athlete, is stronger than we are, and it is to his interest to eat beef for the sake of his muscles; but surely you don't mean that the same diet would be good for weaker men and therefore be right for us?

You are trying to be funny, Socrates. It's a low trick to take my words in the sense you think will be most damaging.

No, no, I protested; but you must explain.

Don't you know, then, that a state may be ruled by a despot, or a democracy, or an aristocracy?

Of course.

And that the ruling element is always the strongest?

Yes.

Well then, in every case the laws are made by the ruling party in its own interest; a democracy makes democratic laws, a despot autocratic ones, and so on. By making these laws they define as 'right' for their subjects whatever is for their own interest, and they call anyone who breaks them a 'wrongdoer' and punish him accordingly. That is what I mean: in all states alike 'right' has the same meaning, namely what is for the interest of the party established in power, and that is the strongest. So the sound conclusion is that what is 'right' is the same everywhere: the interest of the stronger party.

Now I see what you mean, said I; whether it is true or not, I must try to make out. When you define right in terms of interest, you are yourself giving one of those answers you forbade to me; though, to be sure, you add 'to the stronger party.'

An insignificant addition, perhaps!

Its importance is not clear yet; what is clear is that we must find out whether your definition is true. I agree myself that right is in a sense a matter of interest; but when you add 'to the stronger party,' I don't know about that. I must consider.

Go ahead, then.

I will. Tell me this. No doubt you also think it is right to obey the men in power?

I do.

Are they infallible in every type of state, or can they sometimes make a mistake?

Of course they can make a mistake.

In framing laws, then, they may do their work well or badly?

No doubt.

Well, that is to say, when the laws they make are to their own interest; badly, when they are not?

Yes.

But the subjects are to obey any law they lay down, and they will then be doing right?

Of course.

If so, by your account, it will be right to do what is not to the interest of the stronger party, as well as what is so.

What's that you are saying?

Just what you said, I believe; but let us look again. Haven't you admitted that the rulers, when they enjoin certain acts on their subjects, sometimes mistake their own best interests, and at the same time that it is right for the subjects to obey, whatever they may enjoin?

Yes, I suppose so.

Well, that amounts to admitting that it is right to do what is not to the interest of the rulers or the stronger party. They may unwittingly enjoin what is to their own disadvantage; and you say it is right for the others to do as they are told. In that case, their duty must be the opposite of what you said, because the weaker will have been ordered to do what is against the interest of the stronger. You with your intelligence must see how that follows.

Yes, Socrates, said Polemarchus, that is undeniable.

No doubt, Cleitophon broke in, if you are to be a witness on Socrates' side.

No witness is needed, replied Polemarchus; Thrasymachus himself admits that rulers sometimes ordain acts that are to their own disadvantage, and that it is the subjects' duty to do them.

That is because Thrasymachus said it was right to do what you are told by the men in power.

Yes, but he also said that what is to the interest of the stronger party is right; and, after making both these assertions, he admitted that the stronger sometimes command the weaker subjects to act against their interests. From all which it follows that what is in the stronger's interest is no more right than what is not.

No, said Cleitophon; he meant whatever the stronger *believes* to be in his own interest. That is what the subject must do, and what Thrasymachus meant to define as right.

That was not what he said, rejoined Polemarchus.

No matter, Polemarchus, said I; if Thrasymachus says so now, let us take him in that sense. Now, Thrasymachus, tell me, was that what you intended to say—that right means what the stronger thinks is to his interest, whether it really is so or not?

Most certainly not, he replied. Do you suppose I should speak of a man as 'stronger' or 'superior' at the very moment when he is making a mistake?

I did think you said as much when you admitted that rulers are not always infallible.

That is because you are a quibbler, Socrates. Would you say a man deserves to be called a physician at the moment when he makes a mistake in treating his patient and just in respect of that mistake; or a mathematician, when he does a sum wrong and just in so far as he gets a wrong result? Of course we do commonly speak of a physician or a mathematician or a scholar having made a mistake; but really none of these, I should say, is ever mistaken, in so far as he is worthy of the name we give him. So strictly speaking—and you are all for being precise—no one who practises a craft makes mistakes. A man is mistaken when his knowledge fails him; and at that moment he is no craftsman. And what is true of craftsmanship or any sort of skill is true of the ruler: he is never mistaken so long as he is acting as a ruler; though anyone might speak of a ruler making a mistake, just as he might of a physician. You must understand that I was talking in that loose way when I answered your question just now; but the precise statement is this. The ruler, in so far as he is acting as a ruler, makes no mistakes and consequently enjoins what is best for himself; and that is what the subject is to do. So, as I said at first, 'right' means doing what is to the interest of the stronger.

Very well, Thrasymachus, said I. So you think I am quibbling? I am sure you are.

You believe my questions were maliciously designed to damage your position?

I know it. But you will gain nothing by that. You cannot outwit me by cunning, and you are not the man to crush me in the open.

Bless your soul, I answered, I should not think of trying. But, to prevent any more misunderstanding, when you speak of that ruler or stronger party whose interest the weaker ought to serve, please make it clear whether you are using the words in the ordinary way or in that strict sense you have just defined.

I mean a ruler in the strictest possible sense. Now quibble away and be as malicious as you can. I want no mercy. But you are no match for me.

Do you think me mad enough to beard a lion or try to outwit a Thrasymachus?

You did try just now, he retorted, but it wasn't a success.

[*Thrasymachus has already shifted his ground*. At first 'the stronger' meant only the men ruling by superior force; but now their superiority must include the knowledge and ability needed to govern without making mistakes. This knowledge and ability constitute an art of government, comparable to other useful arts or crafts requiring special skill. The ruler in his capacity as ruler, or the craftsman qua craftsman, can also be spoken of as the craft personified, since a craft exists only in the man who embodies it, and we are considering the man only as the embodiment of this special

capacity, neglecting all personal characteristics and any other capac-
ities he may chance to have. When Socrates talks of the art or craft
in this abstract way as having an interest of its own, he means the
same thing as if he spoke of the interest of the craftsman qua *crafts-*
man. Granted that there is, as Thrasymachus suggested, an art of
government exercised by a ruler who, qua *ruler, is infallible and so*
in the full sense 'superior,' the question now is, what his interest
should be, on the analogy of other crafts.]

Enough of this, said I. Now tell me about the <u>physician</u> in that
strict sense you spoke of: is it his business to earn money or to
treat his patients? Remember, I mean your physician who is
worthy of the name.

To treat his patients.

And what of the ship's captain in the true sense? Is he a mere
seaman or the commander of the crew?

The commander.

Yes, we shall not speak of him as a seaman just because he is on
board a ship. That is not the point. He is called captain because
of his skill and authority over the crew.

Quite true.

And each of these people has some special interest? [1]

No doubt.

And the craft in question exists for the very purpose of discovering that interest and providing for it?

Yes.

Can it equally be said of any craft that it has an interest, other
than its own greatest possible perfection?

What do you mean by that?

Here is an illustration. If you ask me whether it is sufficient for
the human body just to be itself, with no need of help from without, I should say, Certainly not; it has weaknesses and defects, and
its condition is not all that it might be. That is precisely why the art

[1] All the persons mentioned have some interest. The craftsman *qua* craftsman
has an interest in doing his work as well as possible, which is the same thing as
serving the interest of the subjects on whom his craft is exercised; and the subjects
have their interest, which the craftsman is there to promote.

of medicine was invented: it was designed to help the body and provide for its interests. Would not that be true?

It would.

But now take the art of medicine itself. Has that any defects or weaknesses? Does any art stand in need of some further perfection, as the eye would be imperfect without the power of vision or the ear without hearing, so that in their case an art is required that will study their interests and provide for their carrying out those functions? Has the art itself any corresponding need of some further art to remedy its defects and look after its interests; and will that further art require yet another, and so on for ever? Or will every art look after its own interests? Or, finally, is it not true that no art needs to have its weaknesses remedied or its interests studied either by another art or by itself, because no art has in itself any weakness or fault, and the only interest it is required to serve is that of its subject-matter? In itself, an art is sound and flawless, so long as it is entirely true to its own nature as an art in the strictest sense—and it is the strict sense that I want you to keep in view. Is not that true?

So it appears.

Then, said I, the art of medicine does not study its own interest, but the needs of the body, just as a groom shows his skill by caring for horses, not for the art of grooming. And so every art seeks, not its own advantage—for it has no deficiencies—but the interest of the subject on which it is exercised.

It appears so.

But surely, Thrasymachus, every art has authority and superior power over its subject.

To this he agreed, though very reluctantly.

So far as arts are concerned, then, no art ever studies or enjoins the interest of the superior or stronger party, but always that of the weaker over which it has authority.

Thrasymachus assented to this at last, though he tried to put up a fight. I then went on:

So the physician, as such, studies only the patient's interest, not his own. For as we agreed, the business of the physician, in the strict sense, is not to make money for himself, but to exercise his power over the patient's body; and the ship's captain, again, considered strictly as no mere sailor, but in command of the crew, will study and enjoin the interest of his subordinates, not his own.

He agreed reluctantly.

And so with government of any kind: no ruler, in so far as he is acting as ruler, will study or enjoin what is for his own interest. All that he says and does will be said and done with a view to what is good and proper for the subject for whom he practises his art.

[*Thrasymachus can hardly challenge this last argument, based as it is on his own 'precise' distinction of the ruler acting in his special capacity with knowledge and ability like the craftsman's and impeccable. Accordingly he takes refuge in an appeal to facts. The ruler, from the Homeric king onwards, had been called the shepherd of the people. Thrasymachus truly remarks that these shepherds have commonly been less concerned with the good of their flock than with shearing and butchering them for their own profit and aggrandizement. This behaviour is called 'injustice' because it means getting more than one's fair share; but the entirely selfish autocrat who practises it on a grand scale is envied and admired; and Thrasymachus himself regards him as the happiest of men. Justice, fairness, honesty, he concludes, never pay; the life of injustice is always more profitable.*

Socrates leaves this more general proposition to be challenged in the next chapter. Here he is still concerned with the art of government. He takes up the analogy of the shepherd and applies once more Thrasymachus' own distinction of 'capacities.' The shepherd qua *shepherd cares for his flock; he receives wages in a different capacity,* qua *wage-earner. The fact that the rulers of mankind expect to be rewarded shows that the proper task of governing is commonly regarded as an irksome and unprofitable business.*]

At this point, when everyone could see that Thrasymachus' definition of justice had been turned inside out, instead of making any reply, he said:

Socrates, have you a nurse?

Why do you ask such a question as that? I said. Wouldn't it be better to answer mine?

Because she lets you go about sniffling like a child whose nose wants wiping. She hasn't even taught you to know a shepherd when you see one, or his sheep either.

What makes you say that?

Why, you imagine that a herdsman studies the interests of his flocks or cattle, tending and fattening them up with some other end in view than his master's profit or his own; and so you don't see that, in politics, the genuine ruler regards his subjects exactly like sheep, and thinks of nothing else, night and day, but the good he can get out of them for himself. You are so far out in your notions of right and wrong, justice and injustice, as not to know that 'right' actually means what is good for someone else, and to be 'just' means serving the interest of the stronger who rules, at the cost of the subject who obeys; whereas injustice is just the reverse, asserting its authority over those innocents who are called just, so that they minister solely to their master's advantage and happiness, and not in the least degree to their own. Innocent as you are yourself, Socrates, you must see that a just man always has the worst of it. Take a private business: when a partnership is wound up, you will never find that the more honest of two partners comes off with the larger share; and in their relations to the state, when there are taxes to be paid, the honest man will pay more than the other on the same amount of property; or if there is money to be distributed, the dishonest will get it all. When either of them hold some public office, even if the just man loses in no other way, his private affairs at any rate will suffer from neglect, while his principles will not allow him to help himself from the public funds; not to mention the offence he will give to his friends and relations by refusing to sacrifice those principles to do them a good turn. Injustice has all the opposite advantages. I am speaking of the type I described just now, the man who can get the better of other people on a large scale: you must fix your eye on him, if you want to judge how much it is to one's own interest not to be just. You can see that best in the most consummate form of injustice, which rewards wrongdoing with supreme welfare and happiness and reduces its victims, if they won't retaliate in kind, to misery. That form is despotism, which uses force or fraud to plunder the goods of others, public or private, sacred or profane, and to do it in a wholesale way. If you are caught committing any one of these crimes on a small scale, you are punished and disgraced; they call it sacrilege, kidnapping, burglary, theft and brigandage. But if, besides taking their property, you turn all your countrymen into slaves, you will hear no more of those ugly names; your countrymen themselves will call you the happiest of men and bless your name, and so will everyone who hears of such a complete triumph of injustice; for when people denounce injustice, it is because they are afraid of suffering wrong, not of doing it. So true is it, Socrates, that injustice, on a grand enough scale, is superior to justice in strength and freedom and autocratic power; and 'right,' as I said at first, means simply what serves the interest of the stronger party; 'wrong' means what is for the interest and profit of oneself.

Having deluged our ears with this torrent of words, as the man at the baths might empty a bucket over one's head, Thrasymachus meant to take himself off; but the company obliged him to stay and defend his position. I was specially urgent in my entreaties.

My good Thrasymachus, said I, do you propose to fling a doctrine like that at our heads and then go away without explaining it properly or letting us point out to you whether it is true or not? Is it so small a matter in your eyes to determine the whole course of conduct which every one of us must follow to get the best out of life?

Don't I realize it is a serious matter? he retorted.

Apparently not, said I; or else you have no consideration for us, and do not care whether we shall lead better or worse lives for being ignorant of this truth you profess to know. Do take the trouble to let us into your secret; if you treat us handsomely, you may be sure it will be a good investment; there are so many of us to show our gratitude. I will make no secret of my own conviction, which is that injustice is not more profitable than justice, even when left free to work its will unchecked. No; let your unjust man have full power to do wrong, whether by successful violence or by escaping detection; all the same he will not convince me that he will gain more than he would by being just. There may be others

here who feel as I do, and set justice above injustice. It is for you
to convince us that we are not well advised.

How can I? he replied. If you are not convinced by what I have
just said, what more can I do for you? Do you want to be fed
with my ideas out of a spoon?

God forbid! I exclaimed; not that. But I do want you to stand
by your own words; or, if you shift your ground, shift it openly
and stop trying to hoodwink us as you are doing now. You see,
Thrasymachus, to go back to your earlier argument, in speaking
of the shepherd you did not think it necessary to keep to that strict
sense you laid down when you defined the genuine physician. You
represent him, in his character of shepherd, as feeding up his flock,
not for their own sake but for the table or the market, as if he
were out to make money as a caterer or a cattle-dealer, rather than
a shepherd. Surely the sole concern of the shepherd's art is to do
the best for the charges put under its care; its own best interest is
sufficiently provided for, so long as it does not fall short of all that
shepherding should imply. On that principle it followed, I thought,
that any kind of authority, in the state or in private life, must, in its
character of authority, consider solely what is best for those under
its care. Now what is your opinion? Do you think that the men
who govern states—I mean rulers in the strict sense—have no reluctance to hold office?

I don't think so, he replied; I know it.

Well, but haven't you noticed, Thrasymachus, that in other positions of authority no one is willing to act unless he is paid wages,
which he demands on the assumption that all the benefit of his action will go to his charges? Tell me: Don't we always distinguish
one form of skill from another by its power to effect some particular result? Do say what you really think, so that we may get on.

Yes, that is the distinction.

And also each brings us some benefit that is peculiar to it: medicine gives health, for example; the art of navigation, safety at sea;
and so on.

Yes.

And wage-earning brings us wages; that is its distinctive product. Now, speaking with that precision which you proposed, you

would not say that the art of navigation is the same as the art of medicine, merely on the ground that a ship's captain regained his health on a voyage, because the sea air was good for him. No more would you identify the practice of medicine with wage-earning because a man may keep his health while earning wages, or a physician attending a case may receive a fee.

No.

And, since we agreed that the benefit obtained by each form of skill is peculiar to it, any common benefit enjoyed alike by all these practitioners must come from some further practice common to them all?

It would seem so.

Yes, we must say that if they all earn wages, they get that benefit in so far as they are engaged in wage-earning as well as in practising their several arts.

He agreed reluctantly.

This benefit, then—the receipt of wages—does not come to a man from his special art. If we are to speak strictly, the physician, as such, produces health; the builder, a house; and then each, in his further capacity of wage-earner, gets his pay. Thus every art has its own function and benefits its proper subject. But suppose the practitioner is not paid; does he then get any benefit from his art?

Clearly not.

And is he doing no good to anyone either, when he works for nothing?

No, I suppose he does some good.

Well then, Thrasymachus, it is now clear that no form of skill or authority provides for its own benefit. As we were saying some time ago, it always studies and prescribes what is good for its subject—the interest of the weaker party, not of the stronger. And that, my friend, is why I said that no one is willing to be in a position of authority and undertake to set straight other men's troubles, without demanding to be paid; because, if he is to do his work well, he will never, in his capacity of ruler, do, or command others to do, what is best for himself, but only what is best for the subject. For that reason, if he is to consent, he must have his recompense, in the shape of money or honour, or of punishment in case of refusal.

What do you mean, Socrates? asked Glaucon. I recognize two of your three kinds of reward; but I don't understand what you mean by speaking of punishment as a recompense.

Then you don't understand the recompense required by the best type of men, or their motive for accepting authority when they do consent. You surely know that a passion for honours or for money is rightly regarded as something to be ashamed of.

Yes, I do.

For that reason, I said, good men are unwilling to rule, either for money's sake or for honour. They have no wish to be called mercenary for demanding to be paid, or thieves for making a secret profit out of their office; nor yet will honours tempt them, for they are not ambitious. So they must be forced to consent under threat of penalty; that may be why a readiness to accept power under no such constraint is thought discreditable. And the heaviest penalty for declining to rule is to be ruled by someone inferior to yourself. That is the fear, I believe, that makes decent people accept power; and when they do so, they face the prospect of authority with no idea that they are coming into the enjoyment of a comfortable berth; it is forced upon them because they can find no one better than themselves, or even as good, to be entrusted with power. If there could ever be a society of perfect men, there might well be as much competition to evade office as there now is to gain it; and it would then be clearly seen that the genuine ruler's nature is to seek only the advantage of the subject, with the consequence that any man of understanding would sooner have another to do the best for him than be at the pains to do the best for that other himself. On this point, then, I entirely disagree with Thrasymachus' doctrine that right means what is to the interest of the stronger.

THRASYMACHUS: IS ~~INJUSTICE MORE PROFITABLE THAN JUSTICE~~?

Socrates now turns from the art of government to Thrasymachus'
whole view of life: that injustice, unlimited self-seeking, pursued
with enough force of character and skill to ensure success, brings
welfare and happiness. This is what he ultimately means by the
interest of the stronger.

Socrates and Thrasymachus have a common ground for argument
in that both accept the notion of an art of living, comparable to the
special crafts in which trained intelligence creates some product.
The goodness, excellence, or virtue of a workman lies in his effi-
ciency, the Greek areté, *a word which, with the corresponding*
adjective agathos, *'good,' never lost its wide application to whatever*
does its work or fulfils its function well, as a good knife is one that
cuts efficiently. The workman's efficiency involves trained intelli-
gence or skill, an old sense of the word sophia, *which also means*
wisdom. None of these words necessarily bears any moral sense;
but they can be applied to the art of living. Here the product to be
aimed at is assumed to be a man's own happiness and well-being.
The efficiency which makes him good at attaining this end is called
'virtue'; the implied knowledge of the end and of the means to it is
like the craftsman's skill and may be called 'wisdom.' But as it
sounds in English almost a contradiction to say that to be unjust
is to be virtuous or good and wise, the comparatively colourless
phrase 'superior in character and intelligence' will be used instead.

Where Socrates and Thrasymachus differ is in their views of the
nature of happiness or well-being. Thrasymachus thinks it consists
in getting more than your fair share of what are commonly called
the good things of life, pleasure, wealth, power. Thus virtue and
wisdom mean to him efficiency and skill in achieving injustice.

HOWEVER, I continued, we may return to that question later. Much
more important is the position Thrasymachus is asserting now:

that a life of injustice is to be preferred to a life of justice. Which side do you take, Glaucon? Where do you think the truth lies?

I should say that the just life is the better worth having.

You heard Thrasymachus' catalogue of all the good things in store for injustice?

I did, but I am not convinced.

Shall we try to convert him, then, supposing we can find some way to prove him wrong?

By all means.

We might answer Thrasymachus' case in a set speech of our own, drawing up a corresponding list of the advantages of justice; he would then have the right to reply, and we should make our final rejoinder; but after that we should have to count up and measure the advantages on each list, and we should need a jury to decide between us. Whereas, if we go on as before, each securing the agreement of the other side, we can combine the functions of advocate and judge. We will take whichever course you prefer.

I prefer the second, said Glaucon.

Come then, Thrasymachus, said I, let us start afresh with our questions. You say that injustice pays better than justice, when both are carried to the furthest point?

I do, he replied; and I have told you why.

And how would you describe them? I suppose you would call one of them an excellence and the other a defect?

Of course.

Justice an excellence, and injustice a defect?

Now is that likely, when I am telling you that injustice pays, and justice does not?

Then what do you say?

The opposite.

That justice is a defect?

No; rather the mark of a good-natured simpleton.

Injustice, then, implies being ill-natured?

No; I should call it good policy.

Do you think the unjust are positively superior in character and intelligence, Thrasymachus?

Yes, if they are the sort that can carry injustice to perfection and make themselves masters of whole cities and nations. Perhaps you think I was talking of pickpockets. There is profit even in that trade, if you can escape detection; but it doesn't come to much as compared with the gains I was describing.

I understand you now on that point, I replied. What astonished me was that you should class injustice with superior character and intelligence and justice with the reverse.

Well, I do, he rejoined.

That is a much more stubborn position, my friend; and it is not so easy to see how to assail it. If you would admit that injustice, however well it pays, is nevertheless, as some people think, a defect and a discreditable thing, then we could argue on generally accepted principles. But now that you have gone so far as to rank it with superior character and intelligence, obviously you will say it is an admirable thing as well as a source of strength, and has all the other qualities we have attributed to justice.

You read my thoughts like a book, he replied.

However, I went on, it is no good shirking; I must go through with the argument, so long as I can be sure you are really speaking your mind. I do believe you are not playing with us now, Thrasymachus, but stating the truth as you conceive it.

Why not refute the doctrine? he said. What does it matter to you whether I believe it or not?

It does not matter, I replied.

[*Socrates attacks separately three points in*]Thrasymachus' *position:* (1) *that the unjust is superior to the just in character ('virtue') and intelligence;* (2) *that injustice is a source of strength;* (3) *that it brings happiness.*

(1) *The first argument* (349 B–350 C) *is omitted here, because only a very loose paraphrase could liberate the meaning from the stiff and archaic form of the original. Thrasymachus has upheld the superman who will try to outdo everyone else and go to any lengths in getting the better of his neighbours. Socrates attacks this ideal of unlimited self-assertion, relying once more on the admitted analogy between the art of living and other arts. The musician, tuning an instrument, knows that there is for each string a certain*

pitch which is absolutely right. He shows his excellence and mastery of the art by aiming at that 'limit' or 'measure' (as the Greeks would call it), and he would be satisfied if he could attain it. In doing so he would be outdoing or 'going one better than' less skilful musicians or the unmusical; but he would not be showing superior skill if he tried to outdo a musician who acknowledged the same measure and had actually attained it. Socrates holds that in moral conduct also there is a measure which is absolutely right, whether we recognize it or not. The just man, who does recognize it, shows a wisdom and virtue corresponding to the skill of the good musician. The unjust, who acknowledges no measure or limit, because there is no limit to getting more and more for yourself at others' expense and that is his object, is, by all analogy, exhibiting rather a lack of intelligence and character. As a man, and therefore a moral agent, he is no more 'wise and good' than an instrumentalist who should refuse to recognize such a thing as the right pitch. Jowett quotes: 'When workmen strive to do better than well, They do confound their skill in covetousness' (K. John iv. 2). Socrates concludes:

'It is evident, then, that it is the just man that is wise and good (superior in character and intelligence), the unjust that is ignorant and bad.'

(2) In the following passage Socrates has little difficulty in showing that unlimited self-assertion is not a source of strength in any association formed for a common purpose. 'Honour among thieves' is common sense, which Thrasymachus cannot challenge. Socrates infers that injustice will have the same effect within the individual soul, dividing a man against himself and destroying unity of purpose. The various desires and impulses in his nature will be in conflict, if each asserts an unlimited claim to satisfaction. This view of justice as a principle of internal order and unity will become clearer when the soul has been analysed into its principal elements.]

Thrasymachus' assent was dragged out of him with a reluctance of which my account gives no idea. He was sweating at every pore, for the weather was hot; and I saw then what I had never seen before—Thrasymachus blushing. However, now that we had agreed that justice implies superior character and intelligence, injustice a deficiency in both respects, I went on:

Good; let us take that as settled. But we were also saying that injustice was a source of strength. Do you remember, Thrasymachus?

I do remember; only your last argument does not satisfy me, and I could say a good deal about that. But if I did, you would tell me I was haranguing you like a public meeting. So either let me speak my mind at length, or else, if you want to ask questions, ask them, and I will nod or shake my head, and say 'Hm?' as we do to encourage an old woman telling us a story.

No, please, said I; don't give your assent against your real opinion.

Anything to please you, he rejoined, since you won't let me have my say. What more do you want?

Nothing. I replied. If that is what you mean to do, I will go on with my questions.

Go on, then.

Well, to continue where we left off. I will repeat my question: What is the nature and quality of justice as compared with injustice? It was suggested, I believe, that injustice is the stronger and more effective of the two; but now we have seen that justice implies superior character and intelligence, it will not be hard to show that it will also be superior in power to injustice, which implies ignorance and stupidity; that must be obvious to anyone. However, I would rather look deeper into this matter than take it as settled off-hand. Would you agree that a state may be unjust and may try to enslave other states or to hold a number of others in subjection unjustly?

Of course it may, he said; above all if it is the best sort of state, which carries injustice to perfection.

I understand, said I; that was your view. But I am wondering whether a state can do without justice when it is asserting its superior power over another in that way.

Not if you are right, that justice implies intelligence; but if I am right, injustice will be needed.

I am delighted with your answer, Thrasymachus; this is much better than just nodding and shaking your head.

It is all to oblige you.

Thank you. Please add to your kindness by telling me whether any set of men—a state or an army or a band of robbers or thieves —who were acting together for some unjust purpose would be likely to succeed, if they were always trying to injure one another. Wouldn't they do better, if they did not?

Yes, they would.

Because, of course, such injuries must set them quarrelling and hating each other. Only fair treatment can make men friendly and of one mind.

Be it so, he said; I don't want to differ from you.

Thank you once more, I replied. But don't you agree that, if injustice has this effect of implanting hatred wherever it exists, it must make any set of people, whether freemen or slaves, split into factions, at feud with one another and incapable of any joint action?

Yes.

And so with any two individuals: injustice will set them at variance and make them enemies to each other as well as to everyone who is just.

It will.

And will it not keep its character and have the same effect, if it exists in a single person?

Let us suppose so.

The effect being, apparently, wherever it occurs—in a state or a family or an army or anywhere else—to make united action impossible because of factions and quarrels, and moreover to set whatever it resides in at enmity with itself as well as with any opponent and with all who are just.

Yes, certainly.

Then I suppose it will produce the same natural results in an individual. He will have a divided mind and be incapable of action, for lack of singleness of purpose; and he will be at enmity with all who are just as well as with himself?

Yes.

And 'all who are just' surely includes the gods?

Let us suppose so.

The unjust man, then, will be a god-forsaken creature; the good-will of heaven will be for the just.

Enjoy your triumph, said Thrasymachus. You need not fear my contradicting you. I have no wish to give offence to the company.

[(3) *The final question is, whether justice (now admitted to be a virtue) or injustice brings happiness. The argument turns on the doctrine (adopted as fundamental in Aristotle's* Ethics) *that man, like any other living species, has a peculiar work or function or activity, in the satisfactory exercise of which his well-being or happiness will consist; and also a peculiar excellence or virtue, namely a state of his soul from which that satisfactory activity will result. Aristotle argues* (Eth. Nic. i. 7) *that, a thing's function being the work or activity of which it alone is capable, man's function will be an activity involving the use of reason, which man alone possesses. Man's virtue is 'the state of character which makes him a good man and makes him do his work well'* (ibid. ii. 6). *It is the quality which enables him to 'live well,' for living is the soul's function; and to live well is to be happy.*

'Here again,' writes Nettleship on the following passage, 'the argument is intensely abstract. We should be inclined to break in on it and say that virtue means something very different in morality from what it means in the case of seeing or hearing, and that by happiness we mean a great many other things besides what seems to be meant here by living well. All depends, in this argument, on the strictness of the terms, upon assuming each of them to have a definite and distinct meaning. The virtues of a man and of a horse are very different, but what is the common element in them which makes us call them virtue? Can we call anything virtue which does not involve the doing well of the function, never mind what, of the agent that possesses the virtue? Is there any other sense in which we can call a thing good or bad, except that it does or does not do well that which it was made to do? Again, happiness in its largest sense, welfare, well-being, or doing well, is a very complex thing, and one cannot readily describe in detail all that goes to *make it up; but does it not necessarily imply that the human soul, man's vital activity as a whole, is in its best state, or is performing well the function it is made to perform? If by virtue and by happiness we mean what it seems we do mean, this consequence follows: when men are agreed that a certain sort of conduct constitutes virtue, if they mean anything at all, they must mean that in that conduct man finds happiness. And if a man says that what he calls virtue has nothing to do with what he calls happiness or wellbeing, then either in calling the one virtue he does not really mean what he says, or in calling the other happiness he does not really mean what he says. This is substantially the position that Plato takes up in this section.'* (Lectures on Plato's Republic, p. 42.)]

You will make my enjoyment complete, I replied, if you will answer my further questions in the same way. We have made out so far that just men are superior in character and intelligence and more effective in action. Indeed without justice men cannot act together at all; it is not strictly true to speak of such people as ever having effected any strong action in common. Had they been thoroughly unjust, they could not have kept their hands off one another; they must have had some justice in them, enough to keep them from injuring one another at the same time with their victims. This it was that enabled them to achieve what they did achieve: their injustice only partially incapacitated them for their careeer of wrongdoing; if perfect, it would have disabled them for any action whatsoever. I can see that all this is true, as against your original position. But there is a further question which we postponed: Is the life of justice the better and happier life? What we have said already leaves no doubt in my mind; but we ought to consider more carefully, for this is no light matter: it is the question, what is the right way to live?

Go on, then.

I will, said I. Some things have a function;[1] a horse, for instance,

---

[1] The word translated 'function' is the common word for 'work.' Hence the need for illustrations to confine it to the narrower sense of 'function,' here defined for the first time.

is useful for certain kinds of work. Would you agree to define a thing's function in general as the work for which that thing is the only instrument or the best one?

I don't understand.

Take an example. We can see only with the eyes, hear only with the ears; and seeing and hearing might be called the functions of those organs.

Yes.

Or again, you might cut vine-shoots with a carving-knife or a chisel or many other tools, but with none so well as with a pruning-knife made for the purpose; and we may call that its function.

True.

Now, I expect, you see better what I meant by suggesting that a thing's function is the work that it alone can do, or can do better than anything else.

Yes, I will accept that definition.

Good, said I; and to take the same examples, the eye and the ear, which we said have each its particular function: have they not also a specific excellence or virtue? Is not that always the case with things that have some appointed work to do?

Yes.

Now consider: is the eye likely to do its work well, if you take away its peculiar virtue and substitute the corresponding defect?

Of course not, if you mean substituting blindness for the power of sight.

I mean whatever its virtue may be; I have not come to that yet. I am only asking, whether it is true of things with a function— eyes or ears or anything else—that there is always some specific virtue which enables them to work well; and if they are deprived of that virtue, they work badly.

I think that is true.

Then the next point is this. Has the soul a function that can be performed by nothing else? Take for example such actions as deliberating or taking charge and exercising control: is not the soul the only thing of which you can say that these are its proper and peculiar work?

That is so.

And again, living—is not that above all the function of the soul?
No doubt.

And we also speak of the soul as having a certain specific excellence or virtue?

Yes.

Then, Thrasymachus, if the soul is robbed of its peculiar virtue, it cannot possibly do its work well. It must exercise its power of controlling and taking charge well or ill according as it is itself in a good or a bad state.

That follows.

And did we not agree that the virtue of the soul is justice, and injustice its defect?

We did.

So it follows that a just soul, or in other words a just man, will live well; the unjust will not.

Apparently, according to your argument.

But living well involves well-being and happiness.

Naturally.

Then only the just man is happy; injustice will involve unhappiness.

Be it so.

But you cannot say it pays better to be unhappy.

Of course not.

Injustice then, my dear Thrasymachus, can never pay better than justice.

Well, he replied, this is a feast-day, and you may take all this as your share of the entertainment.

For which I have to thank you, Thrasymachus; you have been so gentle with me since you recovered your temper. It is my own fault if the entertainment has not been satisfactory. I have been behaving like a greedy guest, snatching a taste of every new dish that comes round before he has properly enjoyed the last. We began by looking for a definition of justice; but before we had found one, I dropped that question and hurried on to ask whether or not it involved superior character and intelligence; and then, as soon as another idea cropped up, that injustice pays better, I could not refrain from pursuing that.

So now the whole conversation has left me completely in the dark; for so long as I do not know what justice is, I am hardly likely to know whether or not it is a virtue, or whether it makes a man happy or unhappy.

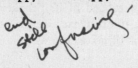

PART II (Books II–IV, 445 b)

JUSTICE IN THE STATE AND IN THE INDIVIDUAL

CHAPTER V (ii. 357 a–367 e)

THE PROBLEM STATED

The question, what Justice or Right ultimately means, being still unanswered, the conversation so far amounts to a preliminary survey of the ground to be covered in the rest of the Republic. *Plato does not pretend that an immoralist like Thrasymachus could be silenced by summary arguments which seem formal and unconvincing until the whole view of life that lies behind them has been disclosed.*

The case which Socrates has to meet is reopened by Glaucon and Adeimantus, young men with a generous belief that justice has a valid meaning, but puzzled by the doctrine, current in intellectual circles, that it is a mere matter of social convention, imposed from without, and is practised as an unwelcome necessity. They demand a proof that justice is not merely useful as bringing external rewards, but intrinsically good as an inward state of the soul, even though the just man be persecuted rather than rewarded. In dealing with inquirers like these, who really wish to discover the truth, Socrates drops his role of ironical critic and becomes constructive.

Glaucon opens with one of the earliest statements of the Social Contract theory. The essence of this is that all the customary rules of religion and moral conduct imposed on the individual by social sanctions have their origin in human intelligence and will and always rest on tacit consent. They are neither laws of nature nor divine enactments, but conventions which man who made them can alter, as laws are changed or repealed by legislative bodies. It is assumed that, if all these artificial restraints were removed, the

41

natural man would be left only with purely egoistic instincts and desires, which he would indulge in all that Thrasymachus commended as injustice.

Adeimantus supplements Glaucon's case by an attack on current moral education and some forms of mystery religion, as tacitly encouraging immorality by valuing justice only for the rewards it brings. Since these can be gained in this life by seeming just without being so, and after death by buying the favour of heaven, the young conclude that the ideal is injustice masked by a good reputation and atoned for by bribery. Both speakers accordingly demand that external rewards shall be ruled out of account and justice proved to be worth having for its own sake. The prospect of rewards and punishments after death is reserved for the myth at the end of the dialogue.

I THOUGHT that, with these words, I was quit of the discussion; but it seems this was only a prelude. Glaucon, undaunted as ever, was not content to let Thrasymachus abandon the field.

Socrates, he broke out, you have made a show of proving that justice is better than injustice in every way. Is that enough, or do you want us to be really convinced?

Certainly I do, if it rests with me.

Then you are not going the right way about it. I want to know how you classify the things we call good. Are there not some which we should wish to have, not for their consequences, but just for their own sake, such as harmless pleasures and enjoyments that have no further result beyond the satisfaction of the moment?

Yes, I think there are good things of that description.

And also some that we value both for their own sake and for their consequences—things like knowledge and health and the use of our eyes?

Yes.

And a third class which would include physical training, medical treatment, earning one's bread as a doctor or otherwise—useful, but burdensome things, which we want only for the sake of the profit or other benefit they bring.

Yes, there is that third class. What then?

In which class do you place justice?

just I should say, in the highest, as a thing which anyone who is to gain happiness must value both for itself and for its results.

Well, that is not the common opinion. Most people would say it was one of those things, tiresome and disagreeable in themselves, which we cannot avoid practising for the sake of reward or a good reputation.

I know, said I; that is why Thrasymachus has been finding fault with it all this time and praising injustice. But I seem to be slow in seeing his point.

Listen to me, then, and see if you agree with mine. There was no need, I think, for Thrasymachus to yield so readily, like a snake you had charmed into submission; and nothing so far said about justice and injustice has been established to my satisfaction. I want to be told what each of them really is, and what effect each has, in itself, on the soul that harbours it, when all rewards and consequences are left out of account. So here is my plan, if you approve. I shall revive Thrasymachus' theory. First, I will state what is commonly held about the nature of justice and its origin; secondly, I shall maintain that it is always practised with reluctance, not as good in itself, but as a thing one cannot do without; and thirdly, that this reluctance is reasonable, because the life of injustice is much the better life of the two—so people say. That is not what I think myself, Socrates; only I am bewildered by all that Thrasymachus and ever so many others have dinned into my ears; and I have never yet heard the case for justice stated as I wish to hear it. You, I believe, if anyone, can tell me what is to be said in praise of justice in and for itself; that is what I want. Accordingly, I shall set you an example by glorifying the life of injustice with all the energy that I hope you will show later in denouncing it and exalting justice in its stead. Will that plan suit you?

Nothing could be better, I replied. Of all subjects this is one on which a sensible man must always be glad to exchange ideas.

Good, said Glaucon. Listen then, and I will begin with my first point: the nature and origin of justice.

What people say is that to do wrong is, in itself, a desirable thing; on the other hand, it is not at all desirable to suffer wrong, and the harm to the sufferer outweighs the advantage to the doer. Consequently, when men have had a taste of both, those who have not the power to seize the advantage and escape the harm decide that they would be better off if they made a compact neither to do wrong nor to suffer it. Hence they began to make laws and covenants with one another; and whatever the law prescribed they called lawful and right. That is what right or justice is and how it came into existence; it stands half-way between the best thing of all—to do wrong with impunity—and the worst, which is to suffer wrong without the power to retaliate. So justice is accepted as a compromise, and valued, not as good in itself, but for lack of power to do wrong; no man worthy of the name, who had that power, would ever enter into such a compact with anyone; he would be mad if he did. That, Socrates, is the nature of justice according to this account, and such the circumstances in which it arose.

The next point is that men practise it against the grain, for lack of power to do wrong. How true that is, we shall best see if we imagine two men, one just, the other unjust, given full licence to do whatever they like, and then follow them to observe where each will be led by his desires. We shall catch the just man taking the same road as the unjust; he will be moved by self-interest, the end which it is natural to every creature to pursue as good, until forcibly turned aside by law and custom to respect the principle of equality.

Now, the easiest way to give them that complete liberty of action would be to imagine them possessed of the talisman found by Gyges, the ancestor of the famous Lydian. The story tells how he was a shepherd in the King's service. One day there was a great storm, and the ground where his flock was feeding was rent by an earthquake. Astonished at the sight, he went down into the chasm and saw, among other wonders of which the story tells, a brazen horse, hollow, with windows in its sides. Peering in, he saw a dead body, which seemed to be of more than human size. It was naked save for a gold ring, which he took from the finger and made his way out. When the shepherds met, as they did every month, to send an account to the King of the state of his flocks, Gyges came wearing the ring. As he was sitting with the others, he happened to turn the bezel of the ring inside his hand. At once he became invisible, and his companions, to his surprise, began to speak of him as if he had left them. Then, as he was fingering the ring, he turned the bezel outwards and became visible again. With that, he set about testing the ring to see if it really had this power, and always with the same result: according as he turned the bezel inside or out he vanished and reappeared. After this discovery he contrived to be one of the messengers sent to the court. There he seduced the Queen, and with her help murdered the King and seized the throne.

Now suppose there were two such magic rings, and one were given to the just man, the other to the unjust. No one, it is commonly believed, would have such iron strength of mind as to stand fast in doing right or keep his hands off other men's goods, when he could go to the market-place and fearlessly help himself to anything he wanted, enter houses and sleep with any woman he chose, set prisoners free and kill men at his pleasure, and in a word go about among men with the powers of a god. He would behave no better than the other; both would take the same course. Surely this would be strong proof that men do right only under compulsion; no individual thinks of it as good for him personally, since he does wrong whenever he finds he has the power. Every man believes that wrongdoing pays him personally much better, and, according to this theory, that is the truth. Granted full licence to do as he liked, people would think him a miserable fool if they found him refusing to wrong his neighbours or to touch their belongings, though in public they would keep up a pretence of praising his conduct, for fear of being wronged themselves. So much for that.

Finally, if we are really to judge between the two lives, the only way is to contrast the extremes of justice and injustice. We can best do that by imagining our two men to be perfect types, and crediting both to the full with the qualities they need for their respective ways of life. To begin with the unjust man: he must be like any consummate master of a craft, a physician or a captain, who, knowing just what his art can do, never tries to do more, and can always retrieve a false step. The unjust man, if he is to reach perfection, must be equally discreet in his criminal attempts, and he must not be found out, or we shall think him a bungler; for the highest pitch of injustice is to seem just when you are not. So we must endow our man with the full complement of injustice; we must allow him to have secured a spotless reputation for virtue while committing the blackest crimes; he must be able to retrieve any mistake, to defend himself with convincing eloquence if his misdeeds are denounced, and, when force is required, to bear down all opposition by his courage and strength and by his command of friends and money.

Now set beside this paragon the just man in his simplicity and nobleness, one who, in Aeschylus' words, 'would be, not seem, the best.' There must, indeed, be no such seeming; for if his character were apparent, his reputation would bring him honours and rewards, and then we should not know whether it was for their sake that he was just or for justice's sake alone. He must be stripped of everything but justice, and denied every advantage the other enjoyed. Doing no wrong, he must have the worst reputation for wrong-doing, to test whether his virtue is proof against all that comes of having a bad name; and under this lifelong imputation of wickedness, let him hold on his course of justice unwavering to the point of death. And so, when the two men have carried their justice and injustice to the last extreme, we may judge which is the happier.

My dear Glaucon, I exclaimed, how vigorously you scour these two characters clean for inspection, as if you were burnishing a couple of statues! [1]

I am doing my best, he answered. Well, given two such characters, it is not hard, I fancy, to describe the sort of life that each of them may expect; and if the description sounds rather coarse, take it as coming from those who cry up the merits of injustice rather than from me. They will tell you that our just man will be

---

[1] At Elis and Athens officials called *phaidryntai*, 'burnishers,' had the duty of cleaning cult statues (A. B. Cook, *Zeus*, iii. 967). At 612 c (p. 339), where this passage is recalled, it is admitted to be an extravagant supposition, that the just and unjust should exchange reputations.

thrown into prison, scourged and racked, will have his eyes burnt out, and, after every kind of torment, be impaled. That will teach him how much better it is to seem virtuous than to be so. In fact those lines of Aeschylus I quoted are more fitly applied to the unjust man, who, they say, is a realist and does not live for appearances: 'he would be, not seem' unjust,

> reaping the harvest sown
> In those deep furrows of the thoughtful heart
> Whence wisdom springs.

With his reputation for virtue, he will hold offices of state, ally himself by marriage to any family he may choose, become a partner in any business, and, having no scruples about being dishonest, turn all these advantages to profit. If he is involved in a lawsuit, public or private, he will get the better of his opponents, grow rich on the proceeds, and be able to help his friends and harm his enemies.[1] Finally, he can make sacrifices to the gods and dedicate offerings with due magnificence, and, being in a much better position than the just man to serve the gods as well as his chosen friends, he may reasonably hope to stand higher in the favour of heaven. So much better, they say, Socrates, is the life prepared for the unjust by gods and men.

Here Glaucon ended, and I was meditating a reply, when his brother Adeimantus exclaimed:

Surely, Socrates, you cannot suppose that that is all there is to be said.

Why, isn't it? said I.

The most essential part of the case has not been mentioned, he replied.

Well, I answered, there is a proverb about a brother's aid. If Glaucon has failed, it is for you to make good his shortcomings; though, so far as I am concerned, he has said quite enough to put me out of the running and leave me powerless to rescue the cause of justice.

Nonsense, said Adeimantus; there is more to be said, and you

---

[1] To help friends and harm enemies, offered as a definition of Justice by Polemarchus (p. 9), now appears as the privilege of the unjust.

must listen to me. If we want a clear view of what I take to be Glaucon's meaning, we must study the opposite side of the case, the arguments used when justice is praised and injustice condemned. When children are told by their fathers and all their pastors and masters that it is a good thing to be just, what is commended is not justice in itself but the respectability it brings. They are to let men see how just they are, in order to gain high positions and marry well and win all the other advantages which Glaucon mentioned, since the just man owes all these to his good reputation.

In this matter of having a good name, they go farther still: they throw in the favourable opinion of heaven, and can tell us of no end of good things with which they say the gods reward piety. There is the good old Hesiod,[1] who says the gods make the just man's oak-trees 'bear acorns at the top and bees in the middle; and their sheep's fleeces are heavy with wool,' and a great many other blessings of that sort. And Homer[2] speaks in the same strain:

As when a blameless king fears the gods and upholds right judgment; then the dark earth yields wheat and barley, and the trees are laden with fruit; the young of his flocks are strong, and the sea gives abundance of fish.

Musaeus and his son Eumolpus[3] enlarge in still more spirited terms upon the rewards from heaven they promise to the righteous. They take them to the other world and provide them with a banquet of the Blest, where they sit for all time carousing with garlands on their heads, as if virtue could not be more nobly recompensed than by an eternity of intoxication. Others, again, carry the rewards of heaven yet a stage farther: the pious man who keeps his oaths is to have children's children and to leave a posterity after him. When they have sung the praises of justice in that strain, with more to same effect, they proceed to plunge the sinners and unrighteous men into a pool of mud in the world below, and set them to fetch water in a sieve. Even in this life, too, they give

[1] *Works and Days,* 232.
[2] *Odyssey,* xix. 109.
[3] Legendary figures, to whom were attributed poems setting forth the doctrines of the mystery religion known as Orphism.

them a bad name, and make out that the unjust suffer all those penalties which Glaucon described as falling upon the good man who has a bad reputation: they can think of no others. That is how justice is recommended and injustice denounced.

Besides all this, think of the way in which justice and injustice are spoken of, not only in ordinary life, but by the poets. All with one voice reiterate that self-control and justice, admirable as they may be, are difficult and irksome, whereas vice and injustice are pleasant and very easily to be had; it is mere convention to regard them as discreditable. They tell us that dishonesty generally pays better than honesty. They will cheerfully speak of a bad man as happy and load him with honours and social esteem, provided he be rich and otherwise powerful; while they despise and disregard one who has neither power nor wealth, though all the while they acknowledge that he is the better man of the two.

Most surprising of all is what they say about the gods and virtue: that heaven itself often allots misfortunes and a hard life to the good man, and gives prosperity to the wicked. Mendicant priests and soothsayers come to the rich man's door with a story of a power they possess by the gift of heaven to atone for any offence that he or his ancestors have committed with incantations and sacrifice, agreeably accompanied by feasting. If he wishes to injure an enemy, he can, at a trifling expense, do him a hurt with equal ease, whether he be an honest man or not, by means of certain invocations and spells which, as they profess, prevail upon the gods to do their bidding. In support of all these claims they call the poets to witness. Some, by way of advertising the easiness of vice, quote the words: 'Unto wickedness men attain easily and in multitudes; smooth is the way and her dwelling is very near at hand. But the gods have ordained much sweat upon the path to virtue'[1] and a long road that is rough and steep.

Others, to show that men can turn the gods from their purpose, cite Homer: 'Even the gods themselves listen to entreaty. Their hearts are turned by the entreaties of men with sacrifice and humble prayers and libation and burnt offering, whensoever anyone

[1] Hesiod, *Works and Days*, 287.

transgresses and does amiss.'[1] They produce a whole farrago of books in which Musaeus and Orpheus, described as descendants of the Muses and the Moon, prescribe their ritual; and they persuade entire communities, as well as individuals, that, both in this life and after death, wrongdoing may be absolved and purged away by means of sacrifices and agreeable performances which they are pleased to call rites of initiation. These deliver us from punishment in the other world, where awful things are in store for all who neglect to sacrifice.

Now, my dear Socrates, when all this stuff is talked about the estimation in which virtue and vice are held by heaven and by mankind, what effect can we suppose it has upon the mind of a young man quick-witted enough to gather honey from all these flowers of popular wisdom and to draw his own conclusions as to the sort of person he should be and the way he should go in order to lead the best possible life? In all likelihood he would ask himself, in Pindar's words: 'Will the way of right or the by-paths of deceit lead me to the higher fortress,' where I may entrench myself for the rest of my life? For, according to what they tell me, I have nothing to gain but trouble and manifest loss from being honest, unless I also get a name for being so; whereas, if I am dishonest and provide myself with a reputation for honesty, they promise me a marvellous career. Very well, then; since 'outward seeming,' as wise men inform me, 'overpowers the truth' and decides the question of happiness, I had better go in for appearances wholeheartedly. I must ensconce myself behind an imposing façade designed to look like virtue, and trail the fox behind me, 'the cunning shifty fox'[2]—Archilochus knew the world as well as any man. You may say it is not so easy to be wicked without ever being found out. Perhaps not; but great things are never easy. Anyhow, if we are to reach happiness, everything we have been told points to this as the road to be followed. We will form secret societies to save us from exposure; besides, there are men who teach the art of winning over popular assemblies and courts of law; so that, one way or another, by persuasion or violence, we shall get the better

[1] *Iliad* ix. 497.
[2] An allusion to a fable by Archilochus.

of our neighbours without being punished. You might object that the gods are not to be deceived and are beyond the reach of violence. But suppose that there are no gods, or that they do not concern themselves with the doings of men; why should we concern ourselves to deceive them? Or, if the gods do exist and care for mankind, all we know or have ever heard about them comes from current tradition and from the poets who recount their family history, and these same authorities also assure us that they can be won over and turned from their purpose 'by sacrifice and humble prayers' and votive offerings. We must either accept both these statements or neither. If we are to accept both, we had better do wrong and use part of the proceeds to offer sacrifice. By being just we may escape the punishment of heaven, but we shall be renouncing the profits of injustice; whereas by doing wrong we shall make our profit and escape punishment into the bargain, by means of those entreaties which win over the gods when we transgress and do amiss. But then, you will say, in the other world the penalty for our misdeeds on earth will fall either upon us or upon our children's children. We can counter that objection by reckoning on the great efficacy of mystic rites and the divinities of absolution, vouched for by the most advanced societies and by the descendants of the gods who have appeared as poets and spokesmen of heavenly inspiration.

What reason, then, remains for preferring justice to the extreme of injustice, when common belief and the best authorities promise us the fulfilment of our desires in this life and the next, if only we conceal our ill-doing under a veneer of decent behaviour? The upshot is, Socrates, that no man possessed of superior powers of mind or person or rank or wealth will set any value on justice; he is more likely to laugh when he hears it praised. So, even one who could prove my case false and were quite sure that justice is best, far from being indignant with the unjust, will be very ready to excuse them. He will know that, here and there, a man may refrain from wrong because it revolts some instinct he is graced with or because he has come to know the truth; no one else is virtuous of his own will; it is only lack of spirit or the infirmity of age or some other weakness that makes men condemn the iniquities they have not the strength to practise. This is easily seen: give such a man the power, and he will be the first to use it to the utmost.

What lies at the bottom of all this is nothing but the fact from which Glaucon, as well as I, started upon this long discourse. We put it to you, Socrates, with all respect, in this way. All you who profess to sing the praises of right conduct, from the ancient heroes whose legends have survived down to the men of the present day, have never denounced injustice or praised justice apart from the reputation, honours, and rewards they bring; but what effect either of them in itself has upon its possessor when it dwells in his soul unseen of gods or men, no poet or ordinary man has ever yet explained No one has proved that a soul can harbour no worse evil than injustice, no greater good than justice. Had all of you said that from the first and tried to convince us from our youth up, we should not be keeping watch upon our neighbours to prevent them from doing wrong to us, but everyone would keep a far more effectual watch over himself, for fear lest by wronging others he should open his doors to the worst of all evils.

That, Socrates, is the view of justice and injustice which Thrasymachus and, no doubt, others would state, perhaps in even stronger words. For myself, I believe it to be a gross perversion of their true worth and effect; but, as I must frankly confess, I have put the case with all the force I could muster because I want to hear the other side from you. You must not be content with proving that justice is superior to injustice; you must make clear what good or what harm each of them does to its possessor, taking it simply in itself and, as Glaucon required, leaving out of account the reputation it bears. For unless you deprive each of its true reputation and attach to it the false one, we shall say that you are praising or denouncing nothing more than the appearances in either case, and recommending us to do wrong without being found out; and that you hold with Thrasymachus that right means what is good for someone else, being the interest of the stronger, and wrong is what really pays, serving one's own interest at the expense of the weaker. You have agreed that justice belongs to that highest class of good things which are worth having not only for their consequences, but much more for their own sakes—things like sight and hearing, knowledge, and health, whose value is genuine and intrinsic, not dependent on opinion. So I want you, in commending justice, to consider only how justice, in itself, benefits a man who has it in him, and how injustice harms him, leaving rewards and reputation out of account. I might put up with others dwelling on those outward effects as a reason for praising the one and condemning the other; but from you, who have spent your life in the study of this question, I must beg leave to demand something better. You must not be content merely to prove that justice is superior to injustice, but explain how one is good, the other evil, in virtue of the intrinsic effect each has on its possessor, whether gods or men see it or not.

CHAPTER VI (II. 367 E-372 A)

THE RUDIMENTS OF SOCIAL ORGANIZATION

Socrates has been challenged to define justice and its effects in the individual soul. Since the life of a political society manifests the life of the men composing it on a larger scale, he proposes to look first for the principle which makes a state just and then to see if the same principle has similar effects in a man. So he starts to build up a social structure from its necessary rudiments.

Plato is not here describing the historical development of any actual state. (In Laws iii he says that civilization has often been destroyed by natural cataclysms, and he traces its growth from a simple pastoral phase on lines quite unlike those followed here.) He takes the type of state in which he lived, the Greek city-state. The construction is based on an analysis of such a society into parts corresponding to fundamental needs of human nature. These parts are put together successively in a logical, not an historical, order.

As against the social contract theory, Plato denies that society is 'unnatural,' either as being the artificial outcome of an arbitrary compact or as thwarting the individual's natural instincts, which

*Thrasymachus assumed to be purely egoistic impulses to unlimited
self-assertion. Men are not born self-sufficient or all alike; hence
an organized society in which they are interdependent and special-
ize according to innate aptitudes is, according to Plato, both natural and advantageous to all the individuals.*

*In this chapter society is considered merely as an economic struc-
ture providing for the lowest of needs, a healthy animal existence.
This aspect is isolated by abstraction from the higher elements of
civilization and culture that will soon be added. The purpose is to
establish the principle of specialization or division of labour as dic-
tated by Nature. This will turn out to be the form that justice takes
on this lowest economic level.*

*Nothing is said here about slaves, perhaps because they would
first appear in the luxurious state of the next chapter. In any case
the slaves (who at Athens made up more than a third of the population) were not citizens and so formed no part of the state. The
institution was universally recognized and Plato seems to assume
that it will continue (for instance at 469 c, p. 172).*

I WAS delighted with these speeches from Glaucon and Adeimantus,
whose gifts I had always admired. How right, I exclaimed, was
Glaucon's lover to begin that poem of his on your exploits at the
battle of Megara by describing you two as the

sons divine
Of Ariston's noble line!

Like father, like sons: there must indeed be some divine quality
in your nature, if you can plead the cause of injustice so eloquently
and still not be convinced yourselves that it is better than justice.
That you are not really convinced I am sure from all I know of
your dispositions, though your words might well have left me in
doubt. But the more I trust you, the harder I find it to reply. How
can I come to the rescue? I have no faith in my own powers, when
I remember that you were not satisfied with the proof I thought I
had given to Thrasymachus that it is better to be just. And yet I
cannot stand by and hear justice reviled without lifting a finger.
I am afraid to commit a sin by holding aloof while I have breath

and strength to say a word in its defence. So there is nothing for it but to do the best I can.

Glaucon and the others begged me to step into the breach and carry through our inquiry into the real nature of justice and injustice, and the truth about their respective advantages. So I told them what I thought. This is a very obscure question, I said, and we shall need keen sight to see our way. Now, as we are not remarkably clever, I will make a suggestion as to how we should proceed. Imagine a rather short-sighted person told to read an inscription in small letters from some way off. He would think it a godsend if someone pointed out that the same inscription was written up elsewhere on a bigger scale, so that he could first read the larger characters and then make out whether the smaller ones were the same.

No doubt, said Adeimantus; but what analogy do you see in that to our inquiry?

I will tell you. We think of justice as a quality that may exist in a whole community as well as in an individual, and the community is the bigger of the two. Possibly, then, we may find justice there in larger proportions, easier to make out. So I suggest that we should begin by inquiring what justice means in a state. Then we can go on to look for its counterpart on a smaller scale in the individual.

That seems a good plan, he agreed.

Well then, I continued, suppose we imagine a state coming into being before our eyes. We might then be able to watch the growth of justice or of injustice within it. When that is done, we may hope it will be easier to find what we are looking for.

Much easier.

Shall we try, then, to carry out this scheme? I fancy it will be no light undertaking; so you had better think twice.

No need for that, said Adeimantus. Don't waste any more time.

My notion is, said I, that a state comes into existence because no individual is self-sufficing; we all have many needs. But perhaps you can suggest some different origin for the foundation of a community?

No, I agree with you.

So, having all these needs, we call in one another's help to satisfy our various requirements; and when we have collected a number of helpers and associates to live together in one place, we call that settlement a state.

Yes.

So if one man gives another what he has to give in exchange for what he can get, it is because each finds that to do so is for his own advantage.

Certainly.

Very well, said I. Now let us build up our imaginary state from the beginning. Apparently, it will owe its existence to our needs, the first and greatest need being the provision of food to keep us alive. Next we shall want a house; and thirdly, such things as clothing.

True.

How will our state be able to supply all these demands? We shall need at least one man to be a farmer, another a builder, and a third a weaver. Will that do, or shall we add a shoemaker and one or two more to provide for our personal wants?

By all means.

The minimum state, then, will consist of four or five men.

Apparently.

Now here is a further point. Is each one of them to bring the product of his work into a common stock? Should our one farmer, for example, provide food enough for four people and spend the whole of his working time in producing corn, so as to share with the rest; or should he take no notice of them and spend only a quarter of his time on growing just enough corn for himself, and divide the other three-quarters between building his house, weaving his clothes, and making his shoes, so as to save the trouble of sharing with others and attend himself to all his own concerns?

The first plan might be the easier, replied Adeimantus.

That may very well be so, said I; for, as you spoke, it occurred to me, for one thing, that no two people are born exactly alike. There are innate differences which fit them for different occupations.

I agree.

And will a man do better working at many trades, or keeping to one only?

Keeping to one.

And there is another point: obviously work may be ruined, if you let the right time go by. The workman must wait upon the work; it will not wait upon his leisure and allow itself to be done in a spare moment. So the conclusion is that more things will be produced and the work be more easily and better done, when every man is set free from all other occupations to do, at the right time, the one thing for which he is naturally fitted.

That is certainly true.

We shall need more than four citizens, then, to supply all those necessaries we mentioned. You see, Adeimantus, if the farmer is to have a good plough and spade and other tools, he will not make them himself. No more will the builder and weaver and shoemaker make all the many implements they need. So quite a number of carpenters and smiths and other craftsmen must be enlisted. Our miniature state is beginning to grow.

It is.

Still, it will not be very large, even when we have added cow-herds and shepherds to provide the farmers with oxen for the plough, and the builders as well as the farmers with draught-animals, and the weavers and shoemakers with wool and leather.

No; but it will not be so very small either.

And yet, again, it will be next to impossible to plant our city in a territory where it will need no imports. So there will have to be still another set of people, to fetch what it needs from other countries.

There will.

Moreover, if these agents take with them nothing that those other countries require in exchange, they will return as empty-handed as they went. So, besides everything wanted for consumption at home, we must produce enough goods of the right kind for the foreigners whom we depend on to supply us. That will mean increasing the number of farmers and craftsmen.

Yes.

And then, there are these agents who are to import and export

all kinds of goods—merchants, as we call them. We must have
them; and if they are to do business overseas, we shall need quite
a number of ship-owners and others who know about that branch
of trading.

We shall.

Again, in the city itself how are the various sets of producers to
exchange their products? That was our object, you will remember,
in forming a community and so laying the foundation of our state.

Obviously, they must buy and sell.

That will mean having a market-place, and a currency to serve
as a token for purposes of exchange.

Certainly.

Now suppose a farmer, or an artisan, brings some of his produce
to market at a time when no one is there who wants to exchange
with him. Is he to sit there idle, when he might be at work?

No, he replied; there are people who have seen an opening here
for their services. In well-ordered communities they are generally
men not strong enough to be of use in any other occupation. They
have to stay where they are in the market-place and take goods for
money from those who want to sell, and money for goods from
those who want to buy.

That, then, is the reason why our city must include a class of
shopkeepers—so we call these people who sit still in the market-
place to buy and sell, in contrast with merchants who travel to
other countries.

Quite so.

There are also the services of yet another class, who have the
physical strength for heavy work, though on intellectual grounds
they are hardly worth including in our society—hired labourers, as
we call them, because they sell the use of their strength for wages.
They will go to make up our population.

Yes.

Well, Adeimantus, has our state now grown to its full size?

Perhaps.

Then, where in it shall we find justice or injustice? If they have
come in with one of the elements we have been considering, can
you say with which one?

I have no idea, Socrates; unless it be somewhere in their dealings with one another.

You may be right, I answered. Anyhow, it is a question which we shall have to face.

CHAPTER VII (II. 372 A–374 E)

THE LUXURIOUS STATE

The answer to Socrates' last question—that justice on the level of economic relations lies in the principle of the division of labour according to natural aptitudes—will be given (433 A, p. 127) only when other aspects of justice have emerged. Here follows a picture of life in a society in which only physical needs are satisfied. It is partly a satire on sentimental nostalgia for a supposed primitive state of nature, to which, had it ever existed, there could, as Plato saw, be no return.[1] But the economic organization of the last chapter (which included manufacture for export and overseas trade) was not a self-contained primitive society; it was only the lowest storey in the structure of a civilized state. To the necessaries of existence there provided are now added the refinements of civilization and culture. These satisfy higher needs, but have also entailed unhealthy elements of luxury. Hence, in contrast with the idyllic picture of the simple life, society as now existing appears morbidly 'inflamed,' needing to be purged until only the features of genuine culture remain. The further construction of the ideal state can thus be treated as a reformation of Athenian society in Plato's own day, 'purging our commonwealth of luxurious excess' (399 E, p. 87). His problem is not to build a Utopia in the air, but to discover the least changes which would radically cure the distempers of Athens.

From this standpoint it is clear why he does not contemplate the abolition of war, which could cease only if all states were united in

[1] A picture of primitive patriarchal society after the Deluge is given in *Laws* iii. 678 ff.

*a world-state or if every state were reformed on Plato's principles.
Neither of these issues is considered even as a possibility. He describes a single city-state, surrounded by others which are unre-
formed and by an outer world of non-hellenic nations. The state
will need to be defended by specialists in the art of war. So we
hear, for the first time, of a distinct order of Guardians.*

LET us begin, then, with a picture of our citizens' manner of life,
with the provision we have made for them. They will be producing
corn and wine, and making clothes and shoes. When they have
built their houses, they will mostly work without their coats or
shoes in summer, and in winter be well shod and clothed. For their
food, they will prepare flour and barley-meal for kneading and
baking, and set out a grand spread of loaves and cakes on rushes or
fresh leaves. Then they will lie on beds of myrtle-boughs and
bryony and make merry with their children, drinking their wine
after the feast with garlands on their heads and singing the praises
of the gods. So they will live pleasantly together; and a prudent
fear of poverty or war will keep them from begetting children beyond their means.

Here Glaucon interrupted me: You seem to expect your citizens
to feast on dry bread.

True, I said; I forgot that they will have something to give it a
relish, salt, no doubt, and olives, and cheese, and country stews of
roots and vegetables. And for dessert we will give them figs and
peas and beans; and they shall roast myrtle-berries and acorns at
the fire, while they sip their wine. Leading such a healthy life in
peace, they will naturally come to a good old age, and leave their
children to live after them in the same manner.

That is just the sort of provender you would supply, Socrates, if
you were founding a community of pigs.

Well, how are they to live, then, Glaucon?

With the ordinary comforts. Let them lie on couches and dine
off tables on such dishes and sweets as we have nowadays.

Ah, I see, said I; we are to study the growth, not just of a state,
but of a luxurious one. Well, there may be no harm in that; the
consideration of luxury may help us to discover how justice and

injustice take root in society. The community I have described
seems to me the ideal one, in sound health as it were: but if you
want to see one suffering from inflammation, there is nothing to
hinder us. So some people, it seems, will not be satisfied to live in
this simple way; they must have couches and tables and furniture
of all sorts; and delicacies too, perfumes, unguents, courtesans,
sweetmeats, all in plentiful variety. And besides, we must not limit
ourselves now to those bare necessaries of house and clothes and
shoes; we shall have to set going the arts of embroidery and painting, and collect rich materials, like gold and ivory.

Yes.

Then we must once more enlarge our community. The healthy
one will not be big enough now; it must be swollen up with a
whole multitude of callings not ministering to any bare necessity:
hunters and fishermen, for instance; artists in sculpture, painting,
and music; poets with their attendant train of professional reciters,
actors, dancers, producers; and makers of all sorts of household
gear, including everything for women's adornment. And we shall
want more servants: children's nurses and attendants, lady's maids,
barbers, cooks and confectioners. And then swineherds—there was
no need for them in our original state, but we shall want them
now; and a great quantity of sheep and cattle too, if people are
going to live on meat.

Of course.

And with this manner of life physicians will be in much greater
request.

No doubt.

The country, too, which was large enough to support the original inhabitants, will now be too small. If we are to have enough
pasture and plough land, we shall have to cut off a slice of our
neighbours' territory; and if they too are not content with necessaries, but give themselves up to getting unlimited wealth, they
will want a slice of ours.

That is inevitable, Socrates.

So the next thing will be, Glaucon, that we shall be at war.

No doubt.

We need not say yet whether war does good or harm, but only

that we have discovered its origin in desires which are the most fruitful source of evils both to individuals and to states.[1]

Quite true.

This will mean a considerable addition to our community—a whole army, to go out to battle with any invader, in defence of all this property and of the citizens we have been describing.

Why so? Can't they defend themselves?

Not if the principle was right, which we all accepted in framing our society. You remember we agreed that no one man can practise many trades or arts satisfactorily.

True.

Well, is not the conduct of war an art, quite as important as shoemaking?

Yes.

But we would not allow our shoemaker to try to be also a farmer or weaver or builder, because we wanted our shoes well made. We gave each man one trade, for which he was naturally fitted; he would do good work, if he confined himself to that all his life, never letting the right moment slip by. Now in no form of work is efficiency so important as in war; and fighting is not so easy a business that a man can follow another trade, such as farming or shoemaking, and also be an efficient soldier. Why, even a game like draughts or dice must be studied from childhood; no one can become a fine player in his spare moments. Just taking up a shield or other weapon will not make a man capable of fighting that very day in any sort of warfare, any more than taking up a tool or implement of some kind will make a man a craftsman or an athlete, if he does not understand its use and has never been properly trained to handle it.

No; if that were so, tools would indeed be worth having.

These guardians of our state, then, inasmuch as their work is the most important of all, will need the most complete freedom from other occupations and the greatest amount of skill and practice.

I quite agree.

And also a native aptitude for their calling.

Certainly.

[1] 'All wars are made for the sake of getting money,' *Phaedo* 66 c.

So it is our business to define, if we can, the natural gifts that fit men to be guardians of a commonwealth, and to select them accordingly. It will certainly be a formidable task; but we must grapple with it to the best of our power.

Yes.

CHAPTER VIII (II. 375 A–376 E)

THE GUARDIAN'S TEMPERAMENT

War has been traced to aggression, consequent on the growth of luxury. With the expurgation of luxury aggression might cease; but the state would still need a force to ward off invasion and to keep internal order. The name 'Guardian' suits these defensive purposes. In Plato's century the citizen militia was found to be no match for professional soldiers; so the Guardians are, in the first instance, to be specialists, fitted by a certain combination of qualities to be at once fierce to the country's enemies and gentle to the citizens in their charge.

The fierceness is characteristic of the 'spirited element' in the soul. This term covers a group of impulses manifested in anger and pugnacity, in generous indignation allied to a sense of honour (439 E, p. 137), and in competitive ambition (581 A, p. 308). Its virtue is courage. Spirit needs to be tamed and controlled by the rational or philosophic element, which will later be seen to predominate in the nature of the higher section of Guardians, the philosophic Rulers, whom the lower section, the warriors, will obey. But for the present the Guardians form a single group, whose elementary education and manner of life will presently be described. The philosophic Rulers will be selected from among them at a later stage and subjected to a more advanced training.

At this point the lowest order—farmers, artisans, and traders— drops almost entirely out of sight. No radical change in their mode of life is proposed. They are already performing their function of satisfying the economic needs of the whole state, and any improvements will be consequent upon the reform of their rulers (425 D, p. 117). No explicit provision is made for their education; but un-

less they share in the early education provided for the Guardians,
there could hardly be opportunities for promoting their most
promising children to a higher order (415 B, p. 107).[1]

DON'T you think then, said I, that, for the purpose of keeping
guard, a young man should have much the same temperament
and qualities as a well-bred watch-dog? I mean, for instance, that
both must have quick senses to detect an enemy, swiftness in pursuing him, and strength, if they have to fight when they have
caught him.

Yes, they will need all those qualities.

And also courage, if they are to fight well.

Of course.

And courage, in dog or horse or any other creature, implies a
spirited disposition. You must have noticed that a high spirit is un-
conquerable. Every soul possessed of it is fearless and indomitable
in the face of any danger.

Yes, I have noticed that.

So now we know what physical qualities our Guardian must
have, and also that he must be of a spirited temper.

Yes.

Then, Glaucon, how are men of that natural disposition to be
kept from behaving pugnaciously to one another and to the rest
of their countrymen?

It is not at all easy to see.

And yet they must be gentle to their own people and dangerous
only to enemies; otherwise they will destroy themselves without
waiting till others destroy them.

True.

What are we to do, then? If gentleness and a high temper are
contraries, where shall we find a character to combine them? Both
are necessary to make a good Guardian, but it seems they are incompatible. So we shall never have a good Guardian.

It looks like it.

---

[1] The lowest order are not the 'working-class' only, but all citizens who are not
chosen to be Guardians, including all owners of property.

Here I was perplexed, but on thinking over what we had been saying, I remarked that we deserved to be puzzled, because we had not followed up the comparison we had just drawn.

What do you mean? he asked.

We never noticed that, after all, there are natures in which these contraries are combined. They are to be found in animals, and not least in the kind we compared to our Guardian. Well-bred dogs, as you know, are by instinct perfectly gentle to people whom they know and are accustomed to, and fierce to strangers. So the combination of qualities we require for our Guardian is, after all, possible and not against nature.

Evidently.

Do you further agree that, besides this spirited temper, he must have a philosophical element in his nature?

I don't see what you mean.

This is another trait you will see in the dog. It is really remarkable how the creature gets angry at the mere sight of a stranger and welcomes anyone he knows, though he may never have been treated unkindly by the one or kindly by the other. Did that never strike you as curious?

I had not thought of it before; but that certainly is how a dog behaves.

Well, but that shows a fine instinct, which is philosophic in the true sense.

How so?

Because the only mark by which he distinguishes a friendly and an unfriendly face is that he knows the one and does not know the other; and if a creature makes that the test of what it finds congenial or otherwise, how can you deny that it has a passion for knowledge and understanding?

Of course, I cannot.

And that passion is the same thing as philosophy—the love of wisdom.[1]

Yes.

[1] The ascription of a philosophic element to dogs is not seriously meant. We might regard man's love of knowledge as rooted in an instinct of curiosity to be

Shall we boldly say, then, that the same is true of human beings? If a man is to be gentle towards his own people whom he knows, he must have an instinctive love of wisdom and understanding.

Agreed.

So the nature required to make a really noble Guardian of our commonwealth will be swift and strong, spirited, and philosophic.

Quite so.

Given those natural qualities, then, how are these Guardians to be brought up and educated? First, will the answer to that question help the purpose of our whole inquiry, which is to make out how justice and injustice grow up in a state? We want to be thorough, but not to draw out this discussion to a needless length.

Glaucon's brother answered: I certainly think it will help.

If so, I said, we must not think of dropping it, though it may be rather a long business.

I agree.

Come on then. We will take our time and educate our imaginary citizens.

Yes, let us do so.

CHAPTER IX (II. 376 E–III. 412 B)

PRIMARY EDUCATION OF THE GUARDIANS

The education of Athenian boys, for which the family, not the state, was responsible, was carried on at private day-schools. It mainly consisted of reading and writing ('Grammatic'); learning and reciting epic and dramatic poetry, lyre-playing and singing lyric poetry, the rudiments of arithmetic and geometry ('Music'); and athletic exercises ('Gymnastic'). 'Music' included all the arts over which the Muses presided: music, art, letters, culture, philosophy. Since the word has now a much restricted meaning, the trans-

found in animals; but curiosity has no connexion with gentleness, and for Plato reason is an independent faculty, existing only in man and not developed from any animal instinct.

lation substitutes a paraphrase. This education might cease at about the age of 15 or be prolonged to 18, when the youth had two years' military training. Plato adopts the system, only removing features which will not help to produce the type of character his Guardians are to have. These simplifying reforms are part of the process of ridding the luxurious state of unhealthy elements in contemporary civilization.

§ 1 (376 E–392 C). CENSORSHIP OF LITERATURE FOR SCHOOL USE

Plato begins with the content of the poetry used in early educa-tion. The Athenian child took his notions of the gods chiefly from Homer and Hesiod, who, as Xenophanes more than a century earlier had complained, attributed to them every sort of immorality. Plato's censorship of the poets as school-books is in line with the practice of modern parents and schoolmasters; but later it develops into a more general attack on poetry.

In the fourth century highly educated men had ceased to believe in the existence of supernatural persons called Zeus, Athena, Apollo, &c., with their mythical attributes and adventures. Myths were not dogma, and no one was required to profess a belief in them. Priests had no authority over belief; they were officials whose duty was to carry out the ritual. The state required only that the cult should be maintained and that the existence of gods, as im-plied by this worship, should not be blatantly denied. Plato does not propose to abolish or to reform the state religion, though in his old age he would have liked to add a cult of the heavenly bodies as symbols of the beauty and harmonious order of the uni-verse, which, he believed, manifested the working of a beneficent intelligence.

He uses the singular 'god' and the plural 'the gods' with an in-difference startling to the modern monotheist. For this reason the translation avoids the expression 'God,' though the reason may be insufficient, since modern philosophers use the term with astonish-ing latitude and often in senses which they neglect to define.

The words 'fiction,' 'fictitious,' are used to represent the Greek pseudos, *which has a much wider sense than our 'lie': it covers any statement describing events which never in fact occurred, and so applies to all works of imagination, all fictitious narratives ('stories') in myth or allegory, fable or parable, poetry or romance. As Plato does not confuse fiction with falsehood or identify truth with literal statements of fact,* pseudos *should be rendered by 'fiction' or 'falsehood' according to the context, and sometimes by 'lie.' It can also mean 'error' when it corresponds to the passive verb* epseusthai = *'to be deceived' or 'mistaken' (as at 382 B 535 E).*

This chapter has been shortened by condensation and by omitting a number of passages from the poets which Plato rejects as impious or immoral.

WHAT is this education to be, then? Perhaps we shall hardly invent a system better than the one which long experience has worked out, with its two branches for the cultivation of the mind and of the body. And I suppose we shall begin with the mind, before we start physical training.

Naturally.

Under that head will come stories; [1] and of these there are two kinds: some are true, others fictitious. Both must come in, but we shall begin our education with the fictitious kind.

I don't understand, he said.

Don't you understand, I replied, that we begin by telling children stories, which, taken as a whole, are fiction, though they contain some truth? Such story-telling begins at an earlier age than physical training; that is why I said we should start with the mind.

You are right.

And the beginning, as you know, is always the most important part, especially in dealing with anything young and tender. That is the time when the character is being moulded and easily takes any impress one may wish to stamp on it.

Quite true.

[1] In a wide sense, tales, legends, myths, narratives in poetry or prose.

Then shall we simply allow our children to listen to any stories that anyone happens to make up, and so receive into their minds ideas often the very opposite of those we shall think they ought to have when they are grown up?

No, certainly not.

It seems, then, our first business will be to supervise the making of fables and legends, rejecting all which are unsatisfactory; and we shall induce nurses and mothers to tell their children only those which we have approved, and to think more of moulding their souls with these stories than they now do of rubbing their limbs to make them strong and shapely. Most of the stories now in use must be discarded.

What kind do you mean?

If we take the great ones, we shall see in them the pattern of all the rest, which are bound to be of the same stamp and to have the same effect.

No doubt; but which do you mean by the great ones?

The stories in Hesiod and Homer and the poets in general, who have at all times composed fictitious tales and told them to mankind.

Which kind are you thinking of, and what fault do you find in them?

The worst of all faults, especially if the story is ugly and immoral as well as false—misrepresenting the nature of gods and heroes, like an artist whose picture is utterly unlike the object he sets out to draw.

That is certainly a serious fault; but give me an example.

A signal instance of false invention about the highest matters is that foul story, which Hesiod repeats, of the deeds of Uranus and the vengeance of Cronos; [1] and then there is the tale of Cronos's doings and of his son's treatment of him. Even if such tales were true, I should not have supposed they should be lightly told to thoughtless young people. If they cannot be altogether suppressed,

---

[1] Hesiod, *Theogony*, 154 ff. A primitive myth of the forcing apart of Sky (Uranus) and Earth (Gaia) by their son Cronos, who mutilated his father. Zeus, again, took vengeance on his father Cronos for trying to destroy his children. These stories were sometimes cited to justify ill-treatment of parents.

they should only be revealed in a mystery, to which access should be as far as possible restricted by requiring the sacrifice, not of a pig, but of some victim such as very few could afford.[1]

It is true: those stories are objectionable.

Yes, and not to be repeated in our commonwealth, Adeimantus. We shall not tell a child that, if he commits the foulest crimes or goes to any length in punishing his father's misdeeds, he will be doing nothing out of the way, but only what the first and greatest of the gods have done before him.

I agree; such stories are not fit to be repeated.

Nor yet any tales of warfare and intrigues and battles of gods against gods, which are equally untrue. If our future Guardians are to think it a disgrace to quarrel lightly with one another, we shall not let them embroider robes with the Battle of the Giants [2] or tell them of all the other feuds of gods and heroes with their kith and kin. If by any means we can make them believe that no one has ever had a quarrel with a fellow citizen and it is a sin to have one, that is the sort of thing our old men and women should tell children from the first; and as they grow older, we must make the poets write for them in the same strain. Stories like those of Hera being bound by her son, or of Hephaestus flung from heaven by his father for taking his mother's part when she was beaten, and all those battles of the gods in Homer, must not be admitted into our state, whether they be allegorical or not. A child cannot distinguish the allegorical sense from the literal, and the ideas he takes in at that age are likely to become indelibly fixed; hence the great importance of seeing that the first stories he hears shall be designed to produce the best possible effect on his character.

Yes, that is reasonable. But if we were asked which of these stories in particular are of the right quality, what should we answer?

I replied: You and I, Adeimantus, are not, for the moment,

[1] The usual sacrifice at the Eleusinian Mysteries was a pig, which was cheap. In a mystery unedifying legends might be given an allegorical interpretation, a method which had been applied to Homer since the end of the sixth century B.C.

[2] Such a robe was woven by maidens for the statue of Athena at the Great Panathenaea.

poets, but founders of a commonwealth. As such, it is not our business to invent stories ourselves, but only to be clear as to the main outlines to be followed by the poets in making their stories and the limits beyond which they must not be allowed to go.

True; but what are these outlines for any account they may give of the gods?

Of this sort, said I. A poet, whether he is writing epic, lyric, or drama, surely ought always to represent the divine nature as it really is. And the truth is that that nature is good and must be described as such.

Unquestionably.

Well, nothing that is good can be harmful; and if it cannot do harm, it can do no evil; and so it cannot be responsible for any evil.

I agree.

Again, goodness is beneficent, and hence the cause of well-being.

Yes.

Goodness, then, is not responsible for everything, but only for what is as it should be. It is not responsible for evil.[1]

Quite true.

It follows, then, that the divine, being good, is not, as most people say, responsible for everything that happens to mankind, but only for a small part; for the good things in human life are far fewer than the evil, and, whereas the good must be ascribed to heaven only, we must look elsewhere for the cause of evils.

I think that is perfectly true.

So we shall condemn as a foolish error Homer's description of Zeus as the 'dispenser of both good and ill.'[2] We shall disapprove when Pandarus' violation of oaths and treaties is said to be the work of Zeus and Athena, or when Themis and Zeus are said to have caused strife among the gods. Nor must we allow our young people to be told by Aeschylus that 'Heaven implants guilt in man, when his will is to destroy a house utterly.' If a poet writes of the sorrows of Niobe or the calamities of the house of Pelops or of

[1] The words of Lachesis in the concluding myth (617 E, p. 357) illustrate Plato's meaning.
[2] Some further instances from Homer are here omitted.

the Trojan war, either he must not speak of them as the work of a god, or, if he does so, he must devise some such explanation as we are now requiring: he must say that what the god did was just and good, and the sufferers were the better for being chastised. One who pays a just penalty must not be called miserable, and his misery then laid at heaven's door. The poet will only be allowed to say that the wicked were miserable because they needed chastisement, and the punishment of heaven did them good. If our commonwealth is to be well-ordered, we must fight to the last against any member of it being suffered to speak of the divine, which is good, being responsible for evil. Neither young nor old must listen to such tales, in prose or verse. Such doctrine would be impious, self-contradictory, and disastrous to our commonwealth.

I agree, he said, and I would vote for a law to that effect.

Well then, that shall be one of our laws about religion. The first principle to which all must conform in speech or writing is that heaven is not responsible for everything, but only for what is good.

I am quite satisfied.

Now what of this for a second principle? Do you think of a god as a sort of magician who might, for his own purposes, appear in various shapes, now actually passing into a number of different forms, now deluding us into believing he has done so; or is his nature simple and of all things the least likely to depart from its proper form?

I cannot say offhand.

Well, if a thing passes out of its proper form, must not the change come either from within or from some outside cause?

Yes.

Is it not true, then, that things in the most perfect condition are the least affected by changes from outside? Take the effect on the body of food and drink or of exertion, or the effect of sunshine and wind on a plant: the healthiest and strongest suffer the least change. Again, the bravest and wisest spirit is least disturbed by external influence. Even manufactured things—furniture, houses, clothes—suffer least from wear and tear when they are well made and in good condition. So this immunity to change from outside is characteristic of anything which, thanks to art or nature or both, is in a satisfactory state.

That seems true.

But surely the state of the divine nature must be perfect in every way, and would therefore be the last thing to suffer transformations from any outside cause.

Yes.

Well then, would a god change or alter himself?

If he changes at all, it can only be in that way.

Would it be a change for the better or for the worse?

It could only be for the worse; for we cannot admit any imperfection in divine goodness or beauty.

True; and that being so, do you think, Adeimantus, that anyone, god or man, would deliberately make himself worse in any respect?

That is impossible.

Then a god cannot desire to change himself. Being as perfect as he can be, every god, it seems, remains simply and for ever in his own form.

That is the necessary conclusion.

If so, my friend, the poets must not tell us that 'the gods go to and fro among the cities of men, disguised as strangers of all sorts from far countries'; nor must they tell any of those false tales of Proteus and Thetis transforming themselves, or bring Hera on the stage in the guise of a priestess collecting alms for 'the life-giving children of Inachus, the river of Argos.'[1] Mothers, again, are not to follow these suggestions and scare young children with mischievous stories of spirits that go about by night in all sorts of outlandish shapes. They would only be blaspheming the gods and at the same time making cowards of their children.

No, that must not be allowed.

But are we to think that the gods, though they do not really change, trick us by some magic into believing that they appear in many different forms?

Perhaps.

---

[1] The allusions are to the *Odyssey* and to a lost play of Aeschylus.

What? said I; would a god tell a falsehood or act one by deluding us with an apparition?

I cannot say.

Do you not know that the true falsehood—if that is a possible expression—is a thing that all gods and men abominate?

What do you mean?

This, I replied: no one, if he could help it, would tolerate the presence of untruth in the most vital part of his nature concerning the most vital matters. There is nothing he would fear so much as to harbour falsehood in that quarter.

Still I do not understand.

Because you think I mean something out of the ordinary. All I mean is the presence of falsehood in the soul concerning reality. To be deceived about the truth of things and so to be in ignorance and error and to harbour untruth in the soul is a thing no one would consent to. Falsehood in that quarter is abhorred above everything.

It is indeed.

Well then, as I was saying, this ignorance in the soul which entertains untruth is what really deserves to be called the true falsehood; for the spoken falsehood is only the embodiment or image of a previous condition of the soul, not pure unadulterated falsity. Is it not so?

It is.

This real falsehood, then, is hateful to gods and men equally. But is the spoken falsehood always a hateful thing? Is it not sometimes helpful—in war, for instance, or as a sort of medicine to avert some fit of folly or madness that might make a friend attempt some mischief? And in those legends we were discussing just now, we can turn fiction to account; not knowing the facts about the distant past, we can make our fiction as good an embodiment of truth as possible.

Yes, that is so.

Well, in which of these ways would falsehood be useful to a god? We cannot think of him as embodying truth in fiction for lack of information about the past.

No, that would be absurd.

So there is no room in his case for poetical inventions. Would he need to tell untruths because he has enemies to fear?

Of course not.

Or friends who are mad or foolish?

No; a fool or a madman could hardly enjoy the friendship of the gods.

Gods, then, have no motive for lying. There can be no falsehood of any sort in the divine nature.

None.

We conclude, then, that a god is a being of entire simplicity and truthfulness in word and in deed. In himself he does not change, nor does he delude others, either in dreams or in waking moments, by apparitions or oracles or signs.

I agree, after all you have said.

You will assent, then, to this as a second principle to guide all that is to be said or written about the gods: that they do not transform themselves by any magic or mislead us by illusions or lies. For all our admiration of Homer, we shall not approve his story of the dream Zeus sent to Agamemnon;[1] nor yet those lines of Aeschylus where Thetis tells how Apollo sang at her wedding:

> Boding good fortune for my child, long life
> From sickness free, in all things blest by heaven,
> His song, so crowned with triumph, cheered my heart.
> I thought those lips divine, with prophecy
> Instinct, could never lie. But he, this guest,
> Whose voice so rang with promise at the feast,
> Even he, has slain my son.

If a poet writes of the gods in this way, we shall be angry and refuse him the means to produce his play. Nor shall we allow such poetry to be used in educating the young, if we mean our Guardians to be godfearing and to reproduce the divine nature in themselves so far as man may.

I entirely agree with your principles, he said, and I would have them observed as laws.

[1] *Iliad* ii. 1 ff.

So far, then, as religion is concerned, we have settled what sorts of stories about the gods may, or may not, be told to children who are to hold heaven and their parents in reverence and to value good relations with one another.

Yes, he said; and I believe we have settled right.

We also want them to be brave. So the stories they hear should be such as to make them unafraid of death. A man with that fear in his heart cannot be brave, can he?

Surely not.

And can a man be free from that fear and prefer death in battle to defeat and slavery, if he believes in a world below which is full of terrors?

No.

Here again, then, our supervision will be needed. The poets must be told to speak well of that other world. The gloomy descriptions they now give must be forbidden, not only as untrue, but as injurious to our future warriors. We shall strike out all lines like these:

I would rather be on earth as the hired servant of another, in the house of a landless man with little to live on, than be king over all the dead;[1]

or these:

Alack, there is, then, even in the house of Death a spirit or a shade; but the wits dwell in it no more.[2]

We shall ask Homer and the poets in general not to mind if we cross out all passages of this sort. If most people enjoy them as good poetry, that is all the more reason for keeping them from children or grown men who are to be free, fearing slavery more than death.

I entirely agree.

We must also get rid of all that terrifying language, the very

---

[1] Spoken by the ghost of Achilles, *Od*. xi. 489.

[2] Spoken by Achilles when the ghost of Patroclus eludes his embrace, *Iliad* xxiii. 103. Other lines from Homer describing the misery of the dead are omitted.

sound of which is enough to make one shiver: 'loathsome Styx,' 'the River of Wailing,' 'infernal spirits,' 'anatomies,' and so on. For other purposes such language may be well enough; but we are afraid that fever consequent upon such shivering fits may melt down the fine-tempered spirit of our Guardians. So we will have none of it; and we shall encourage writing in the opposite strain.

Clearly.

Another thing we must banish is the wailing and lamentations of the famous heroes. For this reason: if two friends are both men of high character, neither of them will think that death has any terrors for his comrade; and so he will not mourn for his friend's sake, as if something terrible had befallen him.

No.

We also believe that such a man, above all, possesses within himself all that is necessary for a good life and is least dependent on others, so that he has less to fear from the loss of a son or brother or of his wealth or any other possession. When such misfortune comes, he will bear it patiently without lamenting.

True.

We shall do well, then, to strike out descriptions of the heroes bewailing the dead, and make over such lamentations to women (and not to women of good standing either) and to men of low character, so that the Guardians we are training for our country may disdain to imitate them.

Quite right.

Once more, then, we shall ask Homer and the other poets not to represent Achilles, the son of a goddess, as 'tossing from side to side, now on his face, now on his back,' and then as rising up and wandering distractedly on the seashore, or pouring ashes on his head with both hands, with all those tears and wailings the poet describes; nor to tell how Priam, who was near akin to the gods, 'rolled in the dung as he made entreaty, calling on each man by name.'[1] Still more earnestly shall we ask them not to represent gods as lamenting, or at any rate not to dare to misrepresent the

---

[1] When Priam saw Achilles maltreating the body of Hector, *Iliad* xxii. 414.

highest god by making him say: 'Woe is me that Sarpedon, whom I love above all men, is fated to die at the hands of Patroclus.' For if our young men take such unworthy descriptions seriously instead of laughing at them, they will hardly feel themselves, who are but men, above behaving in that way or repress any temptation to do so. They would not be ashamed of giving way with complaints and outcries on every trifling occasion; and that would be contrary to the principle we have deduced and shall adhere to, until someone can show us a better.

It would.

Again, our Guardians ought not to be overmuch given to laughter. Violent laughter tends to provoke an equally violent reaction. We must not allow poets to describe men of worth being overcome by it; still less should Homer speak of the gods giving way to 'unquenchable laughter' at the sight of Hephaestus 'bustling from room to room.' That will be against your principles.

Yes, if you choose to call them mine.

Again, a high value must be set upon truthfulness. If we were right in saying that gods have no use for falsehood and it is useful to mankind only in the way of a medicine, obviously a medicine should be handled by no one but a physician.

Obviously.

If anyone, then, is to practise deception, either on the country's enemies or on its citizens, it must be the Rulers of the commonwealth, acting for its benefit; no one else may meddle with this privilege. For a private person to mislead such Rulers we shall declare to be a worse offence than for a patient to mislead his doctor or an athlete his trainer about his bodily condition, or for a seaman to misinform his captain about the state of the ship or of the crew. So, if anyone else in our commonwealth 'of all that practise crafts, physician, seer, or carpenter,' is caught not telling the truth, the Rulers will punish him for introducing a practice as fatal and subversive in a state as it would be in a ship.

It would certainly be as fatal, if action were suited to the word.

Next, our young men will need self-control; and for the mass of mankind that chiefly means obeying their governors, and themselves governing their appetite for the pleasures of eating and drinking and sex. Here again we shall disapprove of much that we find in Homer.[1]

I agree.

Whereas we shall allow the poets to represent any examples of self-control and fortitude on the part of famous men, and admit such lines as these: 'Odysseus smote his breast, chiding his heart: Endure, my heart; thou has borne worse things than these.'

Yes, certainly.

Nor again must these men of ours be lovers of money, or ready to take bribes. They must not hear that 'gods and great princes may be won by gifts.'

No, that sort of thing cannot be approved.

If it were not for my regard for Homer, I should not hesitate to call it downright impiety to make Achilles say to Apollo: 'Thou has wronged me, thou deadliest of gods; I would surely requite thee, if I had but the power.' And all those stories of Achilles dragging Hector round the tomb of Patroclus and slaughtering captives on the funeral pyre we shall condemn as false, and not let our Guardians believe that Achilles, who was the son of a goddess and of the wise Peleus, third in descent from Zeus, and the pupil of the sage Chiron, was so disordered that his heart was a prey to two contrary maladies, mean covetousness and arrogant contempt of gods and men.

You are right.

We have now distinguished the kinds of stories that may and may not be told about gods and demigods, heroes, and the world below. There remains the literature concerned with human life.

Clearly.

We cannot lay down rules for that at our present stage.

Why not?

Because, I suspect, we shall find both poets and prose-writers guilty of the most serious misstatements about human life, making out that wrongdoers are often happy and just men miserable; that

---

[1] In order to save space, illustrations from Homer of the self-indulgence of heroes and gods and of disrespect for rulers are omitted here and below.

injustice pays, if not detected; and that my being just is to another man's advantage, but a loss to myself. We shall have to prohibit such poems and tales and tell them to compose others in the contrary sense. Don't you think so?

I am sure of it.

Well, as soon as you admit that I am right there, may I not claim that we shall have reached agreement on the subject of all this inquiry?

That is a fair assumption.

Then we must postpone any decision as to how the truth is to be told about human life, until we have discovered the real nature of justice and proved that it is intrinsically profitable to its possessor, no matter what reputation he may have in the eyes of the world.

That is certainly true.

§ 2 (392 C–398 B). THE INFLUENCE OF DRAMATIC RECITATION

Plato now passes from the content of literature used in school to its form. The Greek schoolboy was not allowed to repeat Homer or Aeschylus in a perfunctory gabble, but expected to throw himself into the story and deliver the speeches with the tones and gesture of an actor. (The professional reciter, Ion, describes how, when he was reciting Homer, his eyes watered and his hair stood on end, Ion 535 c.) The word for this dramatic representation is mimesis. This has also the wider sense of 'imitation,' and towards the end of this section it is used of the realistic copying of natural sounds and noises in music. But at first Plato is chiefly concerned with the actor's assumption of a character. The actor does not 'imitate' Othello, whom he has never seen; he represents or embodies or reproduces the character created by Shakespeare. In some degree the spectator also identifies himself with a character he admires. Plato held that, in childhood particularly, such imaginative identification may leave its permanent mark on the characters of actor and audience. He will return to this subject in Chapters XXXVI and XXXVII. This section has been considerably abbreviated.

So much for the content of literature. If we consider next the question of form, we shall then have covered the whole field.

I don't understand what you mean by form, said Adeimantus.

I must explain, then, said I. Let me put it in this way. Any story in prose or verse is always a setting forth of events, past, present, or future, isn't it?

Yes.

And that can be done either in pure narrative or by means of representation or in both ways.

I am still rather in the dark.

I seem to be a poor hand at explaining; I had better give a particular illustration.[1] You remember the beginning of the *Iliad,* which describes how Chryses begged Agamemnon to release his daughter, and Agamemnon was angry, and Chryses called on his god to avenge the refusal on the Greeks. So far the poet speaks in his own person, but later on he speaks in the character of Chryses and tries to make us feel that the words come, not from Homer, but from an aged priest. Throughout the *Iliad* and *Odyssey,* the events are set forth in these two different forms. All the time, both in the speeches and in the narrative parts in between, he is telling his story; but where he is delivering a speech in character, he tries to make his manner resemble that of the person he has introduced as speaker. Any poet who does that by means of voice and gesture, is telling his story by way of dramatic representation; whereas, if he makes no such attempt to suppress his own personality, the events are set forth in simple narrative.

Now I understand.

Observe, then, that, if you omit the intervening narrative and leave only the dialogue, you get the opposite form.

Yes, I see; that occurs in tragedy, for instance.

Exactly, said I. Now I think you see the distinction I failed to make clear. All story-telling, in prose or poetry, is in one of three forms. It may be wholly dramatic: tragedy, as you say, or comedy. Or the poet may narrate the events in his own person; perhaps

---

[1] The explanation, necessitated by the ambiguity of the Greek *mimesis,* is shortened in the translation.

the best example of that is the dithyramb.[1] Or again both methods may be used, as in epic and several other kinds of poetry.

Yes, he said, I see now what you meant.

Remember, too, I began by saying that, having done with the
content, we had still to consider the form. I meant that we should
have to decide whether to allow our poets to tell their story in
dramatic form, wholly, or in part (and, if so, in what parts), or not
at all.

You mean, I suspect, the question whether we shall admit tragedy and comedy into our commonwealth.

Perhaps, I replied, or the question may be wider still. I do not
know yet; but we must go wherever the wind of the argument
carries us.[2]

That is good advice.

Here then, Adeimantus, is a question for you to consider: Do
we want our Guardians to be capable of playing many parts? Perhaps the answer follows from our earlier principle that a man can
only do one thing well; if he tries his hand at several, he will fail
to make his mark in any of them. Does not that principle apply to
acting? The same man cannot act many parts so well as he can
act one.

No, he cannot.

Then he will hardly be able to pursue some worthy occupation
and at the same time represent a variety of different characters.
Even in the case of two forms of representation so closely allied as
tragedy and comedy, the same poet cannot write both with equal
success. Again, the recitation of epic poetry and acting on the stage
are distinct professions; and even on the stage different actors perform in tragedy and comedy.

That is so.

And human talent, Adeimantus, seems to be split up into sub-
divisions even minuter than these; so that no man can successfully represent many different characters in the field of art or pursue a corresponding variety of occupations in real life.

---

[1] The most important type of lyric poetry in Plato's time.
[2] In Chap. XXXV poetry and painting will in fact be criticized as 'representation'
in a wider sense.

Quite true.

If, then, we are to hold fast to our original principle that our Guardians shall be set free from all manual crafts to be the artificers of their country's freedom, with the perfect mastery which comes of working only at what conduces to that end, they ought not to play any other part in dramatic representation any more than in real life; but if they act, they should, from childhood upward, impersonate only the appropriate types of character, men who are brave, religious, self-controlled, generous. They are not to do anything mean or dishonourable; no more should they be practised in representing such behaviour, for fear of becoming infected with the reality. You must have noticed how the reproduction of another person's gestures or tones of voice or states of mind, if persisted in from youth up, grows into a habit which becomes second nature.

Yes, I have.

So these charges of ours, who are to grow up into men of worth, will not be allowed to enact the part of a woman, old or young, railing against her husband, or boasting of a happiness which she imagines can rival the gods', or overwhelmed with grief and misfortune; much less a woman in love, or sick, or in labour; nor yet slaves of either sex, going about their menial work; nor men of a low type, behaving with cowardice and all the qualities contrary to those we mentioned, deriding one another and exchanging coarse abuse, whether drunk or sober, and otherwise using language and behaviour that are an offence against themselves as well as their neighbours; nor must they copy the words and actions of madmen. Knowledge they must have of baseness and insanity both in men and women, but not reproduce such behaviour in life or in art.

Quite true.

Again, are they to impersonate men working at some trade, such as a smith's, or rowing a galley or giving the time to the oarsmen?

How should they, when they are not even to take any notice of such occupations?

And may they take part in performances which imitate horses

neighing and bulls bellowing or the noise of rivers and sea and thunder?[1]

We have already forbidden them to represent the ravings of insanity.

If I understand you, then, there are two contrasted forms of expression in which any series of events may be set forth: one which will always be used by a man of fine character and breeding, the other by one whose nature and upbringing are of a very different sort.[2]

Yes, there are those two forms.

One of them involves little change and variety; when the words have been fitted to a suitable musical mode and rhythm, the recitation can keep almost to the same mode and rhythm throughout, the modulations required being slight. The other, on the contrary, involves every sort of variation and demands the use of all the modes and rhythms there are.

Quite true.

Now all writers and composers fall into one or other of these styles, or a mixture of both. What shall we do? Are we to admit into our commonwealth one or other of the extreme styles, or the mixed one, or all three?

If my judgement is to prevail, the simple one which serves to represent a fine character.

On the other hand, Adeimantus, the mixed style has its attractions; and children and their attendants, not to mention the great mass of the public, find the opposite of the one you chose the most attractive of all.

No doubt they do.

[1] This probably refers to the realistic dithyrambic poetry of the fourth century, and more particularly to the musical accompaniment. Philoxenus' dithyramb *Cyclops* represented the bleating of Polyphemus' flock; the *Nautilus* of Timotheus depicted a storm at sea.

[2] Plato's point being now sufficiently clear, the translation omits a passage in which he says that a man of well-regulated character will confine himself to impersonating men of a similar type and will consequently use pure narrative for the most part. A vulgar person, on the other hand, will impersonate any type and even give musical imitations of the cries of animals and inanimate noises. Plato began by speaking of recitation as a part of early education, but he now proposes to exclude poetry and music of the second kind from the state altogether.

But perhaps you think it will not suit our commonwealth, where no man is to be two or more persons or a jack of all trades; this being the reason why ours is the only state in which we shall find a shoemaker who cannot also take command of a ship, a farmer who does not leave his farm to serve on juries, a soldier who is not a tradesman into the bargain.

Quite true.

Suppose, then, that an individual clever enough to assume any character and give imitations of anything and everything should visit our country and offer to perform his compositions, we shall bow down before a being with such miraculous powers of giving pleasure; but we shall tell him that we are not allowed to have any such person in our commonwealth; we shall crown him with fillets of wool, anoint his head with myrrh, and conduct him to the borders of some other country. For our own benefit, we shall employ the poets and story-tellers of the more austere and less attractive type, who will reproduce only the manner of a person of high character and, in the substance of their discourse, conform to those rules we laid down when we began the education of our warriors.

Yes, we shall do that, if it lies in our power.

So now, my dear Adeimantus, we have discussed both the content and the form of literature, and we have finished with that part of education.

Yes, I think so.

§ 3 (398 c–400 c). MUSICAL ACCOMPANIMENT AND METRE

Plato approves of the old practice of writing lyric poetry only to be sung to music, and music only as an accompaniment to song. Hence he speaks of words, musical mode (harmonia), and rhythm (metre in poetry and time in music) as inseparable parts of 'song.' There was no harmony in the modern sense; and the melody followed the words very closely. At first there was normally one note to each syllable, and every syllable was conventionally treated as either 'long' or 'short,' the long being equal to two shorts. By Plato's

time the growing practice of using the poem as a libretto and dis-
torting the words to suit the music had already excited protest.

In the older lyric poetry, of Aeschylus and Pindar for example,
certain rhythms and certain modes were associated with particular
moods of feeling and types of character, and, as the poetry passed
from one mood or type to another, both metre and mode were suit-
ably modulated. Accordingly, the limitations already imposed on
the content of poetry entail corresponding limitations on the choice
of metre and on the musical accompaniment.

This section has been abbreviated by the omission of technicali-
ties of Greek music and metre, which are still imperfectly under-
stood.

There remains the question of style in song and poetry set to
music. It must be easy now for anyone to discover the rules we
must make as to their character, if we are to be consistent.

Glaucon laughed. I am afraid 'anyone' does not include me,
Socrates. At the moment I cannot quite see what the rules should
be, though I have my suspicions.

You can see this much at any rate, that song consists of three
elements: words, musical mode, and rhythm.

Yes.

And so far as the words go, it will make no difference whether
they are set to music or not; in either case they must conform to
the rules we have already made for the content and form of literature.

True.

And the musical mode and the rhythm should fit the words?

Of course.

And we said that we did not want dirges and laments. Which
are the modes that express sorrow? Tell me; you are musical.

Modes like the Mixed Lydian and Hyperlydian.

Then we may discard those; men, and even women of good
standing, will have no use for them.

Certainly.

Again, drunkenness, effeminacy, and inactivity are most unsuitable in Guardians. Which are the modes expressing softness and the ones used at drinking-parties?

There are the Ionian and certain Lydian modes which are called 'slack.'

You will not use them in the training of your warriors?

Certainly not. You seem to have the Dorian and the Phrygian left.

I am not an expert in the modes, I said; but leave me one which will fittingly represent the tones and accents of a brave man in war-like action or in any hard and dangerous task, who, in the hour of defeat or when facing wounds and death, will meet every blow of fortune with steadfast endurance. We shall need another to express peaceful action under no stress of hard necessity; as when a man is using persuasion or entreaty, praying to the gods or instructing and admonishing his neighbour, or again submitting himself to the instruction and persuasion of others; a man who is not overbearing when any such action has proved successful,[1] but behaves always with wise restraint and is content with the outcome. These two modes you must leave: the two which will best express the accents of courage in the face of stern necessity and misfortune, and of temperance in prosperity won by peaceful pursuits.

The modes you want, he replied, are just the two I mentioned.

Our songs and airs, then, will not need instruments of large compass capable of modulation into all the modes, and we shall not maintain craftsmen to make them, in particular the flute, which has the largest compass of all. That leaves the lyre and the cithara for use in the town; and in the country the herdsmen may have some sort of pipe.

That seems to be the conclusion.

At any rate, it is no innovation to prefer Apollo to Marsyas in the choice of instruments.

Surely not.

It strikes me, said I, that, without noticing it, we have been purging our commonwealth of that luxurious excess we said it suffered from.

A wise proceeding, he replied.

---

[1] Omitting καί before μὴ in 399 B 7.

Let us go through with it, then. Next after the modes will come the principle governing rhythm, which will be, not to aim at a great variety of metres, but to discover the rhythms appropriate to a life of courage and self-control; and we shall then adapt metre and melody to the words expressing a life of that sort, not the words to the metre and melody. What these rhythms are, it is for you to explain, as you explained the modes.

Really, he replied, I cannot do that. I have observed that there are three fundamental types of rhythm to which all metres may be reduced, just as there are four intervals at the base of all the modes;[1] but what kind of life each rhythm is suited to express, I cannot say.

Well, said I, we shall consult Damon[2] on this question, which metres are expressive of meanness, insolence, frenzy, and other such evils, and which rhythms we must retain to express their opposites. It would take a long time to settle all that.

It would indeed.

§ 4 (400 C–403 C). THE AIM OF EDUCATION IN POETRY AND MUSIC

Plato here passes from the simplification of poetry and music as used in early education to consider the whole field of art and craftsmanship and its influence on character. In his Protagoras *(326 A), a conversation imagined as taking place in the previous century, Plato had made Protagoras speak of children's training in music as introducing rhythm and harmony into their souls and having a socializing influence; 'for the whole life of man stands in need of rhythm and harmony.' This is not represented as a novel doctrine, but as if it were already a commonplace. The fragments of Damon suggest that it may have been formulated by him.*

The ultimate end of all education is insight into the harmonious

---

[1] The meaning is uncertain, but the three perfect consonances (octave, fourth, fifth) and the tone may be intended.

[2] A famous musician, the friend of Pericles. An obscure account of certain metres is here omitted.

order (cosmos) *of the whole world. This earliest stage ends here in the perception of those 'images' of moral or spiritual excellences which, when combined with bodily beauty in a living person, are the proper object of love* (eros)*. They are apparitions, in the sensible world, of the Forms ('Ideas'), their archetypes in the world of unseen reality, beyond the threshold which the future philosopher will cross at the next stage of his advance* (521 E, p. 237 f.).

One thing, however, is easily settled, namely that grace and seemliness of form and movement go with good rhythm; ungracefulness and unseemliness with bad.

Naturally.

And again, good or bad rhythm and also tunefulness or discord in music go with the quality of the poetry; for they will be modelled after its form, if, as we have said, metre and music must be adapted to the sense of the words.

Well, they must be so adapted.

And the content of the poetry and the manner in which it is expressed depend, in their turn, on moral character.

Of course.

Thus, then, excellence of form and content in discourse [1] and of musical expression and rhythm, and grace of form and movement, all depend on goodness of nature, by which I mean, not the foolish simplicity sometimes called by courtesy 'good nature,' but a nature in which goodness of character has been well and truly established.

Yes, certainly.

So, if our young men are to do their proper work in life, they must follow after these qualities wherever they may be found. And they are to be found in every sort of workmanship, such as painting, weaving, embroidery, architecture, the making of furniture; and also in the human frame and in all the works of nature: in all these grace and seemliness may be present or absent. And the absence of grace, rhythm, harmony is nearly allied to baseness

---

[1] *Eulogia* is given an unusual sense in order to bring in the associations of *eulogos* = 'reasonable,' the poetry being the intellectual element.

of thought and expression and baseness of character; whereas their presence goes with that moral excellence and self-mastery of which they are the embodiment.

That is perfectly true.

Then we must not only compel our poets, on pain of expulsion, to make their poetry the express image of noble character; we must also supervise craftsmen of every kind and forbid them to leave the stamp of baseness, licence, meanness, unseemliness, on painting and sculpture, or building, or any other work of their hands; and anyone who cannot obey shall not practise his art in our commonwealth. We would not have our Guardians grow up among representations of moral deformity, as in some foul pasture where, day after day, feeding on every poisonous weed they would, little by little, gather insensibly a mass of corruption in their very souls. Rather we must seek out those craftsmen whose instinct guides them to whatsoever is lovely and gracious; so that our young men, dwelling in a wholesome climate, may drink in good from every quarter, whence, like a breeze bearing health from happy regions, some influence from noble works constantly falls upon eye and ear from childhood upward, and imperceptibly draws them into sympathy and harmony with the beauty of reason, whose impress they take.

There could be no better upbringing than that.

Hence, Glaucon, I continued, the decisive importance of education in poetry and music: rhythm and harmony sink deep into the recesses of the soul and take the strongest hold there, bringing that grace of body and mind which is only to be found in one who is brought up in the right way. Moreover, a proper training in this kind makes a man quick to perceive any defect or ugliness in art or in nature. Such deformity will rightly disgust him. Approving all that is lovely, he will welcome it home with joy into his soul and, nourished thereby, grow into a man of a noble spirit. All that is ugly and disgraceful he will rightly condemn and abhor while he is still too young to understand the reason; and when reason comes, he will greet her as a friend with whom his education has made him long familiar.

I agree, he said; that is the purpose of education in literature and music.

Now in learning to read, I went on, we were proficient when we could recognize the few letters there are wherever they occur in all the multitude of different words, never thinking them beneath our notice in the most insignificant word, but bent upon distinguishing them everywhere, because we should not be scholars until we had got thus far.

True.

Also we must know the letters themselves before we can recognize images of them, reflected (say) in water or in a mirror. The same skill and practice are needed in either case.

Yes.

Then, is it not true, in the same way, that we and these Guardians we are to bring up will never be fully cultivated until we can recognize the essential Forms of temperance, courage, liberality, high-mindedness, and all other kindred qualities, and also their opposites, wherever they occur.[1] We must be able to discern the presence of these Forms themselves and also of their images in anything that contains them, realizing that, to recognize either, the same skill and practice are required, and that the most insignificant instance is not beneath our notice.

That must surely be so.

And for him who has eyes to see it, there can be no fairer sight than the harmonious union of a noble character in the soul with an outward form answering thereto and bearing the same stamp of beauty.

There cannot.

And the fairest is also the most lovable.

Of course.

So the man who has been educated in poetry and music will be in love with such a person, but never with one who lacks this harmony.

Not if the defect should lie in the soul; if it were only some bodily blemish, he would accept that with patience and goodwill.

I understand, said I; you are or have been in love with a person like that, and I agree. But tell me: is excessive pleasure compatible with temperance?

---

[1] For the Platonic doctrine of Forms see Chap. XIX, p. 179 ff.

How can it be, when it unsettles the mind no less than pain?

Or with virtue in general?

Certainly not.

It has more to do with insolence and profligacy?

Yes.

And is there any pleasure you can name that is greater and keener than sexual pleasure?

No; nor any that is more like frenzy.

Whereas love rightfully is such a passion as beauty combined with a noble and harmonious character may inspire in a temperate and cultivated mind. It must therefore be kept from all contact with licentiousness and frenzy; and where a passion of this rightful sort exists, the lover and his beloved must have nothing to do with the pleasure in question.

Certainly not, Socrates.

It appears, then, that in this commonwealth we are founding you will have a law to the effect that a lover may seek the company of his beloved and, with his consent, kiss and embrace him like a son, with honourable intent, but must never be suspected of any further familiarity, on pain of being thought ill-bred and without any delicacy of feeling.

I quite agree.

Then is not our account of education in poetry and music now complete? It has ended where it ought to end, in the love of beauty.[1]

I agree.

§ 5 (403 C–412 B). PHYSICAL TRAINING. PHYSICIANS AND JUDGES

The physical training suitable for a citizen soldier is briefly contrasted with that of the professional athlete. Simplicity in life produces bodily health, just as it produced temperance in the soul. This analogy leads to the thought that an educated man should be able to manage his own life physically and morally, seldom having recourse to a doctor or a court of law. Incidentally, it is pointed out that, whereas a doctor may be the better for having experienced

---

[1] For the transition from this primary stage of education to the higher intellectual training, see the introductory note to Chap. XXIV, p. 221.

disease in his own person, the experience of wickedness needed by
a good judge is of a different kind. Finally, it appears that physical
training, no less than education in literature and the arts, really has
to do with the soul. The two together should produce a harmoni-
ous development of the spirited and the philosophic elements in
human character.

Next, the upbringing of our young men must include physical
training; and this must be no less carefully regulated throughout
life from childhood onwards. In my view, which I should like you
to consider, it is not true that a sound and healthy body is enough
to produce a sound mind; while, on the contrary, the sound mind
has power in itself to make the bodily condition as perfect as it
can be. What do you say?

I agree with you.

We should do well, then, to leave the care of the body in detail
to those minds which have already been thoroughly cared for themselves. We may save time by giving only a rough outline.

Certainly.

Drunkenness we have already forbidden. A Guardian is surely
the last person to be allowed to get drunk and not know where
he is.

Yes, it would be absurd that a Guardian should need to be
guarded.

What of their food? Our men will be in training for the greatest of all contests. Will the habit of body of the ordinary athlete
be suitable for them?

Perhaps.

But it is rather a drowsy condition, and precarious for health.[1]
You must have noticed how athletes sleep their life away, and fall
seriously ill whenever they depart only slightly from their prescribed diet. A finer sort of training will be needed for our warrior
athletes, who must be as wakeful as watchdogs and have sharp
eyes and ears. On their campaigns too they will be exposed to so
many changes of food and drinking-water and extremes of heat

---

[1] Hippocrates, *Aphorisms*, 1, 3, 'In athletes a perfect condition that is at its
highest pitch is treacherous. Such conditions cannot remain the same or be at rest
and . . . the only possible change is for the worse' (trans. W. H. S. Jones).

and cold that it will not do for their health to be too nicely balanced.

I believe you are right.

Then the best training will be closely akin to that education in poetry and music which we described, in being simple and flexible, especially training for war.

What will it be like?

That, at any rate, may be learnt from Homer. As you know, he gives his heroes on their campaign no fish for their meals, although they are on the shores of the Hellespont, and no boiled meat; nothing but roast, which is convenient for soldiers: they have only to light a fire wherever they may be and not to carry pots and pans about with them. I fancy, too, that Homer never mentions sweets. Even the ordinary athlete knows that you must not eat anything of that sort, if you want to be in good condition.

Yes, they are wise to be so abstemious.

It seems, then, you would not approve of those refinements of Sicilian cookery for which the tables of Syracuse are famous,[1] or of our Athenian confectionery, supposed to be so delicious; and you would not advise a man who is to keep himself fit to take a Corinthian girl as a mistress.

Of course not.

We might, in fact, see an analogy between this luxurious living and that style of music which uses every variation of mode and rhythm. Variety there engendered licence in the soul, and simplicity temperance. So in the body, variety breeds maladies and simplicity health.

That is perfectly true.

In a community where licentiousness and disease are rife, law-courts and dispensaries have their doors constantly open. Law and medicine begin to give themselves airs, when, even among free men, large numbers take too keen an interest in them.

That is inevitable.

[1] The fertility of Sicily, in contrast with Central Greece, led to a growth of luxury which became proverbial and shocked Plato on his first visit to the west, *Epistle* vii. 326 B.

Is it not the surest sign of a disgracefully low state of education that highly skilled physicians and judges should be in request, not merely among the lower classes who work with their hands, but among those who lay claim to a liberal upbringing? Could anything show a more shameful lack of culture than to have so little justice in oneself that one must get it from others, who thus become masters and judges over one?

There could be no worse disgrace.

Or is there a yet lower depth, when, not content with spending most of his life in courts of law as plaintiff or defendant, a man is actually led to take a vulgar pride in being so litigious; one who fancies himself as an expert in dishonesty, up to every turn and twist that will enable him to evade punishment, and all for the sake of trivial or worthless ends, because he does not know how much better it is so to order one's life as never to stand in need of a drowsy judge?

That is indeed a lower depth.

Is it not also disgraceful to need doctoring, not merely for a wound or an attack of some seasonal disorder, but because, through living in idleness and luxury, our bodies are infested with winds and humours, like marsh gas in a stagnant pool, so that the sons of Asclepius [1] are put to inventing for diseases such ingenious names as flatulence and catarrh?

Yes; they are queer, these modern terms.

And not in use, I fancy, in the days of Asclepius himself, to judge from the behaviour of his sons at Troy. When Eurypylus was wounded, they had no fault to find with the woman who gave him a draught of Pramnian wine well sprinkled with barley meal and grated cheese—rather an inflammatory mixture, you might think—nor did they blame Patroclus, who was in charge of the case.

It certainly was an odd drink for a wounded man.

Not if you reflect that in the old days, until the time of Herodicus, the sons of Asclepius had no use for the modern coddling treatment of disease. But Herodicus, who was a gymnastic master and lost his health, combined training and doctoring in such a

[1] Latin Aesculapius, the mythical patron of physicians.

way as to become a plag⌐   ⌐ himself first and foremost and to many others after him.

How?

By lingering out his death. He had a mortal disease, and he spent all his life at its beck and call, with no hope of a cure and no time for anything but doctoring himself. Every departure from his fixed regimen was a torment; and his skill only enabled him to reach old age in a prolonged death struggle.

A fine reward for his art to win him!

Yes, but a suitable one for a man who never understood that, if Asclepius did not reveal these valetudinarian arts to his descendants, it was not from ignorance or lack of experience, but because he realized that in every well-ordered community each man has his appointed task which he must perform; no one has leisure to spend all his life in being ill and doctoring himself. We can see how that is true for an artisan, but absurdly enough we do not see that it applies to the rich, who are supposed to be so fortunate. When a carpenter is ill, he asks his doctor to give him an emetic or a purge to expel the trouble, or to rid him of it by cautery or the knife. But if he is advised to take a long course of treatment, to keep his head wrapped up, and all that sort of thing, he soon replies that he has not time to be ill and it is not worth his while to live in that way, thinking of nothing but his illness and neglecting his proper work. And so he bids good-bye to that kind of doctor and goes back to his ordinary way of life. Then he either regains his health and lives to go about his proper business, or, if his body is not equal to the strain, gets rid of all his troubles by dying.

Yes, we should think that the right attitude towards medicine for a man of his class.

Because he had work to do, and it was not worth his while to live if he could not do it; whereas the rich man, we imagine, has no function such that life will not be worth living if he is prevented from performing it.

I never heard of any.

Why, don't you know that saying of Phocylides, that a man should practise virtue when he has made enough to live on?

I should have thought he might begin sooner.

We need not quarrel with Phocylides on that point. We had better assure ourselves whether the practice of virtue is the rich man's business and his life is not worth living otherwise, or whether that valetudinarianism which prevents any craftsman from attending to his work, does not equally stand in the way of following Phocylides' advice.

Yes, he said. Surely there could be no worse hindrance than this excessive care of the body, over and above the exercise it needs to keep it in health. It becomes a nuisance to anyone who has to manage a household or serve in the field or hold any office at home.

Worst of all, I added, it is prejudicial to learning of all kinds and to thought and meditation. The constant apprehension of headaches and dizziness, for which study is held responsible, is a bar to any exercise or test of intellectual qualities, when a man is always fancying himself ill and never stops being anxious about his body.

Naturally.

Shall we say, then, that Asclepius recognized this and revealed the art of medicine for the benefit of people of sound constitution who normally led a healthy life, but had contracted some definite ailment? He would rid them of their disorders by means of drugs or the knife and tell them to go on living as usual, so as not to impair their usefulness as citizens. But where the body was diseased through and through, he would not try, by nicely calculated evacuations and doses, to prolong a miserable existence and let his patient beget children who were likely to be as sickly as himself. Treatment, he thought, would be wasted on a man who could not live in his ordinary round of duties and was consequently useless to himself and to society.

A statesmanlike person, your Asclepius!

Obviously; and because he was so, his sons, you may observe, not only fought bravely at Troy, but practised medicine in the way I am describing. You will remember how, when Menelaus was shot with an arrow by Pandarus, they 'sucked the blood and spread mild simples' on the wound; but what he was to eat and drink afterwards they no more prescribed for him than for Eurypy

lus. Simples were enough to cure a wounded man who had hitherto lived a regular and healthy life, even if he should drink the
next moment a mixture of meal, wine, and cheese. But if a man
had a sickly constitution and intemperate habits, his life was
worth nothing to himself or to anyone else; medicine was not
meant for such people and they should not be treated, though they
might be richer than Midas.

Shrewd fellows, these sons of Asclepius, by your account.

As they should be, said I; and yet Pindar and the tragedians, in
defiance of our principles, allege that Asclepius, although he was
Apollo's son, took a bribe to raise to life a rich man already at the
point of death, and was struck by a thunderbolt for doing so. As
we said before, we cannot accept both statements; if he was the
son of a god, he was not avaricious; if avaricious, he was not the
son of a god.

All that is certainly true, Socrates; but what do you say to this?
The physicians in our commonwealth must surely be good ones;
and the best, I suppose, would be those who had had the widest
experience in dealing with healthy and sick people; and in the
same way the best judges will be men who have associated with
every type of character.

I agree, we must have good ones. But do you know which I
should call good?

I shall, if you will tell me.

Well, I will try. But your question referred to two different
things as if they were alike. It is true enough of physicians that
the ablest might prove to be men who, from childhood up, besides
mastering their profession, had been in contact with the largest
number of the worst cases, and moreover were not of a robust
constitution and had themselves suffered from every malady. That
is because what they use in taking care of people's bodies is not
their own body; if it were, it would never do for that body to
be in a bad condition; it is their mind, and if that is or has been
in a bad state, it cannot take proper care of anything. But with
a judge it is otherwise; his is the jurisdiction of mind over mind;

and that mind must not have been brought up from childhood in the society of vicious minds and itself have been guilty of the whole catalogue of crimes in order to sharpen its wits in drawing inferences about the crimes of others from its own experience, as was permissible in the case of bodily disease. It can be a sound judge of what is right only if it is itself good and honourable; and to that end it must not have been tainted in youth by familiarity with evil characters. That is, of course, why decent people seem simple-minded when they are young, and are easily taken in by dishonesty: they have no pattern of wickedness in themselves enabling them to detect it in others by their own feelings.

True, they are at a great disadvantage.

For that reason, to make a good judge, a man must be old. The knowledge of what wickedness is should have come late in life, not from a consciousness of its presence in his own soul, but from long practice in observing its evil effects in the souls of others. It should be a matter of knowledge, not of personal experience.

A good portrait of a genuine judge.

Yes, and of the good judge, to whom your question referred; for his merit consists in the goodness of his soul. Your cunning person, who is quick to suspect evil through having been so often guilty of it himself, and fancies himself master of all the tricks, has all his own wickedness to put him on his guard against others, and so he seems formidable, so long as he is dealing with men of his own stamp. But as soon as he comes in contact with honest men older than himself, he appears stupid with his ill-timed suspicions; he cannot recognize a sound character, because he has no soundness in himself to judge by. If he passes in his own eyes and in others' estimation as on the whole more clever than stupid, it is because he falls in with more rogues than honest men.

Quite true.

For a good and understanding judge, then, we must look rather to the other type. Vice can never know both itself and virtue; but virtue, in a well-trained nature, will in time come to a knowledge of vice, as well as of itself. So it is the virtuous man, as I believe, that will make the wise judge.

I agree.

Then you will establish in your state physicians and judges such as we have described. They will look after those citizens whose bodies and souls are constitutionally sound. The physically unsound they will leave to die; and they will actually put to death those who are incurably corrupt in mind.

Yes; that, as we can now see, will be the best thing for them as well as for the community.

And your young men, so long as they keep to that simple education which, we said, engenders temperance, will take good care never to fall in need of legal correction; while if they follow similar lines in physical training, they may, if they choose, become independent of medicine in all but extreme cases.

I think they may.

Now, the ordinary athlete undergoes the rigours of training for the sake of muscular strength; but ours will do so rather with a view to stimulating the spirited element in their nature. So perhaps the purpose of the two established branches of education is not, as some suppose, the improvement of the soul in one case and of the body in the other. Both, it may be, aim chiefly at improving the soul.

How so?

Have you noticed how a life-long devotion to either branch, to the exclusion of the other, affects the mind, resulting in an uncivilized hardness in the one case, and an over-civilized softness in the other?

I have certainly noticed that unmitigated athletics produce a sort of ferocity, and a merely literary and musical education makes men softer than is good for them.

Surely that ferocity is the outcome of the spirited element in our nature. A proper training would produce courage; but if that element is overstrained, it naturally becomes hard and savage. Gentleness, on the other hand, is characteristic of the philosophic disposition. Here again, too much relaxation will result in over-softness; the right training will produce a gentleness that is steady and disciplined. Now we agree that our Guardians must combine both these dispositions; and they will have to be harmonized so that

courage and steadfastness may be united in a soul that would otherwise be either unmanly or boorish.

Certainly.

When a man surrenders himself to music, allowing his soul to
be flooded through the channels of his ears with those sweet and
soft and mournful airs we spoke of, and gives up all his time to
the delights of song and melody, then at first he tempers the high-
spirited part of his nature, like iron whose brittle hardness is sof-
tened to make it serviceable; but if he persists in subduing it to
such incantation, he will end by melting it away altogether. He
will have cut the sinews of his soul and made himself what Homer
calls a faint-hearted warrior. Moreover, this result follows quickly
in a temperament that is naturally spiritless; while a high-spirited
one is rendered weak and unstable, readily flaring up and dying
down again on slight provocation. Such men become rather irri-
table, bad-tempered, and peevish.

Quite so.

On the other hand, there are the consequences of hard bodily exercise and high living, with no attempt to cultivate the mind or
use the intellect in study. At first, the sense of physical fitness fills
a man with self-confidence and energy and makes him twice the
man he was. But suppose he does nothing else and holds aloof
from any sort of culture; then, even if there was something in
him capable of desiring knowledge, it is starved of instruction
and never encouraged to think for itself by taking part in rational
discussion or intellectual pursuits of any kind; and so it grows
feeble for lack of stimulus and nourishment, and deaf and blind
because the darkness that clouds perception is never cleared away.
Such a man ends by being wholly uncultivated and a hater of reason. Having no more use for reasonable persuasion, he gains all
his ends by savage violence, like a brute beast, and he lives in a
dull stupor of ignorance with no touch of inward harmony or
grace.

That is exactly what happens.

There are, then, these two elements in the soul, the spirited and
the philosophic; and it is for their sake, as I should say, and not
(except incidentally) for the sake of soul and body, that heaven

has given to mankind those two branches of education. The purpose is to bring the two elements into tune with one another by adjusting the tension of each to the right pitch. So one who can apply to the soul both kinds of education blended in perfect proportion will be master of a nobler sort of musical harmony than was ever made by tuning the strings of the lyre.

We may well say that, Socrates.

And our commonwealth will need the constant vigilance of such a master, to preserve its constitution.

Certainly, he will be indispensable.

So much, then, for the outlines of education and nurture. We need not go into all the details of their musical performances or of their hunting and athletic contests and races. Obviously these will follow from our principles and can easily be worked out.

Yes, easily.

CHAPTER X (III. 412 B–IV. 421 c)

SELECTION OF RULERS: THE GUARDIANS' MANNER OF LIVING

The education above described will be given to all the Guardians up to the age of twenty (537 B, p. 259). *Plato next indicates the tests (recalling ordeals to which candidates for initiation are subjected) whereby a few will be selected to undergo the higher training of Chapters XXVI-XXVII and to become Rulers whom the lower order of Guardians, now called Auxiliaries,[1] will obey.*

There will thus be three orders in the state: Rulers (legislative and deliberative), Auxiliaries (executive), and Craftsmen (productive). This institution is based, not on birth or wealth, but on natural capacities and attainments; children born in any class are

---

[1] 'Auxiliary,' unsatisfactory as it is, has military associations and is a possible translation of the word ἐπίκουρος. Mr. Crossman's 'Administrator' (*Plato To-day*, 121) has neither of these merits. 'Guards' clashes awkwardly with 'Guardians' and suggests to English ears a purely military body, chiefly associated with ceremonial display and not normally employed in carrying out the decisions of the government.

*to be moved up or down on their merits. It is to be recommended
for popular acceptance by an allegorical myth, the materials for
which are drawn partly from the current belief that certain peoples
were literally 'autochthonous,' born from the soil, partly from
Hesiod's account of the Golden, Silver, and Bronze races which
had succeeded one another before the present age of Iron. The
ancients supposed all myths to be the work of poets, inspired by
the Muses or consciously invented. As we have seen, myths are to
convey important truths in a form that will appeal to the imagination of young or untrained minds.*

*The Guardians are to live with Spartan simplicity under a kind
of military monasticism. The absence of private property (for the
Guardians only) will remove the chief temptations to sacrifice the
welfare of the whole commonwealth to personal interests. (The
abolition of family life for the Guardians will be dealt with later,
Chap. XVI.) They will not use their power, like the tyrants admired by Thrasymachus, to get the best of everything for themselves. They will be happy in the exercise of their natural gifts;
and in any case our aim is not the exclusive happiness of any one
class of citizens.*

Good, said I; and what is the next point to be settled? Is it not the
question, which of these Guardians are to be rulers and which are
to obey?

No doubt.

Well, it is obvious that the elder must have authority over the
young, and that the rulers must be the best.

Yes.

And as among farmers the best are those with a natural turn
for farming, so, if we want the best among our Guardians, we
must take those naturally fitted to watch over a commonwealth.
They must have the right sort of intelligence and ability; and also
they must look upon the commonwealth as their special concern—
the sort of concern that is felt for something so closely bound up
with oneself that its interests and fortunes, for good or ill, are held
to be identical with one's own.

Exactly.

So the kind of men we must choose from among the Guardians will be those who, when we look at the whole course of their lives, are found to be full of zeal to do whatever they believe is for the good of the commonwealth and never willing to act against its interest.

Yes, they will be the men we want.

We must watch them, I think, at every age and see whether they are capable of preserving this conviction that they must do what is best for the community, never forgetting it or allowing themselves to be either forced or bewitched into throwing it over.

How does this throwing over come about?

I will explain. When a belief passes out of the mind, a man may be willing to part with it, if it is false and he has learnt better, or unwilling, if it is true.

I see how he might be willing to let it go; but you must explain how he can be unwilling.

Where is your difficulty? Don't you agree that men are unwilling to be deprived of good, though ready enough to part with evil? Or that to be deceived about the truth is evil, to possess it good? Or don't you think that possessing truth means thinking of things as they really are?

You are right. I do agree that men are unwilling to be robbed of a true belief.

When that happens to them, then, it must be by theft, or violence, or bewitchment.

Again I do not understand.

Perhaps my metaphors are too high-flown. I call it theft when one is persuaded out of one's belief or forgets it. Argument in the one case, and time in the other, steal it away without one's knowing what is happening. You understand now?

Yes.

And by violence I mean being driven to change one's mind by pain or suffering.

That too I understand, and you are right.

And bewitchment, as I think you would agree, occurs when a man is beguiled out of his opinion by the allurements of pleasure or scared out of it under the spell of panic.

Yes, all delusions are like a sort of bewitchment.

As I said just now, then, we must find out who are the best guardians of this inward conviction that they must always do what they believe to be best for the commonwealth. We shall have to watch them from earliest childhood and set them tasks in which they would be most likely to forget or to be beguiled out of this duty. We shall then choose only those whose memory holds firm and who are proof against delusion.

Yes.

We must also subject them to ordeals of toil and pain and watch for the same qualities there. And we must observe them when exposed to the test of yet a third kind of bewitchment. As people lead colts up to alarming noises to see whether they are timid, so these young men must be brought into terrifying situations and then into scenes of pleasure, which will put them to severer proof than gold tried in the furnace. If we find one bearing himself well in all these trials and resisting every enchantment, a true guardian of himself, preserving always that perfect rhythm and harmony of being which he has acquired from his training in music and poetry, such a one will be of the greatest service to the commonwealth as well as to himself. Whenever we find one who has come unscathed through every test in childhood, youth, and manhood, we shall set him as a Ruler to watch over the commonwealth; he will be honoured in life, and after death receive the highest tribute of funeral rites and other memorials. All who do not reach this standard we must reject. And that, I think, my dear Glaucon, may be taken as an outline of the way in which we shall select Guardians to be set in authority as Rulers.

I am very much of your mind.

These, then, may properly be called Guardians in the fullest sense, who will ensure that neither foes without shall have the power, nor friends within the wish, to do harm. Those young men whom up to now we have been speaking of as Guardians, will be better described as Auxiliaries, who will enforce the decisions of the Rulers.

I agree.

Now, said I, can we devise something in the way of those convenient fictions we spoke of earlier, a single bold flight of ~~invention,~~[1] which we may induce the community in general, and if possible the Rulers themselves, to accept?

What kind of fiction?

Nothing new; something like an Eastern tale of what, according to the poets, has happened before now in more than one part of the world. The poets have been believed; but the thing has not happened in our day, and it would be hard to persuade anyone that it could ever happen again.

You seem rather shy of telling this story of yours.

With good reason, as you will see when I have told it.

Out with it; don't be afraid.

Well, here it is; though I hardly know how to find the courage or the words to express it. I shall try to convince, first the Rulers and the soldiers,[2] and then the whole community, that all that nurture and education which we gave them was only something they seemed to experience as it were in a dream. In reality they were the whole time down inside the earth, being moulded and fostered while their arms and all their equipment were being fashioned also; and at last, when they were complete, the earth sent them up from her womb into the light of day. So now they must think of the land they dwell in as a mother and nurse, whom they must take thought for and defend against any attack, and of their fellow citizens as brothers born of the same soil.

You might well be bashful about coming out with your fiction.

No doubt; but still you must hear the rest of the story. It is true, we shall tell our people in this fable, that all of you in this land are brothers; but the god who fashioned you mixed gold in the composition of those among you who are fit to rule, so that they

[1] This phrase is commonly rendered by 'noble lie,' a self-contradictory expression no more applicable to Plato's harmless allegory than to a New Testament parable or the Pilgrim's Progress, and liable to suggest that he would countenance the lies, for the most part ignoble, now called propaganda. For the meaning of *pseudos* see above, p. 68. For γενναῖον = 'on a generous scale' cf. μάζας γενναίας, 372 B, and οὐκ ἀγεννής, *Euthyphr.* 2 c, *Rep.* 529 A.

[2] Note that the Guardians themselves are to accept this allegory, if possible. It is not 'propaganda' foisted on the masses by the Rulers.

are of the most precious quality; and he put silver in the Auxiliaries, and iron and brass in the farmers and craftsmen. Now, since
you are all of one stock, although your children will generally
be like their parents, sometimes a golden parent may have a silver
child or a silver parent a golden one, and so on with all the other
combinations. So the first and chief injunction laid by heaven upon
the Rulers is that, among all the things of which they must show
themselves good guardians, there is none that needs to be so carefully watched as the mixture of metals in the souls of the children.
If a child of their own is born with an alloy of iron or brass, they
must, without the smallest pity, assign him the station proper to
his nature and thrust him out among the craftsmen or the farmers.
If, on the contrary, these classes produce a child with gold or silver
in his composition, they will promote him, according to his value,
to be a Guardian or an Auxiliary. They will appeal to a prophecy
that ruin will come upon the state when it passes into the keeping
of a man of iron or brass. Such is the story; can you think of any
device to make them believe it?

Not in the first generation; but their sons and descendants might
believe it, and finally the rest of mankind.[1]

Well, said I, even so it might have a good effect in making
them care more for the commonwealth and for one another; for I
think I see what you mean.

So, I continued, we will leave the success of our story to the care
of popular tradition; and now let us arm these sons of Earth and
lead them, under the command of their Rulers, to the site of our
city. There let them look round for the best place to fix their camp,
from which they will be able to control any rebellion against the
laws from within and to beat off enemies who may come from
without like wolves to attack the fold. When they have pitched
their camp and offered sacrifice to the proper divinities, they must
arrange their sleeping quarters; and these must be sufficient to
shelter them from winter cold and summer heat.

---

[1] Just as the tradition that the Athenians were 'autochthonous' in a literal sense
was popularly believed, though Plato would suppose it to have been originally invented by some myth-making poet.

Naturally. You mean they are going to live there?

Yes, said I; but live like soldiers, not like men of business.

What is the difference?

I will try to explain. It would be very strange if a shepherd were to disgrace himself by keeping, for the protection of his flock, dogs who were so ill-bred and badly trained that hunger or unruliness or some bad habit or other would set them worrying the sheep and behaving no better than wolves. We must take every precaution against our Auxiliaries treating the citizens in any such way and, because they are stronger, turning into savage tyrants instead of friendly allies; and they will have been furnished with the best of safeguards, if they have really been educated in the right way.

But surely there is nothing wrong with their education.

We must not be too positive about that, my dear Glaucon; but we can be sure of what we said not long ago, that if they are to have the best chance of being gentle and humane to one another and to their charges, they must have the right education, whatever that may be.

We were certainly right there.

Then besides that education, it is only common sense to say that the dwellings and other belongings provided for them must be such as will neither make them less perfect Guardians nor encourage them to maltreat their fellow citizens.

True.

With that end in view, let us consider how they should live and be housed. First, none of them must possess any private property beyond the barest necessaries. Next, no one is to have any dwelling or store-house that is not open for all to enter at will. Their food, in the quantities required by men of temperance and courage who are in training for war, they will receive from the other citizens as the wages of their guardianship, fixed so that there shall be just enough for the year with nothing over; and they will have meals in common and all live together like soldiers in a camp. Gold and silver, we shall tell them, they will not need, having the divine counterparts of those metals always in their souls as a god-given possession, whose purity it is not lawful to sully by the acquisition of that mortal dross, current among mankind, which

No use of metal

has been the occasion of so many unholy deeds. They alone of all
the citizens are forbidden to touch and handle silver or gold, or
to come under the same roof with them, or wear them as orna-
ments, or drink from vessels made of them. This manner of life
will be their salvation and make them the saviours of the commonwealth. If ever they should come to possess land of their own
and houses and money, they will give up their guardianship for
the management of their farms and households and become tyrants
at enmity with their fellow citizens instead of allies. And so they
will pass all their lives in hating and being hated, plotting and
being plotted against, in much greater fear of their enemies at home
than of any foreign foe, and fast heading for the destruction that
will soon overwhelm their country with themselves. For all these
reasons let us say that this is how our Guardians are to be housed
and otherwise provided for, and let us make laws accordingly.

By all means, said Glaucon.

Here Adeimantus interposed. Socrates, he said, how would you
meet the objection that you are not making these people particularly happy? It is their own fault too, if they are not; for they are
really masters of the state, and yet they get no good out of it as
other rulers do, who own lands, build themselves fine houses with
handsome furniture, offer private sacrifices to the gods, and enter-
tain visitors from abroad; who possess, in fact, that gold and silver
you spoke of, with everything else that is usually thought necessary
for happiness. These people seem like nothing so much as a garri-
son of mercenaries posted in the city and perpetually mounting
guard.

Yes, I said, and what is more they will serve for their food only
without getting a mercenary's pay, so that they will not be able
to travel on their own account or to make presents to a mistress
or to spend as they please in other ways, like the people who are
commonly thought happy. You have forgotten to include these
counts in your indictment, and many more to the same effect.

Well, take them as included now.

And you want to hear the answer?

Yes.

We shall find one, I think, by keeping to the line we have followed so far. We shall say that, though it would not be surprising if even these people were perfectly happy under such conditions, our aim in founding the commonwealth was not to make any one class specially happy, but to secure the greatest possible happiness for the community as a whole. We thought we should have the best chance of finding justice in a state so constituted, just as we should find injustice where the constitution was of the worst possible type; we could then decide the question which has been before us all this time. For the moment, we are constructing, as we believe, the state which will be happy as a whole, not trying to secure the well-being of a select few; we shall study a state of the opposite kind presently. It is as if we were colouring a statue [1] and someone came up and blamed us for not putting the most beautiful colours on the noblest parts of the figure; the eyes, for instance, should be painted crimson, but we had made them black. We should think it a fair answer to say: Really, you must not expect us to paint eyes so handsome as not to look like eyes at all. This applies to all the parts: the question is whether, by giving each its proper colour, we make the whole beautiful. So too, in the present case, you must not press us to endow our Guardians with a happiness that will make them anything rather than guardians. We could quite easily clothe our farmers in gorgeous robes, crown them with gold, and invite them to till the soil at their pleasure; or we might set our potters to lie on couches by their fire, passing round the wine and making merry, with their wheel at hand to work at whenever they felt so inclined. We could make all the rest happy in the same sort of way, and so spread this well-being through the whole community. But you must not put that idea into our heads; if we take your advice, the farmer will be no farmer, the potter no longer a potter; none of the elements that make up the community will keep its character. In many cases this does not matter so much: if a cobbler goes to the bad and pretends to be what he is not, he is not a danger to the state; but, as you must surely see, men who make only a vain show of being

---

[1] Greek statues were commonly tinted, wholly or in part.

guardians of the laws and of the commonwealth bring the whole state to utter ruin, just as, on the other hand, its good government and well-being depend entirely on them. We, in fact, are making genuine Guardians who will be the last to bring harm upon the commonwealth; if our critic aims rather at producing a happiness like that of a party of peasants feasting at a fair, what he has in mind is something other than a civic community. So we must consider whether our aim in establishing Guardians is to secure the greatest possible happiness for them, or happiness is something of which we should watch the development in the whole commonwealth. If so, we must compel these Guardians and Auxiliaries of ours to second our efforts; and they, and all the rest with them, must be induced to make themselves perfect masters each of his own craft. In that way, as the community grows into a well-ordered whole, the several classes may be allowed such measure of happiness as their nature will compass.

I think that is an admirable reply.[1]

CHAPTER XI (IV. 421 c–427 c)

THE GUARDIANS' DUTIES

The community of goods is prescribed for the Guardians only; the industrial order, concerned with economic needs, will have private property. But the Guardians must exclude from the state both riches and poverty. Great wealth will not strengthen the state against its enemies, but weaken it by setting up an internal class-war of rich against poor. Unity is all-important, and must further be maintained by not allowing the state to grow too large, and by preserving the principle of promotion by merit; there must be no purely hereditary governing class.

The one essential is to maintain unchanged a system of education which will forestall the growth of lawlessness. To rightly edu-

---

[1] In Chap. XVI (465 D, p. 167) Socrates maintains that the Guardians will be happier than any Olympic victor.

*cated rulers may be safely left all the usual subjects of legislation.
Religious institutions will be regulated by the recognized national
authority, the Oracle at Delphi, which was normally consulted before the foundation of a new city.*

I WONDER whether you will agree on another point closely connected with that and concerned with the craftsmen. Is it not true
that they also are spoilt and turned into bad workmen by wealth
and by poverty alike?

How so?

In this way. When a potter grows rich, will he go on with his
trade? Does he not become idle and careless, and consequently a
worse potter? And equally, if he is too poor to provide himself
with tools and other things he needs for his craft, his work will
be worse, and he will not make such good craftsmen of his sons
and apprentices. So work and workmen suffer from both causes,
poverty and riches as well.

Evidently.

Here, then, are some more evils which must not elude the vigilance of our Guardians and find their way into the commonwealth: riches and poverty. The one produces luxury and idleness,
the other low standards of conduct and workmanship; and both
have a subversive tendency.

True enough. But I should like to know, Socrates, how our state
will be able to go to war, if it has no money, especially if it is
forced to fight a rich and powerful enemy.

Obviously it would be hard to fight one such enemy, but easier to
deal with two.

What do you mean by that?

In the first place, if they have to fight, they will be highly trained
soldiers matched against rich men.

True, so far as that goes.

Well then, Adeimantus, would not a single boxer in perfect
training easily be a match for two wealthy and corpulent antag-
onists who could not box?

Not for both at once perhaps.

Not even if he could give ground and then turn and plant a

blow on whichever came up first? Suppose he kept on doing that under a burning sun, would he not get the better of even more than two?

It would certainly not be surprising.

Well, don't you think that rich people know more of the theory and practice of boxing than of the art of war?

I am sure they do.

In that case it will probably be an easy matter for our trained warriors to fight twice or three times their number.

I will grant you that; I believe you are right.

And now suppose they sent envoys to one of the two enemy countries to tell them what is in fact the truth: 'We have no use for gold and silver; we are not allowed to possess them. But you are allowed; so join forces with us, and you may have the spoils of the other country.'[1] After such an offer would anyone choose to fight against tough, wiry dogs sooner than join the dogs in attacking the fat and tender sheep?

I should say not. But if a single state amasses the wealth of all the others, will not that be a danger to a state that has none?

I congratulate you on your idea that any state other than the one we are constructing deserves the name.

Why, what should the others be called?

By some grander name, for each of them is not one state, but many: two at least, which are at war with one another, one of the rich, the other of the poor, and each of these is divided into many more. To treat them all as a single state is a complete mistake. If you treat them as many and offer to make over to one class the wealth and power and even the persons of the others, you will always find that your allies outnumber your enemies. Consequently, so long as your commonwealth is ordered wisely on the lines we have laid down, it will be the greatest of all; I do not mean the most famous, but greatest in the literal sense, even though it have no more than a thousand men to fight in its defence. You will not easily find in Hellas or elsewhere a state of that size which is really one, though there are plenty which look like single states and are many times as large. Don't you agree?

I do indeed.

[1] This message is in the 'laconic' style of Spartan diplomacy.

Here, then, our Rulers will find the best principle for determining the size of the state and the proportionate amount of territory, beyond which they will not go: the state should be allowed to grow only so far as it can increase in size without loss of unity.

An excellent rule.

So we must lay yet another command on our Guardians: they are to take all possible care that the state shall neither be too small nor yet one that seems great but has no unity.

You think that will be easy!

Not so hard as the duty we mentioned earlier, of moving down any inferior child born to the Guardians into the other classes and promoting from those classes any child who is good enough to be a Guardian. Our intention there was to set the other citizens to work, one man at one task for which his nature fitted him, so that by keeping to that one business he might come to be a single man and not many. In that way the state as a whole would grow to be a single community, and not many.

You may well call that not so easy!

No, but really, my good Adeimantus, we are not laying upon the Guardians a whole number of burdensome duties, as you might suppose. It will all be easy enough, if only they will see to 'the one great thing,' as the saying goes, though I would rather call it the one thing that is sufficient: education and nurture. If a sound education has made them reasonable men, they will easily see their way through all these matters as well as others which we will pass over for the moment, such as the possession of wives, marriage, and child-bearing, and the principle that here we should follow, as far as possible, the proverb which says that friends have all things in common.[1]

Yes, all should go well then.

Moreover, when a community has once made a good start, its growth proceeds in a sort of cycle. If a sound system of nurture and education is maintained, it produces men of a good disposi-

---

[1] This startling proposal is slipped in here and accepted without further remark because Plato wishes to postpone the details to a later chapter (XVI) and not to interrupt his present insistence on the supreme importance of education.

tion; and these in their turn, taking advantage of such education, develop into better men than their forebears, and their breeding qualities improve among the rest, as may be seen in animals.

That is likely enough.

In short, then, those who keep watch over our commonwealth must take the greatest care not to overlook the least infraction of the rule against any innovation upon the established system of education either of the body or of the mind. When the poet says that men care most for 'the newest air that hovers on the singer's lips,' they will be afraid lest he be taken not merely to mean new songs, but to be commending a new style of music. Such innovation is not to be commended, nor should the poet be so understood. The introduction of novel fashions in music is a thing to beware of as endangering the whole fabric of society, whose most important conventions are unsettled by any revolution in that quarter.[1] So Damon declares, and I believe him.

You may count me too among his supporters, said Adeimantus.

It seems, then, said I, that it is here, in the field of music and poetry, that our Guardians must build their watch-tower.

It is certainly there that lawlessness easily creeps in unobserved.

Yes, I said, in the guise of a pastime, which seems so harmless.

It would be harmless, he replied, were it not that, little by little, this lawless spirit gains a lodgement and spreads imperceptibly to manners and pursuits; and from thence with gathering force invades men's dealings with one another, and next goes on to attack the laws and the constitution with wanton recklessness, until it ends by overthrowing the whole structure of public and private life.

Really? said I. Is all that true?

So I believe, he replied.

Our children's pastimes, then, as I began by saying, must be kept from the first within stricter bounds; if any licence be admitted, they will catch the spirit and will never grow into law-abiding and well-conducted men. And so, when children have

---

[1] It seems obvious to Plato, who had not the illusion of perpetual progress, so popular in the nineteenth century, that when once the best possible education has been established, any change must be for the worse.

made a good beginning in their play and musical education has instilled a spirit of order, this reverence for law, in complete contrast to the licence you were describing just now, will attend them in all their doings and foster their growth, restoring any institutions that may earlier have fallen into decay.[1]

That is true.

As a consequence, they will rediscover rules of behaviour which their predecessors have let fall into disuse, including matters supposed to be of little importance: how the young should be silent in the presence of their elders, give up their seats to them, and take dutiful care of their parents; not to mention details of personal appearance, such as the way their hair is cut and the clothes and shoes they wear. It would be silly, I think, to make laws on these matters; such habits cannot be established or kept up by written legislation. It is probable, at any rate, that the bent given by education will determine the quality of later life, by that sort of attraction which like things always have for one another, till they finally mount up to one imposing result, whether for good or ill. For that reason I should not myself be inclined to push legislation to that length.

With good reason.

But now look here, what are we to do about business transactions, dealings between buyers and sellers, contracts with tradesmen, actions for foul language and assault, legal proceedings and the impanelling of juries, collection and payment of any market or harbour dues that may be needed, and generally regulations for markets, police, custom houses, and all that sort of thing? Can we go so far as to legislate on any of these matters?

No; there will be no need to dictate to men of good breeding. They will soon find out for themselves what regulations are needed.

Yes, my friend, I replied, provided that, by the grace of heaven, they preserve the institutions we have already described.

Quite so, he agreed. Otherwise they will spend their lives making a host of petty regulations and amending them in the hope of reaching perfection.

[1] Plato is here thinking of a reformed Athens, rather than of the ideal state.

Living, in fact, like those invalids who are too self-indulgent to give up their unwholesome habits.

Exactly.

And a pretty sort of life they have of it. All they gain from being doctored is that their ailments grow more severe and complicated, though they are always expecting to be cured by every fresh remedy that someone recommends.

Yes, that is a good description of a certain type of invalid.

And another amusing thing about them is that they take for their worst enemy anyone who tells them frankly that until they give up eating and drinking too much and idleness and debauchery, no medicine or surgery and no charms or amulets will do them any good.

I see nothing very amusing in being in a rage with good advice.

You don't seem to be an admirer of people like that.

I certainly am not.

Then neither will you admire the same sort of behaviour in a whole society. You will find something very like those invalids in some states with a bad form of government, which forbid their citizens, under pain of death, to make any radical change in the constitution, and at the same time honour as a good and profoundly wise person any obsequious flatterer who, without attempting such drastic treatment, can minister agreeably to their humours, which he is clever enough to anticipate.

The resemblance is very close, and I have nothing to say for them.

And what of the men who are willing and eager to minister to these invalid states? Have you no admiration for such cool temerity?

Yes, except when they are deluded by popular applause into fancying themselves to be real statesmen.

Why, said I, can't you make some allowances for them? When a man who cannot measure is told by a lot of equally ignorant people that he is six feet high, you cannot expect him not to believe them.

No, not in that instance.

Don't be so hard upon them, then. Surely there is something very amusing in the way they go on enacting their petty laws and amending them, always imagining they will find some way to put an end to fraud in business and in all those other transactions I was speaking of. They have no idea that really they are cutting off the heads of a hydra.

It is true; that is all they are doing.

I should have thought that laws and institutions of that order do not deserve the attention of a law-giver worthy of the name, no matter whether the constitution be good or bad. If it is bad, they are useless and effect nothing; if good, some are such as any-one could devise, and the rest will follow of themselves from the practices we have already instituted.

Then, what is there left for us to do in the way of legislation?

For us, nothing; but there are institutions of the highest worth and importance that must be left to the Delphian Apollo.

What are they?

The founding of temples, sacrifices, and the cults of gods, demi-gods, and heroes; the burial of the dead, and services to propitiate the powers of the other world. These are matters we do not under-stand ourselves, and in founding our commonwealth we shall be wise to consult no other religious authority than our national di-vinity. Indeed in religious matters, the authority of this god, from his seat at the very navel of the earth, may be said to extend to all mankind.[1]

Good. Let us do so.

---

[1] Excavation at Delphi has brought to light in the temple of Apollo the *omphalos* ('navel'), a conical stone which had been supposed to mark the centre of the earth when the earth was imagined to be a circular disk surrounded by the stream of Ocean. The oracle was in fact sometimes consulted by non-Greek states.

CHAPTER XII (IV. 427 C–434 D)

THE VIRTUES IN THE STATE

The original aim in constructing an ideal state was to find in it justice exemplified on a larger scale than in the individual. Assuming that four cardinal qualities make up the whole of virtue, Plato now asks wherein consist the wisdom, courage, temperance, and justice of the state, or, in other words, of the individuals composing the state in their public capacity as citizens.

Wisdom in the conduct of state affairs will be the practical prudence or good counsel of the deliberative body. Only the philosophic Rulers will possess the necessary insight into what is good for the community as a whole. They will have 'right belief' grounded on immediate knowledge of the meaning of goodness in all its forms. The Auxiliaries will have only a right belief accepted on the authority of the Rulers. Their functions will be executive, not deliberative.

The Courage of the state will obviously be manifested in the fighting force. Socrates had defined courage as knowledge of what really is, or is not, to be feared, and he had regarded it as an inseparable part of all virtue, which consists in knowing what things are really good or evil. If the only real evil is moral evil, then poverty, suffering, and all the so-called evils that others can inflict on us, including death itself, are not to be feared, since, if they are met in the right spirit, they cannot make us worse men (cf. the Laches *and the argument at 334 c ff., pp. 12 ff.). This knowledge only the philosophic Rulers will possess to the full. The courage of the Auxiliaries will consist in the power of holding fast to the conviction implanted by their education.*

Temperance is not, as we might expect, the peculiar virtue of the lowest order in the state. As self-mastery, it means the subordination of the lower elements to the higher; but government must be with the willing consent of the governed, and temperance will include the unanimous agreement of all classes as to who should rule and who obey.[1] *It is consequently like a harmony pervading and uniting all parts of the whole, a principle of solidarity. In the* Laws, *which stresses the harmonious union of different and complementary elements, this virtue overshadows even Justice.*

Justice is the complementary principle of differentiation, keeping the parts distinct. It has been before us all through the construction of the state since it first appeared on the economic level as the division of labour based on natural aptitudes (Chap. VI). 'Doing one's own work' now has the larger sense of a concentration on one's peculiar duty or function in the community. This conception of 'doing and possessing what properly belongs to one' is wide enough to cover the justice of the law-courts, assuring to each man his due rights. Injustice will mean invasion and encroachment upon the rights and duties of others.

The virtue described in this chapter is what Plato calls 'civic' or 'popular' virtue. Except in the Rulers, it is not directly based on that ultimate knowledge of good and evil which is wisdom, to be attained only at the end of the higher education of the philosopher.

So now at last, son of Ariston, said I, your commonwealth is established. The next thing is to bring to bear upon it all the light you can get from any quarter, with the help of your brother and Polemarchus and all the rest, in the hope that we may see where justice is to be found in it and where injustice, how they differ, and which of the two will bring happiness to its possessor, no matter whether gods and men see that he has it or not.

Nonsense, said Glaucon; you promised to conduct the search yourself, because it would be a sin not to uphold justice by every means in your power.

That is true; I must do as you say, but you must all help.

We will.

I suspect, then, we may find what we are looking for in this

---

[1] At *Statesman* 276 E the true king is distinguished from the despot by the voluntary submission of his subjects to his rule.

way. I take it that our state, having been founded and built up on
the right lines, is good in the complete sense of the word.

It must be.

Obviously, then, it is wise, brave, temperate, and just.

Obviously.

Then if we find some of these qualities in it, the remainder will
be the one we have not found. It is as if we were looking somewhere for one of any four things, if we detected that one immedi-
ately, we should be satisfied; whereas if we recognized the other
three first, that would be enough to indicate the thing we wanted;
it could only be the remaining one. So here we have four qualities.
Had we not better follow that method in looking for the one we
want?

Surely.

To begin then: the first quality to come into view in our state
seems to be its wisdom; and there appears to be something odd
about this quality.[1]

What is there odd about it?

I think the state we have described really has wisdom; for it
will be prudent in counsel, won't it?

Yes.

And prudence in counsel is clearly a form of knowledge; good
counsel cannot be due to ignorance and stupidity.

Clearly.

But there are many and various kinds of knowledge in our commonwealth. There is the knowledge possessed by the carpenters or
the smiths, and the knowledge how to raise crops. Are we to call
the state wise and prudent on the strength of these forms of skill?

No; they would only make it good at furniture-making or working in copper or agriculture.

Well then, is there any form of knowledge, possessed by some
among the citizens of our new-founded commonwealth, which will
enable it to take thought, not for some particular interest, but for
the best possible conduct of the state as a whole in its internal and
external relations?

Yes, there is.

1 Because the wisdom of the whole resides in the smallest part, as explained below.

What is it, and where does it reside?

It is precisely that art of guardianship which resides in those Rulers whom we just now called Guardians in the full sense.

And what would you call the state on the strength of that knowledge?

Prudent and truly wise.

And do you think there will be more or fewer of these genuine Guardians in our state than there will be smiths?

Far fewer.

Fewer, in fact, than any of those other groups who are called after the kind of skill they possess?

Much fewer.

So, if a state is constituted on natural principles, the wisdom it possesses as a whole will be due to the knowledge residing in the smallest part, the one which takes the lead and governs the rest. Such knowledge is the only kind that deserves the name of wisdom, and it appears to be ordained by nature that the class privileged to possess it should be the smallest of all.

Quite true.

Here then we have more or less made out one of our four qualities and its seat in the structure of the commonwealth.

To my satisfaction, at any rate.

Next there is courage. It is not hard to discern that quality or the part of the community in which it resides so as to entitle the whole to be called brave.

Why do you say so?

Because anyone who speaks of a state as either brave or cowardly can only be thinking of that part of it which takes the field and fights in its defence; the reason being, I imagine, that the character of the state is not determined by the bravery or cowardice of the other parts.

No.

Courage, then, is another quality which a community owes to a certain part of itself. And its being brave will mean that, in this part, it possesses the power of preserving, in all circumstances, a conviction about the sort of things that it is right to be afraid of—

the conviction implanted by the education which the law-giver has established. Is not that what you mean by courage?

I do not quite understand. Will you say it again?

I am saying that courage means preserving something.

Yes, but what?

The conviction, inculcated by lawfully established education, about the sort of things which may rightly be feared. When I added 'in all circumstances,' I meant preserving it always and never abandoning it, whether under the influence of pain or of pleasure, of desire or of fear. If you like, I will give an illustration.

Please do.

You know how dyers who want wool to take a purple dye, first select the white wool from among all the other colours, next treat it very carefully to make it take the dye in its full brilliance, and only then dip it in the vat. Dyed in that way, wool gets a fast colour, which no washing, even with soap, will rob of its brilliance; whereas if they choose wool of any colour but white, or if they neglect to prepare it, you know what happens.

Yes, it looks washed-out and ridiculous.

That illustrates the result we were doing our best to achieve when we were choosing our fighting men and training their minds and bodies. Our only purpose was to contrive influences whereby they might take the colour of our institutions like a dye, so that, in virtue of having both the right temperament and the right education, their convictions about what ought to be feared and on all other subjects might be indelibly fixed, never to be washed out by pleasure and pain, desire and fear, solvents more terribly effective than all the soap and fuller's earth in the world. Such a power of constantly preserving, in accordance with our institutions, the right conviction about the things which ought, or ought not, to be feared, is what I call courage. That is my position, unless you have some objection to make.

None at all, he replied; if the belief were such as might be found in a slave or an animal—correct, but not produced by education—you would hardly describe it as in accordance with our institutions, and you would give it some other name than courage.

Quite true.

Then I accept your account of courage.

You will do well to accept it, at any rate as applying to the courage of the ordinary citizen;[1] if you like we will go into it more fully some other time. At present we are in search of justice, rather than of courage; and for that purpose we have said enough.

I quite agree.

Two qualities, I went on, still remain to be made out in our state, temperance and the object of our whole inquiry, justice. Can we discover justice without troubling ourselves further about temperance?

I do not know, and I would rather not have justice come to light first, if that means that we should not go on to consider temperance. So if you want to please me, take temperance first.

Of course I have every wish to please you.

Do go on then.

I will. At first sight, temperance seems more like some sort of concord or harmony than the other qualities did.

How so?

Temperance surely means a kind of orderliness, a control of certain pleasures and appetites. People use the expression, 'master of oneself,' whatever that means, and various other phrases that point the same way.

Quite true.

Is not 'master of oneself' an absurd expression? A man who was master of himself would presumably be also subject to himself, and the subject would be master; for all these terms apply to the same person.

No doubt.

I think, however, the phrase means that within the man himself, in his soul, there is a better part and a worse; and that he is his own master when the part which is better by nature has the worse under its control. It is certainly a term of praise; whereas it is considered a disgrace, when, through bad breeding or bad

[1] As distinct from the perfect courage of the philosophic Ruler, based on immediate knowledge of values.

company, the better part is overwhelmed by the worse, like a small force outnumbered by a multitude. A man in that condition is called a slave to himself and intemperate.

Probably that is what is meant.

Then now look at our newly founded state and you will find one of these two conditions realized there. You will agree that it deserves to be called master of itself, if temperance and self-mastery exist where the better part rules the worse.

Yes, I can see that is true.

It is also true that the great mass of multifarious appetites and pleasures and pains will be found to occur chiefly in children and women and slaves, and, among free men so called, in the inferior multitude; whereas the simple and moderate desires which, with the aid of reason and right belief, are guided by reflection, you will find only in a few, and those with the best inborn dispositions and the best educated.

Yes, certainly.

Do you see that this state of things will exist in your commonwealth, where the desires of the inferior multitude will be controlled by the desires and wisdom of the superior few? Hence, if any society can be called master of itself and in control of pleasures and desires, it will be ours.

Quite so.

On all these grounds, then, we may describe it as temperate. Furthermore, in our state, if anywhere, the governors and the governed will share the same conviction on the question who ought to rule.[1] Don't you think so?

I am quite sure of it.

Then, if that is their state of mind, in which of the two classes of citizens will temperance reside—in the governors or in the governed?

In both, I suppose.

So we were not wrong in divining a resemblance between temperance and some kind of harmony. Temperance is not like cour-

---

[1] This principle of freedom—government with consent of the governed—is thus recognized. The 'democratic' freedom to 'do whatever you like' will be condemned in Chap. XXXI.

age and wisdom, which made the state wise and brave by residing each in one particular part. Temperance works in a different way; it extends throughout the whole gamut of the state, producing a consonance of all its elements from the weakest to the strongest as measured by any standard you like to take—wisdom, bodily strength, numbers, or wealth. So we are entirely justified in identifying with temperance this unanimity or harmonious agreement between the naturally superior and inferior elements on the question which of the two should govern, whether in the state or in the individual.

I fully agree.

Good, said I. We have discovered in our commonwealth three out of our four qualities, to the best of our present judgment. What is the remaining one, required to make up its full complement of goodness? For clearly this will be justice.

Clearly.

Now is the moment, then, Glaucon, for us to keep the closest watch, like huntsmen standing round a covert, to make sure that justice does not slip through and vanish undetected. It must certainly be somewhere hereabouts; so keep your eyes open for a view of the quarry, and if you see it first, give me the alert.

I wish I could, he answered; but you will do better to give me a lead and not count on me for more than eyes to see what you show me.

Pray for luck, then, and follow me.

I will, if you will lead on.

The thicket looks rather impenetrable, said I; too dark for it to be easy to start up the game. However, we must push on.

Of course we must.

Here I gave the view halloo. Glaucon, I exclaimed, I believe we are on the track and the quarry is not going to escape us altogether.

That is good news.

Really, I said, we have been extremely stupid. All this time the thing has been under our very noses from the start, and we never saw it. We have been as absurd as a person who hunts for something he has all the time got in his hand. Instead of looking at the thing, we have been staring into the distance. No doubt that is why it escaped us.

What do you mean?

I believe we have been talking about the thing all this while without ever understanding that we were giving some sort of account of it.

Do come to the point. I am all ears.

Listen, then, and judge whether I am right. You remember how, when we first began to establish our commonwealth and several times since, we have laid down, as a universal principle, that everyone ought to perform the one function in the community for which his nature best suited him. Well, I believe that that principle, or some form of it, is justice.

We certainly laid that down.

Yes, and surely we have often heard people say that justice means minding one's own business and not meddling with other men's concerns; and we have often said so ourselves.[1]

We have.

Well, my friend, it may be that this minding of one's own business, when it takes a certain form, is actually the same thing as justice. Do you know what makes me think so?

No, tell me.

I think that this quality which makes it possible for the three we have already considered, wisdom, courage, and temperance, to take their place in the commonwealth, and so long as it remains present secures their continuance, must be the remaining one. And we said that, when three of the four were found. the one left over would be justice.

It must be so.

Well now, if we had to decide which of these qualities will contribute most to the excellence of our commonwealth, it would be hard to say whether it was the unanimity of rulers and subjects, or the soldier's fidelity to the established conviction about what is, or

---

[1] If 'justice' here is taken in the wide sense of 'the right way to behave,' 'right conduct,' this has, of course, been stated several times in the *Republic*. But the statement need not refer to any passage in the dialogue.

is not, to be feared, or the watchful intelligence of the Rulers; or
whether its excellence were not above all due to the observance by
everyone, child or woman, slave or freeman or artisan, ruler or
ruled, of this principle that each one should do his own proper
work without interfering with others.

It would be hard to decide, no doubt.

It seems, then, that this principle can at any rate claim to rival
wisdom, temperance, and courage as conducing to the excellence
of a state. And would you not say that the only possible competitor of these qualities must be justice.

Yes, undoubtedly.

Here is another thing which points to the same conclusion. The
judging of law-suits is a duty that you will lay upon your Rulers,
isn't it?

Of course.

And the chief aim of their decisions will be that neither party
shall have what belongs to another or be deprived of what is his
own.

Yes.

Because that is just?

Yes.

So here again justice admittedly means that a man should possess and concern himself with what properly belongs to him.[1]

True.

Again, do you agree with me that no great harm would be done
to the community by a general interchange of most forms of work,
the carpenter and the cobbler exchanging their positions and their
tools and taking on each other's jobs, or even the same man undertaking both?

Yes, there would not be much harm in that.

But I think you will also agree that another kind of interchange
would be disastrous. Suppose, for instance, someone whom nature
designed to be an artisan or tradesman should be emboldened by
some advantage, such as wealth or command of votes or bodily
strength, to try to enter the order of fighting men; or some member of that order should aspire, beyond his merits, to a seat in the

---

[1] Here the legal conception of justice is connected with its moral significance.

council-chamber of the Guardians. Such interference and exchange of social positions and tools, or the attempt to combine all these forms of work in the same person, would be fatal to the common-wealth.

Most certainly.

Where there are three orders, then, any plurality of functions or shifting from one order to another is not merely utterly harmful to the community, but one might fairly call it the extreme of wrongdoing. And you will agree that to do the greatest of wrongs to one's own community is injustice.

Surely.

This, then, is injustice. And, conversely, let us repeat that when each order—tradesman, Auxiliary, Guardian—keeps to its own proper business in the commonwealth and does its own work, that is justice and what makes a just society.

I entirely agree.

CHAPTER XIII (IV. 434 D-441 C)

THE THREE PARTS OF THE SOUL

It has been shown that justice in the state means that the three chief social functions—deliberative and governing, executive, and productive—are kept distinct and rightly performed. Since the qualities of a community are those of the component individuals, we may expect to find three corresponding elements in the individual soul. All three will be present in every soul; but the structure of society is based on the fact that they are developed to different degrees in different types of character.

The existence of three elements or 'parts' of the soul is established by an analysis of the conflict of motives. A simple case is the thirsty man's appetite for drink, held in check by the rational reflection that to drink will be bad for him. That two distinct elements must be at work here follows from the general principle that the same thing cannot act or be affected in two opposite ways at the same

*time. By 'thirst' is meant simply the bare craving for drink; it must
not be confused with a desire for some good (e.g., health or pleasure) expected as a consequence of drinking. This simple craving
says, 'Drink'; Reason says, 'Do not drink': the contradiction shows
that two elements are at work.*

*A third factor is the 'spirited' element, akin to our 'sense of
honour,' manifested in indignation, which takes the side of reason
against appetite, but cannot be identified with reason, since it is
found in children and animals and it may be rebuked by reason.*

*This analysis is not intended as a complete outline of psychology;
that could be reached only by following 'a longer road.' It is concerned with the factors involved in moral behaviour. Later (Chap.
XXXIII, p. 307) they will be represented as three forms of desire,
each with its characteristic object: |wisdom; honour; gain as a
means to the satisfaction of bodily appetites. In Plato's myth of
creation (the* Timaeus) *the three parts are lodged in the head, the
chest, and the belly and organs of generation; and the reason alone
is immortal and separable from the body. But in Chapter XXXVIII,
p. 347, it will be indicated that this mythical picture must not be
taken literally as implying that the soul is like a material thing,
which can be destroyed by being broken up into parts out of which
it has been put together.*

WE must not be too positive yet, said I. If we find that this same
quality when it exists in the individual can equally be identified
with justice, then we can at once give our assent; there will be no
more to be said; otherwise, we shall have to look further. For the
moment, we had better finish the inquiry which we began with
the idea that it would be easier to make out the nature of justice in
the individual if we first tried to study it in something on a larger
scale. That larger thing we took to be a state, and so we set about
constructing the best one we could, being sure of finding justice in
a state that was good. The discovery we made there must now be
applied to the individual. If it is confirmed, all will be well; but if
we find that justice in the individual is something different, we
must go back to the state and test our new result. Perhaps if we

brought the two cases into contact like flint and steel, we might strike out between them the spark of justice, and in its light confirm the conception in our own minds.

A good method. Let us follow it.

Now, I continued, if two things, one large, the other small, are called by the same name, they will be alike in that respect to which the common name applies. Accordingly, in so far as the quality of justice is concerned, there will be no difference between a just man and a just society.

No.

Well, but we decided that a society was just when each of the three types of human character it contained performed its own function; and again, it was temperate and brave and wise by virtue of certain other affections and states of mind of those same types.

True.

Accordingly, my friend, if we are to be justified in attributing those same virtues to the individual, we shall expect to find that the individual soul contains the same three elements and that they are affected in the same way as are the corresponding types in society.

That follows.

Here, then, we have stumbled upon another little problem: Does the soul contain these three elements or not?

Not such a very little one, I think. It may be a true saying, Socrates, that what is worth while is seldom easy.

Apparently; and let me tell you, Glaucon, it is my belief that we shall never reach the exact truth in this matter by following our present methods of discussion; the road leading to that goal is longer and more laborious.[1] However, perhaps we can find an answer that will be up to the standard we have so far maintained in our speculations.

Is not that enough? I should be satisfied for the moment.

Well, it will more than satisfy me, I replied.

Don't be disheartened, then, but go on.

---

[1] Socrates refers to this 'longer road' later, at 504 B, p. 214.

love of money

Surely, I began, we must admit that the same elements and characters that appear in the state must exist in every one of us; where else could they have come from? It would be absurd to imagine that among peoples with a reputation for a high-spirited character, like the Thracians and Scythians and northerners generally, the states have not derived that character from their individual members; or that it is otherwise with the love of knowledge, which would be ascribed chiefly to our own part of the world, or with the love of money, which one would specially connect with Phoenicia and Egypt.

Certainly.

So far, then, we have a fact which is easily recognized. But here the difficulty begins. Are we using the same part of ourselves in all these three experiences, or a different part in each? Do we gain knowledge with one part, feel anger with another, and with yet a third desire the pleasures of food, sex, and so on? Or is the whole soul at work in every impulse and in all these forms of behaviour? The difficulty is to answer that question satisfactorily.

I quite agree.

Let us approach the problem whether these elements are distinct or identical in this way. It is clear that the same thing cannot act in two opposite ways or be in two opposite states at the same time, with respect to the same part of itself, and in relation to the same object. So if we find such contradictory actions or states among the elements concerned, we shall know that more than one must have been involved.

Very well.

Consider this proposition of mine, then. Can the same thing, at the same time and with respect to the same part of itself, be at rest and in motion?

Certainly not.

We had better state this principle in still more precise terms, to guard against misunderstanding later on. Suppose a man is standing still, but moving his head and arms. We should not allow anyone to say that the same man was both at rest and in motion at the same time, but only that part of him was at rest, part in motion. Isn't that so?

Yes.

in parts!

An ingenious objector might refine still further and argue that a peg-top, spinning with its peg fixed at the same spot, or indeed any body that revolves in the same place, is both at rest and in motion as a whole. But we should not agree, because the parts in respect of which such a body is moving and at rest are not the same. It contains an axis and a circumference; and in respect of the axis it is at rest inasmuch as the axis is not inclined in any direction, while in respect of the circumference it revolves; and if, while it is spinning, the axis does lean out of the perpendicular in all directions, then it is in no way at rest.

That is true.

No objection of that sort, then, will disconcert us or make us believe that the same thing can ever act or be acted upon in two opposite ways, or be two opposite things, at the same time, in respect of the same part of itself, and in relation to the same object.

I can answer for myself at any rate.

Well, anyhow, as we do not want to spend time in reviewing all such objections to make sure that they are unsound, let us proceed on this assumption, with the understanding that, if we ever come to think otherwise, all the consequences based upon it will fall to the ground.

Yes, that is a good plan.

Now, would you class such things as assent and dissent, striving after something and refusing it, attraction and repulsion, as pairs of opposite actions or states of mind—no matter which?

Yes, they are opposites.

And would you not class all appetites such as hunger and thirst, and again willing and wishing, with the affirmative members of those pairs I have just mentioned? For instance, you would say that the soul of a man who desires something is striving after it, or trying to draw to itself the thing it wishes to possess, or again, in so far as it is willing to have its want satisfied, it is giving its assent to its own longing, as if to an inward question.

Yes.

And, on the other hand, disinclination, unwillingness, and dislike, we should class on the negative side with acts of rejection or repulsion.

Of course.

That being so, shall we say that ⟨appetites⟩ form one class, the most conspicuous being those we call thirst and hunger?

Yes.

Thirst being desire for drink, hunger for food?

Yes.

Now, is thirst, just in so far as it is thirst, a desire in the soul for anything more than simply drink? Is it, for instance, thirst for hot drink or for cold, for much drink or for little, or in a word for drink of any particular kind? Is it not rather true that you will have a desire for cold drink only if you are feeling hot as well as thirsty, and for hot drink only if you are feeling cold; and if you want much drink or little, that will be because your thirst is a great thirst or a little one? But, just in itself, thirst or hunger is a desire for nothing more than its natural object, drink or food, pure and simple.

Yes, he agreed, each desire, just in itself, is simply for its own natural object. When the object is of such and such a particular kind, the desire will be correspondingly qualified.[1]

We must be careful here, or we might be troubled by the objection that no one desires mere food and drink, but always wholesome food and drink. We shall be told that what we desire is always something that is good; so if thirst is a desire, its object must be, like that of any other desire, something—drink or whatever it may be—that will be good for one.[2]

Yes, there might seem to be something in that objection.

---

[1] The object of the following subtle argument about relative terms is to distinguish thirst as a mere blind craving for drink from a more complex desire whose object includes the pleasure or health expected to result from drinking. We thus forestall the objection that all desires have 'the good' (apparent or real) for their object and include an intellectual or rational element, so that the conflict of motives might be reduced to an intellectual debate, in the same 'part' of the soul, on the comparative values of two incompatible ends.

[2] If this objection were admitted, it would follow that the desire would always be correspondingly qualified. It is necessary to insist that we do experience blind cravings which can be isolated from any judgement about the goodness of their object.

But surely, wherever you have two correlative terms, if one is qualified, the other must always be qualified too; whereas if one is unqualified, so is the other.

I don't understand.

Well, 'greater' is a relative term; and the greater is greater than the less; if it is much greater, then the less is much less; if it is greater at some moment, past or future, then the less is less at that same moment. The same principle applies to all such correlatives, like 'more' and 'fewer,' 'double' and 'half'; and again to terms like 'heavier' and 'lighter,' 'quicker' and 'slower,' and to things like hot and cold.

Yes.

Or take the various branches of knowledge: is it not the same there? The object of knowledge pure and simple is the knowable— if that is the right word—without any qualification; whereas a particular kind of knowledge has an object of a particular kind. For example, as soon as men learnt how to build houses, their craft was distinguished from others under the name of architecture, because it had a unique character, which was itself due to the character of its object; and all other branches of craft and knowledge were distinguished in the same way.

True.

This, then, if you understand me now, is what I meant by saying that, where there are two correlatives, the one is qualified if, and only if, the other is so. I am not saying that the one must have the same quality as the other—that the science of health and disease is itself healthy and diseased, or the knowledge of good and evil is itself good and evil—but only that, as soon as you have a knowledge that is restricted to a particular kind of object, namely health and disease, the knowledge itself becomes a particular kind of knowledge. Hence we no longer call it merely knowledge, which would have for its object whatever can be known, but we add the qualification and call it medical science.

I understand now and I agree.

Now, to go back to thirst: is not that one of these relative terms? It is essentially thirst for something.

Yes, for drink.

And if the drink desired is of a certain kind, the thirst will be correspondingly qualified. But thirst which is just simply thirst is not for drink of any particular sort—much or little, good or bad— but for drink pure and simple.

Quite so.

We conclude, then, that the soul of a thirsty man, just in so far as he is thirsty, has no other wish than to drink. That is the object of its craving, and towards that it is impelled.

That is clear.

Now if there is ever something which at the same time pulls it the opposite way, that something must be an element in the soul other than the one which is thirsting and driving it like a beast to drink; in accordance with our principle that the same thing cannot behave in two opposite ways at the same time and towards the same object with the same part of itself. It is like an archer drawing the bow: it is not accurate to say that his hands are at the same time both pushing and pulling it. One hand does the pushing, the other the pulling.

Exactly.

Now, is it sometimes true that people are thirsty and yet unwilling to drink?

Yes, often.

What, then, can one say of them, if not that their soul contains something which urges them to drink and something which holds them back, and that this latter is a distinct thing and overpowers the other?

I agree.

And is it not true that the intervention of this inhibiting principle in such cases always has its origin in reflection; whereas the impulses driving and dragging the soul are engendered by external influences and abnormal conditions? [1]

Evidently.

We shall have good reason, then, to assert that they are two dis-

---

[1] Some of the most intense bodily desires are due to morbid conditions, e.g. thirst in fever, and even milder desires are caused by a departure from the normal state, which demands 'replenishment' (*Philebus*, 45-46, and Chap. XXXIII below, p. 310 f.).

tinct principles. We may call that part of the soul whereby it reflects, rational; and the other, with which it feels hunger and thirst and is distracted by sexual passion and all the other desires, we will call irrational appetite, associated with pleasure in the replenishment of certain wants.

Yes, there is good ground for that view.

Let us take it, then, that we have now distinguished two elements in the soul. What of that passionate element which makes us feel angry and indignant? Is that a third, or identical in nature with one of those two?

It might perhaps be identified with appetite.

I am more inclined to put my faith in a story I once heard about Leontius, son of Aglaion. On his way up from the Piraeus outside the north wall, he noticed the bodies of some criminals lying on the ground, with the executioner standing by them. He wanted to go and look at them, but at the same time he was disgusted and tried to turn away. He struggled for some time and covered his eyes, but at last the desire was too much for him. Opening his eyes wide, he ran up to the bodies and cried, 'There you are, curse you; feast yourselves on this lovely sight!'

Yes, I have heard that story too.

The point of it surely is that anger is sometimes in conflict with appetite, as if they were two distinct principles. Do we not often find a man whose desires would force him to go against his reason, reviling himself and indignant with this part of his nature which is trying to put constraint on him? It is like a struggle between two factions, in which indignation takes the side of reason. But I believe you have never observed, in yourself or anyone else, indignation make common cause with appetite in behaviour which reason decides to be wrong.

No, I am sure I have not.

Again, take a man who feels he is in the wrong. The more generous his nature, the less can he be indignant at any suffering, such as hunger and cold, inflicted by the man he has injured. He recognizes such treatment as just, and, as I say, his spirit refuses to be roused against it.

That is true.

But now contrast one who thinks it is he that is being wronged. His spirit boils with resentment and sides with the right as he conceives it. Persevering all the more for the hunger and cold and other pains he suffers, it triumphs and will not give in until its gallant struggle has ended in success or death; or until the restraining voice of reason, like a shepherd calling off his dog, makes it relent.

An apt comparison, he said; and in fact it fits the relation of our Auxiliaries to the Rulers: they were to be like watch-dogs obeying the shepherds of the commonwealth.

Yes, you understand very well what I have in mind. But do you see how we have changed our view? A moment ago we were supposing this spirited element to be something of the nature of appetite; but now it appears that, when the soul is divided into factions, it is far more ready to be up in arms on the side of reason.

Quite true.

Is it, then, distinct from the rational element or only a particular form of it, so that the soul will contain no more than two elements, reason and appetite? Or is the soul like the state, which had three orders to hold it together, traders, Auxiliaries, and counsellors? Does the spirited element make a third, the natural auxiliary of reason, when not corrupted by bad upbringing?

It must be a third.

Yes, I said, provided it can be shown to be distinct from reason, as we saw it was from appetite.

That is easily proved. You can see that much in children: they are full of passionate feelings from their very birth; but some, I should say, never become rational, and most of them only late in life.

A very sound observation, said I, the truth of which may also be seen in animals. And besides, there is the witness of Homer in that line I quoted before: 'He smote his breast and spoke, chiding his heart.' The poet is plainly thinking of the two elements as distinct, when he makes the one which has chosen the better course after reflection rebuke the other for its unreasoning passion.

I entirely agree.

THE VIRTUES IN THE INDIVIDUAL

The virtues in the state were the qualities of the citizen, as such, considered as playing the special part in society for which he was qualified by the predominance in his nature of the philosophic, the pugnacious, or the commercial spirit. But all three elements exist in every individual, who is thus a replica of society in miniature. In the perfect man reason will rule, with the spirited element as its auxiliary, over the bodily appetites. Self-control or temperance will be a condition of internal harmony, all the parts being content with their legitimate satisfactions. Justice finally appears, no longer only as a matter of external behaviour towards others, but as an internal order of the soul, from which right behaviour will necessarily follow. Injustice is the opposite state of internal discord and faction. To ask whether justice or injustice pays the better is now seen to be as absurd as to ask whether health is preferable to disease.

AND so, after a stormy passage, we have reached the land. We are fairly agreed that the same three elements exist alike in the state and in the individual soul.

That is so.

Does it not follow at once that state and individual will be wise or brave by virtue of the same element in each and in the same way? Both will possess in the same manner any quality that makes for excellence.

That must be true.

Then it applies to justice: we shall conclude that a man is just in the same way that a state was just. And we have surely not forgotten that justice in the state meant that each of the three orders in it was doing its own proper work. So we may henceforth bear in mind that each one of us likewise will be a just person, fulfilling

139

his proper function, only if the several parts of our nature fulfil
theirs.

Certainly.

And it will be the business of reason to rule with wisdom and
forethought on behalf of the entire soul; while the spirited element
ought to act as its subordinate and ally. The two will be brought
into accord, as we said earlier, by that combination of mental and
bodily training which will tune up one string of the instrument
and relax the other, nourishing the reasoning part on the study
of noble literature and allaying the other's wildness by harmony
and rhythm. When both have been thus nurtured and trained to
know their own true functions, they must be set in command over
the appetites, which form the greater part of each man's soul and
are by nature insatiably covetous. They must keep watch lest this
part, by battening on the pleasures that are called bodily, should
grow so great and powerful that it will no longer keep to its own
work, but will try to enslave the others and usurp a dominion to
which it has no right, thus turning the whole of life upside down.
At the same time, those two together will be the best of guardians
for the entire soul and for the body against all enemies from without: the one will take counsel, while the other will do battle, following its ruler's commands and by its own bravery giving effect
to the ruler's designs.

Yes, that is all true.

And so we call an individual brave in virtue of this spirited part
of his nature, when, in spite of pain or pleasure, it holds fast to
the injunctions of reason about what he ought or ought not to be
afraid of.

True.

And wise in virtue of that small part which rules and issues
these injunctions, possessing as it does the knowledge of what is
good for each of the three elements and for all of them in common.

Certainly.

And, again, temperate by reason of the unanimity and concord of
all three, when there is no internal conflict between the ruling ele-

ment and its two subjects, but all are agreed that reason should be ruler.

Yes, that is an exact account of temperance, whether in the state or in the individual.

Finally, a man will be just by observing the principle we have so often stated.

Necessarily.

Now is there any indistinctness in our vision of justice, that might make it seem somehow different from what we found it to be in the state?

I don't think so.

Because, if we have any lingering doubt, we might make sure by comparing it with some commonplace notions. Suppose, for instance, that a sum of money were entrusted to our state or to an individual of corresponding character and training, would anyone imagine that such a person would be specially likely to embezzle it?

No.

And would he not be incapable of sacrilege and theft, or of treachery to friend or country; never false to an oath or any other compact; the last to be guilty of adultery or of neglecting parents or the due service of the gods?

Yes.

And the reason for all this is that each part of his nature is exercising its proper function, of ruling or of being ruled.

Yes, exactly.

Are you satisfied, then, that justice is the power which produces states or individuals of whom that is true, or must we look further?

There is no need; I am quite satisfied.

And so our dream has come true—I mean the inkling we had that, by some happy chance, we had lighted upon a rudimentary form of justice from the very moment when we set about founding our commonwealth. Our principle that the born shoemaker or carpenter had better stick to his trade turns out to have been an adumbration of justice; and that is why it has helped us. But in reality justice, though evidently analogous to this principle, is not a matter of external behaviour, but of the inward self and of attend-

just
man

ing to all that is, in the fullest sense, a man's proper concern. The just man does not allow the several elements in his soul to usurp one another's functions; he is indeed one who sets his house in order, by self-mastery and discipline coming to be at peace with himself, and bringing into tune those three parts, like the terms in the proportion of a musical scale, the highest and lowest notes and the mean between them, with all the intermediate intervals. Only when he has linked these parts together in well-tempered harmony and has made himself one man instead of many, will he be ready to go about whatever he may have to do, whether it be making money and satisfying bodily wants, or business transactions, or the affairs of state. In all these fields when he speaks of just and honourable conduct, he will mean the behaviour that helps to produce and to preserve this habit of mind; and by wisdom he will mean the knowledge which presides over such conduct. Any action which tends to break down this habit will be for him unjust; and the notions governing it he will call ignorance and folly.

That is perfectly true, Socrates.

Good, said I. I believe we should not be thought altogether mistaken, if we claimed to have discovered the just man and the just state, and wherein their justice consists.

Indeed we should not.

Shall we make that claim, then?

Yes, we will.

Conclusion ? Now, Injustice &

So be it, said I. Next, I suppose, we have to consider injustice.

Evidently.

This must surely be a sort of civil strife among the three elements, whereby they usurp and encroach upon one another's functions and some one part of the soul rises up in rebellion against the whole, claiming a supremacy to which it has no right because its nature fits it only to be the servant of the ruling principle. Such turmoil and aberration we shall, I think, identify with injustice, intemperance, cowardice, ignorance, and in a word with all wickedness.

Exactly.

And now that we know the nature of justice and injustice, we can be equally clear about what is meant by acting justly and again by unjust action and wrongdoing.

How do you mean?

Plainly, they are exactly analogous to those wholesome and unwholesome activities which respectively produce a healthy or unhealthy condition in the body; in the same way just and unjust conduct produce a just or unjust character. Justice is produced in the soul, like health in the body, by establishing the elements concerned in their natural relations of control and subordination, whereas injustice is like disease and means that this natural order is inverted.

Quite so.

It appears, then, that virtue is as it were the health and comeliness and well-being of the soul, as wickedness is disease, deformity, and weakness.

True.

And also that virtue and wickedness are brought about by one's way of life, honourable or disgraceful.

That follows.

So now it only remains to consider which is the more profitable course: to do right and live honourably and be just, whether or not anyone knows what manner of man you are, or to do wrong and be unjust, provided that you can escape the chastisement which might make you a better man.

But really, Socrates, it seems to me ridiculous to ask that question now that the nature of justice and injustice has been brought to light. People think that all the luxury and wealth and power in the world cannot make life worth living when the bodily constitution is going to rack and ruin; and are we to believe that, when the very principle whereby we live is deranged and corrupted, life will be worth living so long as a man can do as he will, and wills to do anything rather than to free himself from vice and wrong-doing and to win justice and virtue?

Yes, I replied, it is a ridiculous question.

PART II, APPENDIX (IV. 445 B–V. 471 C)

THE POSITION OF WOMEN AND THE USAGES OF WAR

Justice being now defined and admitted to be more profitable than injustice, Socrates seems to have answered the challenge of Glaucon and Adeimantus. But Plato more than once hints that the argument so far has been carried on at a superficial level. Virtue is, directly or indirectly, dependent upon that wisdom the love of which is 'philosophy'; we have yet to learn what wisdom is and how it can be attained. This will be the subject of Part III, which will also answer the question whether the ideal state, however desirable, can be realized on earth.

Meanwhile the next three chapters form an interlude, supplementing the institutions described above and only formally connected by the metaphor of the three 'waves' with the account of the philosophic statesman which follows in Part III.

CHAPTER XV (IV. 445 B–V. 457 B)

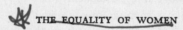 THE EQUALITY OF WOMEN

Before proceeding to the central paradox, the rule of the philosopher-king, Socrates explains how the Guardians are to 'have wives and children in common,' as he hinted earlier (424 A, p. 115). *The common life of the Guardians, it now appears, involves that men and women shall receive the same education and share equally in all public duties: women with the right natural gifts are not to be debarred by difference of sex from fulfilling the highest functions. So when the best Guardians are selected for training as Rulers, the choice may fall upon a woman. At Athens, where women lived in seclusion and took no part in politics, this proposal would appear revolutionary. It is the theme of one of Aristophanes' later comedies,* Women in Parliament (Ecclesiazusae), *which shows that the question of women's rights was in the air as early as* 393 B.C.

144

This topic is introduced as if it were a digression. Socrates is interrupted as he starts upon a description of the degenerate types of constitution and human character, which is not resumed till Chapter XXIX.

NEVERTHELESS, I continued, we are now within sight of the clearest possible proof of our conclusions, and we ought not to slacken our efforts.

No, anything rather than that.

If you will take your stand with me, then, on this point of vantage to which we have climbed, you shall see all the forms that evil takes, or at least all that it seems worth while to look at.

Lead the way and tell me what you see.

What I see is that, whereas there is only one form of excellence, imperfection exists in innumerable shapes, of which there are four that specially deserve notice.

What do you mean?

It looks as if there were as many types of character as there are distinct varieties of political constitution.

How many?

Five of each.

Will you define them?

Yes, I said. One form of constitution will be the form we have been describing, though it may be called by two names: monarchy, when there is one man who stands out above the rest of the Rulers; aristocracy, when there are more than one.[1]

True.

That, then, I regard as a single form; for, so long as they observe our principles of upbringing and education, whether the Rulers be one or more, they will not subvert the important institutions in our commonwealth.

Naturally not.

Such, then, is the type of state or constitution that I call good and right, and the corresponding type of man. By this standard,

[1] The question whether wisdom rules in the person of one man or of several is unimportant. In the sequel the ideal constitution is called kingship or aristocracy (the rule of the best) indifferently. Cf. 540 D, p. 262, and 587 D, p. 315 f.

the other forms in which a state or an individual character may be organized are depraved and wrong. There are four of these vicious forms.

What are they?

Here I was going on to describe these forms in the order in which, as I thought, they develop one from another, when Polemarchus, who was sitting a little way from Adeimantus, reached out his hand and took hold of his garment by the shoulder. Leaning forward and drawing Adeimantus towards him, he whispered something in his ear, of which I only caught the words: What shall we do? Shall we leave it alone?

Certainly not, said Adeimantus, raising his voice.

What is this, I asked, that you are not going to leave alone?

You, he replied.

Why, in particular? I inquired.

Because we think you are shirking the discussion of a very important part of the subject and trying to cheat us out of an explanation. Everyone, you said, must of course see that the maxim 'friends have all things in common' applies to women and children. You thought we should pass over such a casual remark!

But wasn't that right, Adeimantus? said I.

Yes, he said, but 'right' in this case, as in others, needs to be defined. There may be many ways of having things in common, and you must tell us which you mean. We have been waiting a long time for you to say something about the conditions in which children are to be born and brought up and your whole plan of having wives and children held in common. This seems to us a matter in which right or wrong management will make all the difference to society; and now, instead of going into it thoroughly, you are passing on to some other form of constitution. So we came to the resolution which you overheard, not to let you off discussing it as fully as all the other institutions.

I will vote for your resolution too, said Glaucon.

In fact, Socrates, Thrasymachus added, you may take it as carried unanimously.

You don't know what you are doing, I said, in holding me up

like this. You want to start, all over again, on an enormous subject, just as I was rejoicing at the idea that we had done with this form of constitution. I was only too glad that my casual remark should be allowed to pass. And now, when you demand an explanation, you little know what a swarm of questions you are stirring up. I let it alone, because I foresaw no end of trouble.

Well, said Thrasymachus, what do you think we came here for—to play pitch-and-toss or to listen to a discussion?

A discussion, no doubt, I replied; but within limits.

No man of sense, said Glaucon, would think the whole of life too long to spend on questions of this importance. But never mind about us; don't be faint-hearted yourself. Tell us what you think about this question: how our Guardians are to have wives and children in common, and how they will bring up the young in the interval between their birth and education, which is thought to be the most difficult time of all. Do try to explain how all this is to be arranged.

I wish it were as easy as you seem to think, I replied. These arrangements are even more open to doubt than any we have so far discussed. It may be questioned whether the plan is feasible, and even if entirely feasible, whether it would be for the best. So I have some hesitation in touching on what may seem to be an idle dream.

You need not hesitate, he replied. This is not an unsympathetic audience; we are neither incredulous nor hostile.

Thank you, I said; I suppose that remark is meant to be encouraging.

Certainly it is.

Well, I said, it has just the opposite effect. You would do well to encourage me, if I had any faith in my own understanding of these matters. If one knows the truth, there is no risk to be feared in speaking about the things one has most at heart among intelligent friends; but if one is still in the position of a doubting inquirer, as I am now, talking becomes a slippery venture. Not that I am afraid of being laughed at—that would be childish—but I am afraid I may miss my footing just where a false step is most to be dreaded and drag my friends down with me in my fall. I devoutly hope, Glaucon, that no nemesis will overtake me for what I am going to say; for I really believe that to kill a man unintentionally is a lighter offence than to mislead him concerning the goodness and justice of social institutions. Better to run that risk among enemies than among friends; so your encouragement is out of place.

Glaucon laughed at this. No, Socrates, he said, if your theory has any untoward effect on us, our blood shall not be on your head; we absolve you of any intention to mislead us. So have no fear.

Well, said I, when a homicide is absolved of all intention, the law holds him clear of guilt; and the same principle may apply to my case.

Yes, so far as that goes, you may speak freely.

We must go back, then, to a subject which ought, perhaps, to have been treated earlier in its proper place; though, after all, it may be suitable that the women should have their turn on the stage when the men have quite finished their performance, especially since you are so insistent. In my judgement, then, the question under what conditions people born and educated as we have described should possess wives and children, and how they should treat them, can be rightly settled only by keeping to the course on which we started them at the outset. We undertook to put these men in the position of watch-dogs guarding a flock. Suppose we follow up the analogy and imagine them bred and reared in the same sort of way. We can then see if that plan will suit our purpose.

How will that be?

In this way. Which do we think right for watch-dogs: should the females guard the flock and hunt with the males and take a share in all they do, or should they be kept within doors as fit for no more than bearing and feeding their puppies, while all the hard work of looking after the flock is left to the males?

They are expected to take their full share, except that we treat them as not quite so strong.

Can you employ any creature for the same work as another, if you do not give them both the same upbringing and education?

No.

Then, if we are to set women to the same tasks as men, we must teach them the same things. They must have the same two branches of training for mind and body and also be taught the art of war, and they must receive the same treatment.

That seems to follow.

Possibly, if these proposals were carried out, they might be ridiculed as involving a good many breaches of custom.

They might indeed.

The most ridiculous—don't you think?—being the notion of women exercising naked along with the men in the wrestling-schools; some of them elderly women too, like the old men who still have a passion for exercise when they are wrinkled and not very agreeable to look at.

Yes, that would be thought laughable, according to our present notions.

Now we have started on this subject, we must not be frightened of the many witticisms that might be aimed at such a revolution, not only in the matter of bodily exercise but in the training of women's minds, and not least when it comes to their bearing arms and riding on horseback. Having begun upon these rules, we must not draw back from the harsher provisions. The wits may be asked to stop being witty and try to be serious; and we may remind them that it is not so long since the Greeks, like most foreign nations of the present day, thought it ridiculous and shameful for men to be seen naked. When gymnastic exercises were first introduced in Crete and later at Sparta, the humorists had their chance to make fun of them; but when experience had shown that naked-ness is better uncovered than muffled up, the laughter died down and a practice which the reason approved ceased to look ridiculous to the eye. This shows how idle it is to think anything ludicrous but what is base. One who tries to raise a laugh at any spectacle save that of baseness and folly will also, in his serious moments, set before himself some other standard than goodness of what deserves to be held in honour.

Most assuredly.

The first thing to be settled, then, is whether these proposals are feasible; and it must be open to anyone, whether a humorist or serious-minded, to raise the question whether, in the case of mankind, the feminine nature is capable of taking part with the other sex in all occupations, or in none at all, or in some only; and in particular under which of these heads this business of military service falls. Well begun is half done, and would not this be the best way to begin?

Yes.

Shall we take the other side in this debate and argue against ourselves? We do not want the adversary's position to be taken by storm for lack of defenders.

I have no objection.

Let us state his case for him. 'Socrates and Glaucon,' he will say, 'there is no need for others to dispute your position; you yourselves, at the very outset of founding your commonwealth, agreed that everyone should do the one work for which nature fits him.' Yes, of course; I suppose we did. 'And isn't there a very great difference in nature between man and woman?' Yes, surely. 'Does not that natural difference imply a corresponding difference in the work to be given to each?' Yes. 'But if so, surely you must be mistaken now and contradicting yourselves when you say that men and women, having such widely divergent natures, should do the same things?' What is your answer to that, my ingenious friend?

It is not easy to find one at the moment. I can only appeal to you to state the case on our own side, whatever it may be.

This, Glaucon, is one of many alarming objections which I foresaw some time ago. That is why I shrank from touching upon these laws concerning the possession of wives and the rearing of children.

It looks like anything but an easy problem.

True, I said; but whether a man tumbles into a swimming-pool or into mid-ocean, he has to swim all the same. So must we, and try if we can reach the shore, hoping for some Arion's dolphin or other miraculous deliverance to bring us safe to land.[1]

I suppose so.

Come then, let us see if we can find the way out. We did agree that different natures should have different occupations, and that the natures of man and woman are different; and yet we are now saying that these different natures are to have the same occupations. Is that the charge against us?

Exactly.

It is extraordinary, Glaucon, what an effect the practice of debating has upon people.

Why do you say that?

Because they often seem to fall unconsciously into mere disputes which they mistake for reasonable argument, through being unable to draw the distinctions proper to their subject; and so, instead of a philosophical exchange of ideas, they go off in chase of contradictions which are purely verbal.

I know that happens to many people; but does it apply to us at this moment?

Absolutely. At least I am afraid we are slipping unconsciously into a dispute about words. We have been strenuously insisting on the letter of our principle that different natures should not have the same occupations, as if we were scoring a point in a debate; but we have altogether neglected to consider what sort of sameness or difference we meant and in what respect these natures and occupations were to be defined as different or the same. Consequently, we might very well be asking one another whether there is not an opposition in nature between bald and long-haired men, and, when that was admitted, forbid one set to be shoemakers, if the other were following that trade.

That would be absurd.

Yes, but only because we never meant any and every sort of sameness or difference in nature, but the sort that was relevant to the occupations in question. We meant, for instance, that a man and a woman have the same nature if both have a talent for medi-

---

[1] The musician Arion, to escape the treachery of Corinthian sailors, leapt into the sea and was carried ashore at Taenarum by a dolphin, Herod. i. 24.

cine; whereas two men have different natures if one is a born physician, the other a born carpenter.

Yes, of course.

If, then, we find that either the male sex or the female is specially qualified for any particular form of occupation, then that occupation, we shall say, ought to be assigned to one sex or the other. But if the only difference appears to be that the male begets and the female brings forth, we shall conclude that no difference between man and woman has yet been produced that is relevant to our purpose. We shall continue to think it proper for our Guardians and their wives to share in the same pursuits.

And quite rightly.

The next thing will be to ask our opponent to name any profession or occupation in civic life for the purposes of which woman's nature is different from man's.

That is a fair question.

He might reply, as you did just now, that it is not easy to find a satisfactory answer on the spur of the moment, but that there would be no difficulty after a little reflection.

Perhaps.

Suppose, then, we invite him to follow us and see if we can convince him that there is no occupation concerned with the management of social affairs that is peculiar to women. We will confront him with a question: When you speak of a man having a natural talent for something, do you mean that he finds it easy to learn, and after a little instruction can find out much more for himself; whereas a man who is not so gifted learns with difficulty and no amount of instruction and practice will make him even remember what he has been taught? Is the talented man one whose bodily powers are readily at the service of his mind, instead of being a hindrance? Are not these the marks by which you distinguish the presence of a natural gift for any pursuit?

Yes, precisely.

Now do you know of any human occupation in which the male sex is not superior to the female in all these respects? Need I waste time over exceptions like weaving and watching over saucepans and batches of cakes, though women are supposed to be good at such things and get laughed at when a man does them better?

It is true, he replied, in almost everything one sex is easily beaten by the other. No doubt many women are better at many things than many men; but taking the sexes as a whole, it is as you say.

To conclude, then, there is no occupation concerned with the management of social affairs which belongs either to woman or to man, as such. Natural gifts are to be found here and there in both creatures alike; and every occupation is open to both, so far as their natures are concerned, though woman is for all purposes the weaker.

Certainly.

Is that a reason for making over all occupations to men only?

Of course not.

No, because one woman may have a natural gift for medicine or for music, another may not.

Surely.

Is it not also true that a woman may, or may not, be warlike or athletic?

I think so.

And again, one may love knowledge, another hate it; one may be high-spirited, another spiritless?

True again.

It follows that one woman will be fitted by nature to be a Guardian, another will not; because these were the qualities for which we selected our men Guardians. So for the purpose of keeping watch over the commonwealth, woman has the same nature as man, save in so far as she is weaker.

So it appears.

It follows that women of this type must be selected to share the life and duties of Guardians with men of the same type, since they are competent and of a like nature, and the same natures must be allowed the same pursuits.

Yes.

We come round, then, to our former position, that there is nothing contrary to nature in giving our Guardians' wives the same training for mind and body. The practice we proposed to establish was not impossible or visionary, since it was in accordance with nature. Rather, the contrary practice which now prevails turns out to be unnatural.

So it appears.

Well, we set out to inquire whether the plan we proposed was feasible and also the best. That it is feasible is now agreed; we must next settle whether it is the best.

Obviously.

Now, for the purpose of producing a woman fit to be a Guardian, we shall not have one education for men and another for women, precisely because the nature to be taken in hand is the same.

True.

What is your opinion on the question of one man being better than another? Do you think there is no such difference?

Certainly I do not.

And in this commonwealth of ours which will prove the better men—the Guardians who have received the education we described, or the shoemakers who have been trained to make shoes? [1]

It is absurd to ask such a question.

Very well. So these Guardians will be the best of all the citizens?

By far.

And these women the best of all the women?

Yes.

Can anything be better for a commonwealth than to produce in it men and women of the best possible type?

No.

And that result will be brought about by such a system of mental and bodily training as we have described?

Surely.

We may conclude that the institution we proposed was not only practicable, but also the best for the commonwealth.

Yes.

The wives of our Guardians, then, must strip for exercise, since

[1] The elementary education of Chap. IX will be open to all citizens, but presumably carried further (to the age of 17 or 18, see p. 259) in the case of those who show special promise.

they will be clothed with virtue, and they must take their share in war and in the other social duties of guardianship. They are to have no other occupation; and in these duties the lighter part must fall to the women, because of the weakness of their sex. The man who laughs at naked women, exercising their bodies for the best of reasons, is like one that 'gathers fruit unripe,'[1] for he does not know what it is that he is laughing at or what he is doing. There will never be a finer saying than the one which declares that whatever does good should be held in honour, and the only shame is in doing harm.

That is perfectly true.

CHAPTER XVI (v. 457 B–466 D)

ABOLITION OF THE FAMILY FOR THE GUARDIANS

The principle, 'Friends have all things in common,' is now applied by abolishing private homes and families for the Guardians (only), so that they may form a single family. The chief aims are: (1) to breed and rear children of the highest type by the eugenic methods used in breeding domestic animals; (2) to free the Guardians from the temptation to prefer family interests to those of the whole community; (3) to ensure the greatest possible unity in the state.[2] There must be no private property in women and children. It is in this negative sense that wives and children are to be held in common; anything like promiscuity would defeat the eugenic purpose even more than it is now defeated where individuals are allowed free choice of partners. Hence sexual intercourse is to be more strictly controlled and limited by the Rulers than it has ever been in civilized society—a fact which has escaped some hasty readers of in-

[1] An adapted quotation from Pindar (frag. 209, Schr.).

[2] Herodotus iv. 104 records that a northern people, the Agathyrsi, held their women in common, in order that they might all be brothers and kinsmen and have no envy or hatred towards one another. In the *Laws,* 739 B, Plato maintains that complete communism, extended to the whole state, would be ideal. But as a practical proposal he abandons it even for the Rulers.

accurate translations. This throws on the Rulers an invidious task.
They will be protected from the imputation of favouritism or per-
sonal spite by making it appear that the choice of partners is made
by drawing lots, which they will in fact secretly manipulate.

Plato does not seem to have thought out very clearly the details
of his marriage regulations. Some obscure points will be dealt with
in notes.

So far, then, in regulating the position of women, we may claim
to have come safely through with one hazardous proposal, that
male and female Guardians shall have all occupations in common. The consistency of the argument is an assurance that the
plan is a good one and also feasible. We are like swimmers who
have breasted the first wave without being swallowed up.

Not such a small wave either.

You will not call it large when you see the next.

Let me have a look at the next one, then.

Here it is: a law which follows from that principle and all that
has gone before, namely that, of these Guardians, no one man
and one woman are to set up house together privately: wives are
to be held in common by all; so too are the children, and no
parent is to know his own child, nor any child his parent.

It will be much harder to convince people that that is either a
feasible plan or a good one.

As to its being a good plan, I imagine no one would deny the
immense advantage of wives and children being held in common,
provided it can be done. I should expect dispute to arise chiefly
over the question whether it is possible.

There may well be a good deal of dispute over both points.

You mean, I must meet attacks on two fronts. I was hoping to
escape one by running away: if you agreed it was a good plan,
then I should only have had to inquire whether it was feasible.

No, we have seen through that manœuvre. You will have to
defend both positions.

Well, I must pay the penalty for my cowardice. But grant me
one favour. Let me indulge my fancy, like one who entertains
himself with idle day-dreams on a solitary walk. Before he has any

notion how his desires can be realized, he will set aside that question, to save himself the trouble of reckoning what may or may not be possible. He will assume that his wish has come true, and amuse himself with settling all the details of what he means to do then. So a lazy mind encourages itself to be lazier than ever; and I am giving way to the same weakness myself. I want to put off till later that question, how the thing can be done. For the moment, with your leave, I shall assume it to be possible, and ask how the Rulers will work out the details in practice; and I shall argue that the plan, once carried into effect, would be the best thing in the world for our commonwealth and for its Guardians. That is what I shall now try to make out with your help, if you will allow me to postpone the other question.

Very good; I have no objection.

Well, if our Rulers are worthy of the name, and their Auxiliaries likewise, these latter will be ready to do what they are told, and the Rulers, in giving their commands, will themselves obey our laws and will be faithful to their spirit in any details we leave to their discretion.

No doubt.

It is for you, then, as their lawgiver, who have already selected the men, to select for association with them women who are so far as possible of the same natural capacity. Now since none of them will have any private home of his own, but they will share the same dwelling and eat at common tables, the two sexes will be together; and meeting without restriction for exercise and all through their upbringing, they will surely be drawn towards union with one another by a necessity of their nature—necessity is not too strong a word, I think?

Not too strong for the constraint of love, which for the mass of mankind is more persuasive and compelling than even the necessity of mathematical proof.

Exactly. But in the next place, Glaucon, anything like unregulated unions would be a profanation in a state whose citizens lead the good life. The Rulers will not allow such a thing.

No, it would not be right.

Clearly, then, we must have marriages, as sacred as we can make them; and this sanctity will attach to those which yield the best results.[1]

Certainly.

How are we to get the best results? You must tell me, Glaucon, because I see you keep sporting dogs and a great many game birds at your house; and there is something about their mating and breeding that you must have noticed.

What is that?

In the first place, though they may all be of good stock, are there not some that turn out to be better than the rest?

There are.

And do you breed from all indiscriminately? Are you not careful to breed from the best so far as you can?

Yes.

And from those in their prime, rather than the very young or the very old?

Yes.

Otherwise, the stock of your birds or dogs would deteriorate very much, wouldn't it?

It would.

And the same is true of horses or of any animal?

It would be very strange if it were not.

Dear me, said I; we shall need consummate skill in our Rulers, if it is also true of the human race.

Well, it is true. But why must they be so skilful?

Because they will have to administer a large dose of that medicine we spoke of earlier.[2] An ordinary doctor is thought good enough for a patient who will submit to be dieted and can do without medicine; but he must be much more of a man if drugs are required.

True, but how does that apply?

It applies to our Rulers: it seems they will have to give their subjects a considerable dose of imposition and deception for their good.

[1] In the *Laws* 'Plato's view of marriage is very far from being merely physical. It has its moral and even its religious side' (Barker, *Greek Political Theory*, 329).
[2] At 389 B (p. 78).

We said, if you remember, that such expedients would be useful as a sort of medicine.

Yes, a very sound principle.

Well, it looks as if this sound principle will play no small part in this matter of marriage and child-bearing.

How so?

It follows from what we have just said that, if we are to keep our flock at the highest pitch of excellence, there should be as many unions of the best of both sexes, and as few of the inferior, as possible, and that only the offspring of the better unions should be kept.[1] And again, no one but the Rulers must know how all this is being effected; otherwise our herd of Guardians may become rebellious.

Quite true.

We must, then, institute certain festivals at which we shall bring together the brides and the bridegrooms. There will be sacrifices, and our poets will write songs befitting the occasion. The number of marriages we shall leave to the Rulers' discretion. They will aim at keeping the number of the citizens as constant as possible, having regard to losses caused by war, epidemics, and so on; and they must do their best to see that our state does not become either great or small.[2]

Very good.

---

[1] That is, 'kept *as Guardians.*' The inferior children of Guardians were to be 'thrust out among the craftsmen and farmers' (415 c, p. 107), and this is repeated at *Timaeus* 19A. A breeder of race-horses would *keep* (a common meaning of τρέφειν) the best foals, but not kill the rest.

[2] Plato seems to forget that these rules apply only to Guardians. If the much larger third class is to breed without restriction, a substantial rise in their numbers might entail suspension of all childbirth among Guardians, with a dysgenic effect. Plato, however, feared a decline, rather than a rise, in the birth-rate. (The state described in the *Laws* is always to have 5,040 citizens, each holding one inalienable lot of land.)

The 'number of marriages' may include both the number of candidates admitted at each festival and the frequency of the festivals. But it is perhaps likely that the festivals are to be annual, so that women who had borne children since the last festival would be re-marriageable. If so, at each festival a fresh group will be called up, consisting of all who have reached the age of 25 for men or 20 for women since the previous festival. Some or all of these will be paired with one another or with members of older groups. The couples will cohabit during the festival, which might

I think they will have to invent some ingenious system of drawing lots, so that, at each pairing off, the inferior candidate may
blame his luck rather than the Rulers.

Yes, certainly.

Moreover, young men who acquit themselves well in war and
other duties, should be given, among other rewards and privileges,
more liberal opportunities to sleep with a wife,[1] for the further
purpose that, with good excuse, as many as possible of the children
may be begotten of such fathers.

Yes.

As soon as children are born, they will be taken in charge by officers appointed for the purpose, who may be men or women or
both, since offices are to be shared by both sexes. The children of
the better parents they will carry to the crèche to be reared in the
care of nurses living apart in a certain quarter of the city. Those of
the inferior parents and any children of the rest that are born defective will be hidden away, in some appropriate manner that must
be kept secret.[2]

They must be, if the breed of our Guardians is to be kept pure.

These officers will also superintend the nursing of the children.
They will bring the mothers to the crèche when their breasts are
full, while taking every precaution that no mother shall know
her own child; and if the mothers have not enough milk, they will
provide wet-nurses. They will limit the time during which the
mothers will suckle their children, and hand over all the hard
work and sitting up at night to nurses and attendants.

That will make child-bearing an easy business for the Guardians'
wives.

So it should be. To go on with our scheme: we said that chil-

last (say) for a month. The marriages will then be dissolved and the partners remain
celibate until the next festival at earliest. This follows from the statement at 461 D
(p. 162) that the resulting batch of children will all be born between 7 and 10
months after the festival.

[1] Not to have several wives at once, but to be admitted at more frequent intervals
to the periodic marriage festivals, not necessarily with a different wife each time.

[2] Infanticide of defective children was practised at Sparta; but the vague expression used does not imply that all children of inferior Guardians are to be destroyed.
Those not defective would be relegated to the third class. Promotion of children
from that class was provided for at 415 c (p. 107).

dren should be born from parents in the prime of life. Do you agree that this lasts about twenty years for a woman, and thirty for a man? A woman should bear children for the commonwealth from her twentieth to her fortieth year; a man should begin to beget them when he has passed 'the racer's prime in swiftness,' [1] and continue till he is fifty-five.

Those are certainly the years in which both the bodily and the mental powers of man and woman are at their best.

If a man either above or below this age meddles with the begetting of children for the commonwealth, we shall hold it an offence against divine and human law. He will be begetting for his country a child conceived in darkness and dire incontinence, whose birth, if it escape detection, will not have been sanctioned by the sacrifices and prayers offered at each marriage festival, when priests and priestesses join with the whole community in praying that the children to be born may be even better and more useful citizens than their parents.

You are right.

The same law will apply to any man within the prescribed limits who touches a woman also of marriageable age when the Ruler has not paired them. We shall say that he is foisting on the commonwealth a bastard, unsanctioned by law or by religion.

Perfectly right.

As soon, however, as the men and the women have passed the age prescribed for producing children, we shall leave them free to form a connexion with whom they will, except that a man shall not take his daughter or daughter's daughter or mother or mother's mother, nor a woman her son or father or her son's son or father's father; and all this only after we have exhorted them to see that no child, if any be conceived, shall be brought to light, or, if they cannot prevent its birth, to dispose of it on the understanding that no such child can be reared.[2]

[1] A poetical quotation, which may, in its original context, have referred to a racehorse, brought to the stud when he had ceased to run.

[2] The unofficial unions might be permanent. The only unions barred as incestuous are between parents and children, or grandparents and grandchildren (all such are included, since, if a woman cannot marry her father's father, a man cannot marry his son's daughter). It seems to follow that Plato did not regard the much more

That too is reasonable. But how are they to distinguish fathers and daughters and those other relations you mentioned?

They will not, said I. But, reckoning from the day when he becomes a bridegroom, a man will call all children born in the tenth or the seventh month sons and daughters, and they will call him father. Their children again he will call grandchildren, and they will call his group grandfathers and grandmothers; and all who are born within the period during which their mothers and fathers were having children will be called brothers and sisters. This will provide for those restrictions on unions that we mentioned; but the law will allow brothers and sisters to live together, if the lot so falls out and the Delphic oracle also approves.[1]

Very good.

probable connexions of brothers and sisters as incestuous; and if so, he would see no reason against legal marriage of real brothers and sisters, who would not know they were so related. Such unions were regular in Egypt; and some modern authorities deny that they are dysgenic. Greek law allowed marriage between brother and half-sister by a different mother.

[1] This last speech deals with two distinct questions: (1) avoidance of incestuous unions as above defined; (2) legal marriage of brothers and sisters.

(1) Since the elderly people forming unofficial unions are not to know who are their parents or children, they must avoid all persons who could possibly be so related to them. This is easy, if cohabitation in legal marriage is confined to the duration of a marriage festival and the children of any parent must therefore belong to a batch born in the seventh or tenth month after any festival at which that parent has been married. (Most ancient authorities denied that a child could be born in the eighth month.) If a register was kept, a man could be told all the dates in question without being told who were his real children.

(2) After explaining how incestuous unions can be avoided by a man treating certain whole groups as his parents or children or grandparents or grandchildren, Plato adds that all persons 'born within the period during which their mothers and fathers (not *his* father and mother) were having children' will be called 'brothers' and 'sisters.' If unions of real brothers and sisters are not incestuous, this clause has nothing to do with avoidance of incest. It only adds to the definition of nominal parents and children and grandparents and grandchildren, a definition of those who will call one another 'brothers' and 'sisters,' whether they are really so related or not. Probably, it is meant that these will be all the Guardians born in the same generation (in a vague sense). Since there is no question of incest, these persons will never need to inquire about dates of marriage and birth, if they wish to form a union.

The last sentence refers to both topics of the previous one: (1) avoidance of incestuous unions, (2) legal marriage of real brothers and sisters. It has been held that Plato regarded such marriages as incestuous and that the Oracle was to guard against them. But either the Rulers knew how all Guardians were related or they

This, then, Glaucon, is the manner in which the Guardians of your commonwealth are to hold their wives and children in common. Must we not next find arguments to establish that it is consistent with our other institutions and also by far the best plan?

Yes, surely.

We had better begin by asking what is the greatest good at which the lawgiver should aim in laying down the constitution of a state, and what is the worst evil. We can then consider whether our proposals are in keeping with that good and irreconcilable with the evil.

By all means.

Does not the worst evil for a state arise from anything that tends to rend it asunder and destroy its unity, while nothing does it more good than whatever tends to bind it together and make it one?

That is true.

And are not citizens bound together by sharing in the same pleasures and pains, all feeling glad or grieved on the same occasions of gain or loss; whereas the bond is broken when such feelings are no longer universal, but any event of public or personal concern fills some with joy and others with distress?

Certainly.

And this disunion comes about when the words 'mine' and 'not mine,' 'another's' and 'not another's' are not applied to the same things throughout the community. The best ordered state will be the one in which the largest number of persons use these terms in the same sense, and which accordingly most nearly resembles a single person. When one of us hurts his finger, the whole extent of those bodily connexions which are gathered up in the soul and unified by its ruling element is made aware and it all shares as a

did not. If (as seems likely) they did know, they could avoid arranging such marriages without invoking an oracle to negative their own proposals. If they did not (though it would be folly to keep no registers if *any* incest was to be avoided), then how could the Oracle know? Granted that Plato did not hold marriage of brothers and sisters to be incestuous, the Rulers could sometimes knowingly arrange such marriages. The Oracle might be asked once for all to approve the whole scheme of marriage laws, or it might be formally invoked at each festival. If it raised no objection, the Rulers would be protected from any charge of violating religious law.

whole in the pain of the suffering part; hence we say that the man has a pain in his finger. The same thing is true of the pain or pleasure felt when any other part of the person suffers or is relieved.

Yes; I agree that the best organized community comes nearest to that condition.

And so it will recognize as a part of itself the individual citizen to whom good or evil happens, and will share as a whole in his joy or sorrow.

It must, if the constitution is sound.

It is time now to go back to our own commonwealth and see whether these conclusions apply to it more than to any other type of state. In all alike there are rulers and common people, all of whom will call one another fellow citizens.

Yes.

But in other states the people have another name as well for their rulers, haven't they?

Yes; in most they call them masters; in democracies, simply the government.

And in ours?

The people will look upon their rulers as preservers and protectors.

And how will our rulers regard the people?

As those who maintain them and pay them wages.

And elsewhere?

As slaves.

And what do rulers elsewhere call one another?

Colleagues.

And ours?

Fellow Guardians.

And in other states may not a ruler regard one colleague as a friend in whom he has an interest, and another as a stranger with whom he has nothing in common?

Yes, that often happens.

But that could not be so with your Guardians? None of them could ever treat a fellow Guardian as a stranger.

Certainly not. He must regard everyone whom he meets as

brother or sister, father or mother, son or daughter, grandchild or grandparent.

Very good; but here is a further point. Will you not require them, not merely to use these family terms, but to behave as a real family? Must they not show towards all whom they call 'father' the customary reverence, care, and obedience due to a parent, if they look for any favour from gods or men, since to act otherwise is contrary to divine and human law? Should not all the citizens constantly reiterate in the hearing of the children from their earliest years such traditional maxims of conduct towards those whom they are taught to call father and their other kindred?

They should. It would be absurd that terms of kinship should be on their lips without any action to correspond.

In our community, then, above all others, when things go well or ill with any individual everyone will use that word 'mine' in the same sense and say that all is going well or ill with him and his.

Quite true.

And, as we said, this way of speaking and thinking goes with fellow-feeling; so that our citizens, sharing as they do in a common interest which each will call his own, will have all their feelings of pleasure or pain in common.

Assuredly.

A result that will be due to our institutions, and in particular to our Guardians' holding their wives and children in common.

Very much so.

But you will remember how, when we compared a well-ordered community to the body which shares in the pleasures and pains of any member, we saw in this unity the greatest good that a state can enjoy. So the conclusion is that our commonwealth owes to this sharing of wives and children by its protectors its enjoyment of the greatest of all goods.

Yes, that follows.

Moreover, this agrees with our principle that they were not to have houses or lands or any property of their own, but to receive sustenance from the other citizens, as wages for their guardianship, and to consume it in common. Only so will they keep to their true character; and our present proposals will do still more to make them genuine Guardians. They will not rend the community asunder by each applying that word 'mine' to different things and dragging off whatever he can get for himself into a private home, where he will have his separate family, forming a centre of exclusive joys and sorrows. Rather they will all, so far as may be, feel together and aim at the same ends, because they are convinced that all their interests are identical.

Quite so.

Again, if a man's person is his only private possession, lawsuits and prosecutions will all but vanish, and they will be free of those quarrels that arise from ownership of property and from having family ties. Nor would they be justified even in bringing actions for assault and outrage; for we shall pronounce it right and honourable for a man to defend himself against an assailant of his own age, and in that way they will be compelled to keep themselves fit.

That would be a sound law.

And it would also have the advantage that, if a man's anger can be satisfied in this way, a fit of passion is less likely to grow into a serious quarrel.

True.

But an older man will be given authority over all younger persons and power to correct them; whereas the younger will, naturally, not dare to strike the elder or do him any violence, except by command of a Ruler. He will not show him any sort of disrespect. Two guardian spirits, fear and reverence, will be enough to restrain him—reverence forbidding him to lay hands on a parent, and fear of all those others who as sons or brothers or fathers would come to the rescue.

Yes, that will be the result.

So our laws will secure that these men will live in complete peace with one another; and if they never quarrel among themselves, there is no fear of the rest of the community being divided either against them or against itself.[1]

No.

---

[1] Cf. 545 D (p. 269): 'Revolution always starts from the outbreak of internal dissension in the ruling class.'

There are other evils they will escape, so mean and petty that I hardly like to mention them: the poor man's flattery of the rich, and all the embarrassments and vexations of rearing a family and earning just enough to maintain a household; now borrowing and now refusing to repay, and by any and every means scraping together money to be handed over to wife and servants to spend. These sordid troubles are familiar and not worth describing.

Only too familiar.

Rid of all these cares, they will live a more enviable life than the Olympic victor, who is counted happy on the strength of far fewer blessings than our Guardians will enjoy. Their victory is the nobler, since by their success the whole commonwealth is preserved; and their reward of maintenance at the public cost is more complete, since their prize is to have every need of life supplied for themselves and for their children; their country honours them while they live, and when they die they receive a worthy burial.

Yes, they will be nobly rewarded.

Do you remember, then, how someone who shall be nameless reproached us for not making our Guardians happy:[1] they were to possess nothing, though all the wealth of their fellow citizens was within their grasp? We replied, I believe, that we would consider that objection later, if it came in our way: for the moment we were bent on making our Guardians real guardians, and moulding our commonwealth with a view to the greatest happiness, not of one section of it, but of the whole.

Yes, I remember.

Well, it appears now that these protectors of our state will have a life better and more honourable than that of any Olympic victor; and we can hardly rank it on a level with the life of a shoemaker or other artisan or of a farmer.

I should think not.

However, it is right to repeat what I said at the time: if ever a Guardian tries to make himself happy in such a way that he will be a guardian no longer; if, not content with the moderation and security of this way of living which we think the best, he becomes possessed with some silly and childish notion of happiness, impelling him to make his power a means to appropriate all the

[1] Adeimantus' objection at 419 A, p. 109.

citizens' wealth, then he will learn the wisdom of Hesiod's saying [1] that the half is more than the whole.

My advice would certainly be that he should keep to his own way of living.

You do agree, then, that women are to take their full share with men in education, in the care of children, and in the guardianship of the other citizens; whether they stay at home or go out to war, they will be like watch-dogs which take their part either in guarding the fold or in hunting and share in every task so far as their strength allows. Such conduct will not be unwomanly, but all for the best and in accordance with the natural partnership of the sexes.

Yes, I agree.

CHAPTER XVII (v. 466 D–471 C)

USAGES OF WAR

Plato's proposals for mitigating the usages of war are chiefly inspired by a feeling for the unity of the Greek race, which he shared with his rival Isocrates and others who wished to heal the dissensions of the Greek states by uniting them against the Persians. He expresses no humanitarian sympathy extending beyond the borders of Hellas, but he is one of the earliest writers to stand for the rule of international law between independent states.

IT remains to ask whether such a partnership can be established among human beings, as it can among animals, and if so, how.

I was just going to put that question.

---

[1] *Works and Days*, 40. 'Fools, who know not how much more the half is than the whole, nor what happiness there is in mallow and asphodel' (two of the commonest flowers, as we might say, 'buttercups and daisies').

So far as fighting is concerned, it is easy to see how they will go out to war.

How?

Men and women will take the field together [1] and moreover bring with them the children who are sturdy enough, to learn this trade, like any other, by watching what they will have to do themselves when they are grown up; and besides looking on, they will fetch and carry for their fathers and mothers and see to all their needs in time of war. You must have noticed how, in the potter's trade for example, the children watch their fathers and wait on them long before they may touch the wheel. Ought our Guardians to be less careful to train theirs by letting them look on and become familiar with their duties?

No, that would be absurd.

Moreover, any creature will fight better in the presence of its young.

That is so. But in case of defeat, which may always happen in war, there will be serious danger of their children's lives being lost with their own, so that the country could never recover.

True; but, in the first place, do you think we must make sure that they never run any risk?

No, far from it.

Well, if they are ever to take their chance, should it not be on some occasion when, if all goes well, they will be the better for it?

No doubt.

And is it of no importance that men who are to be warriors should see something of war in childhood? Is that not worth some danger?

Yes; it is important.

Granted, then, that the children are to go to war as spectators, all will be well if we can contrive that they shall do so in safety. To begin with, their fathers will not be slow to judge, so far as human foresight can, which expeditions are hazardous and which are safe; and they will be careful not to take the children into

---

[1] Like the Sauromatae, whose women hunted and fought on horseback with the men and wore the same dress. Herod. iv. 116; Hippocr. π. ἀέϱ. 17.

danger. Also they will put them in charge of officers qualified by age and experience to lead and take care of them.

Yes, that would be the proper way.

All the same, the unexpected often happens; and to guard against such chances we must see that they have, from their earliest years, wings to fly away with if need be.

What do you mean by wings?

Horses, which they must be taught to ride at the earliest possible age; then, when they are taken to see the fighting, their mounts must not be spirited chargers but the swiftest we can find and the easiest to manage. In that way they will get a good view of their future business, and in case of need they will be able to keep up with their older leaders and escape in safety.

That seems an excellent plan.

Now, as to the conduct of war and your soldiers' relations to one another and to the enemy: am I right in thinking that anyone guilty of an act of cowardice, such as deserting his post or throwing away his arms, should be reduced to the artisan or farmer class; while if any fall alive into the enemy's hands, we shall make them a present of him, and they may do what they like with their prey?

Certainly.

And what shall be done to the hero who has distinguished himself by his valour? First, should he not be crowned on the field by the youths and children each in turn?

Surely.

And they might shake his hand?

Yes.

But you would stop there, no doubt. I am sure you would not approve of his exchanging kisses with them all?

I am all for that; indeed I would add to the law the provision that, so long as they are on the campaign, no one whom he wishes to kiss may refuse. That would make any soldier who chanced to be in love with a youth or a girl all the more eager to win the prize of valour.

Very well. We have already said that the brave man is to be

selected for marriage more frequently than the rest, so that as
many children as possible may have such a man for their father.
But besides that, these valiant youths may well be rewarded in the
Homeric manner. When Ajax distinguished himself in the war, he
was 'honoured with slices of the chine's full length,' a suitable
compliment to a lusty young hero, and one that would at the same
time strengthen his muscles.

An excellent idea.

Then here at any rate we will follow Homer. At sacrificial feasts
and all such occasions, we shall reward the brave, in proportion
to their merit, not only with songs and those privileges we mentioned but 'with seats of honour, meat, and cups brimful'; and so
at once pay tribute to the bravery of these men and women and
improve their physique.

Nothing could be better.

Good. And of those who are slain in the field, we shall say that
all who fell with honour are of that Golden Race, who, when they
die,

> Dwell here on earth, pure spirits, beneficent,
> Guardians to shield us mortal men from harm.

Shall we not believe those words of Hesiod?[1]

We shall.

Then we shall ask the Oracle with what special rites these men
of more than human mould should be buried, and we shall do as it
prescribes. And for all time to come we shall reverence their tombs
and worship them as demigods.[2] Others, too, who die in the natural course of old age or otherwise shall be honoured in the same
way, if they are judged to have led an exceptionally noble life.

That is but fair.

And next, how will our soldiers deal with enemies?

In what respect?

First take slavery. Is it right that Greek states should sell Greeks
into slavery? Ought they not rather to do all they can to stop this

---

[1] *Works and Days*, 122.

[2] Within Plato's lifetime a hero-cult of the Spartan general Brasidas had been set
up at Amphipolis.

practice and substitute the custom of sparing their own race, for fear of falling into bondage to foreign nations?

That would be better, beyond all comparison.

They must not, then, hold any Greek in slavery themselves, and they should advise the rest of Greece not to do so.[1]

Certainly. Then they would be more likely to keep their hands off one another and turn their energies against foreigners.

Next, is it well to strip the dead, after a victory, of anything but their arms? It only gives cowards an excuse for not facing the living enemy, as if they were usefully employed in poking about over a dead body. Many an army has been lost through this pillaging. There is something mean and greedy in plundering a corpse; and a sort of womanish pettiness in treating the body as an enemy, when the spirit, the real enemy, has flown, leaving behind only the instrument with which he fought. It is to behave no better than a dog who growls at the stone that has hit him and leaves alone the man who threw it.

True.

So we will have no stripping of the slain and we shall not prevent their comrades from burying them. Nor shall we dedicate in the temples trophies of their weapons, least of all those of Greeks, if we are concerned to show loyalty towards the rest of Hellas. We shall rather be afraid of desecrating a sanctuary by bringing to it such spoils of our own people, unless indeed the Oracle should pronounce otherwise.

That is very right.

And what of ravaging Greek lands and burning houses? How will your soldiers deal with their enemies in this matter?

I should like to hear your own opinion.

I think they should do neither, but only carry off the year's harvest. Shall I tell you why?

Please do.

It seems to me that war and civil strife differ in nature as they do in name, according to the two spheres in which disputes may arise: at home or abroad, among men of the same race or with

---

[1] After the capture of Methymna in 406 B.C. the Spartan Callicratidas had declared that no Greek should ever be enslaved if he could prevent it (Xen. *Hell*. i. 6, 14).

foreigners. War means fighting with a foreign enemy; when the enemy is of the same kindred, we call it civil strife.

That is a reasonable distinction.

Is it not also reasonable to assert that Greeks are a single people, all of the same kindred and alien to the outer world of foreigners?

Yes.

Then we shall speak of war when Greeks fight with foreigners, whom we may call their natural enemies. But Greeks are by nature friends of Greeks, and when they fight, it means that Hellas is afflicted by dissension which ought to be called civil strife.

I agree with that view.

Observe, then, that in what is commonly known as civil strife, that is to say, when one of our Greek states is divided against itself, it is thought an abominable outrage for either party to ravage the lands or burn the houses of the other. No lover of his country would dare to mangle the land which gave him birth and nursed him. It is thought fair that the victors should carry off the others' crops, but do no more. They should remember that the war will not last for ever; some day they must make friends again.[1]

That is a much more civilized state of mind.

Well then, is not this commonwealth you are founding a Greek state, and its citizens good and civilized people?

Very much so.

And lovers of Greece, who will think of all Hellas as their home, where they share in one common religion with the rest?[2]

Most certainly.

Accordingly, the Greeks being their own people, a quarrel with them will not be called a war. It will only be civil strife, which they will carry on as men who will some day be reconciled. So they will not behave like a foreign enemy seeking to enslave or destroy, but will try to bring their adversaries to reason by well-meant correction. As Greeks they will not devastate the soil of

---

[1] There was a famous maxim of Bias, one of the Seven Sages: 'Treat a friend as a future enemy, an enemy as a future friend.' Jebb in his appendix on Soph. *Ajax* 679 quotes comments by Bacon, *Aug. Sci.* viii. 2; Montaigne, *Essais,* i. 28; and La Bruyère, *Caractères,* 4, §§ 55, 56.

[2] Herod. viii. 144, makes the Athenians before Plataea speak of Greece as one in blood and speech, in religion, and in culture.

Greece or burn the homesteads; nor will they allow that all the
inhabitants of any state, men, women, and children, are their enemies, but only the few who are responsible for the quarrel. The
greater number are friends, whose land and houses, on all these
accounts, they will not consent to lay waste and destroy. They will
pursue the quarrel only until the guilty are compelled by the innocent sufferers to give satisfaction.

For my part, I agree that our citizens should treat their adversaries in that way, and deal with foreigners as Greeks now deal
with one another.

We will make this a law, then, for our Guardians: they are not
to ravage lands or burn houses.

Yes, we will; it is as satisfactory as all our other laws.

PART III (Books V, 471 c–VII)

THE PHILOSOPHER KING

CAN the ideal state ever be brought into existence? Confronted at last with this question, Socrates states the central paradox of the *Republic*: the smallest change that would effect the revolution would be to put the philosopher in control of society. This Part explains what is meant by a 'philosopher,' and how he might be produced and educated in a reformed state.

What is the wisdom which the philosopher is to seek and to enthrone in human life? Socrates' doctrine, Virtue is Knowledge, had meant that no man could realize the best in himself and thereby become happy unless he knew clearly what life is worth living for. Plato's conception of the knowledge which is virtue goes much farther, to include an understanding, not only of man's end or good, but of the Good itself, the final cause of all that is good in the universe and of its very existence. Few men, if any, can be expected to reach this goal and to become spectators of all time and all existence. But they alone will be really fit to govern; the rest must be schooled by them in 'popular' or 'civic' virtue, based, not on immediate knowledge, but on correct belief.

CHAPTER XVIII (v. 471 c–474 b)

THE PARADOX: PHILOSOPHERS MUST BE KINGS

Challenged to show that the ideal state can exist, Socrates first claims that an ideal is none the worse for not being realizable on earth. The assertion that theory comes closer than practice to truth or reality is characteristically Platonic. The ideal state or man is the true state or man; for if men, who are in fact always imper-

fect, could reach perfection, they would only be realizing all that their nature aims at being and might conceivably be. Further, the realm of ideals is the real world, unchanging and eternal, which can be known by thought. The visible and tangible things commonly called real are only a realm of fleeting appearance, where the ideal is imperfectly manifested in various degrees of approximation. This contrast will be drawn in Chapter XIX.

An ideal has an indispensable value for practice, in that thought thereby gives to action its right aim. So, instead of proving that the ideal state or man can exist here, it is enough to discover the least change, within the bounds of possibility, that would bring the actual state nearest to the ideal. This change would be the union, in the same persons, of political power and the love of wisdom, so as to close the gulf, which had been growing wider since the age of Pericles, between the men of thought and the men of action. The corresponding change in the individual is the supremacy of the reason, the divine element in man, over the rest of our nature.

But really, Socrates, Glaucon continued, if you are allowed to go on like this, I am afraid you will forget all about the question you thrust aside some time ago: whether a society so constituted can ever come into existence, and if so, how. No doubt, if it did exist, all manner of good things would come about. I can even add some that you have passed over. Men who acknowledged one another as fathers, sons, or brothers and always used those names among themselves would never desert one another; so they would fight with unequalled bravery. And if their womenfolk went out with them to war, either in the ranks or drawn up in the rear to intimidate the enemy and act as a reserve in case of need, I am sure all this would make them invincible. At home, too, I can see many advantages you have not mentioned. But, since I admit that our commonwealth would have all these merits and any number more, if once it came into existence, you need not describe it in further detail. All we have now to do is to convince ourselves that it can be brought into being and how.

This is a very sudden onslaught, said I; you have no mercy on my shilly-shallying. Perhaps you do not realize that, after I have barely escaped the first two waves,[1] the third, which you are now bringing down upon me, is the most formidable of all. When you have seen what it is like and heard my reply, you will be ready to excuse the very natural fears which made me shrink from putting forward such a paradox for discussion.

The more you talk like that, he said, the less we shall be willing to let you off from telling us how this constitution can come into existence; so you had better waste no more time.

Well, said I, let me begin by reminding you that what brought us to this point was our inquiry into the nature of justice and injustice.

True; but what of that?

Merely this: suppose we do find out what justice is,[2] are we going to demand that a man who is just shall have a character which exactly corresponds in every respect to the ideal of justice? Or shall we be satisfied if he comes as near to the ideal as possible and has in him a larger measure of that quality than the rest of the world?

That will satisfy me.

If so, when we set out to discover the essential nature of justice and injustice and what a perfectly just and a perfectly unjust man would be like, supposing them to exist, our purpose was to use them as ideal patterns: we were to observe the degree of happiness or unhappiness that each exhibited, and to draw the necessary inference that our own destiny would be like that of the one we most resembled. We did not set out to show that these ideals could exist in fact.

That is true.

Then suppose a painter had drawn an ideally beautiful figure complete to the last touch, would you think any the worse of him, if he could not show that a person as beautiful as that could exist?

No, I should not.

Well, we have been constructing in discourse the pattern of an

[1] The equality of women (Chap. XV) and the abolition of the family (Chap. XVI). The wave metaphor was introduced at 457 B, p. 156.

[2] Justice, as a 'civic' virtue, has been defined in Chaps. XII and XIV; but the wise man's virtue, based on knowledge, has still to be described.

ideal state. Is our theory any the worse, if we cannot prove it possible that a state so organized should be actually founded?

Surely not.

That, then, is the truth of the matter. But if, for your satisfaction, I am to do my best to show under what conditions our ideal would have the best chance of being realized, I must ask you once more to admit that the same principle applies here. Can theory ever be fully realized in practice? Is it not in the nature of things that action should come less close to truth than thought? People may not think so; but do you agree or not?

I do.

ideal society is not realistic

Then you must not insist upon my showing that this construction we have traced in thought could be reproduced in fact down to the last detail. You must admit that we shall have found a way to meet your demand for realization, if we can discover how a state might be constituted in the closest accordance with our description. Will not that content you? It would be enough for me.

And for me too.

What's value of this idea?

Then our next attempt, it seems, must be to point out what defect in the working of existing states prevents them from being so organized, and what is the least change that would effect a transformation into this type of government—a single change if possible, or perhaps two; at any rate let us make the changes as few and insignificant as may be.

By all means.

Well, there is one change which, as I believe we can show, would bring about this revolution—not a small change, certainly, nor an easy one, but possible.

What is it?

I have now to confront what we called the third and greatest wave. But I must state my paradox, even though the wave should break in laughter over my head and drown me in ignominy. Now mark what I am going to say.

Go on.

Unless either philosophers become kings in their countries or those who are now called kings and rulers come to be sufficiently inspired with a genuine desire for wisdom; unless, that is to say, political power and philosophy meet together, while the many natures who now go their several ways in the one or the other direction are forcibly debarred from doing so, there can be no rest from troubles, my dear Glaucon, for states, nor yet, as I believe, for all mankind; nor can this commonwealth which we have imagined ever till then see the light of day and grow to its full stature. This it was that I have so long hung back from saying; I knew what a paradox it would be, because it is hard to see that there is no other way of happiness either for the state or for the individual.

Socrates, exclaimed Glaucon, after delivering yourself of such a pronouncement as that, you must expect a whole multitude of by no means contemptible assailants to fling off their coats, snatch up the handiest weapon, and make a rush at you, breathing fire and slaughter. If you cannot find arguments to beat them off and make your escape, you will learn what it means to be the target of scorn and derision.

Well, it was you who got me into this trouble.

Yes, and a good thing too. However, I will not leave you in the lurch. You shall have my friendly encouragement for what it is worth; and perhaps you may find me more complaisant than some would be in answering your questions. With such backing you must try to convince the unbelievers.

I will, now that I have such a powerful ally.

CHAPTER XIX (v. 474 B-480)

DEFINITION OF THE PHILOSOPHER. THE TWO WORLDS

The word 'philosophy' originally meant curiosity, the desire for fresh experience, such as led Solon to travel and see the world (Herod. i. 30), or the pursuit of intellectual culture, as in Pericles' speech: 'We cultivate the mind (φιλοσοφοῦμεν) *without loss of manliness'* (Thuc. ii. 40). *This sense has to be excluded: the Rulers are not to be dilettanti or mere amateurs of the arts. They are to desire knowledge of the whole of truth and reality, and hence of the world of essential Forms, in contrast with the world of appearances.*

The doctrine of Forms is here more explicitly invoked. Corresponding to the two worlds, the mind has two faculties: Knowledge of the real and Belief in appearances (doxa). Faculties can be distinguished only by (1) the states of mind they produce, and (2) their fields of objects. By both tests Knowledge and Belief differ. (1) Knowledge is infallible (there is no false knowledge); Belief may be true or false. (2) Knowledge, by definition, is of unique, unchanging objects. Just in this respect the Forms resemble the laws of nature sought by modern natural science: a law is an unseen intelligible principle, a unity underlying an unlimited multiplicity of similar phenomena, and supposed to be unalterable. The Forms, however, are not laws of the sequence or coexistence of phenomena, but ideals or patterns, which have a real existence independent of our minds[1] *and of which the many individual things called by their names in the world of appearances are like images or reflections. If we are disposed, with Aristotle, to deny that Platonic Forms or ideals 'exist apart from' individual things in the visible world, we should remember that the essence of the doctrine is the conviction that the differences between good and evil, right and wrong, true and false, beautiful and ugly, are absolute, not 'relative' to the customs or tastes or desires of individual men or social groups. We can know them or (as is commonly the case) not know them; they cannot change or vary from place to place or from time to time. This conviction has been, and is, held by many who cannot accept, at its face value, Plato's mode of expressing it.*

A Form, such as Beauty itself, excludes its opposite, Ugliness: it can never be or become ugly. But any particular beautiful thing may be also ugly in some aspects or situations: it may cease to be beautiful and become ugly; it may seem beautiful to me, ugly to you; and it must begin and cease to exist in time. Such things cannot be objects of knowledge. Our apprehension of these many

---

[1] Hence most modern critics avoid the term 'Idea,' though this is Plato's word, because it now suggests a thought existing only 'in our minds.'

changing things is here called doxa *and compared to dream experience, which is neither wholly real nor utterly non-existent.* Doxa *is usually rendered by 'Opinion.' Here 'Belief' is preferred as having a corresponding verb which, unlike 'opine,' is in common use. But both terms are inadequate.* Doxa *and its cognates denote our apprehension of anything that 'seems':* (1) *what seems to* exist, *sensible appearances, phenomena;* (2) *what seems* true, *opinions, beliefs, whether really true or false;* (3) *what seems* right, *legal and deliberative decisions, and the 'many conventional notions' of current morality* (479 D, p. 188), *which vary from place to place and from time to time. The amateur of the arts and the politician live in the twilight realm of these fluctuating beliefs.*

Now, I continued, if we are to elude those assailants you have described, we must, I think, define for them whom we mean by these lovers of wisdom who, we have dared to assert, ought to be our rulers. Once we have a clear view of their character, we shall be able to defend our position by pointing to some who are naturally fitted to combine philosophic study with political leadership, while the rest of the world should accept their guidance and let philosophy alone.

Yes, this is the moment for a definition.

Here, then, is a line of thought which may lead to a satisfactory explanation. Need I remind you that a man will deserve to be called a lover of this or that, only if it is clear that he loves that thing as a whole, not merely in parts?

You must remind me, it seems; for I do not see what you mean.

That answer would have come better from someone less susceptible to love than yourself, Glaucon. You ought not to have forgotten that any boy in the bloom of youth will arouse some sting of passion in a man of your amorous temperament and seem worthy of his attentions. Is not this your way with your favourites? You will praise a snub nose as piquant and a hooked one as giving a regal air, while you call a straight nose perfectly proportioned; the swarthy, you say, have a manly look, the fair are children of the gods; and what do you think is that word 'honey-pale,' if not the euphemism of some lover who had no fault to find with sal-

lowness on the cheek of youth? In a word, you will carry pretence
and extravagance to any length sooner than reject a single one that
is in the flower of his prime.

If you insist on taking me as an example of how lovers behave,
I will agree for the sake of argument.

Again, do you not see the same behaviour in people with a passion for wine? They are glad of any excuse to drink wine of any
sort. And there are the men who covet honour, who, if they cannot
lead an army, will command a company, and if they cannot win
the respect of important people, are glad to be looked up to by no-
bodies, because they must have someone to esteem them.

Quite true.

Do you agree, then, that when we speak of a man as having a
passion for a certain kind of thing, we mean that he has an appetite for everything of that kind without discrimination?

Yes.

So the philosopher, with his passion for wisdom, will be one who
desires all wisdom, not only some part of it. If a student is particular about his studies, especially while he is too young to know
which are useful and which are not, we shall say he is no lover
of learning or of wisdom; just as, if he were dainty about his food,
we should say he was not hungry or fond of eating, but had a poor
appetite. Only the man who has a taste for every sort of knowledge and throws himself into acquiring it with an insatiable curiosity will deserve to be called a philosopher. Am I not right?

That description, Glaucon replied, would include a large and ill-
assorted company. It is curiosity, I suppose, and a delight in fresh
experience that gives some people a passion for all that is to be
seen and heard at theatrical and musical performances. But they
are a queer set to reckon among philosophers, considering that they
would never go near anything like a philosophical discussion,
though they run round at all the Dionysiac festivals in town or
country as if they were under contract to listen to every company
of performers without fail. Will curiosity entitle all these enthusi-
asts, not to mention amateurs of the minor arts, to be called philosophers?

Certainly not; though they have a certain counterfeit resemblance.

And whom do you mean by the genuine philosophers?

Those whose passion it is to see the truth.

That must be so; but will you explain?

It would not be easy to explain to everyone; but you, I believe, will grant my premiss.

Which is——?

That since beauty and ugliness are opposite, they are two things; and consequently each of them is one. The same holds of justice and injustice, good and bad, and all the essential Forms: each in itself is one; but they manifest themselves in a great variety of combinations, with actions, with material things, and with one another, and so each seems to be many.[1]

That is true.

On the strength of this premiss, then, I can distinguish your amateurs of the arts and men of action from the philosophers we are concerned with, who are alone worthy of the name.

What is your distinction?

Your lovers of sights and sounds delight in beautiful tones and colours and shapes and in all the works of art into which these enter; but they have not the power of thought to behold and to take delight in the nature of Beauty itself. That power to approach Beauty and behold it as it is in itself, is rare indeed.

Quite true.

Now if a man believes in the existence of beautiful things, but not of Beauty itself, and cannot follow a guide who would lead him to a knowledge of it, is he not living in a dream? Consider: does not dreaming, whether one is awake or asleep, consist in mistaking a semblance for the reality it resembles?

I should certainly call that dreaming.

Contrast with him the man who holds that there is such a thing as Beauty itself and can discern that essence as well as the things

---

[1] At 523 A ff., p. 239 f., it is explained how confused impressions of opposite qualities in sense-perception provoke reflection to isolate and define the corresponding universals or Forms.

that partake of its character, without ever confusing the one with the other—is he a dreamer or living in a waking state?

He is very much awake.

So may we say that he knows, while the other has only a belief in appearances; and might we call their states of mind knowledge and belief?

Certainly.

But this person who, we say, has only belief without knowledge may be aggrieved and challenge our statement. Is there any means of soothing his resentment and converting him gently, without telling him plainly that he is not in his right mind?

We surely ought to try.

Come then, consider what we are to say to him. Or shall we ask him a question, assuring him that, far from grudging him any knowledge he may have, we shall be only too glad to find that there is something he knows? But, we shall say, tell us this: When a man knows, must there not be something that he knows? Will you answer for him, Glaucon?

My answer will be, that there must.

Something real or unreal?

Something real; how could a thing that is unreal ever be known?

Are we satisfied, then, on this point, from however many points of view we might examine it: that the perfectly real is perfectly knowable, and the utterly unreal is entirely unknowable?

Quite satisfied.

Good. Now if there is something so constituted that it both *is* and *is not,* will it not lie between the purely real and the utterly unreal?

It will.

Well then, as knowledge corresponds to the real, and absence of knowledge necessarily to the unreal, so, to correspond to this intermediate thing, we must look for something between ignorance and knowledge, if such a thing there be.

Certainly.

Is there not a thing we call belief?

Surely.

A different power from knowledge, or the same?

Different.

Knowledge and belief, then, must have different objects, answering to their respective powers.

Yes.

And knowledge has for its natural object the real—to know the truth about reality. However, before going further, I think we need a definition. Shall we distinguish under the general name of 'faculties'[1] those powers which enable us—or anything else—to do what we can do? Sight and hearing, for instance, are what I call faculties, if that will help you to see the class of things I have in mind.

Yes, I understand.

Then let me tell you what view I take of them. In a faculty I cannot find any of those qualities, such as colour or shape, which, in the case of many other things, enable me to distinguish one thing from another. I can only look to its field of objects and the state of mind it produces, and regard these as sufficient to identify it and to distinguish it from faculties which have different fields and produce different states. Is that how you would go to work?

Yes.

Let us go back, then, to knowledge. Would you class that as a faculty?

Yes; and I should call it the most powerful of all.

And is belief also a faculty?

It can be nothing else, since it is what gives us the power of believing.

But a little while ago you agreed that knowledge and belief are not the same thing.

Yes; there could be no sense in identifying the infallible with the fallible.[2]

Good. So we are quite clear that knowledge and belief are different things?

[1] The Greek here uses only the common word for 'power' (*dynamis*), but Plato is defining the special sense we express by 'faculty.'

[2] This marks one distinction between the two states of mind. Further, even if true, belief, unlike knowledge, is (1) produced by persuasion, not by instruction; (2) cannot 'give an account' of itself; and (3) can be shaken by persuasion (*Timaeus* 51 E).

They are.

If so, each of them, having a different power, must have a different field of objects.

Necessarily.

The field of knowledge being the real; and its power, the power of knowing the real as it is.

Yes.

Whereas belief, we say, is the power of believing. Is its object the same as that which knowledge knows? Can the same things be possible objects both of knowledge and of belief?[1]

Not if we hold to the principles we agreed upon. If it is of the nature of a different faculty to have a different field, and if both knowledge and belief are faculties and, as we assert, different ones, it follows that the same things cannot be possible objects of both.

So if the real is the object of knowledge, the object of belief must be something other than the real.

Yes.

Can it be the unreal? Or is that an impossible object even for belief? Consider: if a man has a belief, there must be something before his mind; he cannot be believing nothing, can he?

No.

He is believing something, then; whereas the unreal could only be called nothing at all.

Certainly.

Now we said that ignorance must correspond to the unreal, knowledge to the real. So what he is believing cannot be real nor yet unreal.

True.

Belief, then, cannot be either ignorance or knowledge.

It appears not.

Then does it lie outside and beyond these two? Is it either more clear and certain than knowledge or less clear and certain than ignorance?

No, it is neither.

---

[1] If 'belief' bore its common meaning, we might answer, yes. But in this context it is essentially belief in *appearances*. It includes perception by the senses, and these can never perceive objects of thought, such as Beauty itself.

It rather seems to you to be something more obscure than knowledge, but not so dark as ignorance, and so to lie between the two extremes?

Quite so.

Well, we said earlier that if some object could be found such that it both *is* and at the same time *is not,* that object would lie between the perfectly real and the utterly unreal; and that the corresponding faculty would be neither knowledge nor ignorance, but a faculty to be found situated between the two.

Yes.

And now what we have found between the two is the faculty we call belief.

True.

It seems, then, that what remains to be discovered is that object which can be said both to be and not to be and cannot properly be called either purely real or purely unreal. If that can be found, we may justly call it the object of belief, and so give the intermediate faculty the intermediate object, while the two extreme objects will fall to the extreme faculties.

Yes.

On these assumptions, then, I shall call for an answer from our friend who denies the existence of Beauty itself or of anything that can be called an essential Form of Beauty remaining unchangeably in the same state for ever, though he does recognize the existence of beautiful things as a plurality—that lover of things seen who will not listen to anyone who says that Beauty is one, Justice is one, and so on. I shall say to him, Be so good as to tell us: of all these many beautiful things is there one which will not appear ugly? Or of these many just or righteous actions, is there one that will not appear unjust or unrighteous?

No, replied Glaucon, they must inevitably appear to be in some way both beautiful and ugly; and so with all the other terms your question refers to.

And again the many things which are doubles are just as much halves as they are doubles. And the things we call large or heavy have just as much right to be called small or light.

Yes; any such thing will always have a claim to both opposite designations.

Then, whatever any one of these many things may be said to be, can you say that it absolutely *is* that, any more than that it *is not* that?

They remind me of those punning riddles people ask at dinner parties, or the child's puzzle about what the eunuch threw at the bat and what the bat was perched on.[1] These things have the same ambiguous character, and one cannot form any stable conception of them either as being or as not being, or as both being and not being, or as neither.

Can you think of any better way of disposing of them than by placing them between reality and unreality? For I suppose they will not appear more obscure and so less real than unreality, or clearer and so more real than reality.

Quite true.

It seems, then, we have discovered that the many conventional notions of the mass of mankind about what is beautiful or honourable or just and so on are adrift in a sort of twilight between pure reality and pure unreality.

We have.

And we agreed earlier that, if any such object were discovered, it should be called the object of belief and not of knowledge. Fluctuating in that half-way region, it would be seized upon by the intermediate faculty.

Yes.

So when people have an eye for the multitude of beautiful things or of just actions or whatever it may be, but can neither behold Beauty or Justice itself nor follow a guide who would lead them to it, we shall say that all they have is beliefs, without any real knowledge of the objects of their belief.

That follows.

But what of those who contemplate the realities themselves as

[1] A man who was not a man (eunuch), seeing and not seeing (seeing imperfectly) a bird that was not a bird (bat) perched on a bough that was not a bough (a reed), pelted and did not pelt it (aimed at it and missed) with a stone that was not a stone (pumice-stone).

they are for ever in the same unchanging state? Shall we not say that they have, not mere belief, but knowledge?

That too follows.

And, further, that their affection goes out to the objects of knowledge, whereas the others set their affections on the objects of belief; for it was they, you remember, who had a passion for the spectacle of beautiful colours and sounds, but would not hear of Beauty itself being a real thing.

I remember.

So we may fairly call them lovers of belief rather than of wisdom—not philosophical, in fact, but philodoxical. Will they be seriously annoyed by that description?

Not if they will listen to my advice. No one ought to take offence at the truth.

The name of philosopher, then, will be reserved for those whose affections are set, in every case, on the reality.

By all means.

CHAPTER XX (vi. 484 a–487 a)

THE PHILOSOPHER'S FITNESS TO RULE

The above definition of the philosopher might suggest an unpractical head-in-air, unfit to control life in the state. But the qualities most valuable in a ruler will follow naturally from the master passion for truth in a nature of the type described earlier (Chap. X), when it is perfected by time and education.

So at last, Glaucon, after this long and weary way, we have come to see who are the philosophers and who are not.

I doubt if the way could have been shortened.

Apparently not. I think, however, that we might have gained a still clearer view, if this had been the only topic to be discussed; but there are so many others awaiting us, if we mean to discover in what ways the just life is better than the unjust.

Which are we to take up now?

Surely the one that follows next in order. Since the philosophers are those who can apprehend the eternal and unchanging, while those who cannot do so, but are lost in the mazes of multiplicity and change, are not philosophers, which of the two ought to be in control of a state?

I wonder what would be a reasonable solution.

To establish as Guardians whichever of the two appear competent to guard the laws and ways of life in society.

True.

Well, there can be no question whether a guardian who is to keep watch over anything needs to be keen-sighted or blind. And is not blindness precisely the condition of men who are entirely cut off from knowledge of any reality, and have in their soul no clear pattern of perfect truth, which they might study in every detail and constantly refer to, as a painter looks at his model, before they proceed to embody notions of justice, honour, and goodness in earthly institutions or, in their character of Guardians, to preserve such institutions as already exist?

Certainly such a condition is very like blindness.

Shall we, then, make such as these our Guardians in preference to men who, besides their knowledge of realities, are in no way inferior to them in experience and in every excellence of character?

It would be absurd not to choose the philosophers, whose knowledge is perhaps their greatest point of superiority, provided they do not lack those other qualifications.

What we have to explain, then, is how those qualifications can be combined in the same persons with philosophy.

Certainly.

The first thing, as we said at the outset, is to get a clear view of their inborn disposition.[1] When we are satisfied on that head, I think we shall agree that such a combination of qualities is possible and that we need look no further for men fit to be in control of a commonwealth. One trait of the philosophic nature we may take as already granted: a constant passion for any knowledge

---

[1] The subject of the present chapter. The next will explain why the other qualifications, of experience and character, are too often lacking.

that will reveal to them something of that reality which endures for ever and is not always passing into and out of existence. And, we may add, their desire is to know the whole of that reality; they will not willingly renounce any part of it as relatively small and insignificant, as we said before when we compared them to the lover and to the man who covets honour.

True.

Is there not another trait which the nature we are seeking cannot fail to possess—truthfulness, a love of truth and a hatred of falsehood that will not tolerate untruth in any form?

Yes, it is natural to expect that.

It is not merely natural, but entirely necessary that an instinctive passion for any object should extend to all that is closely akin to it; and there is nothing more closely akin to wisdom than truth. So the same nature cannot love wisdom and falsehood; the genuine lover of knowledge cannot fail, from his youth up, to strive after the whole of truth.

I perfectly agree.

Now we surely know that when a man's desires set strongly in one direction, in every other channel they flow more feebly, like a stream diverted into another bed. So when the current has set towards knowledge and all that goes with it, desire will abandon those pleasures of which the body is the instrument and be concerned only with the pleasure which the soul enjoys independently —if, that is to say, the love of wisdom is more than a mere pretence. Accordingly, such a one will be temperate and no lover of money; for he will be the last person to care about the things for the sake of which money is eagerly sought and lavishly spent.

That is true.

Again, in seeking to distinguish the philosophic nature, you must not overlook the least touch of meanness. Nothing could be more contrary than pettiness to a mind constantly bent on grasping the whole of things, both divine and human.

Quite true.

And do you suppose that one who is so high-minded and whose thought can contemplate all time and all existence will count this life of man a matter of much concern?

No, he could not.

So for such a man death will have no terrors.

None.

A mean and cowardly nature, then, can have no part in the genuine pursuit of wisdom.

I think not.

And if a man is temperate and free from the love of money, meanness, pretentiousness, and cowardice, he will not be hard to deal with or dishonest. So, as another indication of the philosophic temper, you will observe whether, from youth up, he is fair-minded, gentle, and sociable.

Certainly.

Also you will not fail to notice whether he is quick or slow to learn. No one can be expected to take a reasonable delight in a task in which much painful effort makes little headway. And if he cannot retain what he learns, his forgetfulness will leave no room in his head for knowledge; and so, having all his toil for nothing, he can only end by hating himself as well as his fruitless occupation. We must not, then, count a forgetful mind as competent to pursue wisdom; we must require a good memory.

By all means.

Further, there is in some natures a crudity and awkwardness that can only tend to a lack of measure and proportion; and there is a close affinity between proportion and truth. Hence, besides our other requirements, we shall look for a mind endowed with measure and grace, which will be instinctively drawn to see every reality in its true light.

Yes.

Well then, now that we have enumerated the qualities of a mind destined to take its full part in the apprehension of reality, have you any doubt about their being indispensable and all necessarily going together?

None whatever.

Then have you any fault to find with a pursuit which none can worthily follow who is not by nature quick to learn and to remember, magnanimous and gracious, the friend and kinsman of truth, justice, courage, temperance?

No; Momus[1] himself could find no flaw in it.

Well then, when time and education have brought such characters as these to maturity, would you entrust the care of your commonwealth to anyone else?

CHAPTER XXI (VI. 487 B–497 A)

WHY THE PHILOSOPHIC NATURE IS USELESS OR CORRUPTED IN EXISTING SOCIETY

Adeimantus objects that the above description of the man of thought as gifted with all the qualities of a ruler is only an ideal. In actual fact the better sort of philosophers prove useless to the state, and others who have the natural gifts are demoralized.

Socrates replies: The better sort are useless because a democratic state has no use for men like Socrates and his companions (including Plato); and the corruption of promising natures, like Alcibiades, is ultimately the fault of the public itself.

Socrates was accused at his trial of having 'demoralized the young men' of the upper class, who were concerned in anti-democratic movements during the Peloponnesian War. He was confused in the public mind with the Sophists, and both were thought to have undermined traditional morality and loyalty to the constitution. The Sophists were travelling teachers, who met a growing need for advanced education by lecturing in private houses to young men rich enough to pay their fees. Socrates never taught in private or took fees; he conversed publicly with all comers. The name 'Sophist' had originally meant an expert in any art or a man of special sagacity in practical life or in speculation. But in Plato it has acquired some of the modern meaning and stands for a tendency antagonistic to the Socratic philosophy. The Gorgias defines rhetoric, which many of the Sophists taught, as the art of influencing public assemblies without any real knowledge of right and

---

[1] The spirit of faultfinding, one of the children of Night in Hesiod's *Theogony*.

wrong. The Sophist lives wholly in the world of appearances; he only echoes the conventional notions of the public and teaches the ambitious young how to get on in life by flattering and cajoling the Great Beast. The extreme consequences of such teaching are expressed in Thrasymachus' view of life.

So the disinterested pursuit of truth is abandoned by those promising natures which corrupting influences have diverted to seek power by flattery. Philosophy falls a prey to unworthy aspirants. (It is not known what sort of persons are typified by the 'baldheaded tinker' at 495 E, p. 203.) The faithful few, like Socrates and Plato himself, must stand aside, powerless to help society, and can only save their own souls.

HERE Adeimantus interposed: No one could deny all that, Socrates; but, whenever you talk in this way, your hearers feel a certain misgiving: they think that, because they are inexperienced in your method of question and answer, at each question the reasoning leads them a little farther astray, until at last these slight divergences amount to a serious error and they find themselves contradicting their original position. Just as in draughts the less skilful player is finally hemmed into a corner where he cannot make a move, so in this game where words take the place of counters they feel they are being cornered and reduced to silence, but that does not really prove them in the wrong. I say this with an eye to the present situation. Anyone might say now that at each question you ask there is no contradicting you, but that nevertheless, as a matter of plain fact, the votaries of philosophy, when they carry on the study too long, instead of taking it up in youth as a part of general culture and then dropping it, almost always become decidedly queer, not to say utterly worthless; while even the most respectable are so far the worse for this pursuit you are praising as to become useless to society.

Well, I replied, do you think that charge is untrue?

I do not know, he answered; I should like to hear your opinion. You shall; I think it is true.

Then how can it be right to say that there will be no rest from trouble until states are ruled by these philosophers whom we are now admitting to be of no use to them?

That is a question which needs to be answered by means of a parable.

Whereas you, of course, never talk in parables!

Ah, said I, mocking me, are you? after forcing upon me a thesis that is so hard to prove. But never mind; listen to my parable, and you will see once more what an effort it costs me to scrape one together. The better sort of philosophers are placed in such a cruel position in relation to their country that there is no one thing in nature to be compared to it; I can plead their cause only by collecting materials for my parable from more than one quarter,[1] like an artist drawing a goat-stag or other such composite monster.

Imagine this state of affairs on board a ship or a number of ships. The master is bigger and burlier than any of the crew, but a little deaf and short-sighted and no less deficient in seamanship. The sailors are quarrelling over the control of the helm; each thinks he ought to be steering the vessel, though he has never learnt navigation and cannot point to any teacher under whom he has served his apprenticeship; what is more, they assert that navigation is a thing that cannot be taught at all, and are ready to tear in pieces anyone who says it can. Meanwhile they besiege the master himself, begging him urgently to trust them with the helm; and sometimes, when others have been more successful in gaining his ear, they kill them or throw them overboard, and, after somehow stupefying the worthy master with strong drink or an opiate, take control of the ship, make free with its stores, and turn the voyage, as might be expected of such a crew, into a drunken carousal. Besides all this, they cry up as a skilled navigator and master of seamanship anyone clever enough to lend a hand in persuading or forcing the master to set them in command. Every other kind of man they condemn as useless. They do not under-

---

[1] Perhaps this alludes to comedies, such as Aristophanes' *Knights,* which represented the burly Demos with the shameless politicians competing for his favour, and the *Clouds,* in which Socrates had been shown as a star-gazing head-in-air. In Plato's parable the master of the ship is the sovereign people, Demos, and the crew are the politicians or demagogues, who have no idea that a ruler needs any moral or intellectual training.

stand that the genuine navigator can only make himself fit to command a ship by studying the seasons of the year, sky, stars, and winds, and all that belongs to his craft; and they have no idea that, along with the science of navigation, it is possible for him to gain, by instruction or practice, the skill to keep control of the helm whether some of them like it or not. If a ship were managed in that way, would not those on board be likely to call the expert in navigation a mere star-gazer, who spent his time in idle talk and was useless to them?

They would indeed.

I think you understand what I mean and do not need to have my parable interpreted in order to see how it illustrates the attitude of existing states towards the true philosopher.

Quite so.

Use it, then, to enlighten that critic whom you spoke of as astonished that philosophers are not held in honour by their country. You may try, in the first place, to convince him that it would be far more astonishing if they were; and you may tell him further that he is right in calling the best sort of philosophers useless to the public; but for that he must rather blame those who make no use of them. It is not in the natural course of things for the pilot to beg the crew to take his orders, any more than for the wise to wait on the doorsteps of the rich; the author of that epigram [1] was mistaken. What is natural is that the sick man, whether rich or poor, should wait at the door of the physician, and that all who need to be governed should seek out the man who can govern them; it is not for him to beg them to accept his rule, if there is really any help in him. But our present rulers may fairly be compared to the sailors in our parable, and the useless visionaries, as the politicians call them, to the real masters of navigation.

Quite true.

Under these conditions, the noblest of pursuits can hardly be thought much of by men whose own way of life runs counter to it. But by far the most formidable reproach is brought upon philoso-

---

[1] Simonides was asked by Hiero's queen whether it was better to be wise (a man of genius) or rich. He replied: Rich; for the wise are to be found at the court of the rich.

phy by those professed followers whom your critic no doubt had in mind when he denounced almost all of its votaries as utterly worthless and the best of them as of no use. I admitted the truth of that, did I not?

Yes.

Well, we have explained why the better sort are of no use. Shall we now go on to the question why the majority cannot fail to be worthless, and try to show, if we can, that here again the fault does not lie with philosophy?

Yes, by all means.

Before we begin the discussion, let us recall the point from which we started in describing the inborn disposition required for the making of a noble character. The leading characteristic, if you remember, was truth, which he must always and everywhere follow or else be an impostor with no part in true philosophy. This was one point where the current estimate of the philosopher is very much against us.

It is.

But might we not fairly plead in defence our account of the true lover of knowledge as one born to strive towards reality, who cannot linger among that multiplicity of things which men believe to be real, but holds on his way with a passion that will not faint or fail until he has laid hold upon the essential nature of each thing with that part of his soul which can apprehend reality because of its affinity therewith; and when he has by that means approached real being and entered into union with it, the offspring of this marriage is intelligence and truth; so that at last, having found knowledge and true life and nourishment, he is at rest from his travail?

No defence could be fairer.

Well then, such a one cannot but hate falsehood and love the truth; and when truth takes the lead, we may look to find in its train, not a whole company of defects, but a sound character, in which temperance attends on justice. Nor is there any need to prove once more that a whole array of other qualities must go with the philosophic nature: you will remember how it entailed courage, magnanimity, quickness to learn, and a good memory. Then you objected that, though everyone must assent to all this, yet, if he turned his attention from theory to fact, he would find the actual persons in question to be some of them useless, and most of them having every possible fault. Looking for the grounds of this reproach, we are now inquiring why the majority have these defects; and it was with a view to this problem that we have defined once more the qualities which the genuinely philosophic nature cannot fail to possess.

That is so.

Next then, we must study the influences that corrupt this nature and in many cases completely ruin it, though some few escape, who, as you remark, are said to be of no use, but not altogether worthless. Then we will consider the quality of those counterfeit natures which take to a pursuit too high and too good for them and by their manifold delinquencies have fastened upon philosophy, all the world over, the reputation you spoke of.

What are these corrupting influences?

I will describe them as well as I can. Everyone, I think, would agree that a nature with all the qualities we required to make the perfect philosopher is a rare growth, seldom seen among men.

Extremely rare.

Consider, then, how many grave dangers threaten to destroy these few. Strangest of all, every one of those qualities which we approved—courage, temperance, and all the rest—tends to ruin its possessor and to wrest his mind away from philosophy.

That does sound strange.

And, besides this, all the good things of life, as they are called, corrupt and distract the soul: beauty, wealth, strength, powerful connexions, and so forth—you know the sort of thing I mean.

Yes, but I should like you to explain in more detail.

The matter will be clear enough, and what I have just said will not seem so strange, when you have grasped the underlying principle. We know it to be true of any seed or growing thing, whether plant or animal, that if it fails to find its proper nourishment or climate or soil, then the more vigorous it is, the more it will lack the qualities it should possess. Evil is a worse enemy to the good than to the indifferent; so it is natural that bad conditions of nurture should be peculiarly uncongenial to the finest nature and that it should come off worse under them than natures of an insignificant order.

That is so.

Is not the same principle true of the mind, Adeimantus: if their early training is bad, the most gifted turn out the worst. Great crimes and unalloyed wickedness are the outcome of a nature full of generous promise, ruined by bad upbringing; no great harm, or great good either, will ever come of a slight or feeble disposition.

That is true.

So is it, then, with this temperament we have postulated for the philosopher: given the right instruction, it must grow to the full flower of excellence; but if the plant is sown and reared in the wrong soil, it will develop every contrary defect, unless saved by some miracle. Or do you hold the popular belief that, here and there, certain young men are demoralized by the private instructions of some individual sophist? Does that sort of influence amount to much? Is not the public itself the greatest of all sophists, training up young and old, men and women alike, into the most accomplished specimens of the character it desires to produce?

When does that happen?

Whenever the populace crowds together at any public gathering, in the Assembly, the law-courts, the theatre, or the camp, and sits there clamouring its approval or disapproval, both alike excessive, of whatever is being said or done; booing and clapping till the rocks ring and the whole place redoubles the noise of their applause and outcries. In such a scene what do you suppose will be a young man's state of mind? What sort of private instruction will have given him the strength to hold out against the force of such a torrent, or will save him from being swept away down the stream, until he accepts all their notions of right and wrong, does as they do, and comes to be just such a man as they are?

Yes, Socrates, such influence must be irresistible.

And I have said nothing of the most powerful engines of persuasion which the masters in this school of wisdom bring to bear when words have no effect. As you know, they punish the recalcitrant with disfranchisement, fines, and death.

They do.

How could the private teaching of any individual sophist avail in counteracting theirs? It would be great folly even to try; for no instruction aiming at an ideal contrary to the training they give has ever produced, or ever will produce, a different type of character—on the level, that is to say, of common humanity: one must always make an exception of the superhuman; and you may be sure that, in the present state of society, any character that escapes and comes to good can only have been saved by some miraculous interposition.[1]

I quite agree.

Then I hope you will also agree to this. Every one of these individuals who make a living by teaching in private and whom the public are pleased to call sophists and to regard as their rivals, is teaching nothing else than the opinions and beliefs expressed by the public itself when it meets on any occasion; and that is what he calls wisdom. It is as if the keeper of some huge and powerful creature should make a study of its moods and desires, how it may best be approached and handled, when it is most savage or gentle and what makes it so, the meaning of its various cries and the tones of voice that will soothe or provoke its anger; and, having mastered all this by long familiarity, should call it wisdom, reduce it to a system, and set up a school. Not in the least knowing which of these humours and desires is good or bad, right or wrong, he will fit all these terms to the fancies of the great beast and call what it enjoys good and what vexes it bad. He has no other account to give of their meaning; for him any action will be 'just' and 'right' that is done under necessity,[2] since he is too blind to tell how great is the real difference between what must

---

[1] This speech has been variously interpreted. Adam explains: 'Cities are either actual or ideal. In the ideal city, education does not produce a type of character which conflicts with public opinion, because public opinion is itself formed by education. In actual cities, education must conform to the same standard if it is to exist at all.' As things are, Plato accounts for the occasional appearance of a good statesman by suggesting (sometimes ironically) that, like poets and prophets, they are inspired by a sort of irrational genius or 'divine' afflatus.

[2] From Socrates' next speech it appears that the necessity of conforming to the Beast's humours is meant.

be and what ought to be. It would be a queer sort of education that such a person could offer, would it not?

It would indeed.

And is there anything to choose between him and one who thinks it is wisdom to have studied the moods and tastes of the assembled multitude, either in painting and music or in politics? Certainly, no one can go into such mixed company and submit to their judgement a poem or a work of art or some service he would render to the state, thus going out of his way to make the public his masters, without falling under the fatal necessity to give them whatever they like and do whatever they approve; but have you ever heard any argument which was not beneath contempt to show that what they admire is really beautiful or what they approve really good?

No; and I do not expect to hear one.

Now, with all this in mind, recall that distinction we drew earlier, between Beauty itself and the multiplicity of beautiful things. Is it conceivable that the multitude should ever believe in the existence of any real essence, as distinct from its many manifestations, or listen to anyone who asserts such a reality?

Assuredly not.

If that is so, the multitude can never be philosophical. Accordingly it is bound to disapprove of all who pursue wisdom; and so also, of course, are those individuals who associate with the mob and set their hearts on pleasing it.

That is clear.

What hope can you see, then, that a philosophic nature should be saved to persevere in the pursuit until the goal is reached? Remember how we agreed that the born philosopher will be distinguished by quickness of understanding, good memory, courage, and generosity. With such gifts, already as a boy he will stand out above all his companions, especially if his person be a match for his mind; and when he grows older, his friends and his fellow citizens will no doubt want to make use of him for their own purposes. They will fawn upon him with their entreaties and promises of advancement, flattering beforehand the power that will some day be his.

Yes, that happens often enough.

What will become of a youth so circumstanced, above all if he belongs to a great country and is conspicuous there for his birth and wealth, as well as for a tall and handsome person? Will he not be filled with unbounded ambition, believing himself well able to manage the affairs of all the world, at home and abroad, and thereupon give himself airs and be puffed up with senseless self-conceit?[1]

No doubt.

Now suppose that while this frame of mind is gaining upon him, someone should come and quietly tell him the truth, that there is no sense in him and that the only way to get the understanding he needs is to work for it like a slave: will he find it easy to listen, surrounded by all these evil influences?

Certainly not.

Perhaps, however, because there is something in a fine nature that responds to the voice of reason, he might be sensitive to the force which would draw him towards philosophy and begin to yield. But then those friends of his will see that they are in danger of losing one who might do so much for their party. Sooner than let him be won over, there is no engine of force or persuasion, from private intrigue to prosecution in the courts, that they will not bring to bear either upon him or upon his counsellor. How can he ever become a lover of wisdom?

He never will.

You see, then, I was not wrong in saying that, in a way, the very qualities which make up the philosopher's nature may, with a bad upbringing, be the cause of his falling away, no less than wealth and all other so-called advantages.

Yes, you were right.

These, then, are the dangers which threaten the noblest natures,

[1] The description fits Alcibiades, for whose disastrous career Socrates was held responsible by his enemies. In the dialogue *Alcibiades I*, Socrates takes him to task for his senseless conceit and ambition, and in the *Symposium* Alcibiades himself describes his admiration for Socrates' character and the wisdom of his advice. At the same time Plato may well be thinking also of his own youth, distracted between the influence of Socrates and the importunities of his political friends (Introd., p. xviii).

rare enough in any case, and spoil them for the highest of all pursuits. And among men of this type will be found those who do the greatest harm or, if the current should chance to set the other way, the greatest good, to society and to individuals; whereas no great good or harm will come to either from a little mind.

Quite true.

So Philosophy is left forlorn, like a maiden deserted by her nearest kin; and while these apostates take to a life that is no true life for them, she, bereft of her natural protectors, is dishonoured by unworthy interlopers, who fasten on her the reproach you have repeated, that some who have to do with her are worthless and most of them deserve heavy punishment.

That is what people say.

Naturally enough; when any poor creature who has proved his cleverness in some mechanical craft, sees here an opening for a pretentious display of high-sounding words and is glad to break out of the prison of his paltry trade and take sanctuary in the shrine of philosophy. For as compared with other occupations, philosophy, even in its present case, still enjoys a higher prestige, enough to attract a multitude of stunted natures, whose souls a life of drudgery has warped and maimed no less surely than their sedentary crafts have disfigured their bodies. For all the world they are like some little bald-headed tinker, who, having come into some money, has just got out of prison, had a good wash at the baths, and dressed himself up in a new coat as a bridegroom, ready to marry his master's daughter, who has been left poor and friendless. Could the issue of such a match ever be anything but pitiful base-born creatures? And, by the same token, what sort of ideas and opinions will be begotten of the misalliance of Philosophy with men incapable of culture? Not any true-born child of wisdom; the only right name for them will be sophistry.

Quite true.

So, Adeimantus, the remnant who are worthy to consort with Philosophy will be small indeed: perhaps some noble and well-nurtured character, saved by exile from those influences which would have impaired his natural impulse to be constant in her service; or it may be a great mind born in a petty state whose affairs are beneath its notice; and, possibly, a gifted few who have turned to philosophy from some other calling which they rightly disdain. Some, again, might be held back like our friend Theages, who, with every temptation to abandon study for a public life, has been restrained by ill health.[1] Of my own case there is little need to speak; the warning of the divine sign, I dare say, has come to few men, if any, before me.[2] One who has joined this small company and tasted the happiness that is their portion; who has watched the frenzy of the multitude and seen that there is no soundness in the conduct of public life, nowhere an ally at whose side a champion of justice could hope to escape destruction; but that, like a man fallen among wild beasts, if he should refuse to take part in their misdeeds and could not hold out alone against the fury of all, he would be destined, before he could be of any service to his country or his friends, to perish, having done no good to himself or to anyone else—one who has weighed all this keeps quiet and goes his own way, like the traveller who takes shelter under a wall from a driving storm of dust and hail; and seeing lawlessness spreading on all sides, is content if he can keep his hands clean from iniquity while this life lasts, and when the end comes take his departure, with good hopes, in serenity and peace.[3]

Surely, said Adeimantus, that would be no small achievement.

Yes; but far less than he might achieve, if his lot were cast in a society congenial to his nature, where he could grow to his full height and save his country as well as himself.

[1] The text here has the phrase 'the bridle of Theages,' which became proverbial.

[2] One of those supernatural intimations which came to Socrates had forbidden him to take more than the necessary part in public life. At *Apology* 31 D Socrates says: 'It is this sign which opposes my taking part in politics. And well for me that it does so; for you may be sure that, if I had, I should have perished long ago and done no good to you or to myself.'

[3] This last sentence alludes to the position of Plato himself, after he had renounced his early hopes of a political career and withdrawn to his task of training philosophic statesmen in the Academy. See Introduction, p. xxiii.

CHAPTER XXII (VI. 497 A–502 C)

A PHILOSOPHIC RULER IS NOT AN IMPOSSIBILITY

The pessimism of the last chapter is now redeemed by a ray of hope. The public might be reconciled to the rule of a philosopher, if we could make them see what the love of wisdom means and produce even a single man capable of remoulding human character after the pattern which he alone can know.

Plato alludes to hopes, perhaps conceived on his first visit to southern Italy and Syracuse (388/7 B.C.), of a reform of society from above by an enlightened despot or by some philosophic statesman trained at the Academy. But the philosopher king will not be like the ordinary absolute ruler, free 'to do whatever he likes.' On the contrary, he is compared to an artist working with constant reference to an unchanging model, which irrevocably determines the outline and basic principles of his work.

WELL then, I went on, enough has been said about the prejudice against philosophy, why it exists and how unfair it is, unless you have anything to add.

No, nothing on that head. But is there any existing form of society that you would call congenial to philosophy?

Not one. That is precisely my complaint: no existing constitution is worthy of the philosophic nature; that is why it is perverted and loses its character. As a foreign seed sown in a different soil yields to the new influence and degenerates into the local variety, so this nature cannot now keep its proper virtue, but falls away and takes on an alien character. If it can ever find the ideal form of society, as perfect as itself, then we shall see that it is in reality something divine, while all other natures and ways of life are merely human. No doubt you will ask me next what this ideal society is.

You are mistaken, he replied; I was going to ask whether you meant the commonwealth we have been founding.

Yes, in all points but one: our state must always contain some authority which will hold to the same idea of its constitution that you had before you in framing its laws. We did, in fact, speak of that point before, but not clearly enough; you frightened me with your objections, which have shown that the explanation is a long and difficult matter; and the hardest part is still to come.

What is that?

The question how a state can take in hand the pursuit of philosophy without disaster; for all great attempts are hazardous, and the proverb is only too true, that what is worth while is never easy.

All the same, this point must be cleared up to complete your account.

If I fail, it will not be for want of goodwill; 'yourself shall see me do my uttermost.'[1] In proof of which I shall at once be rash enough to remark that the state should deal with this pursuit, not as it does now, but in just the opposite way. As things are, those who take it up at all are only just out of their childhood. In the interval before they set up house and begin to earn their living, they are introduced to the hardest part—by which I mean abstract discussions—and then, when they have done with that, their philosophic education is supposed to be complete. Later, they think they have done much if they accept an invitation to listen to such a discussion, which is, in their eyes, to be taken as a pastime; and as age draws on, in all but a very few the light is quenched more effectually than the sun of Heraclitus,[2] inasmuch as it is never rekindled.

And what would be the right plan?

Just the opposite. Boys and youths should be given a liberal education suitable to their age; and, while growing up to manhood, they should take care to make their bodies into good instruments for the service of philosophy. As the years go on in which the mind begins to reach maturity, intellectual training should be in-

---

[1] The iambic rhythm and the word παρών, otnerwise hard to account for, suggest a quotation from tragedy. *Rep.* 533 A, *Symp.* 210 A, and *Meno* 77 A (all associated with the revelation of a mystery) may allude to the same context, which perhaps also included the words τὰ γὰρ δὴ μεγάλα πάντ' ἐπισφαλῆ (497 D).

[2] Heraclitus said 'there is a new sun every day,' since all things change and nothing remains the same.

tensified. Finally, when strength fails and they are past civil and military duties, let them range at will, free from all serious business but philosophy; for theirs is to be a life of happiness, crowned after death with a fitting destiny in the other world.

You really do seem to be doing your uttermost, Socrates. But I fancy most of your hearers will be even more in earnest on the other side. They are not at all likely to agree; least of all Thrasymachus.

Don't try to make a quarrel between Thrasymachus and me, when we have just become friends—not that we were enemies before. You and I will spare no effort until we convince him and the rest of the company, or at least take them some way with us, against the day when they may find themselves once more engaged in discussions like ours in some future incarnation.

Rather a distant prospect!

No more than a moment in the whole course of time. However, it is no wonder that most people have no faith in our proposals, for they have never seen our words come true in fact. They have heard plenty of eloquence, not like our own unstudied discourse, but full of balanced phrases and artfully matched antitheses;[1] but a man with a character so finely balanced as to be a match for the ideal of virtue in word and deed, ruling in a society as perfect as himself—that they have never yet seen in a single instance.

They have not.

Nor yet have they cared to listen seriously to frank discussion of the nobler sort that is entirely bent on knowing the truth for its own sake and leaves severely alone those tricks of special pleading in the law-court or the lecture-room which aim only at influencing opinion or winning a case.

Quite true.

These, then, were the obstacles I foresaw when, in spite of my fears, truth compelled me to declare that there will never be a

---

[1] Refers to the political speeches and tracts of Isocrates, whose school for future statesmen was a rival of Plato's Academy, and who taught his pupils a very elegant style. Plato contrives to parody one of its artificial devices with a play upon words that defies translation.

perfect state or constitution, nor yet a perfect man, until some happy circumstance compels these few philosophers who have escaped corruption but are now called useless, to take charge, whether they like it or not, of a state which will submit to their authority; or else until kings and rulers or their sons are divinely inspired with a genuine passion for true philosophy. If either alternative or both were impossible, we might justly be laughed at as idle dreamers; but, as I maintain, there is no ground for saying so. Accordingly, if ever in the infinity of time, past or future, or even to-day in some foreign region far beyond our horizon, men of the highest gifts for philosophy are constrained to take charge of a commonwealth, we are ready to maintain that, then and there, the constitution we have described has been realized, or will be realized when once the philosophic muse becomes mistress of a state. For that might happen. Our plan is difficult—we have admitted as much—but not impossible.

I agree to that.

But the public, you are going to say, think otherwise?

Perhaps.

My dear Adeimantus, you must not condemn the public so sweepingly; they will change their opinion, if you avoid controversy and try gently to remove their prejudice against the love of learning. Repeat our description of the philosopher's nature and of his pursuits, and they will see that you do not mean the sort of person they imagine. It is only ill-temper and malice in oneself that call out those qualities in others who are not that way inclined; and I will anticipate you by declaring that, in my belief, the public with a few exceptions is not of such an unyielding temper.

Yes, I agree with you there.

Will you also agree that, if it is ill-disposed towards philosophy, the blame must fall on that noisy crew of interlopers who are always bandying abuse and spiteful personalities—the last thing of which a philosopher can be guilty? For surely, Adeimantus, a man whose thoughts are fixed on true reality has no leisure to look downwards on the affairs of men, to take part in their quarrels, and to catch the infection of their jealousies and hates. He contemplates a world of unchanging and harmonious order, where reason governs and nothing can do or suffer wrong; and, like one who imitates an admired companion, he cannot fail to fashion himself in its likeness. So the philosopher, in constant companionship with the divine order of the world, will reproduce that order in his soul and, so far as man may, become godlike; though here, as everywhere, there will be scope for detraction.

Quite true.

Suppose, then, he should find himself compelled to mould other characters besides his own and to shape the pattern of public and private life into conformity with his vision of the ideal, he will not lack the skill to produce such counterparts of temperance, justice, and all the virtues as can exist in the ordinary man. And the public, when they see that we have described him truly, will be reconciled to the philosopher and no longer disbelieve our assertion that happiness can only come to a state when its lineaments are traced by an artist working after the divine pattern.

Yes, they will be reconciled when once they understand. But how will this artist set to work?

He will take society and human character as his canvas, and begin by scraping it clean. That is no easy matter; but, as you know, unlike other reformers, he will not consent to take in hand either an individual or a state or to draft laws, until he is given a clean surface to work on or has cleansed it himself.[1]

Quite rightly.

Next, he will sketch in the outline of the constitution. Then, as the work goes on, he will frequently refer to his model, the ideals of justice, goodness, temperance, and the rest, and compare with them the copy of those qualities which he is trying to create in human society. Combining the various elements of social life as a painter mixes his colours, he will reproduce the complexion of true humanity, guided by that divine pattern whose likeness Homer saw in the men he called godlike. He will rub out and paint in again this or that feature, until he has produced, so far as may be, a type of human character that heaven can approve.

---

[1] At 540 E, p. 262, Plato proposes to rusticate the whole population above the age of ten. Contrast the piecemeal tinkering at reform satirized at 425 E, p. 116.

No picture could be more beautiful than that.

Are we now making any impression on those assailants who, you said, would fall upon us so furiously when we spoke in praise of the philosopher and proposed to give him control of the state? Will they be calmer now that we have told them we mean an artist who will use his skill in this way to design a constitution?

They ought to be, if they have any sense.

Yes, for what ground is left for dispute? It would be absurd to deny that a philosopher is a lover of truth and reality; or that his nature, as we have described it, is allied to perfection; or again, that given the right training, no other will be so completely good and enlightened. They will hardly give the preference to those impostors whom we have ruled out.

Surely not.

So they will no longer be angry with us for saying that, until philosophers hold power, neither states nor individuals will have rest from trouble, and the commonwealth we have imagined will never be realized.

Less angry perhaps.

I suggest that, if we go farther and assume them to be completely pacified and convinced, then, perhaps, they might agree with us for very shame.

Certainly they might.

Granted, then, that they are convinced so far, no one will dispute our other point, that kings and hereditary rulers might have sons with a philosophic nature, and these might conceivably escape corruption. It would be hard to save them, we admit; but can anyone say that, in the whole course of time, not a single one could be saved?

Surely not.

Well, one would be enough to effect all this reform that now seems so incredible, if he had subjects disposed to obey; for it is surely not impossible that they should consent to carry out our laws and customs when laid down by a ruler.[1] It would be no miracle if others should think as we do; and we have, I believe,

---

[1] At *Laws* 709 E Plato again suggests the conjunction of a lawgiver with a young, intelligent, and self-controlled despot.

sufficiently shown that our plan, if practicable, is the best. So, to conclude: our institutions would be the best, if they could be realized, and to realize them, though hard, is not impossible.

Yes, that is the conclusion.

CHAPTER XXIII (VI. 502 C–509 C)

THE GOOD AS THE HIGHEST OBJECT OF KNOWLEDGE

Granted that a Philosopher-King might possibly be produced, how is he to be trained? The rest of this Part describes the higher education in mathematics and moral philosophy which the prospective Rulers, after the elementary education of Chapter IX and two or three years of intensive physical training, will receive from the age of twenty to thirty-five (537 B, p. 259). The account may also be taken as a sort of ideal programme of studies at the Academy.

Plato first defines the ultimate goal, the knowledge of the Good. For the saviour of society the one thing needful is a certain and immediate knowledge of values, the ends which all life, private or public, should realize. Both Plato (Charmides, 173, Euthydemus, 288 D ff.) and Aristotle (Ethics, I. i) picture social life as a domain in which all forms of 'art' or specialized skill have their several fields, each with its peculiar end: medicine producing health, the art of war victory, business wealth, and so on. Above them all is the Royal Art, or Art of Statesmanship ('Politics'), which sees these special ends as means to, or elements in, the ultimate end or perfection (telos) of life, human well-being or happiness, 'the Good for man.' All effort will be perverted and falsely orientated if this end is misconceived—if a statesman, e.g., believes that his nation should aim at imperial domination or unlimited wealth, or if an individual imagines that wealth or power or pleasure will suffice to make him happy. It is of this 'Human Good' that Plato first speaks, as the most important object of knowledge. He rejects the popular belief that it is pleasure. The more refined view, that it is 'knowledge' (insight, wisdom) may be attributed to the Socrates

*pictured in Plato's early dialogues. He held that man's happiness
consists in the full realization of his characteristic virtue and function (Chap. IV), and that his virtue, as a rational being, is a clear
insight into the true end of life, 'knowledge of the Good.' Such
knowledge, once attained, cannot fail to determine will and action.*

*But in the latter part of this chapter (506 B ff., p. 216) 'the Good'
receives the much wider meaning it bears in Plato's own theory of
Forms ('Ideas'). In Greek 'the Good' is normally synonymous with
'Goodness itself.' This is the supreme Form or Essence manifested
not only in the special kinds of moral goodness, Justice, Courage,
&c., but throughout all Nature (for every living creature has its
own 'good') and especially in the beautiful and harmonious order
of the heavenly bodies (592 B, p. 320). The knowledge of the Good,
on which well-being depends, is now to include an understanding
of the moral and physical order of the whole universe. As the object
of a purpose attributed to a divine Reason operating in the world,
this supreme Good makes the world intelligible, as a work of human craftsmanship becomes intelligible when we see the purpose
it is designed to serve. As thus illuminating and accounting for the
rational aspect of the universe, the Good is analogous to the Sun,
which, as the source of light, is the cause of vision and of visibility,
and also of all mortal existence.*

*Socrates refuses to define this supreme Good. The apprehension
of it is rather to be thought of as a revelation which can only fol-
low upon a long intellectual training (540 A, p. 262). Neither
Glaucon nor the readers of the* Republic *have been so prepared.
Also Plato would never commit his deepest thoughts to writing*
(Epistle vii. 341 c).

ONE difficulty, then, has been surmounted. It remains to ask how
we can make sure of having men who will preserve our constitution. What must they learn, and at what age should they take up
each branch of study?

Yes, that is the next point.

I gained nothing by my cunning in putting off those thorny
questions of the possession of wives and children and the appointment of Rulers. I knew that the ideal plan would give offence and

be hard to carry out; none the less I have had to discuss these matters. We have now disposed of the women and children, but we must start all over again upon the training of the Rulers. You remember how their love for their country was to be proved, by the tests of pain and pleasure, to be a faith that no toil or danger, no turn of fortune could make them abandon.[1] All who failed were to be rejected; only the man who came out flawless, like gold tried in the fire, was to be made a Ruler with privileges and rewards in life and after death. So much was said, when our argument turned aside, as if hoping, with veiled face, to slip past the danger that now lies in our path.

Quite true, I remember.

Yes, I shrank from the bold words which have now been spoken; but now we have ventured to declare that our Guardians in the fullest sense must be philosophers.[2] So much being granted, you must reflect how few are likely to be available. The natural gifts we required will rarely grow together into one whole; they tend to split apart.

How do you mean?

Qualities like ready understanding, a good memory, sagacity, quickness, together with a high-spirited, generous temper, are seldom combined with willingness to live a quiet life of sober constancy. Keen wits are apt to lose all steadiness and to veer about in every direction. On the other hand, the steady reliable characters, whose impassivity is proof against the perils of war, are equally proof against instruction. Confronted with intellectual work, they become comatose and do nothing but yawn.

That is true.

But we insist that no one must be given the highest education or hold office as Ruler, who has not both sets of qualities in due measure. This combination will be rare. So, besides testing it by hardship and danger and by the temptations of pleasure, we may now add that its strength must be tried in many forms of study,

---

[1] Chap. X, pp. 103 ff.

[2] The constancy of *belief* required of all Guardians in the earlier passage referred to (413, p. 105) is not enough for those few who will be the Rulers obeyed by the rest. They must have the philosopher's immediate *knowledge* of the Good.

to see whether it has the courage and endurance to pursue the highest kind of knowledge, without flinching as others flinch under physical trials.

By all means; but what kinds of study do you call the highest?

You remember how we deduced the definitions of justice, temperance, courage, and wisdom by distinguishing three parts of the soul?

If I had forgotten that, I should not deserve to hear any more.

Do you also remember my warning you beforehand[1] that in order to gain the clearest possible view of these qualities we should have to go round a longer way, although we could give a more superficial account in keeping with our earlier argument. You said that would do; and so we went on in a way which seemed to me not sufficiently exact; whether you were satisfied, it is for you to say.

We all thought you gave us a fair measure of truth.

No measure that falls in the least degree short of the whole truth can be quite fair in so important a matter. What is imperfect can never serve as a measure; though people sometimes think enough has been done and there is no need to look further.

Yes, indolence is common enough.

But the last quality to be desired in the Guardian of a commonwealth and its laws. So he will have to take the longer way and work as hard at learning as at training his body; otherwise he will never reach the goal of the highest knowledge, which most of all concerns him.

Why, are not justice and the other virtues we have discussed the highest? Is there something still higher to be known?

There is; and of those virtues themselves we have as yet only a rough outline, where nothing short of the finished picture should content us. If we strain every nerve to reach precision and clearness in things of little moment, how absurd not to demand the highest degree of exactness in the things that matter most.

Certainly. But what do you mean by the highest kind of knowledge and with what is it concerned? You cannot hope to escape that question.

[1] At 435 D, p. 131.

I do not; you may ask me yourself. All the same, you have been told many a time; but now either you are not thinking or, as I rather suspect, you mean to put me to some trouble with your insistence. For you have often been told that the highest object of knowledge is the essential nature of the Good, from which everything that is good and right derives its value for us. You must have been expecting me to speak of this now, and to add that we have no sufficient knowledge of it. I need not tell you that, without that knowledge, to know everything else, however well, would be of no value to us, just as it is of no use to possess anything without getting the good of it. What advantage can there be in possessing everything except what is good, or in understanding everything else while of the good and desirable we know nothing?

None whatever.

Well then, you know too that most people identify the Good [1] with pleasure, whereas the more enlightened think it is knowledge.

Yes, of course.

And further that these latter cannot tell us what knowledge they mean, but are reduced at last to saying, 'knowledge of the Good.'

That is absurd.

It is; first they reproach us with not knowing the Good, and then tell us that it is knowledge of the Good, as if we did after all understand the meaning of that word 'Good' when they pronounce it.

Quite true.

What of those who define the Good as pleasure? Are they any less confused in their thoughts? They are obliged to admit that there are bad pleasures; from which it follows that the same things are both good and bad. [2]

Quite so.

Evidently, then, this is a matter of much dispute. It is also evident that, although many are content to do what seems just or honourable without really being so, and to possess a mere sem-

---

[1] Here 'the Good' obviously means 'the Human Good' or end of human life.

[2] This admission is extracted in the *Gorgias* (499 B) from Callicles, who has maintained extreme hedonism.

blance of these qualities, when it comes to good things, no one is satisfied with possessing what only seems good: here all reject the appearance and demand the reality.

Certainly.

A thing, then, that every soul pursues as the end of all her actions, dimly divining its existence, but perplexed and unable to grasp its nature with the same clearness and assurance as in dealing with other things, and so missing whatever value those other things might have—a thing of such supreme importance is not a matter about which those chosen Guardians of the whole fortunes of our commonwealth can be left in the dark.

Most certainly not.

At any rate, institutions or customs which are desirable and right will not, I imagine, find a very efficient guardian in one who does not know in what way they are good. I should rather guess that he will not be able to recognize fully that they are right and desirable.

No doubt.

So the order of our commonwealth will be perfectly regulated only when it is watched over by a Guardian who does possess this knowledge.

That follows. But, Socrates, what is your own account of the Good? Is it knowledge, or pleasure, or something else? [1]

There you are! I exclaimed; I could see all along that you were not going to be content with what other people think.

Well, Socrates, it does not seem fair that you should be ready to repeat other people's opinions but not to state your own, when you have given so much thought to this subject.

And do you think it fair of anyone to speak as if he knew what he does not know?

No, not as if he knew, but he might give his opinion for what it is worth.

Why, have you never noticed that opinion without knowledge is always a shabby sort of thing? At the best it is blind. One who

---

[1] Here it begins to appear that the discussion is not confined to the 'Human Good' but extends to the supreme Form, 'Goodness itself.'

holds a true belief without intelligence is just like a blind man who happens to take the right road, isn't he? [1]

No doubt.

Well, then, do you want me to produce one of these poor blind cripples, when others could discourse to you with illuminating eloquence?

No, really, Socrates, said Glaucon, you must not give up within sight of the goal. We should be quite content with an account of the Good like the one you gave us of justice and temperance and the other virtues.

So should I be, my dear Glaucon, much more than content! But I am afraid it is beyond my powers; with the best will in the world I should only disgrace myself and be laughed at. No, for the moment let us leave the question of the real meaning of good; to arrive at what I at any rate believe it to be would call for an effort too ambitious for an inquiry like ours. However, I will tell you, though only if you wish it, what I picture to myself as the offspring of the Good and the thing most nearly resembling it.

Well, tell us about the offspring, and you shall remain in our debt for an account of the parent.

I only wish it were within my power to offer, and within yours to receive, a settlement of the whole account. But you must be content now with the interest only; [2] and you must see to it that, in describing this offspring of the Good, I do not inadvertently cheat you with false coin.

We will keep a good eye on you. Go on.

First we must come to an understanding. Let me remind you of the distinction we drew earlier and have often drawn on other occasions, [3] between the multiplicity of things that we call good or beautiful or whatever it may be and, on the other hand, Good-

[1] At *Meno* 97 the man who has a correct belief at second-hand about the way from Athens to Larisa is contrasted with one who has certain knowledge of the road from having travelled by it himself.

[2] The Greek has a play on two meanings of the word *tokos*—'offspring' and 'interest' on a loan, 'a breed for barren metal.'

[3] Perhaps an allusion to the *Phaedo* (especially 78 E ff.), where the theory of Forms was first explicitly stated in similar terms. The earlier passage in the *Republic* is at 475 E ff., p. 183.

ness itself or Beauty itself and so on. Corresponding to each of these sets of many things, we postulate a single Form or real essence, as we call it.

Yes, that is so.

Further, the many things, we say, can be seen, but are not objects of rational thought; whereas the Forms are objects of thought, but invisible.

Yes, certainly.

And we see things with our eyesight, just as we hear sounds with our ears and, to speak generally, perceive any sensible thing with our sense-faculties.

Of course.

Have you noticed, then, that the artificer who designed the senses has been exceptionally lavish of his materials in making the eyes able to see and their objects visible?

That never occurred to me.

Well, look at it in this way. Hearing and sound do not stand in need of any third thing, without which the ear will not hear nor sound be heard; [1] and I think the same is true of most, not to say all, of the other senses. Can you think of one that does require anything of the sort?

No, I cannot.

But there is this need in the case of sight and its objects. You may have the power of vision in your eyes and try to use it, and colour may be there in the objects; but sight will see nothing and the colours will remain invisible in the absence of a third thing peculiarly constituted to serve this very purpose.

By which you mean——?

Naturally I mean what you call light; and if light is a thing of value, the sense of sight and the power of being visible are linked together by a very precious bond, such as unites no other sense with its object.

No one could say that light is not a precious thing.

And of all the divinities in the skies [2] is there one whose light,

----

[1] Plato held that the hearing of sound is caused by blows inflicted by the air (*Timaeus* 67 B, 80 A); but the air is hardly analogous to light.

[2] Plato held that the heavenly bodies are immortal living creatures, i.e. gods.

above all the rest, is responsible for making our eyes see perfectly and making objects perfectly visible?

There can be no two opinions: of course you mean the Sun.

And how is sight related to this deity? Neither sight nor the eye which contains it is the Sun, but of all the sense-organs it is the most sun-like; and further, the power it possesses is dispensed by the Sun, like a stream flooding the eye.[1] And again, the Sun is not vision, but it is the cause of vision and also is seen by the vision it causes.

Yes.

It was the Sun, then, that I meant when I spoke of that offspring which the Good has created in the visible world, to stand there in the same relation to vision and visible things as that which the Good itself bears in the intelligible world to intelligence and to intelligible objects.

How is that? You must explain further.

You know what happens when the colours of things are no longer irradiated by the daylight, but only by the fainter luminaries of the night: when you look at them, the eyes are dim and seem almost blind, as if there were no unclouded vision in them. But when you look at things on which the Sun is shining, the same eyes see distinctly and it becomes evident that they do contain the power of vision.

Certainly.

Apply this comparison, then, to the soul. When its gaze is fixed upon an object irradiated by truth and reality, the soul gains understanding and knowledge and is manifestly in possession of intelligence. But when it looks towards that twilight world of things that come into existence and pass away, its sight is dim and it has only opinions and beliefs which shift to and fro, and now it seems like a thing that has no intelligence.

That is true.

[1] Plato's theory of vision involves three kinds of fire or light: (1) daylight, a body of pure fire diffused in the air by the Sun; (2) the visual current or 'vision,' a pure fire similar to daylight, contained in the eye-ball and capable of issuing out in a stream directed towards the object seen; (3) the colour of the external object, 'a flame streaming off from every body, having particles proportioned to those of the visual current, so as to yield sensation' when the two streams meet and coalesce (*Timaeus*, 45 B, 67 c).

This, then, which gives to the objects of knowledge their truth and to him who knows them his power of knowing, is the Form or essential nature of Goodness. It is the cause of knowledge and truth; and so, while you may think of it as an object of knowledge, you will do well to regard it as something beyond truth and knowledge and, precious as these both are, of still higher worth. And, just as in our analogy light and vision were to be thought of as like the Sun, but not identical with it, so here both knowledge and truth are to be regarded as like the Good, but to identify either with the Good is wrong. The Good must hold a yet higher place of honour.

You are giving it a position of extraordinary splendour, if it is the source of knowledge and truth and itself surpasses them in worth. You surely cannot mean that it is pleasure.

Heaven forbid, I exclaimed. But I want to follow up our analogy still further. You will agree that the Sun not only makes the things we see visible, but also brings them into existence and gives them growth and nourishment; yet he is not the same thing as existence.[1] And so with the objects of knowledge: these derive from the Good not only their power of being known, but their very being and reality; and Goodness is not the same thing as being, but even beyond being, surpassing it in dignity and power.

Glaucon exclaimed with some amusement at my exalting Goodness in such extravagant terms.

It is your fault, I replied; you forced me to say what I think.

Yes, and you must not stop there. At any rate, complete your comparison with the Sun, if there is any more to be said.

There is a great deal more, I answered.

Let us hear it, then; don't leave anything out.

I am afraid much must be left unspoken. However, I will not, if I can help it, leave out anything that can be said on this occasion.

Please do not.

---

[1] The ambiguity of *genesis* can hardly be reproduced. The Sun 'gives things their *genesis*' (generation, birth), but 'is not itself *genesis*' (becoming, the existence in time of things which begin and cease to exist, as opposed to the real being of eternal things in the intelligible world).

CHAPTER XXIV (VI. 509 D–511 E)

FOUR STAGES OF COGNITION. THE LINE

Chapter XIX contrasted the realm of sensible appearances and shifting beliefs with the realm of eternal and unchanging Forms, dominated (as we now know) by the Good. The philosopher was he whose affections were set on knowledge of that real world. The Guardians' primary education in literature and art was mainly confined to the world of appearance and belief, though it culminated in the perception of 'images' of the moral ideals, the beauty of which would excite love for the individual person in whose soul they dwelt (402, p. 91). The higher intellectual training now to be described is to detach the mind from appearances and individuals and to carry it across the boundary between the two worlds and all the way beyond to the vision of the Good. It thus corresponds to the 'greater mysteries' of which Diotima speaks in the Symposium *(210), where* Eros, *detached from its individual object, advances to the vision of Beauty itself (the Good considered as the object of desire). The next chapter will give an allegorical picture of this progress.*

The allegory is here prefaced by a diagram. A line is divided into two parts, whose inequality symbolizes that the visible world has a lower degree of reality and truth than the intelligible. Each part is then subdivided in the same proportion as the whole line, (thus $A + B : C + D = A : B = C : D$*). The four sections correspond to four states of mind or modes of cognition, each clearer and more certain than the one below.*

The lower part $(A + B)$ *is at first called 'the Visible,' but elsewhere the field of* doxa *in the wide sense explained above (p. 181); and so it includes the 'many conventional notions of the multitude' about morality (479 D, p. 188). It is the physical and moral world as apprehended by those 'lovers of appearance' who do not recognize the absolute ideals which Plato calls real (p. 189).*

Asg to assent to real Knowledge

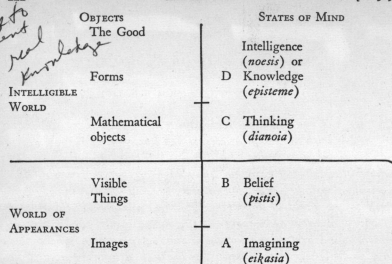

OBJECTS		STATES OF MIND
The Good		
		Intelligence (*noesis*) or
Forms	D	Knowledge (*episteme*)
INTELLIGIBLE WORLD		
Mathematical objects	C	Thinking (*dianoia*)
Visible Things	B	Belief (*pistis*)
WORLD OF APPEARANCES		
Images	A	Imagining (*eikasia*)

(*A*) *The lowest form of cognition is called* eikasia. *The word defies translation, being one of those current terms to which Plato gives a peculiar sense, to be inferred from the context. It is etymologically connected with* eikon = *image, likeness, and with* eikos = *likely, and it can mean either likeness (representation) or likening (comparison) or estimation of likelihood (conjecture). Perhaps 'imagining' is the least unsatisfactory rendering. It seems to be the wholly unenlightened state of mind which takes sensible appearances and current moral notions at their face value—the condition of the unreleased prisoners in the Cave allegory below, who see only images of images.*

(*B*) *The higher section stands for common-sense belief* (pistis) *in the reality of the visible and tangible things commonly called substantial. In the moral sphere it would include 'correct beliefs without knowledge' (506 c, p. 216), such as the young Guardians were taught to hold. True beliefs are sufficient guides for action, but are insecure until based on knowledge of the reasons for them* (Meno 97).

Higher education is to effect an escape from the prison of appearances by training the intellect, first in mathematics, and then in moral philosophy. (*C*) *The lower section of the intelligible con-*

tains the subject-matter of the mathematical sciences (511 B, p. 225).[1] *Two characteristics of mathematical procedure are mentioned:* (a) *the use of visible diagrams and models as imperfect illustrations of the objects and truths of pure thought. Here is a sort of bridge carrying the mind across from the visible thing to the intelligible reality, which it must learn to distinguish.* (b) *Each branch of mathematics starts from unquestioned assumptions* (*postulates, axioms, definitions*) *and reasons from them deductively. The premises may be true and the conclusions may follow, but the whole structure hangs in the air until the assumptions themselves shall have been shown to depend on an unconditional principle.* (*This may be conjectured to be Unity itself, an aspect of the Good.*) *Meanwhile the state of mind is* dianoia, *the ordinary word for 'thought' or 'thinking,' here implying a degree of understanding which falls short of perfect knowledge* (533 D, p. 254). Dianoia *suggests discursive thinking or reasoning from premiss to conclusion, whereas* noesis *is constantly compared to the immediate act of vision and suggests rather the direct intuition or apprehension of its object.*

(D) *The higher method is called Dialectic, a word which since Hegel has acquired misleading associations. In the* Republic *it simply means the technique of philosophic conversation* (*dialogue*) *carried on by question and answer and seeking to render, or to receive from a respondent, an 'account'* (logos) *of some Form, usually a moral Form such as Justice in this dialogue. At this stage visible illustrations are no longer available, and the movement at first is not downward, deducing conclusions from premises, but upward, examining the premises themselves and seeking the ultimate principle on which they all depend. It is suggested that, if the mind could ever rise to grasp the supreme Form, it might then descend by a deduction confirming the whole structure of moral and mathematical knowledge. The state of mind is called intelligence or rational intuition* (noesis) *and knowledge* (episteme, 533 E, p. 254) *in the full sense. The procedure of Dialectic will be further described in Chapter XXVII.*

---

[1] The interpretation of the higher part of the Line is the subject of a long controversy which cannot be pursued here.

CONCEIVE, then, that there are these two powers I speak of, the Good reigning over the domain of all that is intelligible, the Sun over the visible world—or the heaven as I might call it; only you would think I was showing off my skill in etymology.[1] At any rate you have these two orders of things clearly before your mind: the visible and the intelligible?

I have.

Now take a line divided into two unequal parts, one to represent the visible order, the other the intelligible; and divide each part again in the same proportion, symbolizing degrees of comparative clearness or obscurity. Then (A) one of the two sections in the visible world will stand for images. By images I mean first shadows, and then reflections in water or in close-grained, polished surfaces, and everything of that kind, if you understand.

Yes, I understand.

Let the second section (B) stand for the actual things of which the first are likenesses, the living creatures about us and all the works of nature or of human hands.

So be it.

Will you also take the proportion in which the visible world has been divided as corresponding to degrees of reality and truth, so that the likeness shall stand to the original in the same ratio as the sphere of appearances and belief to the sphere of knowledge?

Certainly.

Now consider how we are to divide the part which stands for the intelligible world. There are two sections. In the first (C) the mind uses as images those actual things which themselves had images in the visible world; and it is compelled to pursue its inquiry by starting from assumptions and travelling, not up to a principle, but down to a conclusion. In the second (D) the mind moves in the other direction, from an assumption up towards a principle which is not hypothetical; and it makes no use of the images employed in the other section, but only of Forms, and conducts its inquiry solely by their means.

I don't quite understand what you mean.

---

[1] Some connected the word for heaven (οὐρανός) with ὁρᾶν 'to see' (*Cratylus*, 396 Β). It is sometimes used for the whole of the visible universe.

Then we will try again; what I have just said will help you to understand. (C) You know, of course, how students of subjects like geometry and arithmetic begin by postulating odd and even numbers, or the various figures and the three kinds of angle, and other such data in each subject. These data they take as known; and, having adopted them as assumptions, they do not feel called upon to give any account of them to themselves or to anyone else, but treat them as self-evident. Then, starting from these assumptions, they go on until they arrive, by a series of consistent steps, at all the conclusions they set out to investigate.

Yes, I know that.

You also know how they make use of visible figures and discourse about them, though what they really have in mind is the originals of which these figures are images: they are not reasoning, for instance, about this particular square and diagonal which they have drawn, but about *the* Square and *the* Diagonal; and so in all cases. The diagrams they draw and the models they make are actual things, which may have their shadows or images in water; but now they serve in their turn as images, while the student is seeking to behold those realities which only thought can apprehend.[1]

True.

This, then, is the class of things that I spoke of as intelligible, but with two qualifications: first, that the mind, in studying them, is compelled to employ assumptions, and, because it cannot rise above these, does not travel upwards to a first principle; and second, that it uses as images those actual things which have images of their own in the section below them and which, in comparison with those shadows and reflections, are reputed to be more palpable and valued accordingly.

I understand: you mean the subject-matter of geometry and of the kindred arts.

(D) Then by the second section of the intelligible world you

---

[1] Conversely, the fact that the mathematician can use visible objects as illustrations indicates that the realities and truths of mathematics are embodied, though imperfectly, in the world of visible and tangible things; whereas the counterparts of the moral Forms can only be beheld by thought.

may understand me to mean all that unaided reasoning apprehends
by the power of dialectic, when it treats its assumptions, not as
first principles, but as *hypotheses* in the literal sense, things 'laid
down' like a flight of steps up which it may mount all the way
to something that is not hypothetical, the first principle of all; and
having grasped this, may turn back and, holding on to the consequences which depend upon it, descend at last to a conclusion,
never making use of any sensible object, but only of Forms, moving through Forms from one to another, and ending with Forms.

I understand, he said, though not perfectly; for the procedure
you describe sounds like an enormous undertaking. But I see that
you mean to distinguish the field of intelligible reality studied by
dialectic as having a greater certainty and truth than the subject-
matter of the 'arts,' as they are called, which treat their assumptions
as first principles. The students of these arts are, it is true, compelled to exercise thought in contemplating objects which the senses
cannot perceive; but because they start from assumptions without
going back to a first principle, you do not regard them as gaining
true understanding about those objects, although the objects themselves, when connected with a first principle, are intelligible. And
I think you would call the state of mind of the students of geometry
and other such arts, not intelligence, but thinking, as being something between intelligence and mere acceptance of appearances.

You have understood me quite well enough, I replied. And now
you may take, as corresponding to the four sections, these four
states of mind: *intelligence* for the highest, *thinking* for the second, *belief* for the third, and for the last *imagining*.[1] These you
may arrange as the terms in a proportion, assigning to each a degree of clearness and certainty corresponding to the measure in
which their objects possess truth and reality.

I understand and agree with you. I will arrange them as you say.

---

[1] Plato never uses hard and fast technical terms. The four here proposed are not
defined or strictly employed in the sequel.

CHAPTER XXV (VII. 514 A–521 B)

THE ALLEGORY OF THE CAVE

The progress of the mind from the lowest state of unenlightenment to knowledge of the Good is now illustrated by the famous parable comparing the world of appearance to an underground Cave. In Empedocles' religious poem the powers which conduct the soul to its incarnation say, 'We have come under this cavern's roof.' The image was probably taken from mysteries held in caves or dark chambers representing the underworld, through which the candidates for initiation were led to the revelation of sacred objects in a blaze of light. The idea that the body is a prison-house, to which the soul is condemned for past misdeeds, is attributed by Plato to the Orphics.

One moral of the allegory is drawn from the distress caused by a too sudden passage from darkness to light. The earlier warning against plunging untrained minds into the discussion of moral problems (498 A, p. 206), as the Sophists and Socrates himself had done, is reinforced by the picture of the dazed prisoner dragged out into the sunlight. Plato's ten years' course of pure mathematics is to habituate the intellect to abstract reasoning before moral ideas are called in question (537 E, ff., p. 259).

NEXT, said I, here is a parable to illustrate the degrees in which our nature may be enlightened or unenlightened. Imagine the condition of men living in a sort of cavernous chamber underground, with an entrance open to the light and a long passage all down the cave.[1] Here they have been from childhood, chained by the leg and also by the neck, so that they cannot move and can see only what is in front of them, because the chains will not let them turn their heads. At some distance higher up is the light of a fire burning behind them; and between the prisoners and the

---

[1] The *length* of the 'way in' (*eisodos*) to the chamber where the prisoners sit is an essential feature, explaining why no daylight reaches them.

fire is a track [1] with a parapet built along it, like the screen at a puppet-show, which hides the performers while they show their puppets over the top.

I see, said he.

Now behind this parapet imagine persons carrying along various artificial objects, including figures of men and animals in wood or stone or other materials, which project above the parapet. Naturally, some of these persons will be talking, others silent. [2]

It is a strange picture, he said, and a strange sort of prisoners.

Like ourselves, I replied; for in the first place prisoners so confined would have seen nothing of themselves or of one another, except the shadows thrown by the fire-light on the wall of the Cave facing them, would they?

Not if all their lives they had been prevented from moving their heads.

And they would have seen as little of the objects carried past.

Of course.

Now, if they could talk to one another, would they not suppose that their words referred only to those passing shadows which they saw? [3]

Necessarily.

And suppose their prison had an echo from the wall facing them? When one of the people crossing behind them spoke, they could only suppose that the sound came from the shadow passing before their eyes.

No doubt.

[1] The track crosses the passage into the cave at right angles, and is *above* the parapet built along it.

[2] A modern Plato would compare his Cave to an underground cinema, where the audience watch the play of shadows thrown by the film passing before a light at their backs. The film itself is only an image of 'real' things and events in the world outside the cinema. For the film Plato has to substitute the clumsier apparatus of a procession of artificial objects carried on their heads by persons who are merely part of the machinery, providing for the movement of the objects and the sounds whose echo the prisoners hear. The parapet prevents these persons' shadows from being cast on the wall of the Cave.

[3] Adam's text and interpretation. The prisoners, having seen nothing but shadows, cannot think their words refer to the objects carried past behind their backs. For them shadows (images) are the only realities.

In every way, then, such prisoners would recognize as reality nothing but the shadows of those artificial objects.[1]

Inevitably.

Now consider what would happen if their release from the chains and the healing of their unwisdom should come about in this way. Suppose one of them set free and forced suddenly to stand up, turn his head, and walk with eyes lifted to the light; all these movements would be painful, and he would be too dazzled to make out the objects whose shadows he had been used to see. What do you think he would say, if someone told him that what he had formerly seen was meaningless illusion, but now, being somewhat nearer to reality and turned towards more real objects, he was getting a truer view? Suppose further that he were shown the various objects being carried by and were made to say, in reply to questions, what each of them was. Would he not be perplexed and believe the objects now shown him to be not so real as what he formerly saw?[2]

Yes, not nearly so real.

And if he were forced to look at the fire-light itself, would not his eyes ache, so that he would try to escape and turn back to the things which he could see distinctly, convinced that they really were clearer than these other objects now being shown to him?

Yes.

And suppose someone were to drag him away forcibly up the steep and rugged ascent and not let him go until he had hauled him out into the sunlight, would he not suffer pain and vexation at such treatment, and, when he had come out into the light, find his eyes so full of its radiance that he could not see a single one of the things that he was now told were real?

Certainly he would not see them all at once.

He would need, then, to grow accustomed before he could see things in that upper world.[3] At first it would be easiest to make out shadows, and then the images of men and things reflected in

---

[1] The state of mind called *eikasia* in the previous chapter.

[2] The first effect of Socratic questioning is perplexity. Cf. p. 8.

[3] Here is the moral—the need of habituation by mathematical study before discussing moral ideas and ascending through them to the Form of the Good.

water, and later on the things themselves. After that, it would be easier to watch the heavenly bodies and the sky itself by night, looking at the light of the moon and stars rather than the Sun and the Sun's light in the day-time.

Yes, surely.

Last of all, he would be able to look at the Sun and contemplate its nature, not as it appears when reflected in water or any alien medium, but as it is in itself in its own domain.

No doubt.

And now he would begin to draw the conclusion that it is the Sun that produces the seasons and the course of the year and controls everything in the visible world, and moreover is in a way the cause of all that he and his companions used to see.

Clearly he would come at last to that conclusion.

Then if he called to mind his fellow prisoners and what passed for wisdom in his former dwelling-place, he would surely think himself happy in the change and be sorry for them. They may have had a practice of honouring and commending one another, with prizes for the man who had the keenest eye for the passing shadows and the best memory for the order in which they followed or accompanied one another, so that he could make a good guess as to which was going to come next.[1] Would our released prisoner be likely to covet those prizes or to envy the men exalted to honour and power in the Cave? Would he not feel like Homer's Achilles, that he would far sooner 'be on earth as a hired servant in the house of a landless man'[2] or endure anything rather than go back to his old beliefs and live in the old way?

Yes, he would prefer any fate to such a life.

Now imagine what would happen if he went down again to take his former seat in the Cave. Coming suddenly out of the sunlight, his eyes would be filled with darkness. He might be required once more to deliver his opinion on those shadows, in com-

---

[1] The empirical politician, with no philosophic insight, but only a 'knack of remembering what usually happens' (*Gorg.* 501 A). He has *eikasia* = conjecture as to what is likely (*eikos*).

[2] This verse (already quoted at 386 c, p. 76), being spoken by the ghost of Achilles, suggests that the Cave is comparable with Hades.

petition with the prisoners who had never been released, while his eyesight was still dim and unsteady; and it might take some time to become used to the darkness. They would laugh at him and say that he had gone up only to come back with his sight ruined; it was worth no one's while even to attempt the ascent. If they could lay hands on the man who was trying to set them free and lead them up, they would kill him.[1]

Yes, they would.

Every feature in this parable, my dear Glaucon, is meant to fit our earlier analysis. The prison dwelling corresponds to the region revealed to us through the sense of sight, and the fire-light within it to the power of the Sun. The ascent to see the things in the upper world you may take as standing for the upward journey of the soul into the region of the intelligible; then you will be in possession of what I surmise, since that is what you wish to be told. Heaven knows whether it is true; but this, at any rate, is how it appears to me. In the world of knowledge, the last thing to be perceived and only with great difficulty is the essential Form of Goodness. Once it is perceived, the conclusion must follow that, for all things, this is the cause of whatever is right and good; in the visible world it gives birth to light and to the lord of light, while it is itself sovereign in the intelligible world and the parent of intelligence and truth. Without having had a vision of this Form no one can act with wisdom, either in his own life or in matters of state.

So far as I can understand, I share your belief.

Then you may also agree that it is no wonder if those who have reached this height are reluctant to manage the affairs of men. Their souls long to spend all their time in that upper world—naturally enough, if here once more our parable holds true. Nor, again, is it at all strange that one who comes from the contemplation of divine things to the miseries of human life should appear awkward and ridiculous when, with eyes still dazed and not yet accustomed to the darkness, he is compelled, in a law-court or else-

---

[1] An allusion to the fate of Socrates.

where, to dispute about the shadows of justice or the images that cast those shadows, and to wrangle over the notions of what is right in the minds of men who have never beheld Justice itself.[1]

It is not at all strange.

No; a sensible man will remember that the eyes may be confused in two ways—by a change from light to darkness or from darkness to light; and he will recognize that the same thing happens to the soul. When he sees it troubled and unable to discern anything clearly, instead of laughing thoughtlessly, he will ask whether, coming from a brighter existence, its unaccustomed vision is obscured by the darkness, in which case he will think its condition enviable and its life a happy one; or whether, emerging from the depths of ignorance, it is dazzled by excess of light. If so, he will rather feel sorry for it; or, if he were inclined to laugh, that would be less ridiculous than to laugh at the soul which has come down from the light.

That is a fair statement.

If this is true, then, we must conclude that education is not what it is said to be by some, who profess to put knowledge into a soul which does not possess it, as if they could put sight into blind eyes. On the contrary, our own account signifies that the soul of every man does possess the power of learning the truth and the organ to see it with; and that, just as one might have to turn the whole body round in order that the eye should see light instead of darkness, so the entire soul must be turned away from this changing world, until its eye can bear to contemplate reality and that supreme splendour which we have called the Good. Hence there may well be an art whose aim would be to effect this very thing, the conversion of the soul, in the readiest way; not to put the power of sight into the soul's eye, which already has it, but to ensure that, instead of looking in the wrong direction, it is turned the way it ought to be.

Yes, it may well be so.

It looks, then, as though wisdom were different from those ordinary virtues, as they are called, which are not far removed from

---

[1] In the *Gorgias* 486 A, Callicles, forecasting the trial of Socrates, taunts him with the philosopher's inability to defend himself in a court.

bodily qualities, in that they can be produced by habituation and exercise in a soul which has not possessed them from the first. Wisdom, it seems, is certainly the virtue of some diviner faculty, which never loses its power, though its use for good or harm depends on the direction towards which it is turned. You must have noticed in dishonest men with a reputation for sagacity the shrewd glance of a narrow intelligence piercing the objects to which it is directed. There is nothing wrong with their power of vision, but it has been forced into the service of evil, so that the keener its sight, the more harm it works.

Quite true.

And yet if the growth of a nature like this had been pruned from earliest childhood, cleared of those clinging overgrowths which come of gluttony and all luxurious pleasure and, like leaden weights charged with affinity to this mortal world, hang upon the soul, bending its vision downwards; if, freed from these, the soul were turned round towards true reality, then this same power in these very men would see the truth as keenly as the objects it is turned to now.

Yes, very likely.

Is it not also likely, or indeed certain after what has been said, that a state can never be properly governed either by the uneducated who know nothing of truth or by men who are allowed to spend all their days in the pursuit of culture? The ignorant have no single mark before their eyes at which they must aim in all the conduct of their own lives and of affairs of state; and the others will not engage in action if they can help it, dreaming that, while still alive, they have been translated to the Islands of the Blest.

Quite true.

It is for us, then, as founders of a commonwealth, to bring compulsion to bear on the noblest natures. They must be made to climb the ascent to the vision of Goodness, which we called the highest object of knowledge; and, when they have looked upon it long enough, they must not be allowed, as they now are, to remain on the heights, refusing to come down again to the prisoners or to take any part in their labours and rewards, however much or little these may be worth.

Shall we not be doing them an injustice, if we force on them a worse life than they might have?

You have forgotten again, my friend, that the law is not concerned to make any one class specially happy, but to ensure the welfare of the commonwealth as a whole. By persuasion or constraint it will unite the citizens in harmony, making them share whatever benefits each class can contribute to the common good; and its purpose in forming men of that spirit was not that each should be left to go his own way, but that they should be instrumental in binding the community into one.

True, I had forgotten.

You will see, then, Glaucon, that there will be no real injustice in compelling our philosophers to watch over and care for the other citizens. We can fairly tell them that their compeers in other states may quite reasonably refuse to collaborate: there they have sprung up, like a self-sown plant, in despite of their country's institutions; no one has fostered their growth, and they cannot be expected to show gratitude for a care they have never received. 'But,' we shall say, 'it is not so with you. We have brought you into existence for your country's sake as well as for your own, to be like leaders and king-bees in a hive; you have been better and more thoroughly educated than those others and hence you are more capable of playing your part both as men of thought and as men of action. You must go down, then, each in his turn, to live with the rest and let your eyes grow accustomed to the darkness. You will then see a thousand times better than those who live there always; you will recognize every image for what it is and know what it represents, because you have seen justice, beauty, and goodness in their reality; and so you and we shall find life in our commonwealth no mere dream, as it is in most existing states, where men live fighting one another about shadows and quarrelling for power, as if that were a great prize; whereas in truth government can be at its best and free from dissension only where the destined rulers are least desirous of holding office.'

Quite true.

Then will our pupils refuse to listen and to take their turns at sharing in the work of the community, though they may live together for most of their time in a purer air?

No; it is a fair demand, and they are fair-minded men. No doubt, unlike any ruler of the present day, they will think of holding power as an unavoidable necessity.

Yes, my friend; for the truth is that you can have a well-governed society only if you can discover for your future rulers a better way of life than being in office; then only will power be in the hands of men who are rich, not in gold, but in the wealth that brings happiness, a good and wise life. All goes wrong when, starved for lack of anything good in their own lives, men turn to public affairs hoping to snatch from thence the happiness they hunger for. They set about fighting for power, and this internecine conflict ruins them and their country.[1] The life of true philosophy is the only one that looks down upon offices of state; and access to power must be confined to men who are not in love with it; otherwise rivals will start fighting. So whom else can you compel to undertake the guardianship of the commonwealth, if not those who, besides understanding best the principles of government, enjoy a nobler life than the politician's and look for rewards of a different kind?

There is indeed no other choice.

CHAPTER XXVI (VII. 521 c–531 c)

HIGHER EDUCATION. MATHEMATICS

The Pythagorean Archytas, Plato's contemporary, enumerates as sister subjects (mathemata) *geometry, arithmetic, astronomy, and music. Plato adopts these four, adding solid geometry. These sciences are here described and criticized with respect to their*

---

[1] Aristotle, *Politics* iii. 6: 'Nowadays men seek to be always in office for the sake of the advantages to be gained from office and from the public revenues.' Thucydides, iii. 82 (on the revolution at Corcyra): 'The cause of all these things was the pursuit of office for motives of greed and ambition.'

power of turning the soul's eye from the material world to objects
of pure thought. They are the only disciplines recognized by Plato
as sciences in the proper sense, yielding a priori *certain knowledge*
of immutable and eternal objects and truths. For him there could
be no 'natural science,' no exact knowledge of perishable and ever-
changing sensible things. The modern technique of seeking laws of
phenomena in the sensible world by observation and experiment
was unknown to the ancients. Knowledge, Plato thought, was to be
found, not by starting from 'facts' observed by the senses, framing
tentative generalizations, and then returning to the facts for con-
firmation, but by turning away and escaping as fast as possible
from all sensible appearances. Mathematical knowledge might be
even better achieved by a disembodied soul which had no sensible
experience. Information about the facts or events of human or
natural history was not knowledge in the strict sense.

The introductory section describes a feature of sensible experience
which stimulates reflection on objects of pure thought, like num-
bers and Forms. This is the confused perception of two contrary
qualities (e.g. big and small, light and heavy) coexisting in the
same thing, which may be at once big or heavy as compared with
one thing and small or light as compared with another. Such prop-
erties are not conceived as relations between *things, but as inherent*
qualities: the same thing partakes of two distinct Forms, Bigness
itself and Smallness itself. These Forms are absolute and unmixed:
Bigness itself is not small, nor Smallness big; nor can either change
and become its own opposite, whereas a small thing can become
big. When we have learnt to think about Bigness and Smallness
themselves, and to ask what they are, we are dealing with intel-
ligible objects and have left sensible things behind.

SHALL we next consider how men of this quality are to be produced
and how they may be led upward to the light, as some are fabled
to have ascended from the underworld to the gods?

By all means.

It is a question of 'night or day,' to be determined not, as in the

children's game,[1] by spinning a shell, but by the turning about of
the soul from a day that is like night to the veritable day, that
journey up to the real world which we shall call the true pursuit
of wisdom. We have to ask what studies will have this effect.

Yes.

What form of study is there, Glaucon, that would draw the soul
from the world of change to reality? At this moment it occurs to
me that our young men were to be trained warriors; so the study
we are looking for ought to be not without use in warfare as well.

Yes, if possible.

Now, of the two branches of their earlier education, physical
training is certainly concerned with perishable things, for bodily
strength grows and decays. So this cannot be the study we are in
search of. Can it be education in poetry and music carried to the
point we laid down earlier?

No, he replied; that, if you remember, was the counterpart of
bodily training. It educated our Guardians by the influence of
habit, imparting no real knowledge, but only a kind of measure
and harmony by means of melody and rhythm, and forming the
character in similar ways through the content of the literature,
fabulous or true. It taught nothing useful for so high a purpose
as you now have in view.

Quite true; your memory is very exact. But where shall we find
what we want? The manual crafts, we agreed, were all rather degrading.

Yes, of course. But if you exclude them as well as all that early
education, what is there left to study?

Well, if we cannot find anything over and above these subjects,
suppose we take something that has a bearing upon them all. There
is one, for instance, which is universally useful in all crafts and
in every form of knowledge and intellectual operation—the first
thing everyone has to learn.

What do you mean?

[1] The players formed two groups. A shell, black on one side and white on the
other, was thrown between them by a boy who cried 'Night or day.' According as
white or black came up, one side ran away, the other gave chase.

A simple matter: learning to tell the difference between one, two, and three, or, to put it shortly, number and calculation. Is it not true that this is something which no art or science can dispense with?

Certainly.

Including the art of war. On the stage, at any rate, Agamemnon is made to look a very ridiculous sort of general. You must remember how often the tragedians make Palamedes claim to have invented number and by that means to have marshalled the ranks of the army at Troy and counted the ships and everything. Apparently nothing could be counted before, and Agamemnon could not even tell how many feet he had—an odd kind of general, don't you think?

Very odd, if that is really true.

So we may conclude that a soldier must know how to count and calculate?

He must, or he could not be a human being at all, to say nothing of marshalling an army.[1]

Does it strike you, then, that this study is one of those we are looking for, which naturally awaken the power of thought, though no one makes a right use of its tendency to draw us towards reality?

How do you mean?

I will try to explain how I distinguish in my own mind the things which have that tendency. If you will consider them too and say whether or not you agree, we shall see if I am right in my surmise.

Please explain.

Take our perceptions, then. I can point to some of these which do not provoke thought to reflect upon them, because we are satisfied with the judgement of the senses. But in other cases percep-

---

[1] Plato rejects the traditional belief that numbers (or language, writing, and other arts) were invented by some 'culture-hero' like Palamedes or Prometheus. He thought that 'the sight of day and night, of months and the revolving years, of equinox and solstice, has caused the invention of number and bestowed on us the notion of time and the study of the nature of the world, whence we have derived all philosophy,' *Timaeus,* 47 A.

tion seems to yield no trustworthy result, and reflection is instantly demanded.

You mean objects seen from a great distance, or illusory effects in scene-painting.

No, you have not understood me. I mean that reflection is provoked when perception yields a contradictory impression, presenting two opposite qualities with equal clearness, no matter whether the object be distant or close at hand. When there is no such contradiction, we are not encouraged to reflect. Let me illustrate what I mean. Here are three fingers, the middle finger, the third, and the little one. I am assuming that you have a close view of them. The point is this. Each one of them presents itself equally as a finger, and in this respect it makes no difference whether we see it at either end of the row or in the middle, as fair or dark, thick or thin, and so on. In any case we see it as a finger, and the ordinary mind is not driven to call in its power of reflection and ask for a definition of 'finger,' because at no stage has the sense of sight intimated that the finger is at the same moment the opposite of a finger. So an impression of this kind naturally has no tendency to arouse reflection.

Naturally.

But now take the size of these fingers. Can sight satisfactorily distinguish their bigness and smallness, and does it make no difference whether any particular one of them is at the end of the row or in between? [1] Or can touch discriminate between thick and thin or hard and soft? In reporting on qualities like these all the senses are deficient. They seem to work in this way. The sense which takes cognizance of hardness must also take cognizance of softness, and it reports to the mind that it feels the same thing as both hard and soft.

That is true.

In such cases, then, the mind must be at a loss to know what this sensation means by hard, since it declares the same thing to be also soft; or what sensations of lightness and heaviness mean

[1] We might call the middle finger big, the little finger small; but the third finger, between them, looks small as compared with the middle finger and big as compared with the little one.

by light and heavy, if they intimate that what is light is heavy and what is heavy is light.

Yes; these reports strike the mind as paradoxical and they do call for reflection.

So it is natural in these circumstances for the mind to invoke the help of reason with its power of calculation,[1] to consider whether any given message it receives refers to a single thing or two. If there appear to be two things, each of them will appear as one thing, distinct from the other; and accordingly, each being one and both together making two, the mind will conceive them as separate; otherwise it would think of them not as two, but as one.

Quite so.

Now sight, too, as we said, perceives both big and little; only not as separate, but in a confused impression. In order to clear up this confusion, intelligence was driven to look at bigness and smallness in the opposite way, as distinct things. It is some such experience as this that first prompts us to ask what is meant by bigness or smallness. And that is how we came to distinguish what we call the object of intelligence from the thing seen.

Exactly.

Well then, that is the distinction I was trying to express just now, when I defined as provocative of thought impressions of sense in which opposites are combined; whereas, if there is no contradictory impression, there is nothing to awaken reflection.

I understand now and I agree.

§ 1 (524 D–526 C). ARITHMETIC

The Greeks distinguished the art of calculating or doing sums (logistic) *from the theory of number* (arithmetic). *Calculation, dealing with collections of tangible things which can be counted, added together, divided, &c., is useful in the vulgar sense to the soldier and for other practical purposes. In the earliest education*

---

[1] *Logismos,* like 'calculation' or 'reckoning,' can mean either the operations of arithmetic (*logistikē*) or the activity of the rational element (*logistikon*) in the soul.

of children kindergarten methods are recommended at Laws 819 B: *they will divide up apples, arrange competitors in byes and pairs, &c. But the true utility lies in the escape from reckoning with material objects to the study of pure numbers in Arithmetic. A number was defined as a plurality of units, and the mathematical unit was held to be essentially indivisible, unlike a material thing, which is both one and also many, as being indefinitely divisible into parts. Fractions, such as* ⅓ *or* ¾, *were interpreted as standing for one out of a collection of three units or three out of a collection of four, and so on, not as parts of the unit.*

Now what about unity and number? To which of those two classes do they belong?

I cannot be sure.

What we have just said should help you to a conclusion. If unity can be satisfactorily apprehended, just by itself, by sight or any other sense, as we said of the finger, then it will not have the quality of drawing the mind towards reality. But if it is always seen in some contradictory combination, so as to appear no more one than the opposite of one, then a judge will be needed to decide; the mind will be forced to seek a way out of the difficulty, setting thought in motion and asking what unity means. In this way the study of unity would be one of those which convert the soul and lead it to the contemplation of reality.

Well, unity is a case in which sight certainly does present a contradiction. We see the same thing as both one and also indefinitely many.

Then if that is true of unity, all number has the same property, hasn't it?

Yes.

Well now, number is the subject of the whole art of calculation and of the science of number; and since the properties of number appear to have the power of leading us towards reality, these must be among the studies we are in search of. The soldier must learn them in order to marshal his troops; the philosopher, because he must rise above the world of change and grasp true being, or he will never become proficient in the calculations of reason.[1] Our Guardian is both soldier and philosopher; so this will be a suitable study for our law to prescribe. Those who are to take part in the highest functions of state must be induced to approach it, not in an amateur spirit, but perseveringly, until, by the aid of pure thought, they come to see the real nature of number. They are to practise calculation, not like merchants or shopkeepers for purposes of buying and selling, but with a view to war and to help in the conversion of the soul itself from the world of becoming to truth and reality.

Excellent.

Moreover, talking of this study, it occurs to me now what a fine thing it is and in how many ways it will further our intentions, if it is pursued for the sake of knowledge and not for commercial ends. As we were saying, it has a great power of leading the mind upwards and forcing it to reason about pure numbers, refusing to discuss collections of material things which can be seen and touched. Good mathematicians, as of course you know, scornfully reject any attempt to cut up the unit itself into parts: if you try to break it up small, they will multiply it up again, taking good care that the unit shall never lose its oneness and appear as a multitude of parts.

Quite true.

And if they are asked what are these numbers they are talking about, in which every unit, as they claim, is exactly equal to every other and contains no parts, what would be their answer?

This, I should say: that the numbers they mean can only be conceived by thought: there is no other way of dealing with them.

You see, then, that this study is really indispensable for our purpose, since it forces the mind to arrive at pure truth by the exercise of pure thought.

Yes, it has a powerful effect of that kind.

Have you noticed, too, how people with a talent for calculation are naturally quick at learning almost any other subject; and how

[1] Plato plays on the double sense of 'becoming *logistikos*': 'arithmetician' and 'rational.'

a training in it makes a slow mind quicker, even if it does no other good?

That is true.

Also, it would not be easy to find many branches of study which require more effort from the learner. For all these reasons we cannot do without this form of training for the most gifted natures.

I agree.

§ 2 (526 C–527 C). GEOMETRY

Once more Plato emphasizes the eternal and unchanging character of mathematical objects, though mathematicians talk of 'processes' and 'operations.' Heath (Gk. Maths. i, 287) accepts Plutarch's story that Plato blamed Eudoxus, Archytas, and Menaechmus for trying to reduce the duplication of the cube to mechanical constructions by means of instruments, because 'the good of geometry is thereby lost and destroyed, as it is brought back to things of sense instead of being directed upward and grasping at eternal and incorporeal things' (Qu. Conv. 718 F). Proclus (on Euclid i, p. 77 Friedlein) records a difference of opinion among mathematicians at the Academy about the distinction between problems and theorems. Speusippus and Amphinomus held that all propositions should be called theorems because 'there is no becoming in things eternal,' whereas the problem 'promises the generation and making of what has not before existed, e.g. the construction of an equilateral triangle.'

It is settled, then, that arithmetic is to be one of our subjects. Have we any use for the one that comes next?

You mean geometry?

I do.

Obviously, so much of it as bears on warlike operations will concern us. For pitching a camp, occupying a position, closing up or deploying troops, and for other formations in battle or on the march, a knowledge of geometry will be an advantage.

But still, I replied, for such purposes a small amount of geometry and arithmetic will be enough. We have to ask whether a much more advanced study will help towards a comprehension of the essential Form of Goodness. Any study, as we said, will have that tendency, if it forces the soul to turn towards the region of that beatific reality, which it must by all means behold. So geometry will be suitable or not, according as it makes us contemplate reality or the world of change.

That is our view.

In this respect, then, no one who has even a slight acquaintance with geometry will deny that the nature of this science is in flat contradiction with the absurd language used by mathematicians, for want of better terms. They constantly talk of 'operations' like 'squaring,' 'applying,' 'adding,' and so on, as if the object were to *do* something, whereas the true purpose of the whole subject is knowledge—knowledge, moreover, of what eternally exists, not of anything that comes to be this or that at some time and ceases to be.

Yes, that will be readily agreed: geometry is knowledge of the eternally existent.

If so, it will tend to draw the soul towards truth and to direct upwards the philosophic intelligence which is now wrongly turned earthwards.

There is no doubt about that.

Then there can be no doubt that geometry must by no means be neglected by the citizens of your Callipolis.[1] It has incidental advantages, too, which are not to be despised. There are its uses in war, which you mentioned; and also we know that a training in geometry makes all the difference in preparing the mind for any kind of study.

It does indeed.

Then we will make this the second subject of study for our young men.

We will.

§ 3 (527 D–528 E). SOLID GEOMETRY

After proposing to take astronomy next, Socrates retracts and inserts solid geometry as an independent subject which should logically fill the gap between plane geometry and the study of solid bodies in motion. Plato indicates that stereometry was in a very

[1] Callipolis, 'Fair City,' was the name of more than one Greek city.

undeveloped state at the dramatic date of the Republic. *It was substantially advanced by Theaetetus and others at the Academy, where, he hints, a competent director of further research was to be found.*

Shall we put astronomy third? Do you agree?

Certainly I do. It is important for military purposes, no less than for agriculture and navigation, to be able to tell accurately the times of the month or year.

I am amused by your evident fear that the public will think you are recommending useless knowledge. True, it is quite hard to realize that every soul possesses an organ better worth saving than a thousand eyes, because it is our only means of seeing the truth; and that when its light is dimmed or extinguished by other interests, these studies will purify the hearth and rekindle the sacred fire.[1] Those who believe in this faculty will approve of your proposals without reserve; all who are unaware of its existence will of course think them nonsense, because they can see in such knowledge no ulterior profit worth mentioning. So you had better decide at once which party you mean to reason with. Or you may ignore both and carry on the discussion chiefly for your own satisfaction, though anyone who can benefit by it may be welcome to do so.

I would rather go on with the conversation for my own sake in the main.

Well then, we must retrace our steps. We made a mistake just now about the subject that comes next after geometry. From plane geometry we went straight on to the study of solid bodies in circular motion. We ought first to take solid bodies in themselves; for the third dimension should come after the second, and that brings us to the cube and all the figures which have depth.

That is so. But this subject, Socrates, seems not to have been investigated.

There are two reasons for that. These inquiries, difficult as they

---

[1] When the Greeks purified the sacred places polluted by the Persian invaders, they put out all the fires in the country and had them relit from the sacred hearth at Delphi. Plato, it must be remembered, held that the eye contains the fire which forms the visual ray (p. 219, above).

are, languish because no state thinks them worth encouraging. Secondly, students are not likely to make discoveries without a director, who is hard to find, and supposing him found, as matters now stand,[1] the men with a gift for these researches would be too proud to accept his guidance. They would be amenable only if a whole community were to conceive a respect for such work and give a director its support. The problems might then be solved by continuous and energetic investigation. Even now, despised as the subject is by the public and curtailed by students who do not take account of its true utility, in spite of everything it is gaining ground, thanks to its inherent charm; and it would not be surprising if inquiry should succeed in bringing the truth to light.

Yes, he agreed, it has a remarkable charm. But please explain further. Just now you spoke of geometry as the study of plane surfaces, and you put astronomy next. But then you went back on that.

Yes, I was in too great a hurry to cover all the ground; more haste less speed. The study of solids should have come next; I passed it over because it is in such a pitiable state, and went on to astronomy, which studies the motion of solid bodies.

True.

§ 4 (528 E–530 C). ASTRONOMY

Astronomy is treated as a branch of pure mathematics. Some Pythagoreans called it 'Sphaerics,' since it dealt with the motions of the heavenly bodies considered as perfect spheres moving in perfect circles: there was no question of physical forces causing the movements. Plato's approach is similar. The stars as material objects are parts of the visible world and share in its imperfection. Their motions must show accidental irregularities and variations. No two days or months can be exactly of the same length. Gazing at the stars and trying (with no instruments of precision) to measure the periods of planetary revolutions will bring us no nearer to exact knowledge. The visible heavens will serve only as an orrery.

---

[1] Heath, *Gk. Math.* I, 12, points out the ambiguity of these words. Besides the obvious sense, they might mean that the director who was not to be found at the dramatic date of the *Republic* is to be found now, at the time of writing, in Plato himself or one of his colleagues at the Academy.

In any case, Plato's primary purpose here is not to advance physical science, but to train the mind to think abstractly. On the other hand, he seems to be feeling after a pure mathematical science of motion, much wider than astronomy and equal in exactness to geometry. But the laws of motion were not discovered in antiquity. The first steps towards a science of mechanics were taken by his contemporary Archytas, but seem to have been limited to attempts to explain mathematically the surprising powers of a few very simple machines, like the lever or the capstan.

Then let us put astronomy fourth, assuming the subject now neglected to have been established, provided that the state will take it up.

That may well happen. And now, Socrates, I will praise astronomy on your own principles, instead of commending its usefulness in the vulgar spirit for which you upbraided me. Anyone can see that this subject forces the mind to look upwards, away from this world of ours to higher things.

Anyone except me, perhaps, I replied. I do not agree.

Why not?

As it is now handled by those who are trying to lead us up to philosophy, I think it simply turns the mind's eye downwards.

What do you mean?

You put a too generous construction on the study of 'higher things.' Apparently you would think a man who threw his head back to contemplate the decorations on a ceiling was using his reason, not his eyes, to gain knowledge. Perhaps you are right and my notion is foolish; but I cannot think of any study as making the mind look upwards, except one which has to do with unseen reality. No one, I should say, can ever gain knowledge of any sensible object by gaping upwards any more than by shutting his eyes and searching for it on the ground, because there can be no knowledge of sensible things. His mind will be looking downwards, though he may pursue his studies lying on his back or floating on the sea.

I deserve to be rebuked, he answered. But how did you mean

the study of astronomy to be reformed, so as to serve our purposes?

In this way. These intricate traceries in the sky are, no doubt, the loveliest and most perfect of material things, but still part of the visible world, and therefore they fall far short of the true realities—the real relative velocities, in the world of pure number and all perfect geometrical figures, of the movements which carry round the bodies involved in them.[1] These, you will agree, can be conceived by reason and thought, not seen by the eye.

Exactly.

Accordingly, we must use the embroidered heaven as a model to illustrate our study of those realities, just as one might use diagrams exquisitely drawn by some consummate artist like Daedalus. An expert in geometry, meeting with such designs, would admire their finished workmanship, but he would think it absurd to study them in all earnest with the expectation of finding in their proportions the exact ratio of any one number to another.

Of course it would be absurd.

The genuine astronomer, then, will look at the motions of the stars with the same feelings. He will admit that the sky with all that it contains has been framed by its artificer with the highest perfection of which such works are capable. But when it comes to the proportions of day to night, of day and night to month, of month to year, and of the periods of other stars to Sun and Moon and to one another, he will think it absurd to believe that these visible material things go on for ever without change or the slightest deviation, and to spend all his pains on trying to find exact truth in them.

Now you say so, I agree.

If we mean, then, to turn the soul's native intelligence to its proper use by a genuine study of astronomy, we shall proceed, as

---

[1] At *Gorgias* 451 c Socrates defines astronomy as concerned with 'the relative speeds of the motions of the sun, moon, and stars.' Here he explains that, if the science is to serve our present purpose, the mathematician must get beyond observation to the ideal (i.e. 'real') abstract relations of velocities exactly expressed in numbers, and to perfect figures, such as the circle, which will never be traced with absolute exactness by the actual movement of any star.

we do in geometry, by means of problems, and leave the starry heavens alone.

That will make the astronomer's labour many times greater than it is now.

Yes; and if we are to be of any use as lawgivers, the other tasks we set will be no less burdensome.

§ 5 (530 C–531 C). HARMONICS

Harmonics is treated on the same principle as astronomy. The Pythagoreans (probably Pythagoras himself) had discovered that the perfect consonances of the musical scale (harmonia) could be exactly expressed by ratios: the octave being 2 : 1, the fifth 3 : 2, the fourth 4 : 3. The discovery would be made by measuring, on a monochord with a movable bridge, the lengths of string required to yield the various notes. Plato apparently wishes to extend the science beyond the consonances exemplified in a few agreeable combinations of sounds within the accidental range of our hearing to a general theory of 'consonant numbers.'

And now, I went on, have you any further suitable study to suggest?

Not at the moment.

Yet there is more than one variety of motion, I fancy. An expert would be able to name them all; but even people like us can distinguish two.

What are they?

Besides the motion studied in astronomy, there is its counterpart, the harmonious movement for which our ears are framed, as our eyes are for the study of the stars. These are sister sciences, so the Pythagoreans say, and we may agree with them. This is a large subject and we will ask what they have to tell us about it, and perhaps about some other questions. Only we must constantly hold by our own principle, not to let our pupils take up any study in an imperfect form, stopping short of that higher region to which all studies should attain, as we said just now in speaking of astronomy. As you will know, the students of harmony make the same sort of mistake as the astronomers: they waste their time in measuring audible concords and sounds one against another.

Yes, said Glaucon, they are absurd enough, with their talk of 'groups of quarter-tones' and all the rest of it. They lay their ears to the instrument as if they were trying to overhear the conversation from next door. One says he can still detect a note in between, giving the smallest possible interval, which ought to be taken as the unit of measurement, while another insists that there is now no difference between the two notes. Both prefer their ears to their intelligence.

You are thinking of those worthy musicians who tease and torture the strings, racking them on the pegs.[1] I will not push the metaphor so far as to picture the musician beating them with the plectrum and charging them with faults which the strings deny or brazen out. I will drop the comparison and tell you that I am thinking rather of those Pythagoreans whom we were going to consult about harmony. They are just like the astronomers—intent upon the numerical properties embodied in these audible consonances: they do not rise to the level of formulating problems and inquiring which numbers are inherently consonant and which are not, and for what reasons.

That sounds like a superhuman undertaking.

I would rather call it a 'useful' study; but useful only when pursued as a means to the knowledge of beauty and goodness.

No doubt.

CHAPTER XXVII (VII. 531 C–535 A)

DIALECTIC

After a ten-years' training in mathematics the philosophers are to be exercised from the age of 30 to 35 in Dialectic. The brief description given in Chapter XXIV (the Line) is now expanded in

[1] In order to extort from them a confession of *the truth*. Greek law allowed the torture of slaves for this purpose at trials.

*terms of the imagery of the Cave. Mathematics will drag the pris-
oner out of the darkness to the point where he can look at the
shadows and reflections of real things, but not yet at the things
themselves or the Sun. The defect of these studies is that the various branches are not seen 'synoptically' as one connected whole*
(531 D, 537 C, pp. 252, 259), *but pursued separately, each starting
from the assumption of its own unquestioned premisses. Thus each
mathematical science is a separate chain of deductive reasoning,
self-consistent but not linked at the upper end to any absolutely
self-evident and unconditional principle. The object of Dialectic,
as applied in this field, is to secure this final confirmation and the
synoptic view of all mathematical knowledge in connexion with the
whole of reality* (533 C, p. 253 f.). *It may be conjectured that Plato
contemplated a possible deduction of all pure mathematics starting
from the concept of Unity, one aspect of the Good. (At* Parmenides
142 D ff. *the existence of the infinite series of numbers is deduced
from the conception of a 'One Being' or 'Existent Unity.')*

*Dialectic is also applicable to the moral Forms, which are more
obviously partial aspects of the Good. Astronomy and Harmonics
have just been represented as useful in so far as they conduce to
a knowledge of beauty and goodness. They lead the mind to contemplate the beautiful and harmonious order manifested in the
visible heavens and in the harmonies of sound (cf.* Timaeus 46 E).
*Since the purpose is the assimilation of the philosopher's soul to this
order* (500 C, p. 208 f.), *harmony has both a physical and a moral
significance and provides a transition to moral philosophy. In this
field the Forms will be studied by the method of question and answer which Plato inherited from Socrates, the respondent putting
forward his 'hypothetical' attempts at definition, the questioner demanding an 'account' of his meaning and subjecting his suggestions
to examination and refutation* (elenchus) *and so leading him on to
amend them. Such a procedure, covering the whole field of moral
conceptions, would ideally lead up to a perfect vision of the nature
of Goodness itself. Plato refuses to give a detailed account of this
method for the same reasons that made him refuse to give a definition of Goodness* (p. 212).

FURTHER, I continued, this whole course of study will, I believe, contribute to the end we desire and not be labour wasted, only if it is carried to the point at which reflection can take a comprehensive view of the mutual relations and affinities which bind all these sciences together.

So I suspect; but it is an enormous task, Socrates.

What do you refer to? The prelude? Do we not know that all this is no more than an introduction to the main theme which has yet to be learnt? Surely you would not regard experts in mathematics as masters of dialectic.

Certainly not, except a very few of those I have met.

Well, can the knowledge we are demanding ever be attained by people who cannot give a rational account of their statements or make others give an account of theirs?

Once more I should say No.

Here at last, then, we come to the main theme, to be developed in philosophic discussion. It falls within the domain of the intelligible world; but its progress is like that of the power of vision in the released prisoner of our parable. When he had reached the stage of trying to look at the living creatures outside the Cave, then at the stars, and lastly at the Sun himself, he arrived at the highest object in the visible world. So here, the summit of the intelligible world is reached in philosophic discussion by one who aspires, through the discourse of reason unaided by any of the senses, to make his way in every case to the essential reality and perseveres until he has grasped by pure intelligence the very nature of Goodness itself. This journey is what we call Dialectic.

Yes, certainly.

There was also that earlier stage when the prisoner, set free from his chains, turned from the shadows to the images which cast them and to the fire-light, and climbed up out of the cavern into the sunshine. When there, he was still unable to look at the animals and plants and the sunlight; he could only see the shadows of things and their reflections in water, though these, it is true, are works of divine creation and come from real things, not mere shadows of images thrown by the light of the fire, which was itself only an image as compared with the Sun. Now the whole course of study in the arts we have reviewed has the corresponding effect of leading up the noblest faculty of the soul towards the contemplation of the highest of all realities, just as in our allegory the bodily organ which has the clearest perceptions was led up towards the brightest of visible things in the material world.

I agree to what you are saying, Glaucon replied; I find it very hard to accept, but in another way no less hard to deny. However, there will be many other opportunities to reconsider it; so let us assume for the moment that it is true, and go on to develop what you call the main theme as fully as we have treated the prelude. I want you to describe the function of philosophic discussion, into what divisions it falls, and what are its methods; for here, it seems, we have come to the procedure which should lead to the resting-place at our journey's end.

My dear Glaucon, said I, you will not be able to follow me farther, though not for want of willingness on my part. It would mean that, instead of illustrating the truth by an allegory, I should be showing you the truth itself, at least as it appears to me. I cannot be sure whether or not I see it as it really is; but we can be sure that there is some such reality which it concerns us to see. Is not that so?

No doubt.

And also that it can be revealed only to one who is trained in the studies we have discussed, and to him only by the power of dialectic?

That also we can assert.

At any rate, no one will maintain against us that there is any other method of inquiry which systematically attempts in every case to grasp the nature of each thing as it is in itself. The other arts are nearly all concerned with human opinions and desires, or with the production of natural and artificial things, or with the care of them when produced. There remain geometry and those other allied studies which, as we said, do in some measure apprehend reality; but we observe that they cannot yield anything clearer than a dream-like vision of the real so long as they leave the assumptions they employ unquestioned and can give no account of them. If your premiss is something you do not really know and your conclusion and the intermediate steps are a tissue of things you do not really know, your reasoning may be consistent with itself, but how can it ever amount to knowledge?

It cannot.

So, said I, the method of dialectic is the only one which takes this course, doing away with assumptions and travelling up to the first principle of all, so as to make sure of confirmation there. When the eye of the soul is sunk in a veritable slough of barbarous ignorance,[1] this method gently draws it forth and guides it upwards, assisted in this work of conversion by the arts we have enumerated. From force of habit we have several times spoken of these as branches of knowledge; but they need some other name implying something less clear than knowledge, though not so dim as the apprehension of appearances. 'Thinking,' I believe, was the term we fixed on earlier; but in considering matters of such high importance we shall not quarrel about a name.

Certainly not.

We shall be satisfied, then, with the names we gave earlier [2] to our four divisions: first, knowledge; second, thinking; third, belief; and fourth, imagining. The last two taken together constitute the apprehension of appearances in the world of Becoming; the first two, intelligence concerned with true Being. Finally, as Being is to Becoming, so is intelligence to the apprehension of appearances; and in the same relation again stand knowledge to belief, and thinking to imagining. We had better not discuss the corresponding objects, the intelligible world and the world of appearance, or the twofold division of each of those provinces and the proportion in which the divisions stand. We might be involved in a discussion many times as long as the one we have already had.

Well, I certainly agree on those other points, so far as I can follow you.[3]

---

[1] This bold metaphor recalls mysteries in which sinners were dramatically represented as plunged in a pool of mud in Hades (363 D, p. 48).

[2] In the diagram of the Line, Chap. XXIV, p. 226.

[3] The above passage seems to describe the special use of dialectical method to criticize and finally confirm the premisses of the mathematical sciences, thus 'doing

And by a master of dialectic do you also mean one who demands an account of the essence of each thing? And would you not say that, in so far as he can render no such account to himself or to others, his intelligence is at fault?

I should.

And does not this apply to the Good? He must be able to distinguish the essential nature of Goodness, isolating it from all other Forms; he must fight his way through all criticisms, determined to examine every step by the standard, not of appearances and opinions, but of reality and truth, and win through to the end without sustaining a fall. If he cannot do this, he will know neither Goodness itself nor any good thing; if he does lay hold upon some semblance of good, it will be only a matter of belief, not of knowledge; and he will dream away his life here in a sleep which has no awakening on this side of that world of Death where he will sleep at last for ever.

I do most earnestly agree with you.

Well then, if you should ever be charged in actual fact with the upbringing and education of these imaginary children of yours, you will not allow them, I suppose, to bear rule in your commonwealth so long as their minds are, as a mathematician might say, irrational quantities, not commensurate with the highest responsibilities.[1] So you will make a law that they must devote themselves especially to the discipline which will make them masters of the technique of asking and answering questions.

Yes, I will, with your collaboration.

May we conclude, then, that our account of the subjects of study is now complete? Dialectic will stand as the coping-stone of the whole structure; there is no other study that deserves to be put above it.

Yes, I agree.

away' with their hypothetical character. Socrates now passes on to the application of dialectic to moral ideas in the highest section of the intelligible realm.

[1] Plato puns on the phrase 'irrational (incommensurable) lines,' commonly illustrated by the diagonal and side of the square.

CHAPTER XXVIII (VII. 535 A–541 B)

The whole course of education has now been traced. It remains to fix the age for entering on each successive stage.

(1) Up to 17 or 18, the early training in literature and music and in elementary mathematics will be carried on with as little compulsion as possible. (2) From 17 or 18 to 20, an intensive course of physical and military training will leave no leisure for study. (3) From 20 to 30, a select few will go through the advanced course in mathematics outlined in Chapter XXVI, with a view to grasping the connexions between the several branches of mathematics and their relation to reality. (4) After a further selection, the years from 30 to 35 will be given wholly to Dialectic, and especially to the ultimate principles of morality. Plato once more insists on the danger of a too early questioning of these principles. (5) From 35 to 50, practical experience of life will be gained by public service in subordinate posts. (6) At 50 the best will reach the vision of the Good and thereafter divide their time between study and governing the state as the supreme council.

The question, asked at the beginning of this Part, how, if ever, the ideal state might come into being, is now answered. It can exist, if the philosophic statesman can be produced and educated and given a free hand to remould society.

It only remains, then, to draw up a scheme showing how, and to whom, these studies are to be allotted.

Clearly.

You remember what sort of people we chose earlier to be Rulers? [1]

Of course I do.

In most respects, then, natures of that quality are to be selected:

[1] 412 B ff., p. 103 f.

we shall prefer the steadiest, the bravest, and, so far as possible, the handsomest persons. But, besides that, we must look not only for generous and virile characters, but for gifts fitting them for this sort of education. They must be eager students and learn with ease, because the mind is more apt to shrink from severe study than from hard physical exercise, in which part of the burden falls upon the body. Also we must demand a good memory and a dogged appetite for hard work of every kind. How else can you expect a man to undergo all the hardships of bodily training and, on the top of that, to carry through such a long course of study?

He will certainly need every natural advantage.

At any rate, this explains what is wrong now with the position of Philosophy and why she has fallen into disrepute: as I said before,[1] she ought never to have been wooed by the base-born, who are unworthy of her favours. To begin with, the genuine aspirant should not be one-sided in his love of work, liking one half of it and neglecting the other; as happens with one who throws himself into athletics and hunting and all sorts of bodily exertion, but hates the trouble of learning anything from others or of thinking for himself. His industry goes halting on one foot; and so it does too if it takes the opposite direction.

Quite true.

Also with regard to truth, we shall count as equally crippled a mind which, while it hates deliberate falsehood, cannot bear to tell lies, and is very angry when others do so, yet complacently tolerates involuntary error and is in no way vexed at being caught wallowing in swinish ignorance. We must be no less on the watch to distinguish the base metal from the true in respect of temperance, courage, highmindedness, and every kind of virtue. A state which chooses its rulers, or a man who chooses his friends, without a searching eye for these qualities will find themselves, in respect of one or another of them, cheated by a counterfeit or leaning on a broken reed. So all such precautions are very much our concern. If we can find, for this long course of training and study, men who are at all points sound of limb and sound in mind, then

[1] 495 c, p. 202 f.

Justice herself will have no fault to find with us and we shall en-sure the safety of our commonwealth and its institutions. We should only ruin it by choosing pupils of a different stamp; and moreover we should bring down upon philosophy an even greater storm of ridicule.

That would be a discreditable result.

It would. But at the moment I seem to be inviting ridicule my-self.

In what way?

By speaking with so much warmth and forgetting that these speculations are only an amusement for our leisure. As I spoke, I seemed to see Philosophy suffering undeserved insults, and was so vexed with her persecutors that I lost my temper and became too vehement.

I did not think so as I listened.

No, but I felt it myself. However, here is something we must not forget. When we spoke earlier of selecting Rulers, we said we should choose old men;[1] but that will not do for the selection we are making now. We must not let Solon persuade us that a man can learn many things as he grows old;[2] he could sooner learn to run. Youth is the time for hard work of all sorts.

Undoubtedly.

Arithmetic, then, and geometry and all branches of the prelimi-nary education which is to pave the way for Dialectic should be introduced in childhood; but not in the guise of compulsory in-struction, because for the free man there should be no element of slavery in learning. Enforced exercise does no harm to the body, but enforced learning will not stay in the mind. So avoid com-pulsion, and let your children's lessons take the form of play. This will also help you to see what they are naturally fitted for.

That is a reasonable plan.

You remember, too, our children were to be taken to the wars on horseback to watch the fighting, and, when it was safe, brought close up like young hounds to be given a taste of blood.

I remember.

[1] At 412 c, p. 103.
[2] Solon, frag. 22 (Diehl): 'I go on learning many things as I grow old.'

Then we must make a select list including everyone who shows forwardness in all these studies and exercises and dangers.

At what age?

As soon as they are released from the necessary physical training. This may take two or three years, during which nothing else can be done; for weariness and sleep are unfavourable to study. And at the same time, these exercises will provide not the least important test of character.

No doubt.

When that time is over, then, some of those who are now twenty years old will be selected for higher privileges. The detached studies in which they were educated as children will now be brought together in a comprehensive view of their connexions with one another and with reality.

Certainly that is the only kind of knowledge which takes firm root in the mind.

Yes, and the chief test of a natural gift for Dialectic, which is the same thing as the ability to see the connexions of things.

I agree.

You will keep an eye, then, on these qualities and make a further selection of those who possess them in the highest degree and show most steadfastness in study as well as in warfare and in their other duties. When they reach thirty they will be promoted to still higher privileges and tested by the power of Dialectic, to see which can dispense with sight and the other senses and follow truth into the region of pure reality. And here, my friend, you will need the greatest watchfulness.

Why in particular?

You must have seen how much harm is done now by philosophical discussion—how it infects people with a spirit of lawlessness.

Yes, I have.

Does that surprise you? Can you not make allowances for them? Imagine a child brought up in a rich family with powerful connexions and surrounded by a host of flatterers; and suppose that, when he comes to manhood, he learns that he is not the son of those who call themselves his parents and his true father and mother are not to be found. Can you guess how he would feel towards his supposed parents and towards his flatterers before he knew about his parentage and after learning the truth? Or shall I tell you what I should expect?

Please do.

I should say that, so long as he did not know the truth, he would have more respect for his reputed parents and family than for the flatterers, and be less inclined to neglect them in distress or to be insubordinate in word or deed; and in important matters the flatterers would have less influence with him. But when he learnt the facts, his respect would be transferred to them; their influence would increase, and he would openly associate with them and adopt their standards of behaviour, paying no heed to his reputed father and family, unless his disposition were remarkably good.

Yes; all that would be likely to happen. But how does your illustration apply to people who are beginning to take part in philosophical discussions?

In this way. There are certain beliefs about right and honourable conduct, which we have been brought up from childhood to regard with the same sort of reverent obedience that is shown to parents. In opposition to these, other courses attract us with flattering omises of pleasure; though a moderately good character will resist such blandishments and remain loyal to the beliefs of his fathers. But now suppose him confronted by the question, What does 'honourable' mean? He gives the answer he has been taught by the lawgiver, but he is argued out of his position. He is refuted again and again from many different points of view and at last reduced to thinking that what he called honourable might just as well be called disgraceful. He comes to the same conclusion about justice, goodness, and all the things he most revered. What will become now of his old respect and obedience?

Obviously they cannot continue as before.

And when he has disowned these discredited principles and failed to find the true ones, naturally he can only turn to the life which flatters his desires; and we shall see him renounce all morality and become a lawless rebel. If this is the natural consequence of plunging the young into philosophical discussion, ought we not to make allowances, as I said before?

Yes, and be sorry for them too.

Then, if you do not want to be sorry for those pupils of yours who have reached the age of thirty, you must be very careful how you introduce them to such discussions. One great precaution is to forbid their taking part while they are still young. You must have seen how youngsters, when they get their first taste of it, treat argument as a form of sport solely for purposes of contradiction. When someone has proved them wrong, they copy his methods to confute others, delighting like puppies in tugging and tearing at anyone who comes near them. And so, after a long course of proving others wrong and being proved wrong themselves, they rush to the conclusion that all they once believed is false; and the result is that in the eyes of the world they discredit, not themselves only, but the whole business of philosophy. An older man will not share this craze for making a sport of contradiction. He will prefer to take for his model the conversation of one who is bent on seeking truth, and his own reasonableness will bring credit on the pursuit. We meant to ensure this result by all that we said earlier against the present practice of admitting anybody, however unfit, to philosophic discussions, and about the need for disciplined and steadfast character.

Certainly.

If a man, then, is to devote himself to such discussion as continuously and exclusively as he gave himself up earlier to the corresponding training of his body, will twice as long a time be enough?

Do you mean six years or four?

No matter; let us say five. For after that they must be sent down again into that Cave we spoke of and compelled to take military commands and other offices suitable to the young, so that they may not be behind their fellow citizens in experience. And at this stage they must once more be tested to see whether they will stand firm against all seductions.

How much time do you allow for this?

Fifteen years. Then, when they are fifty, those who have come safely through and proved the best at all points in action and in study must be brought at last to the goal. They must lift up the eye of the soul to gaze on that which sheds light on all things; and when they have seen the Good itself, take it as a pattern for the right ordering of the state and of the individual, themselves included. For the rest of their lives, most of their time will be spent in study; but they will all take their turn at the troublesome duties of public life and act as Rulers for their country's sake, not regarding it as a distinction, but as an unavoidable task. And so, when each generation has educated others like themselves to take their place as Guardians of the commonwealth, they will depart to dwell in the Islands of the Blest. The state will set up monuments for them and sacrifices, honouring them as divinities, if the Pythian Oracle approves, or at least as men blest with a godlike spirit.

That is a fine portrait of our Rulers, Socrates.

Yes, Glaucon, and you must not forget that some of them will be women. All I have been saying applies just as much to any women who are found to have the necessary gifts.

Quite right, if they are to share equally with the men in everything, as we said.

Well then, said I, do you agree that our scheme of a commonwealth and its constitution has not been a mere day-dream? Difficult it may be, but possible, though only on the one condition we laid down, that genuine philosophers—one or more of them—shall come into power in a state; men who will despise all existing honours as mean and worthless, caring only for the right and the honours to be gained from that, and above all for justice as the one indispensable thing in whose service and maintenance they will reorganize their own state.

How will they do that?

They must send out into the country all citizens who are above ten years old, take over the children, away from the present habits and manners of their parents, and bring them up in their own ways under the institutions we have described. Would not that be the quickest and easiest way in which our polity could be established, so as to prosper and be a blessing to any nation in which it might arise?

Yes, certainly; and I think, Socrates, you have satisfactorily explained how, if ever, it might come into being.

Have we now said enough, then, about this commonwealth and also about the corresponding type of man; for it must be clear what sort of person we shall expect him to be?

It is clear; and, to answer your question, I believe our account is complete.

PART IV (Books VIII–IX)

THE DECLINE OF SOCIETY AND OF THE SOUL. COMPARISON OF THE JUST AND UNJUST LIVES

At the outset of Part II Socrates was challenged to set side by side the perfectly just and the perfectly unjust man and to show that, apart from external rewards and reputation, justice is better both for its own sake and for the happiness it brings to its possessor. In Part III he has completed his picture of the ideal state where justice would flourish, and of the ideal man, the philosophic Ruler, whose soul is ordered on an analogous pattern. It remains to describe the ideally evil condition of society and of the individual soul. This is an inverted economy, in which the basest elements of human nature have set up an absolute despotism or 'tyranny' over the higher, the very negation of that principle of justice whereby each element, by doing its proper work, contributes to the well-being of the whole.

As in the earlier part what was really a logical analysis of society was cast into the more vivid form of an historical development, so here, instead of directly confronting the best condition with the worst, Plato imagines a gradual decline through intermediate forms of constitution and types of character, arranged, on psychological grounds, in an order of merit, not in the order in which Greek political society had normally evolved.[1] Each of the constitutions he describes is animated by a certain spirit, the outcome of some tendency in human nature, nowhere existing in pure isolation, but capable of being portrayed as dominant in a corresponding type of individual. Every type is to be found in every society; but where one type prevails in numbers and influence the political constitution will exhibit its characteristic traits on a larger scale.

[1] Barker, however, notes that 'the communes of mediaeval Italy exactly followed Plato's sequence: the oligarchical *commune* either succumbed before the democratic *popolo*, or admitted it to a share in the government; and in either case a division of classes still survived, acute enough to paralyse the State and ultimately introduce a tyranny, open or concealed' (*Greek Political Theory*, 245).

THE FALL OF THE IDEAL STATE. TIMOCRACY AND THE TIMOCRATIC MAN

'*In the infinity of time, past or future*' *the Ideal State may never have existed or be destined to exist* (499 c, p. 207 f.); *but if we suppose it realised, nothing in this world of mortality and change can last for ever. Most students of history would admit that the flow and ebb of collective vitality which accompany the rise and fall of successive forms of culture has not yet been explained. Aware that here is an equally unanswerable question, Plato veils his account in poetical and even mock-heroic language, hinting at some predestined correspondence between the cycle of life in animals and plants and the periodicity of the heavenly bodies. The wisest of Rulers, entrusted with the regulation of marriage and childbirth, may well fail to understand and observe this principle, and then children will be born who are worse than their parents. The decline of society will set in with the outbreak of dissension within the ruling order. This is at all times the cause of revolution.*

The first degenerate form of constitution is called Timocracy, a state in which the ambitious man's love of honour (timé), *the motive of the 'spirited' part, usurps the rule of reason. Plato expressly regards this principle as exemplified in Spartan institutions, from which he had borrowed several features in prescribing the mode of life of his Auxiliaries (Chap. X). But at Sparta private property had nourished the secret growth of avarice, intellect was distrusted, and an exaggerated cult of military efficiency aimed at holding down a population of helots. (Aristotle describes Spartan and Cretan institutions in the* Politics, Bk. ii. Chap. 9-10.) *This type of state might emerge, if Plato's Auxiliaries should begin to oust the philosophic Rulers from supreme control. The history and character of the timocratic individual closely reflect those of the state.*

The argument here goes back to the point, at the beginning of

Chapter XV, where Socrates professed to be 'within sight of the clearest possible proof' of the superiority of the just life to the un-just—the proof which will be given at the end of this Part. The whole of Part III, the central and most important section of the Republic, *is treated as if it were a digression.*

VERY well, I continued. So far, then, Glaucon, we agree that in a state destined to reach the height of good government wives and children must be held in common; men and women must have the same education throughout and share all pursuits, warlike or peaceful; and those who have proved themselves the best both in philosophy and in war are to be kings among them. Further, the Rulers, as soon as they are appointed, will lead the soldiers and settle them in quarters such as we prescribed, common to all, with nothing private about them; and besides these dwellings we agreed, if you remember, how far they should have anything they could call their own.

Yes, I remember we thought they should have no property in the ordinary sense, but, as Guardians in training for war, they should receive as wages from the other citizens enough to keep them for the year while they fulfilled their duty of watching over the community, themselves included.

That is right. But when we had done with those matters, we went off into the digression which has brought us to this point. Let us go back now into our old path. Where did we leave it?

That is easy to remember. You were talking, very much as you are now, as if your description of the state were complete, and telling us that such a constitution and the corresponding type of man were what you would call good; although, as it now appears, you had it in your power to tell of a state and an individual of a still higher quality.[1] But at any rate you said that, if this consti-tution were right, all others must be wrong, mentioning, if I re-member, four varieties as worth considering with an eye to their defects. We were also to look at all the corresponding types of in-dividual character, decide which was the best and which the worst,

---

[1] Plato speaks as if the account of the philosophic ruler had brought out the full merits of the ideal state outlined in the earlier part.

and then consider whether or not the best is also the happiest, the worst the most miserable. I was asking what these four constitutions were, when Polemarchus and Adeimantus interrupted us; and so you entered on the discussion which has brought us to this point.

Your memory is very accurate, I replied.

Let us be like wrestlers, then, who go back to the same grip after an indecisive fall. If I repeat my question, try to give me the answer you were going to make.

I will do my best.

Well, I am just as eager to hear what are the four types of government you meant.

There is no difficulty about that; they are the types which have names in common use. First there is the constitution of Crete and Sparta, which is so commonly admired; second and next in esteem oligarchy, as it is called, a constitution fraught with many evils; next follows its antagonist, democracy; then despotism, which is thought so glorious and goes beyond them all as the fourth and final disease of society. Can you mention any other type of government, I mean any that is obviously a distinct species? There are, of course, types like hereditary monarchy, and states where the highest offices can be bought;[1] but these are rather intermediate forms, to be found quite as frequently outside Greece as within it.

True, one hears of many strange varieties.

Do you see, then, that there must be as many types of human character as there are forms of government? Constitutions cannot come out of stocks and stones; they must result from the preponderance of certain characters which draw the rest of the community in their wake. So if there are five forms of government, there must be five kinds of mental constitution among individuals.

Naturally.

Now we have already described the man whom we regard as in the full sense good and just and who corresponds to aristocracy, the government of the best. We have next to consider the inferior types: the competitive and ambitious temperament, answering to

---

[1] This was so at Carthage, according to Aristotle, *Pol.* 1273 a 36, and Polybius vi. 56, 4. Plato confines himself to Greek institutions.

the Spartan constitution, and then the oligarchic, democratic, and despotic characters, in order that, by setting the extreme examples in contrast, we may finally answer the question how pure justice and pure injustice stand in respect of the happiness or misery they bring, and so decide to pursue the one or the other, according as we listen to Thrasymachus or to the argument we are now developing.

Yes, that is the next thing to be done.

When we were studying moral qualities earlier, we began with the state, because they stood out more clearly there than in the individual. On the same principle we had better now take, in each case, the constitution first, and then, in the light of our results, examine the corresponding character. We shall start with the constitution dominated by motives of ambition—it has no name in common use that I know of; let us call it timarchy or timocracy—and then go on to oligarchy and democracy, and lastly visit a state under despotic government and look into the despot's soul. We ought then to be in a position to decide the question before us.

Yes, such a systematic review should give us the materials for judgement.

Come then, let us try to explain how the government of the best might give place to a timocracy. Is it not a simple fact that in any form of government revolution always starts from the outbreak of internal dissension in the ruling class? The constitution cannot be upset so long as that class is of one mind, however small it may be.[1]

That is true.

Then how, Glaucon, will trouble begin in our commonwealth? How will our Auxiliaries and Rulers come to be divided against each other or among themselves? Shall we, like Homer, invoke the Muses to tell us 'how first division came,' and imagine them amusing themselves at our expense by talking in high-flown language, as one teases a child with a pretence of being in earnest?

What have they to say?

Something of this sort. 'Hard as it may be for a state so framed

---

[1] This principle was asserted earlier at 465 B, p. 166.

to be shaken, yet, since all that comes into being must decay, even a fabric like this will not endure for ever, but will suffer dissolution. In this manner: not only for plants that grow in the earth, but also for all creatures that move thereon, there are seasons of fruitfulness and unfruitfulness for soul and body alike, which come whenever a certain cycle is completed, in a period [1] short or long according to the length of life of each species. For your own race, the rulers you have bred for your commonwealth, wise as they are, will not be able, by observation and reckoning, to hit upon the times propitious or otherwise for birth; some day the moment will slip by and they will beget children out of due season. For the divine creature there is a period embraced by a perfect number; [2] while for the human there is a geometrical number determining the better or worse quality of the births.[3] When your Guardians, from ignorance of this, bring together brides and bridegrooms out of season, their children will not be well-endowed or fortunate. The best of these may be appointed by the elder generation; but when they succeed to their fathers' authority as Guardians, being un-

---

[1] This period has been taken to be the period of gestation, at the end of which the seed of the living creature ('soul and body') either comes successfully to birth or miscarries. Aristotle (*On the Generation of Animals*, iv. 10, 777 b 16) remarks: 'In all animals the time of gestation and development and the length of life aim at being measured by naturally complete periods. By a natural period I mean, e.g. a day and night, a month, a year, and the greater times measured by these, and also the periods (phases) of the moon.'

[2] The 'divine creature' is the visible universe, which is called a 'created god' in the cosmological myth of the *Timaeus*. The perfect number is probably the number of days in a Great Year, which is completed when all the heavenly bodies come back to the same relative positions (*Tim.* 39 D).

[3] The extremely obscure description of this number, which has been variously interpreted, is omitted. Ancient evidence points to some relation between two numbers, both ultimately based on the factors 3, 4, 5, representing the sides of the 'Pythagorean' or 'zoogonic' right-angled triangle. (1) One is $216 = 3^3 + 4^3 + 5^3 = 6^3$. This was called the 'psychogonic cube,' as expressing the number of days in the gestation period of the seven-months' child. The period of the nine-months' child was obtained by adding $60 = 3 \times 4 \times 5$. (2) The other number is $12,960,000 = 3,600^2 = (3 \times 4 \times 5)^4$, the number of days in a Great Year, reckoned as 36,000 solar years of 360 days each. If Plato does describe two numbers, and not (as some hold) the second only, he has not explained how the two should be brought into relation. The serious idea behind this seemingly fanciful passage is the affinity and correspondence of macrocosm and microcosm and the embodiment of mathematical principles in both.

worthy, they will begin to neglect us and to think too lightly first of the cultivation of the mind, and then of bodily training, so that your young men will come to be worse educated. Then Rulers appointed from among them will fail in their duty as Guardians to try the mettle of your citizens, those breeds of gold and silver, brass and iron that Hesiod told of; [1] and when the silver is alloyed with iron and the gold with brass, diversity, inequality, and disharmony will beget, as they always must, enmity and war. Such, everywhere, is the birth and lineage of civil strife.'

Yes, we will take that as a true answer to our question.

How could it be otherwise, when it comes from the Muses?

And what will they go on to tell us?

Once civil strife is born, the two parties begin to pull different ways: the breed of iron and brass towards money-making and the possession of house and land, silver and gold; while the other two, wanting no other wealth than the gold and silver in the composition of their souls, try to draw them towards virtue and the ancient ways. But the violence of their contention ends in a compromise: they agree to distribute land and houses for private ownership; they enslave their own people who formerly lived as free men under their guardianship and gave them maintenance; and, holding them as serfs and menials, devote themselves to war and to keeping these subjects under watch and ward.

I agree: that is how the transition begins.

And this form of government will be midway between the rule of the best and oligarchy,[2] will it not?

Yes.

Such being the transition, how will the state be governed after the change? Obviously, as intermediate between the earlier constitution and oligarchy, it will resemble each of these in some respects and have some features of its own.

True.

[1] Cf. the allegory at 415 A ff., p. 106 f.

[2] By oligarchy, as will appear in the next chapter, Plato means government by the rich, plutocracy. The first step towards this is taken when the ruling order begins to acquire private property.

It will be like the earlier constitution in several ways. Authority will be respected; the fighting class will abstain from any form of business, farming, or handicrafts; they will keep up their common meals and give their time to physical training and martial exercises.

Yes.

On the other hand, it will have some peculiar characteristics. It will be afraid to admit intellectuals to office. The men of that quality now at its disposal will no longer be single-minded and sincere; it will prefer simpler characters with plenty of spirit, better suited for war than for peace. War will be its constant occupation, and military tricks and stratagems will be greatly admired.

Yes.

At the same time, men of this kind will resemble the ruling class of an oligarchy in being avaricious, cherishing furtively a passionate regard for gold and silver; for they will now have private homes where they can hoard their treasure in secret and live ensconced in a nest of their own, lavishing their riches on their women or whom they please. They will also be miserly, prizing the money they may not openly acquire, though prodigal enough of other people's wealth for the satisfaction of their desires. They will enjoy their pleasures in secret, like truant children, in defiance of the law; because they have been educated not by gentle influence but under compulsion, cultivating the body in preference to the mind and caring nothing for the spirit of genuine culture which seeks truth by the discourse of reason.

The society you describe is certainly a mixture of good and evil.

Yes, it is a mixture; but, thanks to the predominance of the spirited part of our nature, it has one most conspicuous feature: ambition and the passion to excel.

Quite so.

Such, then, is the origin and character of this form of government. We have given only an outline, for no more finished picture is needed for the purpose of setting before our eyes the perfect types of just and unjust men. It would be an endless task to go through all the forms of government and of human character without omitting any detail.

True.

And now what of the corresponding individual? How does he come into being, and what is he like?

I imagine, said Adeimantus, his desire to excel, so far as that goes, would make him rather like Glaucon.

Perhaps, said I; but in other ways the likeness fails. He must be more self-willed than Glaucon and rather uncultivated, though fond of music; one who will listen readily, but is no speaker. Not having a properly educated man's consciousness of superiority to slaves, he will treat them harshly; though he will be civil to free men, and very obedient to those in authority. Ambitious for office, he will base his claims, not on any gifts of speech, but on his exploits in war and the soldierly qualities he has acquired through his devotion to athletics and hunting. In his youth he will despise money, but the older he grows the more he will care for it, because of the touch of avarice in his nature; and besides his character is not thoroughly sound, for lack of the only safeguard that can preserve it throughout life, a thoughtful and cultivated mind.[1]

Quite true.

If that is the sort of young man whose character reflects a timocratical régime, his history will be something like this. He may be the son of an excellent father who, living in an ill-governed state, holds aloof from public life because he would sooner forgo some of his rights than take part in the scramble for office or be troubled with going to law. His son's character begins to take shape when he hears his mother complaining that she is slighted by the other women because her husband has no official post. She sees too that he cares little for money, and is indifferent to all the scurrilous battle of words that goes on in the Assembly and the law-courts; and she finds him always absorbed in his thoughts, without much regard for her, or disregard either. Nursing all these grievances, she tells her son that his father is not much of a man and far too easy-going, and has all the other weaknesses that the wives of such men are fond of harping on.

Yes, we hear plenty of these feminine complaints.

Besides, as you know, servants who are esteemed loyal to the

---

[1] This speech represents an Athenian's view of a typical Spartan.

family sometimes talk privately to the sons in the same way. If they see the father taking no action against a swindler or a defaulting debtor, they urge the son, when he is grown up, to stand up for his rights and be more of a man than his father. When the boy goes out, he sees and hears the same sort of thing: one man is made light of as a fool for minding his own business, whereas another who has a finger in every pie is praised and respected. All this experience affects the young man, and on the other hand he listens to his father's conversation and can see at close quarters how his way of life compares with other people's; and so he is pulled both ways. His father tends the growth of reason in his soul, while the rest of the world is fostering the other two elements, ambition and appetite. By temperament he is not a bad man, but he has fallen into bad company, and the two contrary influences result in a compromise: he gives himself up to the control of the middle principle of high-spirited emulation and becomes an arrogant and ambitious man.

That is a good account of his history, I think.

So now we have an idea of the second form of government and the corresponding individual.

Yes.

CHAPTER XXX (VIII. 550 C–555 B)

OLIGARCHY (PLUTOCRACY) AND THE OLIGARCHIC MAN

In Timocracy the illegitimate institution of private property for the Guardians stimulated ambition, under cover of which the still lower passion for wealth was released from the control of reason. The love of money is the most reputable motive characterizing the third element in human nature, the 'multifarious' group of appetites for the satisfactions, necessary or unnecessary, which money can buy. Oligarchy, the 'government of the few,' or, as Xenophon (Mem. iv, 6, 12) calls it, Plutocracy, is the constitution which results when power passes into the hands of men for whom wealth is the end of life. The state now suffers a further loss of unity by the out-

break of that class war of rich against poor which Plato sought to avert by denying all private property to the ruling order and limiting the acquisition of wealth by tradesmen and farmers (Chap. XI, p. 112). The plutocrat, as a mere consumer of goods, is compared to the drone; and when he has squandered his money he sinks into the dangerous class of paupers and criminals (stingdrones).

In the oligarchic individual, the drone-like appetites have gained some ground against reason; but they are still held in check by the dominant passion for wealth, which calls for an outward respectability.

SHALL we go on then, as Aeschylus might say, to tell of 'another man, matched with another state,' [1] or rather keep to our plan of taking the state first?

By all means.

Then I suppose the next type of constitution will be oligarchy.

What sort of régime do you mean?

The one which is based on a property qualification, where the rich are in power and the poor man cannot hold office.

I see.

We must start, then, by describing the transition from timocracy to oligarchy. No one could fail to see how that happens. The downfall of timocracy is due to the flow of gold into those private stores we spoke of. In finding new ways of spending their money, men begin by stretching the law for that purpose, until they and their wives obey it no longer. Then, as each keeps an envious eye on his neighbour, their rivalry infects the great mass of them; and as they go to further lengths in the pursuit of riches, the more they value money and the less they care for virtue. Virtue and wealth are balanced against one another in the scales; as the rich rise in social esteem, the virtuous sink. These changes of valuation, moreover, are always reflected in practice. So at last the competitive spirit of ambition in these men gives way to the passion for gain; they despise the poor man and promote to power the rich, who

---

[1] Alludes to the messenger's descriptions of the champions who appeared before the gates of Thebes in Aeschylus' *Seven against Thebes.*

wins all their praise and admiration. At this point they fix by stat-
ute the qualification for privilege in an oligarchy, an amount of
wealth which varies with the strength of the oligarchical principle;
no one may hold office whose property falls below the prescribed
sum. This measure is carried through by armed force, unless they
have already set up their constitution by terrorism. That, then, is
how an oligarchy comes to be established.

Yes, said Adeimantus; but what is the character of this régime,
and what are the defects we said it would have?

In the first place, I replied, the principle on which it limits
privilege. How would it be, if the captain of a ship were appointed
on a property qualification, and a poor man could never get a
command, though he might know much more about seamanship?

The voyage would be likely to end in disaster.

Is not the same true of any position of authority? Or is the government of a state an exception?

Anything but an exception, inasmuch as a state is the hardest
thing to govern and the most important.

So this is one serious fault of oligarchy.

Evidently.

Is it any less serious that such a state must lose its unity and
become two, one of the poor, the other of the rich, living together
and always plotting against each other?

Quite as serious.

Another thing to its discredit is that they may well be unable to
carry on a war. Either they must call out the common people or
not. If they do, they will have more to fear from the armed multitude than from the enemy; and if they do not, in the day of battle
these oligarchs will find themselves only too literally a government
of the few. Also, their avarice will make them unwilling to pay
war-taxes.

True.

And again, is it right that the same persons should combine
many occupations, agriculture, business, and soldiering? We condemned that practice some time ago.

No, not at all right.

Worst of all, a man is allowed to sell all he has to another and then to go on living in a community where he plays no part as tradesman or artisan or as a soldier capable of providing his own equipment; he is only what they call a pauper. This is an evil which first becomes possible under an oligarchy, or at least there is nothing to prevent it; otherwise there would not be some men excessively wealthy and others destitute.

True.

Now think of this pauper in his earlier days when he was well off. By spending his money, was he doing any more good to the community in those useful ways I mentioned? He seemed to belong to the ruling class, but really he was neither ruling the state nor serving it; he was a mere consumer of goods. His house might be compared to one of those cells in the honeycomb where a drone is bred to be the plague of the hive. Some drones can fly, and these were all created without stings; others, which cannot fly, are of two sorts: some have formidable stings, the rest have none.[1] In society, the stingless drones end as beggars in their old age; the ones which have stings become what is known as the criminal class. It follows that, in any community where beggars are to be seen, there are also thieves and pickpockets and temple-robbers and other such artists in crime concealed somewhere about the place. And you will certainly see beggars in any state governed by an oligarchy.

Yes, nearly everywhere, outside the ruling class.

Then we may assume that there are also plenty of drones with stings, criminals whom the government takes care to hold down by force; and we shall conclude that they are bred by lack of education, bad upbringing, and a vicious form of government.

Yes.

Such, then, is the character of a state ruled by an oligarchy. It has all these evils and perhaps more.

Very likely.

[1] Aristotle, *Hist. Anim.* ix. 40, describes drones as living on the honey made by the working bees. If the king-bee dies, drones are said to be reared by the workers in their own cells and to become more spirited; hence they are called sting-drones, though they really have no stings, but only the wish to use such weapons. Drones and robber-bees, if caught damaging the work of the other bees, are killed or driven from the hive.

We have finished, then, with the constitution known as oligarchy, where power is held on a property qualification, and we may turn now to the history and character of the corresponding individual.

Yes, let us do so.

The transition from the timocratic type to the oligarchical happens somewhat in this way. The timocratical man has a son, who at first emulates his father and follows in his steps. Then suddenly he sees him come up against society, like a ship striking a sunken rock, and founder with all his possessions; he may have held some high office or command and then have been brought to trial by informers and put to death or banished or outlawed with the loss of all his property.

All this might well happen.

The son is terror-stricken at the sight of this ruin, in which his own fortunes are involved. At once that spirit of eager ambition which hitherto ruled in his heart is thrust headlong from the throne. Humbled by poverty, he turns to earning his living and, little by little, through hard work and petty savings, scrapes together a fortune. And now he will instal another spirit on the vacant throne, the money-loving spirit of sensual appetite, like an eastern monarch with diadem and golden chain and scimitar girt at his side. At its footstool, on either hand, will crouch the two slaves he has forced into subjection: Reason, whose thought is now confined to calculating how money may breed more money, and Ambition, suffered to admire and value nothing but wealth and its possessors and to excel in nothing but the struggle to gain money by any and every means.

There is no swifter and surer way by which an ambitious young man may be transformed into a lover of money.

Is this, then, our oligarchical type?

Well, at any rate, the type from which he has developed corresponded to the constitution from which oligarchy arose.

Let us see, then, whether he will not have the same sort of character. The first point of resemblance is that he values wealth above everything. Another is that he is niggardly and a worker who satisfies only his necessary wants and will go to no further expense; his other desires he keeps in subjection as leading nowhere. There is something squalid about him, with his way of always expecting to make a profit and add to his hoard—the sort of person who is much admired by the vulgar. Surely there is a likeness here to the state under an oligarchy?

I think there is, especially in the way that money is valued above everything.

Because, I suspect, he has never thought of cultivating his mind.

Never; or he would not have promoted the blind god of Wealth [1] to lead the dance.

Good; and here is another point. As a consequence of his lack of education, appetites will spring up in him, comparable to those drones in society whom we classified as either beggars or criminals, though his habitual carefulness will keep them in check. If you want to see his criminal tendencies at work, you must look to any occasions, such as the guardianship of orphans, where he has a chance to be dishonest without risk. It will then be clear that in his other business relations, where his apparent honesty gives him a good reputation, he is only exercising a sort of enforced moderation. The base desires are there, not tamed by a reasonable conviction that it is wrong to gratify them, but only held down under stress of fear, which makes him tremble for the safety of his whole fortune. Moreover, you may generally be sure of discovering these drone-like appetites whenever men of this sort have other people's money to spend.

That is very true.

Such a man, then, will not be single-minded but torn in two by internal conflict, though his better desires will usually keep the upper hand over the worse. Hence he presents a more decent appearance than many; but the genuine virtue of a soul in peace and harmony with itself will be utterly beyond his reach.

I agree.

Further, his stinginess weakens him as a competitor for any personal success or honourable distinction. He is unwilling to spend his money in a struggle for that sort of renown, being afraid to stir up his expensive desires by calling upon them to second his

---

[1] Plutus is blind in Aristophanes' play of that name and elsewhere.

ambition. So, like a true oligarch, fighting with only a small part of his forces, he is usually beaten and remains a rich man.

Quite so.

Have we any further doubts, then, about the likeness between a state under an oligarchy and this parsimonious money-getter?

None at all.

CHAPTER XXXI (VIII. 555 B–562 A)

DEMOCRACY AND THE DEMOCRATIC MAN

The type of democracy whose defects Plato has in view could exist only in a small city-state like Athens. It was not the rule of the majority through elected representatives, but was based on the theory that every adult male citizen had an equal right to take a personal part in the government through the Assembly and the law-courts and was capable of holding any office. (It must be remembered that more than half the population were either slaves with no civic rights or resident aliens.) At Athens the members of the Council of five hundred, which prepared the business and carried out the resolutions of the Assembly, were appointed by lot from among the candidates who presented themselves. The Assembly was nominally the whole body of citizens over eighteen, a quorum of 6,000 being required for certain purposes. It was the sovereign administrative power, though it could not alter the constitutional laws, under whose impersonal sovereignty the Greek citizen conceived himself to live, without the co-operation of another popular judicial body, the Heliaea, *composed nominally of all citizens over thirty who had taken an oath to observe the constitution and been declared by the nine Archons to be duly qualified. The ideals of Athenian democracy are set down in the Funeral Speech of Pericles (Thuc. ii, 35). In Plato's view, the direct rule of the many violated the fundamental principle of 'justice,' that men, being born with different capacities, should do only the work for which they are fitted. Fitness to govern is, he has argued, the last achievement of the highest natures.*

Oligarchy, by making wealth the end of life and failing to check the accumulation of property in a few hands and the ravages of usury, so weakens itself that the poor see their opportunity to wrest power from the degenerate rich.

In the democratic temperament the principle of freedom and equal rights for all is applied to the whole mob of appetites in the lowest part of the soul. Ignoring the distinction between the necessary, profitable desires, indulged by the thrifty plutocrat without loss of respectability, and the unnecessary, prodigal desires, the democratic man gives himself up to the pleasure of the moment, everything by turns and nothing long.

In a later dialogue, The Statesman, *Plato regards even the more lawless type of democracy as superior to oligarchy, though not to timocracy.*

DEMOCRACY, I suppose, should come next. A study of its rise and character should help us to recognize the democratic type of man and set him beside the others for judgement.

Certainly that course would fit in with our plan.

If the aim of life in an oligarchy is to become as rich as possible, that insatiable craving would bring about the transition to democracy. In this way: since the power of the ruling class is due to its wealth, they will not want to have laws restraining prodigal young men from ruining themselves by extravagance. They will hope to lend these spendthrifts money on their property and buy it up, so as to become richer and more influential than ever. We can see at once that a society cannot hold wealth in honour and at the same time establish a proper self-control in its citizens. One or the other must be sacrificed.

Yes, that is fairly obvious.

In an oligarchy, then, this neglect to curb riotous living sometimes reduces to poverty men of a not ungenerous nature. They settle down in idleness, some of them burdened with debt, some disfranchised, some both at once; and these drones are armed and can sting. Hating the men who have acquired their property and conspiring against them and the rest of society, they long for a revolution. Meanwhile the usurers, intent upon their own business, seem unaware of their existence; they are too busy planting their own stings into any fresh victim who offers them an opening to inject the poison of their money; and while they multiply their capital by usury, they are also multiplying the drones and the paupers. When the danger threatens to break out, they will do nothing to quench the flames, either in the way we mentioned, by forbidding a man to do what he likes with his own, or by the next best remedy, which would be a law enforcing a respect for right conduct. If it were enacted that, in general, voluntary contracts for a loan should be made at the lender's risk,[1] there would be less of this shameless pursuit of wealth and a scantier crop of those evils I have just described.

Quite true.

But, as things are, this is the plight to which the rulers of an oligarchy, for all these reasons, reduce their subjects. As for themselves, luxurious indolence of body and mind makes their young men too lazy and effeminate to resist pleasure or to endure pain; and the fathers, neglecting everything but money, have no higher ideals in life than the poor. Such being the condition of rulers and subjects, what will happen when they are thrown together, perhaps as fellow-travellers by sea or land to some festival or on a campaign, and can observe one another's demeanour in a moment of danger? The rich will have no chance to feel superior to the poor. On the contrary, the poor man, lean and sunburnt, may find himself posted in battle beside one who, thanks to his wealth and indoor life, is panting under his burden of fat and showing every mark of distress. 'Such men,' he will think, 'are rich because we are cowards'; and when he and his friends meet in private, the word will go round: 'These men are no good: they are at our mercy.'

Yes, that is sure to happen.

This state, then, is in the same precarious condition as a person

---

[1] At *Laws* 742 E, Plato proposes a law: 'No one shall deposit money with anyone he does not trust, nor lend at interest, since it is permissible for the borrower to refuse entirely to pay back either interest or principal' (trans. R. G. Bury).

so unhealthy that the least shock from outside will upset the balance or, even without that, internal disorder will break out. It falls sick and is at war with itself on the slightest occasion, as soon as one party or the other calls in allies from a neighbouring oligarchy or democracy; and sometimes civil war begins with no help from without.

Quite true.

And when the poor win, the result is a democracy. They kill some of the opposite party, banish others, and grant the rest an equal share in civil rights and government, officials being usually appointed by lot.

Yes, that is how a democracy comes to be established, whether by force of arms or because the other party is terrorized into giving way.

Now what is the character of this new régime? Obviously the way they govern themselves will throw light on the democratic type of man.

No doubt.

First of all, they are free. Liberty and free speech are rife everywhere; anyone is allowed to do what he likes.

Yes, so we are told.

That being so, every man will arrange his own manner of life to suit his pleasure. The result will be a greater variety of individuals than under any other constitution. So it may be the finest of all, with its variegated pattern of all sorts of characters. Many people may think it the best, just as women and children might admire a mixture of colours of every shade in the pattern of a dress. At any rate if we are in search of a constitution, here is a good place to look for one. A democracy is so free that it contains a sample of every kind; and perhaps anyone who intends to found a state, as we have been doing, ought first to visit this emporium of constitutions and choose the model he likes best.

He will find plenty to choose from.

Here, too, you are not obliged to be in authority, however competent you may be, or to submit to authority, if you do not like it; you need not fight when your fellow citizens are at war, nor remain at peace when they do, unless you want peace; and though you may have no legal right to hold office or sit on juries, you will do so all the same if the fancy takes you. A wonderfully pleasant life, surely, for the moment.

For the moment, no doubt.

There is a charm, too, in the forgiving spirit shown by some who have been sentenced by the courts. In a democracy you must have seen how men condemned to death or exile stay on and go about in public, and no one takes any more notice than he would of a spirit that walked invisible. There is so much tolerance and superiority to petty considerations; such a contempt for all those fine principles we laid down in founding our commonwealth, as when we said that only a very exceptional nature could turn out a good man, if he had not played as a child among things of beauty and given himself only to creditable pursuits. A democracy tramples all such notions under foot; with a magnificent indifference to the sort of life a man has led before he enters politics, it will promote to honour anyone who merely calls himself the people's friend.

Magnificent indeed.

These then, and such as these, are the features of a democracy, an agreeable form of anarchy with plenty of variety and an equality of a peculiar kind for equals and unequals alike.

All that is notoriously true.

Now consider the corresponding individual character. Or shall we take his origin first, as we did in the case of the constitution?

Yes.

I imagine him as the son of our miserly oligarch, brought up under his father's eye and in his father's ways. So he too will enforce a firm control over all such pleasures as lead to expense rather than profit—unnecessary pleasures, as they have been called. But, before going farther, shall we draw the distinction between necessary and unnecessary appetites, so as not to argue in the dark? [1]

Please do so.

---

[1] A classification of appetites is needed because oligarchy, democracy, and despotism are based on the supremacy of three sorts of appetite: (1) the necessary, (2) the unnecessary and spendthrift, and (3) the lawless, distinguished later at 571 A, p. 297 ff.

There are appetites which cannot be got rid of, and there are all those which it does us good to fulfil. Our nature cannot help seeking to satisfy both these kinds; so they may fairly be described as necessary. On the other hand, 'unnecessary' would be the right name for all appetites which can be got rid of by early training and which do us no good and in some cases do harm. Let us take an example of each kind, so as to form a general idea of them. The desire to eat enough plain food—just bread and meat—to keep in health and good condition may be called necessary. In the case of bread the necessity is twofold, since it not only does us good but is indispensable to life; whereas meat is only necessary in so far as it helps to keep us in good condition. Beyond these simple needs the desire for a whole variety of luxuries is unnecessary. Most people can get rid of it by early discipline and education; and it is as prejudicial to intelligence and self-control as it is to bodily health. Further, these unnecessary appetites might be called expensive, whereas the necessary ones are rather profitable, as helping a man to do his work. The same distinctions could be drawn in the case of sexual appetite and all the rest.

Yes.

Now, when we were speaking just now of drones, we meant the sort of man who is under the sway of a host of unnecessary pleasures and appetites, in contrast with our miserly oligarch, over whom the necessary desires are in control. Accordingly, we can now go back to describe how the democratic type develops from the oligarchical. I imagine it usually happens in this way. When a young man, bred, as we were saying, in a stingy and uncultivated home, has once tasted the honey of the drones and keeps company with those dangerous and cunning creatures, who know how to purvey pleasures in all their multitudinous variety, then the oligarchical constitution of his soul begins to turn into a democracy. The corresponding revolution was effected in the state by one of the two factions calling in the help of partisans from outside. In the same way one of the conflicting sets of desires in the soul of this youth will be reinforced from without by a group of kindred passions; and if the resistance of the oligarchical faction in him is strengthened by remonstrances and reproaches coming from his father, perhaps, or his friends, the opposing parties will soon be battling within him. In some cases the democratic interest yields to the oligarchical: a sense of shame gains a footing in the young man's soul, and some appetites are crushed, others banished, until order is restored.

Yes, that happens sometimes.

But then again, perhaps, owing to the father's having no idea how to bring up his son, another brood of desires, akin to those which were banished, are secretly nursed up until they become numerous and strong. These draw the young man back into clandestine commerce with his old associates, and between them they breed a whole multitude. In the end, they seize the citadel of the young man's soul, finding it unguarded by the trusty sentinels which keep watch over the minds of men favoured by heaven. Knowledge, right principles, true thoughts, are not at their post; and the place lies open to the assault of false and presumptuous notions. So he turns again to those lotus-eaters and now throws in his lot with them openly. If his family send reinforcements to the support of his thrifty instincts, the impostors who have seized the royal fortress shut the gates upon them, and will not even come to parley with the fatherly counsels of individual friends. In the internal conflict they gain the day; modesty and self-control, dishonoured and insulted as the weaknesses of an unmanly fool, are thrust out into exile; and the whole crew of unprofitable desires take a hand in banishing moderation and frugality, which, as they will have it, are nothing but churlish meanness. So they take possession of the soul which they have swept clean, as if purified for initiation into higher mysteries; and nothing remains but to marshal the great procession [1] bringing home Insolence, Anarchy, Waste, and Impudence, those resplendent divinities crowned with garlands, whose praises they sing under flattering names: Insolence they call good breeding, Anarchy freedom, Waste magnificence, and Impudence a manly spirit. Is not that a fair account of the revolution which gives free rein to unnecessary and harmful pleasures in a

---

[1] Using once more the imagery of the Eleusinian Mysteries, Plato alludes to the evening procession which conducted the image of Iacchus from Athens home to Eleusis.

young man brought up in the satisfaction only of the necessary desires?

Yes, it is a vivid description.

In his life thenceforward he spends as much time and pains and money on his superfluous pleasures as on the necessary ones. If he is lucky enough not to be carried beyond all bounds, the tumult may begin to subside as he grows older. Then perhaps he may recall some of the banished virtues and cease to give himself up entirely to the passions which ousted them; and now he will set all his pleasures on a footing of equality, denying to none its equal rights and maintenance, and allowing each in turn, as it presents itself, to succeed, as if by the chance of the lot, to the government of his soul until it is satisfied. When he is told that some pleasures should be sought and valued as arising from desires of a higher order, others chastised and enslaved because the desires are base, he will shut the gates of the citadel against the messengers of truth, shaking his head and declaring that one appetite is as good as another and all must have their equal rights. So he spends his days indulging the pleasure of the moment, now intoxicated with wine and music, and then taking to a spare diet and drinking nothing but water; one day in hard training, the next doing nothing at all, the third apparently immersed in study. Every now and then he takes a part in politics, leaping to his feet to say or do whatever comes into his head. Or he will set out to rival someone he admires, a soldier it may be, or, if the fancy takes him, a man of business. His life is subject to no order or restraint, and he has no wish to change an existence which he calls pleasant, free, and happy.

That well describes the life of one whose motto is liberty and equality.

Yes, and his character contains the same fine variety of pattern that we found in the democratic state; it is as multifarious as that epitome of all types of constitution. Many a man, and many a woman too, will find in it something to envy. So we may see in him the counterpart of democracy, and call him the democratic man.

We may.

CHAPTER XXXII (VIII. 562 A–IX. 576 B)

DESPOTISM AND THE DESPOTIC MAN

The Greeks called an absolute, unconstitutional ruler a 'tyrant,' but the word by no means always bore the sinister associations which are now gathering round its modern equivalent, the once honourable name of 'dictator.' A tyrant might be, like Peisistratus at Athens, a comparatively benevolent champion of the common people against the oppression of a landed aristocracy; but then, as now, Acton's saying was true: 'all power corrupts; absolute power corrupts absolutely.' Little as Plato valued what he has described as democratic liberty, no democrat could surpass him in detestation of the despotism which is the triumph of injustice and the very negation of the liberty he did believe in.

Democratic anarchy, carried to the extreme, divides society into three classes: a growing number of ruined spendthrift and desperadoes; the capitalists, quietly amassing wealth; and the mass of country people, working their own small farms and uninterested in politics. The most unscrupulous 'drones' lead an attack upon property, which drives the capitalists in self-defence to form a reactionary party. The people then put forward a champion who, having tasted blood, is fated to become a human wolf, the enemy of mankind. Threatened with assassination, he successfully demands a bodyguard or private army, seizes absolute power, and makes the people his slaves. This account of the rise of despotism is adapted to Plato's psychological standpoint, rather than to the normal course of Greek history. At Athens, for example, the 'tyranny' of Peisistratus broke the power of the landed nobility and prepared the way for democracy. On the other hand democracy sometimes passed into despotism, as at Syracuse in Plato's time.

A picture follows of the miserable condition to which the despot is driven to reduce himself by murdering his opponents and possible rivals, till he is left with only scoundrels for company and

287

loathed by the people when they realize how they have been en-
slaved.

In the individual soul despotism means the dominion of one
among those unlawful appetites whose existence, even in decent
people, is revealed in dreams. The democratic man allowed equal
rights to all his desires; but this balance is easily destroyed by the
growth of a master passion, which will gradually enslave every
other element in the soul. So at last the portrait of the perfectly un-
just man is completed for comparison with the perfectly just phi-
losopher-king.

Now there remains only the most admired of all constitutions and
characters—despotism and the despot. How does despotism arise?
That it comes out of democracy is fairly clear. Does the change take
place in the same sort of way as the change from oligarchy to
democracy? Oligarchy was established by men with a certain aim
in life: the good they sought was wealth, and it was the insatiable
appetite for money-making to the neglect of everything else that
proved its undoing. Is democracy likewise ruined by greed for what
it conceives to be the supreme good?

What good do you mean?

Liberty. In a democratic country you will be told that liberty *is*
its noblest possession, which makes it the only fit place for a free
spirit to live in.

True; that is often said.

Well then, as I was saying, perhaps the insatiable desire for this
good to the neglect of everything else may transform a democracy
and lead to a demand for despotism. A democratic state may fall
under the influence of unprincipled leaders, ready to minister to
its thirst for liberty with too deep draughts of this heady wine;
and then, if its rulers are not complaisant enough to give it un-
stinted freedom, they will be arraigned as accursed oligarchs and
punished. Law-abiding citizens will be insulted as nonentities who
hug their chains; and all praise and honour will be bestowed, both
publicly and in private, on rulers who behave like subjects and
subjects who behave like rulers. In such a state the spirit of liberty
is bound to go to all lengths.

Inevitably.

It will make its way into the home, until at last the very animals catch the infection of anarchy. The parent falls into the habit of behaving like the child, and the child like the parent: the father is afraid of his sons, and they show no fear or respect for their parents, in order to assert their freedom. Citizens, resident aliens, and strangers from abroad are all on an equal footing. To descend to smaller matters, the schoolmaster timidly flatters his pupils, and the pupils make light of their masters as well as of their attendants. Generally speaking, the young copy their elders, argue with them, and will not do as they are told; while the old, anxious not to be thought disagreeable tyrants, imitate the young and condescend to enter into their jokes and amusements. The full measure of popular liberty is reached when the slaves of both sexes are quite as free as the owners who paid for them; and I had almost forgotten to mention the spirit of freedom and equality in the mutual relations of men and women.

Well, to quote Aeschylus, we may as well speak 'the word that rises to our lips.'

Certainly; so I will. No one who had not seen it would believe how much more freedom the domestic animals enjoy in a democracy than elsewhere. The very dogs behave as if the proverb 'like mistress, like maid' applied to them; and the horses and donkeys catch the habit of walking down the street with all the dignity of freemen, running into anyone they meet who does not get out of their way. The whole place is simply bursting with the spirit of liberty.

No need to tell me that. I have often suffered from it on my way out of the town.

Putting all these items together, you can see the result: the citizens become so sensitive that they resent the slightest application of control as intolerable tyranny, and in their resolve to have no master they end by disregarding even the law, written or unwritten.

Yes, I know that only too well.

Such then, I should say, is the seed, so full of fair promise, from which springs despotism.

Promising indeed. But what is the next stage?

The same disease that destroyed oligarchy breaks out again here, with all the more force because of the prevailing licence, and enslaves democracy. The truth is that, in the constitution of society, quite as much as in the weather or in plants and animals, any excess brings about an equally violent reaction. So the only outcome of too much freedom is likely to be excessive subjection, in the state or in the individual; which means that the culmination of liberty in democracy is precisely what prepares the way for the cruellest extreme of servitude under a despot. But I think you were asking rather about the nature of that disease which afflicts democracy in common with oligarchy and reduces it to slavery.

Yes, I was.

What I had in mind was that set of idle spendthrifts, among whom the bolder spirits take the lead. We compared these leaders, if you remember, to drones armed with stings, the stingless drones being their less enterprising followers. In any society where these two groups appear they create disorder, as phlegm and bile do in the body. Hence the lawgiver, as a good physician of the body politic, should take measures in advance, no less than the prudent bee-keeper who tries to forestall the appearance of drones, or, failing that, cuts them out, cells and all, as quickly as he can.

Quite true.

Then, to gain a clearer view of our problem, let us suppose the democratic commonwealth to be divided into three parts, as in fact it is. One consists of the drones we have just described. Bred by the spirit of licence, in a democracy this class is no less numerous and much more energetic than in an oligarchy, where it is despised and kept out of office and so remains weak for lack of exercise. But in a democracy it furnishes all the leaders, with a few exceptions; its keenest members make the speeches and transact the business, while the other drones settle on the benches round, humming applause to drown any opposition. Thus nearly the whole management of the commonwealth is in its hands.

Quite true.

Meanwhile, a second group is constantly emerging from the mass. Where everyone is bent upon making money, the steadiest characters tend to amass the greatest wealth. Here is a very convenient source from which the drones can draw an abundance of honey.

No doubt; they cannot squeeze any out of men of small means.

'The rich,' I believe, is what they call this class which provides provender for the drones.

Yes.

The third class will be the 'people,' comprising all the peasantry who work their own farms, with few possessions and no interest in politics. In a democracy this is the largest class and, when once assembled, its power is supreme.

Yes, but it will not often meet, unless it gets some share of the honey.

Well, it always does get its share, when the leaders are distributing to the people what they have taken from the well-to-do, always provided they can keep the lion's share for themselves.[1] The plundered rich are driven to defend themselves in debate before the Assembly and by any measures they can compass; and then, even if they have no revolutionary designs, the other party accuse them of plotting against the people and of being reactionary oligarchs. At last, when they see the people unwittingly misled by such denunciation into attempts to treat them unjustly, then, whether they wish it or not, they become reactionaries in good earnest. There is no help for it; the poison is injected by the sting of those drones we spoke of. Then follow impeachments and trials, in which each party arraigns the other.

Quite so.

And the people always put forward a single champion of their interests, whom they nurse to greatness. Here, plainly enough, is the root from which despotism invariably springs.[2]

Yes.

[1] Pericles had introduced the payment of a small fee to enable country people to come to Athens for service on juries. This was later increased to an amount compensating for the loss of a day's work. After the Peloponnesian War, citizens were paid for attending the Assembly. There were also distributions of surplus revenue, corn-doles, and payments for festivals.

[2] Aristotle (*Politics*, v. 5) observes that in the old days most despots had risen from being demagogues. Cf. Herod. iii. 82.

How does the transformation of the people's champion into a despot begin? You have heard the legend they tell of the shrine of Lycaean Zeus in Arcadia: how one who tastes a single piece of human flesh mixed in with the flesh of the sacrificial victims is fated to be changed into a wolf. In the same way the people's champion, finding himself in full control of the mob, may not scruple to shed a brother's blood; dragging him before a tribunal with the usual unjust charges, he may foully murder him, blotting out a man's life and tasting kindred blood with unhallowed tongue and lips; he may send men to death or exile with hinted promises of debts to be cancelled and estates to be redistributed. Is it not thenceforth his inevitable fate either to be destroyed by his enemies or to seize absolute power and be transformed from a human being into a wolf?

It is.

Here, then, we have the party-leader in the civil war against property. If he is banished, and then returns from exile in despite of his enemies, he will come back a finished despot. If they cannot procure his banishment or death by denouncing him to the state, they will conspire to assassinate him. Then comes the notorious device of all who have reached this stage in the despot's career, the request for a bodyguard to keep the people's champion safe for them. The request is granted, because the people, in their alarm on his account, have no fear for themselves.

Quite true.

This is a terrifying sight for the man of property, who is charged with being not merely rich but the people's enemy. He will follow the oracle's advice to Croesus,

> To flee by Hermus' pebbly shore,
> Dreading the coward's shame no more.[1]

Well, he would have little chance to dread it a second time.

True; if he is caught, no doubt he will be done to death; whereas our champion himself does not, like Hector's charioteer,[2] 'measure his towering length in dust,' but on the contrary, overthrows a host

---

[1] Herodotus, i. 55.   [2] *Iliad*, xvi. 776.

of rivals and stands erect in the chariot of the state, no longer pro-
tector of the people, but its absolute master.

Yes, it must come to that.

And now shall we describe the happy condition of the man and
of the country which harbours a creature of this stamp?

By all means.

In the early days he has a smile and a greeting for everyone he
meets; disclaims any absolute power; makes large promises to his
friends and to the public; sets about the relief of debtors and the
distribution of land to the people and to his supporters; and as-
sumes a mild and gracious air towards everybody. But as soon as
he has disembarrassed himself of his exiled enemies by coming to
terms with some and destroying others, he begins stirring up one
war after another, in order that the people may feel their need
of a leader, and also be so impoverished by taxation that they will
be forced to think of nothing but winning their daily bread, instead
of plotting against him. Moreover, if he suspects some of cherishing
thoughts of freedom and not submitting to his rule, he will find
a pretext for putting them at the enemy's mercy and so making
away with them. For all these reasons a despot must be constantly
provoking wars.

He must.

This course will lead to his being hated by his countrymen
more and more. Also, the bolder spirits among those who have
helped him to power and now hold positions of influence will begin
to speak their mind to him and among themselves and to criticize
his policy. If the despot is to maintain his rule, he must gradually
make away with all these malcontents, until he has not a friend or
an enemy left who is of any account. He will need to keep a
sharp eye open for anyone who is courageous or high-minded or
intelligent or rich; it is his happy fate to be at war with all such,
whether he likes it or not, and to lay his plans against them until
he has purged the commonwealth.[1]

[1] At *Gorg.* 510 B Socrates remarks that a despot cannot make friends with his
betters, whom he will fear, or with his inferiors, whom he will despise, but only
with men of like character, who will truckle to him. In *Ep.* vii 332 C Plato says

A fine sort of purgation!

Yes, the exact opposite of the medical procedure, which removes the worst elements in the bodily condition and leaves the best.

There seems to be no choice, if he is to hold his power.

No; he is confined to the happy alternatives of living with people most of whom are good for nothing and who hate him into the bargain, or not living at all. And the greater the loathing these actions inspire in his countrymen, the more he will need trustworthy recruits to strengthen his bodyguard. Where will he turn to find men on whom he can rely?

They will come flocking of their own accord, if he offers enough pay.

Foreigners of all sorts, you mean—yet another swarm of drones. But why not draw upon the home supply? He could rob the citizens of their slaves, emancipate them, and enroll them in his bodyguard.

No doubt they would be the most faithful adherents he could find.

What an enviable condition for the despot, to put his trust in such friends as these, when he has made away with his earlier supporters! He will, of course, be the admiration of all this band of new-made citizens, whose company he will enjoy when every decent person shuns him with loathing. It is not for nothing that the tragic drama is thought to be a storehouse of wisdom, and above all Euripides, whose profundity of thought appears in the remark that 'despots grow wise by converse with the wise,' meaning no doubt by the wise these associates we have described.

Yes, and Euripides praises absolute power as godlike, with much more to the same effect. So do the other poets.[1]

That being so, the tragedians will give a further proof of their wisdom if they will excuse us and all states whose constitution resembles ours, when we deny them admittance on the ground that they sing the praises of despotism. At the same time, I expect

that Dionysius I was too clever to trust anyone, and 'there is no surer sign of moral character than the lack of trustworthy friends.'

[1] The ancients often quote lines from the tragedians, as many people now quote Shakespeare, without regard to the context or the fact that a dramatist is not responsible for all the sentiments expressed by his characters.

they will go the round of other states, where they will hire actors
with fine sonorous voices to sway the inclination of the assembled
crowd towards a despotic or a democratic constitution. Naturally
they are honoured and well paid for these services, by despots
chiefly, and in a less degree by democracies. But the higher they
mount up the scale of commonwealths, the more their reputation
flags, like a climber who gives in for lack of breath. However, we
are wandering from our subject. Let us go back to the despot's
army. How is he to maintain this fine, ever-shifting array of non-
descripts?

No doubt he will spend any treasure there may be in the
temples,[1] so long as it will last, as well as the property of his victims, thus lightening the war-taxes imposed on the people.

And when that source fails?

Clearly he will support himself, with his boon-companions, min-
ions, and mistresses, from his parent's estate.

I understand: the despot and his comrades will be maintained
by the common people which gave him birth.

Inevitably.

But how if the people resent this and say it is not right for the
father to support his grown-up son—it ought to be the other way
about; they did not bring him into being and set him up in
order that, when he had grown great, they should be the slaves
of their own slaves and support them together with their master
and the rest of his rabble; he was to be the champion to set them
free from the rich and the so-called upper class. Suppose they
now order him and his partisans to leave the country, as a father
might drive his son out of the house along with his riotous friends?

Then, to be sure, the people will learn what sort of a creature
it has bred and nursed to greatness in its bosom, until now the
child is too strong for the parent to drive out.

Do you mean that the despot will dare to lay violent hands on
this father of his and beat him if he resists?

Yes, when once he has disarmed him.

So the despot is a parricide, with no pity for the weakness of

---

[1] In the ancient world temples were to some extent used like banks for the safe
deposit of valuables, since robbery would involve the additional guilt of sacrilege.

age. Here, it seems, is absolutism openly avowed. The people, as they say, have escaped the smoke only to fall into the fire, exchanging service to free men for the tyranny of slaves. That freedom which knew no bounds must now put on the livery of the most harsh and bitter servitude, where the slave has become the master.

Yes, that is what happens.

May we say, then, that we have now sufficiently described the transition from democracy to despotism, and what despotism is like when once established?

Yes, quite sufficiently.

Last comes the man of despotic character. It remains to ask how he develops from the democratic type, what he is like, and whether his life is one of happiness or of misery.

Yes.

Here I feel the need to define, more fully than we have so far done, the number and nature of the appetites. Otherwise it will not be so easy to see our way to a conclusion.

Well, it is not too late.

Quite so. Now, about the appetites, here is the point I want to make plain. Among the unnecessary pleasures and desires,[1] some, I should say, are unlawful. Probably they are innate in everyone; but when they are disciplined by law and by the higher desires with the aid of reason, they can in some people be got rid of entirely, or at least left few and feeble, although in others they will be comparatively strong and numerous.

What kind of desires do you mean?

Those which bestir themselves in dreams, when the gentler part of the soul slumbers and the control of reason is withdrawn; then the wild beast in us, full-fed with meat or drink, becomes rampant and shakes off sleep to go in quest of what will gratify its own instincts. As you know, it will cast away all shame and prudence at such moments and stick at nothing. In phantasy it will not shrink from intercourse with a mother or anyone else, man, god,

---

[1] Distinguished at 558 D, p. 284 f.

or brute, or from forbidden food or any deed of blood. In a word, it will go to any length of shamelessness and folly.

Quite true.

It is otherwise with a man sound in body and mind, who, before he goes to sleep, awakens the reason within him to feed on high thoughts and questionings in collected meditation. If he has neither starved nor surfeited his appetites, so that, lulled to rest, no delights or griefs of theirs may trouble that better part, but leave it free to reach out, in pure and independent thought, after some new knowledge of things past, present, or to come; if, likewise, he has soothed his passions so as not to fall asleep with his anger roused against any man; if, in fact, he does not take his rest until he has quieted two of the three elements in his soul and awakened the third wherein wisdom dwells, then he is in a fair way to grasp the truth of things, and the visions of his dreams will not be unlawful. However, we have been carried away from our point, which is that in every one of us, even those who seem most respectable, there exist desires, terrible in their untamed lawlessness, which reveal themselves in dreams. Do you agree?

I do.

Remember, then, our account of the democratic man, how his character was shaped by his early training under a parsimonious father, who respected only the businesslike desires, dismissing the unnecessary ones as concerned with frivolous embellishments. Then, associating with more sophisticated people who were a prey to those lawless appetites we have just described, he fell into their ways, and hatred of his father's miserliness drove him into every sort of extravagance. But, having a better disposition than his corrupters, he came to a compromise between the two conflicting ways of life, making the best of both with what he called moderation and avoiding alike the meanness of the one and the licence of the other. So the oligarchical man was transformed into the democratic type.

Yes, I hold by that description.

Now imagine him grown old in his turn, with a young son bred in his ways, who is exposed to the same influences, drawn towards the utter lawlessness which his seducers call perfect freedom, while on the other side his father and friends lend their support to the compromise. When those terrible wizards who would conjure up an absolute ruler in the young man's soul begin to doubt the power of their spells, in the last resort they contrive to engender in him a master passion, to champion the mob of idle appetites which are for dividing among themselves all available plunder—a passion that can only be compared to a great winged drone. Like a swarm buzzing round this creature, the other desires come laden with incense and perfumes, garlands and wine, feeding its growth to the full on the pleasures of a dissolute life, until they have implanted the sting of a longing that cannot be satisfied.[1] Then at last this passion, as leader of the soul, takes madness for the captain of its guard and breaks out in frenzy; if it can lay hold upon any thoughts or desires that are of good report and still capable of shame, it kills them or drives them forth, until it has purged the soul of all sobriety and called in the partisans of madness to fill the vacant place.

That is a complete picture of how the despotic character develops.

Is not this the reason why lust has long since been called a tyrant? A drunken man, too, has something of this tyrannical spirit; and so has the lunatic who dreams that he can lord it over all mankind and heaven besides. Thus, when nature or habit or both have combined the traits of drunkenness, lust, and lunacy, then you have the perfect specimen of the despotic man.

Quite true.

Such, then, being his origin and character, what will his life be like?

I give it up. You must tell me.

I will. When a master passion is enthroned in absolute dominion over every part of the soul, feasting and revelling with courtesans and all such delights will become the order of the day. And every day and night a formidable crop of fresh appetites springs up,

---

[1] The winged drone, it will be remembered, is naturally stingless (552 c, p. 277). The word translated by 'passion' is *Eros,* and *Eros* was commonly pictured with wings.

whose numerous demands quickly consume whatever income there may be. Soon he will be borrowing and trenching on his capital; and when all resources fail, the lusty brood of appetites will crowd about him clamouring. Goaded on to frenzy by them and above all by that ruling passion to which they serve as a sort of body-guard, he will look out for any man of property whom he can rob by fraud or violence. Money he must have, no matter how, if he is not to suffer torments.

All that is inevitable.

Now, just as a succession of new pleasures asserted themselves in his soul at the expense of the older ones, so this young man will claim the right to live at his parents' expense and help himself to their property when his own portion is spent. If they resist, he will first try to cheat them; and failing that, he will rob them by force. If the old people still hold out, will any scruple restrain him from behaving like a despot?

I should not have much hope for the parents of such a son.

And yet consider, Adeimantus: his father and mother have been bound to him by the closest ties all his life; and now that they are old and faded, would he really be ready to beat them for the sake of the charms of some new-found mistress or favourite who has no sort of claim on him? Is he going to bring these creatures under the same roof and let them lord it over his parents?

I believe he would.

It is no very enviable lot, then, to give birth to a despotic son.

It is not.

And now suppose that his parents' resources begin to fail, while his appetites for new pleasures have mustered into a great swarm in his soul; he will begin by breaking into someone's house or robbing a traveller by night, and go on to sweep some temple clean of its treasures. Meanwhile, the old approved beliefs about right and wrong which he had as a child will be overpowered by thoughts, once held in subjection, but now emancipated to second that master passion whose bodyguard they form. In his democratic days when he was still under the control of his father and of the laws, they broke loose only in sleep; but now that this passion has set up an absolute dominion, he has become for all his waking life the man he used to be from time to time in his dreams, ready to shed blood or eat forbidden food or do any dreadful deed. The desire that lives in him as sole ruler in a waste of lawless disrule will drive him, as a tyrant would drive his country, into any desperate venture which promises to maintain it with its horde of followers, some of whom evil communication has brought in from without, while others have been released from bondage by the same evil practices within. Is that a fair account of his manner of life?

Yes.

If there are a few such characters in a country where most men are law-abiding, they will go elsewhere to join some despot's bodyguard or serve as mercenaries in any war that is toward. In quiet times of peace, they stay at home and commit crimes on a small scale, as thieves, burglars, pickpockets, temple-robbers, kidnappers; or, if they have a ready tongue, they may take to selling their services as informers and false witnesses.

Such crimes will be a small matter, you mean, so long as the criminals are few in number.

Small is a relative term; and all of them put together do not, as they say, come within sight of the degradation and misery of society under a despot. When the number of such criminals and their hangers-on increases and they become aware of their strength, then it is they who, helped by the folly of the common people, create the despot out of that one among their number whose soul is itself under the most tyrannical despotism.

Yes, such a state of mind would naturally be his best qualification.

All goes smoothly if men are ready to submit. But the country may resist; and then, just as he began by calling his father and mother to order, so now he will discipline his once loved fatherland, or motherland as the Cretans call it, and see that it shall live in subjection to the new-found partisans he has called in to enslave it. So this man's desires come to their fulfilment.

Yes, that is true.

In private life, before they gain power, men of this stamp either consort with none but parasites ready to do them any service, or, if they have a favour to beg, they will not hesitate themselves to cringe and posture in simulated friendliness, which soon cools off when their end is gained. So, throughout life, the despotic character has not a friend in the world; he is sometimes master, sometimes slave, but never knows true friendship or freedom. There is no faithfulness in him; and, if we were right in our notion of justice, he is the perfect example of the unjust man.

Certainly.

CHAPTER XXXIII (IX. 576 B–588 A)

THE JUST AND UNJUST LIVES COMPARED IN RESPECT OF HAPPINESS

By tracing the portraits of the philosopher-king and of the despot, Socrates has now set in contrast the ideally just man and the ideally unjust, in response to the original demand of Glaucon and Adeimantus (Chap. V). It remains to point out which life is the happiest. Three arguments are advanced.

(1) The man whose soul is under the despotism of a master passion is the unhappiest by three tests of well-being: freedom, wealth, and security from fear. His unlimited licence to 'do what he likes' is not genuine freedom, which consists in doing what the true, i.e. the reasonable, self wills for the good of the whole man. (In the Gorgias 466 ff. Socrates argues against Polus that the autocrat is least of all men able to do what he wills in this sense.) No man is rich whose desires can never be satisfied. The despot, moreover, as the enemy of mankind, must live haunted by fear.

(2) When the two lives are compared in respect of pleasantness, the best judge is the philosopher, who alone has experienced the peculiar pleasures of all three parts of the soul, and whose experience is supported by insight and reasoning. (It appears here, more clearly than elsewhere, that each part of the soul has its characteristic desire, and that desires are defined by differences in their objects. This fits in with the suggestion at 485 D (p. 191)

that desire is a single fund of energy which can be turned from one object to another 'like a stream diverted into another bed.')

(3) *The third proof turns on the distinction between pure or positive pleasure and pleasure which is illusory because exaggerated by contrast with a preceding pain of want. Thus the pleasure of eating is enhanced by the pain of hunger which it relieves; and this is said to be true of most sensual pleasures, but not (it is implied) of the pleasures enjoyed by the soul independently of the body. Intellectual satisfactions are also more real, in proportion as the mind and the truth it feeds on are more real than the body and its earthly food. The despot, being enslaved to the lowest of all desires and appetites, is at the farthest remove from the pure and real pleasures accessible to the philosophic ruler. (The distinctions between true and false, or pure and mixed, pleasures are drawn in greater detail in the* Philebus.)

To sum up, then: this worst type of man is he who behaves in waking life as we said men do in their dreams. The born despot who gains absolute power must come to this, and the longer he lives as a tyrant, the more this character grows upon him.

Inevitably, said Glaucon, who now took his turn to answer.

Now shall we find that the lowest depth of wickedness goes with the lowest depth of unhappiness, and that the misery of the despot is really in proportion to the extent and duration of his power, though the mass of mankind may hold many different opinions?

Yes, that much is certain.

It is true, is it not? that each type of individual—the despotic, the democratic, and so on—resembles the state with the corresponding type of constitution, and will be good and happy in a corresponding degree.

Yes, of course.

In point of excellence, then, how does a state under a despotism compare with the one governed by kings, such as we first described?

They are at opposite extremes: the best and the worst.

I shall not ask which is which, for that is obvious. Is your esti-

mate the same with respect to their degrees of happiness or misery?
We must not let our eyes be dazzled by fixing them only on the
despot himself and some few of his supporters; we should not decide until we have looked into every corner and inspected the life
of the whole community.

That is a fair demand. Everyone must see that a state is most
wretched under a despot and happiest under a true king.

And in judging between the corresponding individuals, is it not
equally fair to demand the verdict of one who is not dazzled, like
a child, by the outward pomp and parade of absolute power, but
whose understanding can enter into a man's heart and see all that
goes on within? Should we not all do well to listen to such a competent judge, if he had also lived under the same roof and wit-
nessed the despot's behaviour, not only in the emergencies of public
life, but towards intimates in his own household, where he can
best be seen stripped of his theatrical garb? We might then ask
for a report on the happiness or misery of the despot as compared
with the rest of the world.

Yes, that would be perfectly fair.

Shall we, then, make believe that we ourselves are qualified to
judge from having been in contact with despots, so that we may
have someone to answer our questions? [1]

By all means.

Bearing in mind, then, the analogy between state and individual,
you shall tell me what you think of the condition of each in turn.
To begin with the state: is it free under a despot, or enslaved?

Utterly enslaved.

And yet you see it contains some who are masters and free men.

Yes, a few; but almost the whole of it, including the most respectable part, is degraded to a miserable slavery.

If the individual, then, is analogous to the state, we shall find
the same order of things in him: a soul labouring under the mean-
est servitude, the best elements in it being enslaved, while a small

---

[1] Plato, it is generally agreed, here implies that he himself is qualified to judge
by his experience of living at the court of Dionysius I of Syracuse on his first visit
to the West in 388/7 B.C. Introd., p. xxv.

part, which is also the most frenzied and corrupt, plays the master. Would you call such a condition of the soul freedom or slavery?

Slavery, of course.

And just as a state enslaved to a tyrant cannot do what it really wishes, so neither can a soul under a similar tyranny do what it wishes as a whole. Goaded on against its will by the sting of desire, it will be filled with confusion and remorse. Like the corresponding state, it must always be poverty-stricken, unsatisfied, and haunted by fear. Nowhere else will there be so much lamentation, groaning, and anguish as in a country under a despotism, and in a soul maddened by the tyranny of passion and lust.

It cannot be otherwise.

These, I think, were the considerations that made you judge such a state to be the most unhappy of all.

Was I not right?

Certainly. But, in view of the same facts, what would you say of the despotic type of individual?

That he is by far the most miserable of men.

There I think you are wrong. You will perhaps agree that there is a still lower depth of misery, to be found in a man of this temperament who has not the good fortune to remain in a private station but is thrust by circumstance into the position of an actual despot.

Judging by what we have said already, I should think that must be true.

Yes; but this is the most important of all questions, the choice between a good and an evil life; and we must be content with nothing short of a reasoned conviction. Am I right in thinking that some light may be gained from considering those wealthy private individuals who own a large number of slaves? In that respect they are like the despot, though his subjects are still more numerous. Now, as you know, they do not live in terror of their servants.

No; what have they to fear?

Nothing. But do you see why?

Yes; it is because the individual is protected by the whole community.

True; but imagine a man owning fifty or more slaves, miraculously caught up with his wife and children and planted, along with all his household goods and servants, in some desert place where there were no freemen to come to his rescue. Would he not be horribly afraid that his servants would make away with him and his family? He would be driven to fawn upon some of the slaves with liberal promises and give them their freedom, much against his will. So he would become a parasite, dependent on his own henchmen.

That would be his only way to escape destruction.

Moreover, the place he was transported to might be surrounded by neighbours who would not tolerate the claims of one man to lord it over others, but would retaliate fiercely on anyone they caught in such an attempt.

In that case he would be in still more desperate straits, hemmed in on all sides by enemies.

Is not that a picture of the prison to which the despot is confined? His nature is such as we have described, infested with all manner of fears and lusts. However curious he may be, he alone can never travel abroad to attend the great festivals which every freeman wants to witness, but must live like a woman ensconced in the recesses of his house, envying his countrymen who can leave their homes to see what is worth seeing in foreign lands. You spoke just now of the despotic character, ill governed in his own soul, as the most miserable of men; but these disadvantages I have mentioned add to his wretchedness when he is driven by ill luck out of his private station to become an actual despot and undertake to rule others when he is not his own master. You might as well force a paralytic to leave the sheltered life of an invalid and spend his days in fighting or in trials of physical strength.

Quite true, Socrates; that is a fair comparison.

So the despot's condition, my dear Glaucon, is supremely wretched, even harder than the life you pronounced the hardest of all. Whatever people may think, the actual tyrant is really the most abject slave, a parasite of the vilest scoundrels. Never able to satisfy his desires, he is always in need, and, to an eye that sees a soul in its entirety, he will seem the poorest of the poor.

His condition is like that of the country he governs, haunted throughout life by terrors and convulsed with anguish. Add to this what we said before, that power is bound to exaggerate every fault and make him ever more envious, treacherous, unjust, friendless, impure, harbouring every vice in his bosom, and hence only less of a calamity to all about him than he is to himself.

No man of sense will dispute that.

Then the time has come for you, as the final judge in this competition, to decide who stands first in point of happiness and to arrange in order all our five types of character, the kingly, the timocratic, the oligarchic, the democratic, the despotic.

The decision is easy. In respect both of goodness and of happiness I range them in the order in which they have entered the lists.

Shall we hire a herald, then, or shall I myself proclaim that, in the judgement of the son of Ariston, the happiest man is he who is first in goodness and justice, namely the true king who is also king over himself; and the most miserable is that lowest example of injustice and vice, the born despot whose tyranny prevails in his own soul and also over his country.

Yes, you may proclaim that.

May I add that it would make no difference if the true character of both should remain unknown to heaven and to mankind?

You may.

Very well, said I; that may stand as one of our proofs. But I want to consider a second one, which can, I think, be based on our division of the soul into three parts, corresponding to the three orders in the state. Each part seems to me to have its own form of pleasure and its peculiar desire; and any one of the three may govern the soul.

How do you mean?

There was the part with which a man gains knowledge and understanding, and another whereby he shows spirit. The third was so multifarious that we could find no single appropriate name; we called it after its chief and most powerful characteristic 'appetite,' because of the intensity of all the appetites connected with eating and drinking and sex and so on. We also called it money-loving,

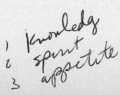

1 Knowledg
2 spirit
3 appetite

because money is the principal means of satisfying desires of this kind. Gain is the source of its pleasures and the object of its affection; so 'money-loving' or 'gain-loving' might be the best single expression to sum up the nature of this part of the soul for the purpose of our discussion.

I agree.

The spirited element, again, we think of as wholly bent upon winning power and victory and a good name. So we might call it honour-loving or ambitious.

Very suitably.

Whereas the part whereby we gain knowledge and understanding is least of all concerned with wealth or reputation. Obviously its sole endeavour is to know the truth, and we may speak of it as loving knowledge and philosophic.

Quite so.

And the human soul is sometimes governed by this principle, sometimes by one of the other two, as the case may be. Hence we recognise three main classes of men, the philosophic, the ambitious, and the lovers of gain. So there will also be three corresponding forms of pleasure.

Certainly.

Now, if you choose to ask men of these three types, which of their lives is the pleasantest, each in turn will praise his own above the rest. The man of business will say that, as compared with profit-making, the pleasures of winning a high reputation or of learning are worthless, except in so far as they bring in money. The ambitious man will despise the pleasure derived from money as vulgar, and the pleasure of learning, if it does not bring fame, as moonshine. The philosopher, again, will think that the satisfaction of knowing the truth and always gaining fresh understanding is beyond all comparison with those other pleasures, which he will call 'necessary' in the fullest sense; for he would have no use for them, if they were not unavoidable. In this dispute about the pleasures of each class and as to which of the three lives as a whole is not merely better and nobler but actually pleasanter or less painful, how is one to know whose judgement is the truest?

I am not prepared to say.

Well, think of it in this way. What is required for a sound judgement? Can it rest on any better foundation than experience, or insight, or reasoning?

Surely not.

Take experience, then. Which of our three men has the fullest acquaintance with all the pleasures we have mentioned? Has the lover of gain such an understanding of the truth as to know by experience the pleasure of knowledge better than the philosopher knows the pleasure of gain?

No, all the advantage lies with the philosopher, who cannot help experiencing both the other kinds of pleasure from childhood up; whereas the lover of gain is under no necessity to taste the sweetness of understanding the truth of things; rather he would not find it easy to gain that experience, however hard he should try.

In experience of both sorts of pleasure, then, the philosopher has the advantage over the lover of gain. How does he compare with the ambitious man? Is he less well acquainted with the pleasures of honour than the other is with the pleasures of wisdom?

No, honour comes to them all, if they accomplish their several purposes; the rich man is esteemed by many people, and so are the brave man and the wise. So the pleasure of being honoured is familiar to them all; but only the philosopher can know how sweet it is to contemplate the truth.

Then, so far as experience goes, he is the best judge of the three.

Yes, by far.

And the only one in whom experience is seconded by insight.[1]

Yes.

Further, we agreed that the decision must be reached by means of reasoning; and this is peculiarly the tool of the philosopher, not of the money-lover or of the ambitious man.

No doubt.

Now, if wealth and profit were the most satisfactory criteria, the judgements of value passed by the lover of gain would be nearest to the truth; and if honour, courage, and success were the test,

---

[1] Insight or intelligence will help him to learn more from a less amount of experience.

the best judge would be the man who lives for honour and victory; but since the tests are experience, insight, and reasoning—?

The truest values must be those approved by the philosopher, who uses reason for the pursuit of wisdom.

Of the three kinds of pleasure, then, the sweetest will belong to that part of the soul whereby we gain understanding and knowledge, and the man in whom that part predominates will have the pleasantest life.

It must be so; in praising his own life the wise man speaks with authority.

What life or form of pleasure will this judge rank second?

Obviously, that of the warlike and ambitious temperament. It comes nearer than the business man's to his own.

And the pleasure of gain will come last, it seems.

Surely.

So now the just man has scored a second victory over the unjust. There remains the third round, for which the wrestlers at the Great Games invoke Olympian Zeus, the Preserver;[1] and a fall in this bout should be decisive. I seem to have heard some wise man say that only the pleasures of intelligence are entirely true and pure; all the others are illusory.

That should settle the matter. But what does it mean?

I shall discover the meaning, if you will help me by answering my questions. We speak of pain as the contrary of pleasure. Is there not also a neutral state between the two, in which the mind feels neither pleasure nor pain, but is as it were at rest from both?

Yes.

Well, you must have heard people say, when they are ill, that nothing is pleasanter than to be well, though they never knew it until they were ill; and people in great pain will tell you that relief from pain is the greatest pleasure in the world. There are many such cases in which you find the sufferer saying that the

---

[1] At banquets the third libation was offered to Zeus the Preserver. This passage seems to imply that competitors at the Olympic Games had a corresponding custom. Plato is fond of quoting the phrase 'the third (libation) to the Preserver,' where his arguments culminate at the third stage.

height of pleasure is not positive enjoyment, but the peace which comes with the absence of pain.

Yes; I suppose at such moments the state of rest becomes pleasurable and all that can be desired.

In the same way, then, when enjoyment comes to an end, the cessation of pleasure will be painful.

I suppose so.

If so, that state of rest which, we said, lies between pleasure and pain, will be sometimes one, sometimes the other. But if it is neither of the two, how can it become both?

I do not think it can.

And besides, both pleasure and pain are processes of change [1] which take place in the mind, are they not? whereas the neutral condition appeared to be a state of rest between the two. So can it be right to regard the absence of pain as pleasant or the absence of enjoyment as painful?

No, it cannot.

It follows, then, that the state of rest is not really either pleasant or painful, but only appears so in these cases by contrast. There is no soundness in these appearances; by the standard of true pleasure they are a sort of imposture.

That seems to be the conclusion.

You might be tempted, in these instances, to suppose that pleasure is the same thing as relief from pain, and pain the same as the cessation of pleasure; but, as an instance to the contrary, consider pleasures which do not follow on pain. There are plenty of them; the best example is the pleasures of smell. These occur suddenly with extraordinary intensity; they are not preceded by any pain and they leave no pain behind when they cease.

Quite true.

We are not to be persuaded, then, that relief from pain is the same thing as pure pleasure, or cessation of pleasure the same as pure pain.

No.

On the other hand, the class of pleasures which do involve some

---

[1] Plato is thinking specially of pleasures, like that of satisfying hunger, which accompany the physical process of restoring the normal (neutral) state, which has been depleted with accompanying pain.

sort of relief from pain may be said to include the great majority
and the most intense of all the pleasures, so called, which reach
the mind by way of the body; and the same description applies to
the pleasures or pains of anticipation which precede them.

Yes.

Here is an analogy, to illustrate their nature. You think of the
world as divided into an upper region and a lower, with a centre
between them.[1] Now if a person were transported from below to
the centre, he would be sure to think he was moving 'upwards';
and when he was stationed at the centre and looking in the direction he had come from, he would imagine he was in the upper
region, if he had never seen the part which is really above the
centre. And supposing he were transported back again, he would
think he was travelling 'downwards,' and this time he would be
right. His mistake would be due to his ignorance of the real distinctions between the upper and lower regions and the centre.

Clearly.

You will not be surprised, then, if people whose ignorance of
truth and reality gives them many unsound ideas, are similarly
confused about pleasure and pain and the intermediate state. When
the movement is towards a painful condition, they are right in
believing that the pain is real; but when they are passing from a
state of pain to the neutral point, they are firmly convinced that
they are approaching the pleasure of complete satisfaction. In their
ignorance of true pleasure, they are deceived by the contrast between pain and the absence of pain, just as one who had never
seen white might be deceived by the contrast between black and
grey.

Certainly; I should be much more surprised if it were not so.

Then look at it in this way. As hunger and thirst are states of
bodily inanition, which can be replenished by food, so ignorance
and unwisdom in the soul are an emptiness to be filled by gaining understanding. Of the two sorts of nourishment, will not the
more real yield the truer satisfaction?

Clearly.

Which kind of nourishment, then, has the higher claim to pure

[1] A popular view, adopted for purposes of illustration here, but corrected at
Timaeus 62 c.

reality—food-stuffs like bread and meat and drink, or such things as true belief, knowledge, reason, and in a word all the excellences of the mind? You may decide by asking yourself whether something which is closely connected with the unchanging and immortal world of truth and itself shares that nature together with the thing in which it exists, has more or less reality than something which, like the thing which contains it, belongs to a world of mortality and perpetual change.

No doubt it is much more real.

And a higher or lower degree of reality goes with a greater or less measure of knowledge and so of truth? [1]

Necessarily.

And is there not, to speak generally, less of truth and reality in the things which serve the needs of the body than in those which feed the soul?

Much less.

And, again, less in the body itself than in the soul?

Certainly.

And in proportion as the sustenance and the thing sustained by it are more real, the satisfaction itself is a more real satisfaction.

Of course.

Accordingly, if the appropriate satisfaction of natural needs constitutes pleasure, there will be more real enjoyment of true pleasure in such a case; whereas in the opposite case the satisfaction is not so genuine or secure and the pleasure is less true and trustworthy.

Inevitably.

To conclude, then: those who have no experience of wisdom and virtue and spend their whole time in feasting and self-indul-

---

[1] The text here is corrupt and much disputed. With the slight change of εἰ to ἤ at 585 c 12 the MS. text can be literally rendered as follows: 'And does the substance of an always unchanging thing partake any more of reality than of knowledge?—No.—Or of truth?—No. (In other words, the substance of an always unchanging thing partakes of knowledge and so of truth *just as much as* it does of reality.) ἤ δὲ (sc. οὐσία) ἀληθείας ἧττον (μετέχει), οὐ καὶ οὐσίας (ἧττον μετέχει); And does not the substance which partakes less of truth, also partake less of reality?—Necessarily.' ('To partake of knowledge' here seems to mean 'to be knowable.')

gence are all their lives, as it were, fluctuating downwards from the central point and back to it again, but never rise beyond it into the true upper region, to which they have not lifted their eyes. Never really satisfied with real nourishment, the pleasure they taste is uncertain and impure. Bent over their tables, they feed like cattle with stooping heads and eyes fixed upon the ground; so they grow fat and breed, and in their greedy struggle kick and butt one another to death with horns and hoofs of steel, because they can never satisfy with unreal nourishment that part of themselves which is itself unreal and incapable of lasting satisfaction.

Your description of the way most people live is quite in the oracular style, Socrates.

Does it not follow that the pleasures of such a life are illusory phantoms of real pleasure, in which pleasure and pain are so combined that each takes its colour and apparent intensity by contrast with the other? Hence the frenzied desire they implant in the breasts of fools, who fight for them as Stesichorus says the combatants at Troy fought, in their blindness, for a phantom Helen.[1]

Yes, that is bound to be so.

Take, again, the satisfaction of the spirited element in our nature. Must not that be no less illusory, when a man seeks, at all costs, to gratify his ambition by envy, his love of victory by violence, and his ill-temper by outbursts of passion, without sense or reason?

It must.

What then? May we boldly assert that all the desires both of the gain-loving and of the ambitious part of our nature will win the truest pleasures of which they are capable, if they accept the guidance of knowledge and reason and pursue only those pleasures which wisdom approves? Such pleasures will be true, because truth is their guide, and will also be proper to their nature, if it is a

---

[1] At *Phaedrus* 243 A Plato refers to the legend that the poet Stesichorus, divinely punished with blindness for defaming Helen, regained his sight only by writing a recantation declaring that she never went to Troy, but was all the while in Egypt. Euripides' *Helen* is based on this story.

fact that a thing always finds in what is best for it something akin to its real self.

Well, that is certainly a fact.

To conclude, then, each part of the soul will not only do its own work and be just when the whole soul, with no inward conflict, follows the guidance of the wisdom-loving part, but it also will enjoy the pleasures that are proper to it and the best and truest of which it is capable;[1] whereas if either of the other two parts gains the upper hand, besides failing to find its own proper pleasure, it will force the others to pursue a false pleasure uncongenial to their nature.

Yes.

Now would not these evil effects be most of all produced by the elements farthest removed from philosophy and reason, that is to say, from subordination to law? Such, we have seen, are the lustful and despotic appetites; whereas the orderly and kingly desires stand nearest to the controlling reason. Accordingly, the despot is at the farthest remove from the true pleasure proper to man's nature, and his life is the least pleasant, in contrast with the king's, who stands at the opposite extreme. Have you any notion how much less pleasant it is?

No, tell me.

There are, it seems, three kinds of pleasure, one genuine and two spurious.[2] The despot, in his flight from law and reason, goes beyond the bounds even of the spurious kinds, to surround himself with pleasures comparable to a bodyguard of slaves.[3] The measure of his inferiority can hardly be expressed, unless perhaps in this way. The despot, you remember, was at the third remove from the oligarch; for the democratic man came between. If that was right, the pleasure he enjoys will be a phantom three times less real than the oligarch's. And the oligarch himself was third in rank below the king, if we identify kingship with the rule of the best.

---

[1] Note that Plato does not hold that lower desires should be altogether suppressed or mortified.

[2] Corresponding to the three parts of the soul and to the king, the timocrat, and the oligarch.

[3] As described at 573 D, p. 299 f.

So the number representing the distance that separates this phantom pleasure of the despot from reality will be three times three; and when that number is squared and cubed, calculation will show how great the interval becomes. Conversely, you will find that, in respect of truth and reality, the kingly life is seven hundred and twenty-nine times the pleasanter, and the despot's more painful by the same amount.[1]

I feel quite overwhelmed by your estimate of the difference between the just and unjust man, on the score of pleasure and pain.

All the same, my figure is correct and applicable to the lives of men as surely as the reckoning of days and nights, months, and years.[2] And if the good and just man is so far superior to the bad and unjust in point of pleasure, there is no saying by how much more his life will surpass the other's in grace, nobility, and virtue.

I entirely agree.

CHAPTER XXXIV (IX. 588 B–592 B)

JUSTICE, NOT INJUSTICE, IS PROFITABLE

Socrates now gives the final answer to Thrasymachus' contention, restated in Glaucon's opening speech at 360 E ff., p. 45, that injustice pays when it goes unpunished. The question of rewards and punishments after death, expressly excluded at the outset, is still reserved for the closing myth in Chapter XL.

[1] The translation here simplifies the text, which is perhaps intentionally obscure. It is not explained why 9 is to be raised to the third power, 729. J. A. Stewart, *Myths of Plato*, 349, notes the importance attached later to this number, which is the square of 27 as well as the cube of 9. Plutarch makes it the number of the Sun (*de anim. proc.* 31), which stands for Reason (*nous*) in *de fac. in orbe lunae*, 28.

[2] According to Censorinus *de die nat.* 18-19 (Diels-Kranz, *Vors.*⁵ 44 A 22) the Pythagorean Philolaus reckoned 364½ days (and presumably the same number of nights) to the year, and $2 \times 364\frac{1}{2} = 729$. This may explain 'days and nights.' He had also a 'great year' of 729 months. These numerical correspondences between macrocosm and microcosm, which seem to us fantastic, may not be literally meant but they cannot have been mere nonsense to Plato.

This chapter ends with a doubt whether the ideal state can ever be founded on earth. There is more hope that, here and there, some man may come near to realizing the ideal of justice in the economy of his own soul. Plato had before him the example of Socrates himself, the one man he knew who seemed to have found complete happiness in 'living well.'

Good, said I. And now that the argument has brought us to this point, let us recall something that was said at the outset, namely, if I remember aright, that wrongdoing is profitable when a man is completely unjust but has a reputation for justice.

Yes, that position was stated.

Well, we are now agreed about the real meaning and consequences of doing wrong as well as of doing right, and the time has come to point out to anyone who maintains that position what his statement implies. We may do so by likening the soul to one of those many fabulous monsters said to have existed long ago, such as the Chimaera or Scylla or Cerberus, which combined the forms of several creatures in one. Imagine, to begin with, the figure of a multifarious and many-headed beast, girt round with heads of animals, tame and wild, which it can grow out of itself and transform at will.

That would tax the skill of a sculptor; but luckily the stuff of imagination is easier to mould than wax.

Now add two other forms, a lion and a man. The many-headed beast is to be the largest by far, and the lion next to it in size. Then join them in such a way that the three somehow grow together into one. Lastly, mould the outside into the likeness of one of them, the man, so that, to eyes which cannot see inside the outward sheath, the whole may look like a single creature, a human being.

Very well. What then?

We can now reply to anyone who says that for this human creature wrongdoing pays and there is nothing to be gained by doing right. This simply means, we shall tell him, that it pays to feed up and strengthen the composite beast and all that belongs to the lion, and to starve the man till he is so enfeebled that the other two can drag him whither they will, and he cannot bring them to live together in peace, but must leave them to bite and struggle and devour one another. On the other hand, to declare that justice pays is to assert that all our words and actions should tend towards giving the man within us complete mastery over the whole human creature, and letting him take the many-headed beast under his care and tame its wildness, like the gardener who trains his cherished plants while he checks the growth of weeds. He should enlist the lion as his ally, and, caring for all alike, should foster their growth by first reconciling them to one another and to himself.

Yes, such are the implications when justice or injustice is commended.

From every point of view, then, whether of pleasure or reputation or advantage, one who praises justice speaks the truth; he who disparages it does not know what it is that he idly condemns.

I agree; he has no conception.

But his error is not wilful; so let us reason with him gently. We will ask him on what grounds conduct has come to be approved or disapproved by law and custom. Is it not according as conduct tends to subdue the brutish parts of our nature to the human—perhaps I should rather say to the divine in us—or to enslave our humanity to the savagery of the beast? Will he agree?

Yes, if he has any regard for my opinion.

On that showing, then, can it profit a man to take money unjustly, if he is thereby enslaving the best part of his nature to the vilest? No amount of money could make it worth his while to sell a son or daughter as slaves into the hands of cruel and evil men; and when it is a matter of ruthlessly subjugating all that is most godlike in himself to whatsoever is most ungodly and despicable, is not the wretch taking a bribe far more disastrous than the necklace Eriphyle took as the price of her husband's life? [1]

Far more, said Glaucon, if I may answer on his behalf.

You will agree, too, with the reasons why certain faults have

[1] Eriphyle was bribed with a necklace by Polynices to persuade her husband, the seer Amphiaraos, to become one of the seven champions who made war on Thebes and of whom all but one lost their lives.

always been condemned: profligacy, because it gives too much licence to the multiform monster; self-will and ill temper, when the lion and serpent [1] part of us is strengthened till its sinews are overstrung: luxury and effeminacy, because they relax those sinews till the heart grows faint; flattery and meanness, in that the heart's high spirit is subordinated to the turbulent beast, and for the sake of money to gratify the creature's insatiable greed the lion is browbeaten and schooled from youth up to become an ape. Why, again, is mechanical toil discredited as debasing? Is it not simply when the highest thing in a man's nature is naturally so weak that it cannot control the animal parts but can only learn how to pamper them?

I suppose so.

Then, if we say that people of this sort ought to be subject to the highest type of man, we intend that the subject should be governed, not, as Thrasymachus thought, to his own detriment, but on the same principle as his superior, who is himself governed by the divine element within him. It is better for everyone, we believe, to be subject to a power of godlike wisdom residing within himself, or, failing that, imposed from without, in order that all of us, being under one guidance, may be so far as possible equal and united. This, moreover, is plainly the intention of the law in lending its support to every member of the community, and also of the government of children; for we allow them to go free only when we have established in each one of them as it were a constitutional ruler, whom we have trained to take over the guardianship from the same principle in ourselves.

True.

On what ground, then, can we say that it is profitable for a man to be unjust or self-indulgent or to do any disgraceful act which will make him a worse man, though he may gain money and power? Or how can it profit the wrongdoer to escape detection and punishment? He will only grow still worse; whereas if he is found out, chastisement will tame the brute in him and lay it to rest, while the gentler part is set free; and thus the entire soul, restored to its native soundness, will gain, in the temperance and

[1] The serpent, perhaps a symbol of cunning, occurs here only (if the text is sound).

righteousness which wisdom brings, a condition more precious than the strength and beauty which health brings to the body, in proportion as the soul itself surpasses the body in worth. To this end the man of understanding will bend all his powers through life, prizing in the first place those studies only which will fashion these qualities in his soul; and, so far from abandoning the care of his bodily condition to the irrational pleasures of the brute and setting his face in that direction, he will not even make health his chief object. Health, strength, and beauty he will value only in so far as they bring soundness of mind, and you will find him keeping his bodily frame in tune always for the sake of the resulting concord in the soul.

Yes, if he is to have true music in him.

And in the matter of acquiring wealth he will order his life in harmony with the same purpose. He will not be carried away by the vulgar notion of happiness into heaping up an unbounded store which would bring him endless troubles. Rather, in adding to or spending his substance, he will, to the best of his power, be guided by watchful care that neither want nor abundance may unsettle the constitution set up in his soul. Again, in accepting power and honours he will keep the same end in view, ready to enjoy any position in public or private life which he thinks will make him a better man, and avoiding any that would break down the established order within him.

Then, if that is his chief concern, he will have no wish to take part in politics.

Indeed he will, in the politics of his own commonwealth, though not perhaps in those of his country, unless some miraculous chance should come about.

I understand, said Glaucon: you mean this commonwealth we have been founding in the realm of discourse; for I think it nowhere exists on earth.

No, I replied; but perhaps there is a pattern set up in the heavens [1] for one who desires to see it and, seeing it, to found one in

[1] 'The heavens' probably means the visible order (cosmos) of the universe (sometimes called 'the heaven') and in particular of the heavenly bodies, which preserves the stars from wrong and manifests, though imperfectly, the divine order which the

himself. But whether it exists anywhere or ever will exist is no matter; for this is the only commonwealth in whose politics he can ever take part.

I suspect you are right.

philosopher tries to reproduce in himself (500 B ff., p. 208 f. Cf. the account of the Astronomer-Guardians in *Laws* xii. 965 ff.). The word has not the Christian associations of 'heaven' or of the kingdom of heaven. But this passage inspired both Stoics and Christians with the idea of the City of God.

PART V (Book X, 595 A–608 B)

THE QUARREL BETWEEN PHILOSOPHY AND POETRY

THE attack on poetry in this Part has the air of an appendix, only superficially linked with the preceding and following context. Possibly the strictures on dramatic poetry in Chapter IX had become known [1] and provoked criticism to which Plato wished to reply. In discussing the early education of the Guardians he began by limiting the dramatic recitations of school-children to the impersonation (*mimesis*) of appropriate types of character and forbidding the realistic imitation (also *mimesis*) of animals' cries and lifeless noises. Then, somewhat unexpectedly, he proposed to banish altogether from his commonwealth all poetry which did not conform to these standards, in terms which suggested the complete exclusion of tragedy and comedy (p. 85).

The excuse for returning to the subject of poetry is that, since that earlier passage, we have had (1) the metaphysical distinction of the intelligible world of Forms known to the philosopher and the sensible world which alone is recognized by the lover of sights and sounds (Chapters XIX and XXIV); and (2) the analysis of the soul into three elements (Chapter XIII). These furnish the basis for a wider attack (1) on poetry and art in general as far removed from any apprehension of reality and (2) on dramatic poetry as psychologically injurious.

CHAPTER XXXV (x. 595 A–602 B)

HOW REPRESENTATION IN ART IS RELATED TO TRUTH

Readers who take this chapter as stating, for its own sake, an aesthetic theory of the nature of art are surprised and shocked: the

---

[1] Since books were not printed or published at a fixed date, MS. copies of parts of a long work might be circulated privately and pass out of the author's control. In the *Parmenides* Zeno complains that this had happened to an early treatise of his own, which he would have preferred to suppress.

point of view seems as perverse, and even stupid, as Tolstoy's in What is Art? *The main object of attack, however, is the claim, currently made by sophists and professional reciters of the Homeric poems,[1] that Homer in particular, and in a less degree the tragedians, were masters of all technical knowledge, from wagon-building or chariot-driving to strategy, and also moral and religious guides to the conduct of life.[2] As such, the poet becomes the rival of the philosopher as conceived by Plato, and the study of poetry an alternative to the severe intellectual training of the Academy. If wisdom is to be gained only through knowledge of the real world of Forms disclosed by Dialectic, the claim that the poet can educate mankind to virtue must be as hollow as the pretence that the artist knows all about shoemaking because he can paint a life-like picture of a shoemaker. How much knowledge of ultimate values does the poet need in order to paint in words his pictures of human life?*

The painter is taken first by way of illustration. A picture of a bed is a two-dimensional representation of the appearance of a solid object seen at a certain angle. The object itself is only a particular bed, which, as a part of the material world, is not a wholly real thing, since it comes into being and perishes and is perpetually changing; it belongs to the realm of Becoming characterized in Chapter XIX. This actual bed, however, is nearer `to reality than the picture, because it is one of many embodiments of the essential nature common to all beds. Beds can be made of wood or iron or canvas and may vary indefinitely in size, shape, colour, etc. But they cannot be called beds at all unless they serve the purpose of a bed, a thing designed to be slept on. This purpose, however hard to define, may be called the essence or Form of Bed, and in Plato's view it is the unique and unvarying reality which must be, however imperfectly, embodied in any bed, and is in one sense the meaning of the word 'Bed.' (Plato speaks here of this essential Bed as 'in the nature of things,' i.e. in the real world of Forms, and as made by a god, though the Forms are elsewhere described as not made by

---

[1] Such as Ion in Plato's dialogue of that name.
[2] In Xenophon's *Symposium*, iii. 5, Niceratus says his father made him learn all Homer by heart in order that he might become a good man.

anyone, but eternal, and there is a difficulty in supposing eternal Forms of the products of human workmanship. These points, however, need not be pressed. The bed was perhaps chosen for illustrative purposes because beds are obviously made by a practical craftsman, whom Plato wishes to contrast with the fine artist, whereas the maker of natural objects, the divine Demiurge of the Timaeus, is a mythical figure who could not be introduced without a long explanation.) The upshot is that the artist's picture of a bed is at two removes from the essential Form. It is only as it were a mirror-image of a sensible thing, which itself is only one embodiment (with many accidental features) of the real Form, the object of knowledge.

Poetry is like a picture in words, a representation of life. However skilfully executed, it is no evidence that the poet really possessed the knowledge required for the right conduct of actual life. This knowledge is not to be gained by studying his portraits of heroic characters, any more than we can learn how to drive a chariot or conduct a campaign from his descriptions of a chariot-race or of the Trojan war. Socrates' examination of the poets had convinced him that they worked, not with conscious intelligence, but from inspiration, like seers and oracle-mongers who do not understand the meaning of the fine language they use (Apology, 22 B).

In this chapter mimesis has a wider sense than dramatic impersonation: the nearest English word is 'representation,' applicable to many forms of fine art. The usual rendering 'imitation' is misleading. We do not say that Garrick, still less that Shakespeare, imitated the character of Hamlet; or that Raphael imitated Julius II; or that the Passion music imitates religious emotion. In all these cases mimesis would be used. The substantive mimetes can be rendered in this context by 'artist.' On the other hand, mimesis does also mean 'imitation,' and this encourages the suggestion that tragic acting is on a level with mimicry and that fine art in general is no more than a copying of external appearances. The view that a work of art is an image or likeness (eikon) of some original, or holds a mirror up to nature, became prominent towards the end of the fifth century together with the realistic drama of Euripides and

the illusionistic painting of Zeuxis. Plato's attack adopts this theory.
The art which claims to be 'realistic' is, in his view, as far as pos-
sible from reality. See T. B. L. Webster, 'Greek Theories of Art
and Literature down to 400 B.C.,' Classical Quarterly, xxxiii (1939),
166.

INDEED, I continued, our commonwealth has many features which
make me think it was based on very sound principles, especially
our rule not on any account to admit the poetry of dramatic representation.[1] Now that we have distinguished the several parts of
the soul, it seems to me clearer than ever that such poetry must be
firmly excluded.

What makes you say so?

Between ourselves—for you will not denounce me to the tragedians and the other dramatists—poetry of that sort seems to be
injurious to minds which do not possess the antidote in a knowledge of its real nature.

What have you in mind?

I must speak out, in spite of a certain affection and reverence I
have had from a child for Homer, who seems to have been the
original master and guide of all this imposing company of tragic
poets.[2] However, no man must be honoured above the truth; so, as
I say, I must speak my mind.

Do, by all means.

Listen then, or rather let me ask you a question. Can you tell
me what is meant by representation in general? I have no very
clear notion myself.

So you expect me to have one!

Why not? It is not always the keenest eye that is the first to see
something.

----

[1] At 398 A (p. 85) Plato seemed to exclude all dramatic poetry because this
contains no narrative but involves the impersonation (*mimesis*) of all types of character, good or bad; whereas epic, for instance, can limit speeches in character to the
representation of virtuous or heroic types. He will now argue that all poetry and
other forms of art are essentially *mimesis*. The meaning of the word is obviously
enlarged where he speaks just below of 'representation in general.'

[2] The plots of Greek tragedy were normally stories borrowed from epic poetry.
Hence Homer was spoken of as the first tragic poet.

True; but when you are there I should not be very desirous to tell what I saw, however plainly. You must use your own eyes.

Well then, shall we proceed as usual and begin by assuming the existence of a single essential nature or Form for every set of things which we call by the same name? Do you understand?

I do.

Then let us take any set of things you choose. For instance there are any number of beds or of tables, but only two Forms, one of Bed and one of Table.

Yes.

And we are in the habit of saying that the craftsman, when he makes the beds or tables we use or whatever it may be, has before his mind the Form [1] of one or other of these pieces of furniture. The Form itself is, of course, not the work of any craftsman. How could it be?

It could not.

Now what name would you give to a craftsman who can produce all the things made by every sort of workman?

He would need to have very remarkable powers!

Wait a moment, and you will have even better reason to say so. For, besides producing any kind of artificial thing, this same craftsman can create all plants and animals, himself included, and earth and sky and gods and the heavenly bodies and all the things under the earth in Hades.

That sounds like a miraculous feat of virtuosity.

Are you incredulous? Tell me, do you think there could be no such craftsman at all, or that there might be someone who could create all these things in one sense, though not in another? [2] Do you not see that you could do it yourself, in a way?

In what way, I should like to know.

---

[1] 'Form' does not mean 'shape,' but the essential properties which constitute what the thing, by definition, is.

[2] The divine Demiurge of the creation-myth in the *Timaeus* is pictured as fashioning the whole visible world after the likeness of the eternal Forms, which he does not create but uses as models. He is thus the maker of natural objects, corresponding to the carpenter who makes artificial objects; and both, as makers of actual things, are superior to the painter or poet, who makes all things only 'in a way,' by creating mere semblances like images in a mirror.

There is no difficulty; in fact there are several ways in which the thing can be done quite quickly. The quickest perhaps would be to take a mirror and turn it round in all directions. In a very short time you could produce sun and stars and earth and yourself and all the other animals and plants and lifeless objects which we mentioned just now.

Yes, in appearance, but not the actual things.

Quite so; you are helping out my argument. My notion is that a painter is a craftsman of that kind. You may say that the things he produces are not real; but there is a sense in which he too does produce a bed.

Yes, the appearance of one.

And what of the carpenter? Were you not saying just now that he only makes a particular bed, not what we call the Form or essential nature of Bed?

Yes, I was.

If so, what he makes is not the reality, but only something that resembles it. It would not be right to call the work of a carpenter or of any other handicraftsman a perfectly real thing, would it?

Not in the view of people accustomed to thinking on these lines.[1]

We must not be surprised, then, if even an actual bed is a somewhat shadowy thing as compared with reality.

True.

Now shall we make use of this example to throw light on our question as to the true nature of this artist who represents things? We have here three sorts of bed: one which exists in the nature of things and which, I imagine, we could only describe as a product of divine workmanship; another made by the carpenter; and a third by the painter. So the three kinds of bed belong respectively to the domains of these three: painter, carpenter, and god.

Yes.

Now the god made only one ideal or essential Bed, whether by choice or because he was under some necessity not to make more

---

[1] Familiar with the Platonic doctrine, as opposed to current materialism, which regards the beds we sleep on as real things and the Platonic Form as a mere 'abstraction' or notion existing only in our minds.

than one; at any rate two or more were not created, nor could they possibly come into being.

Why not?

Because, if he made even so many as two, then once more a single ideal Bed would make its appearance, whose character those two would share; and that one, not the two, would be the essential Bed. Knowing this, the god, wishing to be the real maker of a real Bed, not a particular manufacturer of one particular bed, created one which is essentially unique.

So it appears.

Shall we call him, then, the author of the true nature of Bed, or something of that sort?

Certainly he deserves the name, since all his works constitute the real nature of things.

And we may call the carpenter the manufacturer of a bed?

Yes.

Can we say the same of the painter?

Certainly not.

Then what is he, with reference to a bed?

I think it would be fairest to describe him as the artist who represents the things which the other two make.

Very well, said I; so the work of the artist is at the third remove from the essential nature of the thing?

Exactly.

The tragic poet, too, is an artist who represents things; so this will apply to him: he and all other artists are, as it were, third in succession from the throne of truth.[1]

Just so.

We are in agreement, then, about the artist. But now tell me about our painter: which do you think he is trying to represent— the reality that exists in the nature of things, or the products of the craftsman?

The products of the craftsman.

[1] Jowett and Campbell quote from Dante Virgil's description of human art as the 'grandchild of God,' since art is said to copy nature, and nature is the child of God: *si che vostr' arte a Dio quasi è nipote,* Inferno xi. 105.

As they are, or as they appear? You have still to draw that distinction.[1]

How do you mean?

I mean: you may look at a bed or any other object from straight in front or slantwise or at any angle. Is there then any difference in the bed itself, or does it merely look different?

It only looks different.

Well, that is the point. Does painting aim at reproducing any actual object as it is, or the appearance of it as it looks? In other words, is it a representation of the truth or of a semblance?

Of a semblance.

The art of representation, then, is a long way from reality; and apparently the reason why there is nothing it cannot reproduce is that it grasps only a small part of any object, and that only an image. Your painter, for example, will paint us a shoemaker, a carpenter, or other workman, without understanding any one of their crafts;[2] and yet, if he were a good painter, he might deceive a child or a simple-minded person into thinking his picture was a real carpenter, if he showed it them at some distance.

No doubt.

But I think there is one view we should take in all such cases. Whenever someone announces that he has met with a person who is master of every trade and knows more about every subject than any specialist, we should reply that he is a simple fellow who has apparently fallen in with some illusionist and been tricked into thinking him omniscient, because of his own inability to discriminate between knowledge and ignorance and the representation of appearances.

Quite true.

Then it is now time to consider the tragic poets and their master, Homer, because we are sometimes told that they understand

---

[1] The distinction is needed to exclude another possible sense of *mimesis*, the production of a complete replica.

[2] Knowledge of carpentry is the essence of the carpenter, what makes him a carpenter. The painter could not reproduce this knowledge in his picture, even if he possessed it himself. This may sound absurd as an objection to art, but Plato is thinking rather of the application to the poet, for whom it was claimed that he both possessed technical and moral knowledge and reproduced it in his work.

not only all technical matters but also all about human conduct, good or bad, and about religion; for, to write well, a good poet, so they say, must know his subject; otherwise he could not write about it. We must ask whether these people have not been deluded by meeting with artists who can represent appearances, and in contemplating the poets' work have failed to see that it is at the third remove from reality, nothing more than semblances, easy to produce with no knowledge of the truth. Or is there something in what they say? Have the good poets a real mastery of the matters on which the public thinks they discourse so well?

It is a question we ought to look into.

Well then, if a man were able actually to do the things he represents as well as to produce images of them, do you believe he would seriously give himself up to making these images and take that as a completely satisfying object in life? I should imagine that, if he had a real understanding of the actions he represents, he would far sooner devote himself to performing them in fact. The memorials he would try to leave after him would be noble deeds, and he would be more eager to be the hero whose praises are sung than the poet who sings them.

Yes, I agree; he would do more good in that way and win a greater name.

Here is a question, then, that we may fairly put to Homer or to any other poet. We will leave out of account all mere matters of technical skill: we will not ask them to explain, for instance, why it is that, if they have a knowledge of medicine and not merely the art of reproducing the way physicians talk, there is no record of any poet, ancient or modern, curing patients and bequeathing his knowledge to a school of medicine, as Asclepius did. But when Homer undertakes to tell us about matters of the highest importance, such as the conduct of war, statesmanship, or education, we have a right to inquire into his competence. 'Dear Homer,' we shall say, 'we have defined the artist as one who produces images at the third remove from reality. If your knowledge of all that concerns human excellence was really such as to raise you above him to the second rank, and you could tell what courses of conduct will make men better or worse as individuals or as citizens, can you name any country which was better governed thanks to your efforts? Many states, great and small, have owed much to a good lawgiver, such as Lycurgus at Sparta, Charondas in Italy and Sicily, and our own Solon. Can you tell us of any that acknowledges a like debt to you?'

I should say not, Glaucon replied. The most devout admirers of Homer make no such claim.

Well, do we hear of any war in Homer's day being won under his command or thanks to his advice?

No.

Or of a number of ingenious inventions and technical contrivances, which would show that he was a man of practical ability like Thales of Miletus or Anacharsis the Scythian?[1]

Nothing of the sort.

Well, if there is no mention of public services, do we hear of Homer in his own lifetime presiding, like Pythagoras, over a band of intimate disciples who loved him for the inspiration of his society and handed down a Homeric way of life, like the way of life which the Pythagoreans called after their founder and which to this day distinguishes them from the rest of the world?

No; on the contrary, Homer's friend with the absurd name, Creophylus,[2] would look even more absurd when considered as a product of the poet's training, if the story is true that he completely neglected Homer during his lifetime.

Yes, so they say. But what do you think, Glaucon? If Homer had really possessed the knowledge qualifying him to educate people and make them better men, instead of merely giving us a poetical representation of such matters, would he not have attracted a host of disciples to love and revere him? After all, any number of private teachers like Protagoras of Abdera and Prodicus

---

[1] Thales (early sixth cent.) made a fortune out of a corner in oil-mills when his knowledge of the stars enabled him to predict a large olive harvest, thus proving that wise men could be rich if they chose (Aristotle, *Politics,* i. 11). Anacharsis was said to have invented the anchor and the potter's wheel (Diog. Laert. i. 105).

[2] Creophylus' name is supposed to be derived from two words meaning 'flesh' and 'tribe.' He is said to have been an epic poet from Chios.

of Ceos[1] have succeeded in convincing their contemporaries that they will never be fit to manage affairs of state or their own households unless these masters superintend their education; and for this wisdom they are so passionately admired that their pupils are all but ready to carry them about on their shoulders. Can we suppose that Homer's contemporaries, or Hesiod's, would have left them to wander about reciting their poems, if they had really been capable of helping their hearers to be better men? Surely they would sooner have parted with their money and tried to make the poets settle down at home; or failing that, they would have danced attendance on them wherever they went, until they had learnt from them all they could.

I believe you are quite right, Socrates.

We may conclude, then, that all poetry, from Homer onwards, consists in representing a semblance of its subject, whatever it may be, including any kind of human excellence, with no grasp of the reality. We were speaking just now of the painter who can produce what looks like a shoemaker to the spectator who, being as ignorant of shoemaking as he is himself, judges only by form and colour. In the same way the poet, knowing nothing more than how to represent appearances, can paint in words his picture of any craftsman so as to impress an audience which is equally ignorant and judges only by the form of expression; the inherent charm of metre, rhythm, and musical setting is enough to make them think he has discoursed admirably about generalship or shoemaking or any other technical subject. Strip what the poet has to say of its poetical colouring, and I think you must have seen what it comes to in plain prose. It is like a face which was never really handsome, when it has lost the fresh bloom of youth.

Quite so.

Here is a further point, then. The artist, we say, this maker of images, knows nothing of the reality, but only the appearance. But that is only half the story. An artist can paint a bit and bridle, while the smith and the leather-worker can make them. Does the painter understand the proper form which bit and bridle ought to

---

[1] Two of the most famous Sophists of the fifth century. Plato's *Protagoras* gives a vivid picture of them on a visit to a rich patron at Athens.

have? Is it not rather true that not even the craftsmen who make them know that, but only the horseman who understands their use? [1]

Quite true.

May we not say generally that there are three arts concerned with any object—the art of using it, the art of making it, and the art of representing it?

Yes.

And that the excellence or beauty or rightness of any implement or living creature or action has reference to the use for which it is made or designed by nature? [2]

Yes.

It follows, then, that the user must know most about the performance of the thing he uses and must report on its good or bad points to the maker. The flute-player, for example, will tell the instrument-maker how well his flutes serve the player's purpose, and the other will submit to be instructed about how they should be made. So the man who uses any implement will speak of its merits and defects with knowledge, whereas the maker will take his word and possess no more than a correct belief, which he is obliged to obtain by listening to the man who knows.

Quite so.

But what of the artist? Has he either knowledge or correct belief? Does he know from direct experience of the subjects he portrays whether his representations are good and right or not? Has he even gained a correct belief by being obliged to listen to someone who does know and can tell him how they ought to be represented?

No, he has neither.

If the artist, then, has neither knowledge nor even a correct belief about the soundness of his work, what becomes of the poet's wisdom in respect of the subjects of his poetry?

---

[1] In the *Parmenides* (127 A) Plato's half-brother Antiphon, who had transferred his interest from philosophy to horses, is discovered instructing a smith about making a bit. Ancient craftsmen were far less specialized than ours. A blacksmith and a cobbler to-day might need instructions from a jockey.

[2] This recalls the association of a thing's peculiar excellence or 'virtue' with its function, 352 D, p. 37 f.

It will not amount to much.

And yet he will go on with his work, without knowing in what way any of his representations is sound or unsound. He must, apparently, be reproducing only what pleases the taste or wins the approval of the ignorant multitude.[1]

Yes, what else can he do?

We seem, then, so far to be pretty well agreed that the artist knows nothing worth mentioning about the subjects he represents, and that art is a form of play, not to be taken seriously. This description, moreover, applies above all to tragic poetry, whether in epic or dramatic form.

Exactly.[2]

CHAPTER XXXVI (x. 602 c–605 c)

DRAMATIC POETRY APPEALS TO THE EMOTIONS, NOT TO THE REASON

The psychological objections to poetry in this and the following chapter are based on the earlier division of the soul into three parts, and apply especially to the drama and the element of dramatic impersonation in epic poetry. The appeal of dramatic poetry is not to the reason but to a lower part, the emotions, which, like the senses, are subject to illusions. As optical and other such illusions can be corrected by the calculating and reflective part (logistikon) *which ascertains the true facts by measurement, so illusory exaggerations of feeling should be corrected by reflection. But the dramatist is concerned rather to rouse sympathetic emotion than to check its excesses, and while we enter into the joys or sorrows of a*

[1] Living in the world of appearances, the poet reproduces only 'the many conventional notions of the mass of mankind about what is beautiful or honourable or just' (479 D, p. 188).

[2] It should now be clear that this chapter is not concerned with aesthetic criticism, but with extravagant claims for the poets as moral teachers. It may leave the impression that Plato has been irritated by some contemporary controversy, and is overstating his case with a slightly malicious delight in paradox. At p. 341 he speaks of all this Part as a 'defence' of his earlier exclusion of poetry.

hero on the stage, the reason is held in abeyance. Thus drama is as far removed as visual art from true reality and from wisdom.

BUT now look here, said I; the content of this poetical representation is something at the third remove from reality, is it not?

Yes.

On what part of our human nature, then, does it produce its effect?

What sort of part do you mean?

Let me explain by an analogy. An object seen at a distance does not, of course, look the same size as when it is close at hand; a straight stick looks bent when part of it is under water; and the same thing appears concave or convex to an eye misled by colours. Every sort of confusion like these is to be found in our minds; and it is this weakness in our nature that is exploited, with a quite magical effect, by many tricks of illusion, like scene-painting and conjuring.

True.

But satisfactory means have been found for dispelling these illusions by measuring, counting, and weighing. We are no longer at the mercy of apparent differences of size and quantity and weight; the faculty which has done the counting and measuring or weighing takes control instead. And this can only be the work of the calculating or reasoning element in the soul.

True.

And when this faculty has done its measuring and announced that one quantity is greater than, or equal to, another, we often find that there is an appearance which contradicts it. Now, as we have said, it is impossible for the same part of the soul to hold two contradictory beliefs at the same time. Hence the part which agrees with the measurements must be a different part from the one which goes against them; and its confidence in measurement and calculation is a proof of its being the highest part; the other which contradicts it must be an inferior one.

It must.

This, then, was the conclusion I had in view when I said that paintings and works of art in general are far removed from reality, and that the element in our nature which is accessible to art and responds to its advances is equally far from wisdom. The offspring of a connexion thus formed on no true or sound basis must be as inferior as the parents. This will be true not only of visual art, but of art addressed to the ear, poetry as we call it.

Naturally.

Then, instead of trusting merely to the analogy from painting, let us directly consider that part of the mind to which the dramatic element in poetry [1] appeals, and see how much claim it has to serious worth. We can put the question in this way. Drama, we say, represents the acts and fortunes of human beings. It is wholly concerned with what they do, voluntarily or against their will, and how they fare, with the consequences which they regard as happy or otherwise, and with their feelings of joy and sorrow in all these experiences. That is all, is it not?

Yes.

And in all these experiences has a man an undivided mind? Is there not an internal conflict which sets him at odds with himself in his conduct, much as we were saying that the conflict of visual impressions leads him to make contradictory judgements? However, I need not ask that question; for, now I come to think of it, we have already agreed [2] that innumerable conflicts of this sort are constantly occurring in the mind. But there is a further point to be considered now. We have said [3] that a man of high character will bear any stroke of fortune, such as the loss of a son or of anything else he holds dear, with more equanimity than most people. We may now ask: will he feel no pain, or is that impossible? Will he not rather observe due measure in his grief?

Yes, that is nearer the truth.

Now tell me: will he be more likely to struggle with his grief and resist it when he is under the eyes of his fellows or when he is alone?

---

[1] That ἡ τῆς ποιήσεως μιμητική is here once more restricted to drama and the dramatic element in other poetry is clear from the definition of its content as 'the acts and fortunes of human beings' (πράττειν means both 'to act' and 'to fare' well or ill).

[2] In the analysis of the conflict of motives at 439 c ff., p. 136.

[3] At 387 D, p. 77.

He will be far more restrained in the presence of others.

Yes; when he is by himself he will not be ashamed to do and say much that he would not like anyone to see or hear.

Quite so.

What encourages him to resist his grief is the lawful authority of reason, while the impulse to give way comes from the feeling itself; and, as we said, the presence of contradictory impulses proves that two distinct elements in his nature must be involved. One of them is law-abiding, prepared to listen to the authority which declares that it is best to bear misfortune as quietly as possible without resentment, for several reasons: it is never certain that misfortune may not be a blessing; nothing is gained by chafing at it; nothing human is matter for great concern; and, finally, grief hinders us from calling in the help we most urgently need. By this I mean reflection on what has happened, letting reason decide on the best move in the game of life that the fall of the dice permits. Instead of behaving like a child who goes on shrieking after a fall and hugging the wounded part, we should accustom the mind to set itself at once to raise up the fallen and cure the hurt, banishing lamentation with a healing touch.

Certainly that is the right way to deal with misfortune.

And if, as we think, the part of us which is ready to act upon these reflections is the highest, that other part which impels us to dwell upon our sufferings and can never have enough of grieving over them is unreasonable, craven, and faint-hearted.

Yes.

Now this fretful temper gives scope for a great diversity of dramatic representation; whereas the calm and wise character in its unvarying constancy is not easy to represent, nor when represented is it readily understood, especially by a promiscuous gathering in a theatre, since it is foreign to their own habit of mind. Obviously, then, this steadfast disposition does not naturally attract the dramatic poet, and his skill is not designed to find favour with it. If he is to have a popular success, he must address himself to the fretful type with its rich variety of material for representation.

Obviously.

We have, then, a fair case against the poet and we may set him down as the counterpart of the painter, whom he resembles in two ways: his creations are poor things by the standard of truth and reality, and his appeal is not to the highest part of the soul, but to one which is equally inferior. So we shall be justified in not admitting him into a well-ordered commonwealth, because he stimulates and strengthens an element which threatens to undermine the reason. As a country may be given over into the power of its worst citizens while the better sort are ruined, so, we shall say, the dramatic poet sets up a vicious form of government in the individual soul: he gratifies that senseless part which cannot distinguish great and small, but regards the same things as now one, now the other; and he is an image-maker whose images are phantoms far removed from reality.

Quite true.

CHAPTER XXXVII (x. 605 c–608 b)

THE EFFECT OF DRAMATIC POETRY ON CHARACTER

A further psychological objection is that dramatic poetry, tragic or comic, by encouraging the sympathetic indulgence of emotions which we are ashamed to give way to in our own lives, undermines the character. If poetry cannot be defended from this charge, it must be restricted to celebrating the praises of the gods and of good men.

But, I continued, the heaviest count in our indictment is still to come. Dramatic poetry has a most formidable power of corrupting even men of high character, with a few exceptions.

Formidable indeed, if it can do that.

Let me put the case for you to judge. When we listen to some hero in Homer or on the tragic stage moaning over his sorrows in a long tirade, or to a chorus beating their breasts as they chant a lament, you know how the best of us enjoy giving ourselves up to follow the performance with eager sympathy. The more a poet can move our feelings in this way, the better we think him. And yet when the sorrow is our own, we pride ourselves on being able to bear it quietly like a man, condemning the behaviour we admired in the theatre as womanish. Can it be right that the spectacle of a man behaving as one would scorn and blush to behave oneself should be admired and enjoyed, instead of filling us with disgust?

No, it really does not seem reasonable.

It does not, if you reflect that the poet ministers to the satisfaction of that very part of our nature whose instinctive hunger to have its fill of tears and lamentations is forcibly restrained in the case of our own misfortunes. Meanwhile the noblest part of us, insufficiently schooled by reason or habit, has relaxed its watch over these querulous feelings, with the excuse that the sufferings we are contemplating are not our own and it is no shame to us to admire and pity a man with some pretensions to a noble character, though his grief may be excessive. The enjoyment itself seems a clear gain, which we cannot bring ourselves to forfeit by disdaining the whole poem. Few, I believe, are capable of reflecting that to enter into another's feelings must have an effect on our own: the emotions of pity our sympathy has strengthened will not be easy to restrain when we are suffering ourselves.

That is very true.

Does not the same principle apply to humour as well as to pathos? You are doing the same thing if, in listening at a comic performance or in ordinary life to buffooneries which you would be ashamed to indulge in yourself, you thoroughly enjoy them instead of being disgusted with their ribaldry. There is in you an impulse to play the clown, which you have held in restraint from a reasonable fear of being set down as a buffoon; but now you have given it rein, and by encouraging its impudence at the theatre you may be unconsciously carried away into playing the comedian in your private life. Similar effects are produced by poetic representation of love and anger and all those desires and feelings of pleasure or pain which accompany our every action. It waters the growth of passions which should be allowed to wither away and sets them up in control, although the goodness and happiness of our lives depend on their being held in subjection.

I cannot but agree with you.

If so, Glaucon, when you meet with admirers of Homer who tell you that he has been the educator of Hellas and that on questions of human conduct and culture he deserves to be constantly studied as a guide by whom to regulate your whole life, it is well to give a friendly hearing to such people, as entirely well-meaning according to their lights, and you may acknowledge Homer to be the first and greatest of the tragic poets; but you must be quite sure that we can admit into our commonwealth only the poetry which celebrates the praises of the gods and of good men. If you go further and admit the honeyed muse in epic or in lyric verse, then pleasure and pain will usurp the sovereignty of law and of the principles always recognized by common consent as the best.

Quite true.

So now, since we have recurred to the subject of poetry, let this be our defence: it stands to reason that we could not but banish such an influence from our commonwealth. But, lest poetry should convict us of being harsh and unmannerly, let us tell her further that there is a long-standing quarrel between poetry and philosophy. There are countless tokens of this old antagonism, such as the lines which speak of 'the cur which at his master yelps,' or 'one mighty in the vain talk of fools' or 'the throng of all-too-sapient heads,' or 'subtle thinkers all in rags.'[1] None the less, be it declared that, if the dramatic poetry whose end is to give pleasure can show good reason why it should exist in a well-governed society, we for our part should welcome it back, being ourselves conscious of its charm; only it would be a sin to betray what we believe to be the truth. You too, my friend, must have felt this charm, above all when poetry speaks through Homer's lips.

I have indeed.

It is fair, then, that before returning from exile poetry should publish her defence in lyric verse or some other measure; and I

---

[1] The source of these poetical attacks on philosophy is unknown. The earliest philosophers to denounce Homer and Hesiod had been Xenophanes and Heraclitus, about the beginning of the fifth century.

suppose we should allow her champions who love poetry but are not poets to plead for her in prose, that she is no mere source of pleasure but a benefit to society and to human life. We shall listen favourably; for we shall clearly be the gainers, if that can be proved.

Undoubtedly.

But if it cannot, then we must take a lesson from the lover who renounces at any cost a passion which he finds is doing him no good. The love for poetry of this kind, bred in us by our own much admired institutions, will make us kindly disposed to believe in her genuine worth; but so long as she cannot make good her defence we shall, as we listen, rehearse to ourselves the reasons we have just given, as a counter-charm to save us from relapsing into a passion which most people have never outgrown. We shall reiterate that such poetry has no serious claim to be valued as an apprehension of truth. One who lends an ear to it should rather beware of endangering the order established in his soul, and would do well to accept the view of poetry which we have expressed.

I entirely agree.

Yes, Glaucon; for much is at stake, more than most people suppose: it is a choice between becoming a good man or a bad; and poetry, no more than wealth or power or honours, should tempt us to be careless of justice and virtue.

Your argument has convinced me, as I think it would anyone else.

PART VI (Book X, 608 c–end)

IMMORTALITY AND THE REWARDS OF JUSTICE

SOCRATES now passes abruptly to claim for justice those rewards, in this life and after death, which it was originally agreed to exclude until the nature of justice and injustice and their inherent effects on the soul should have been defined. By the end of Part IV it had been shown that perfect justice would mean complete happiness, and perfect injustice the extreme of misery. Socrates, having thus met the challenge of Glaucon and Adeimantus by recommending justice purely for its own sake, is now entitled to bring in the question of external rewards. He first supports the immortality of the soul by a new proof. Then he argues that, on the whole, justice does pay in this life. Finally, the rewards and punishments which may await the soul in the unseen world and in other lives on earth are pictured in a myth illustrating the doctrine of reincarnation.

CHAPTER XXXVIII (x. 608 c–612 a)

A PROOF OF IMMORTALITY

The arguments for immortality in the Phaedo *are here supplemented by a proof based on the idea that everything has some peculiar evil or vicious condition which tends to destroy it. This is the opposite of its peculiar excellence or goodness* (areté), *which is defined by its function (353 B, 601 D, pp. 38 f., 333 f.), and can be thought of as constituting its essential nature. The soul's peculiar evil is moral evil or vice; and if anything could destroy the soul, it would be this denial of its true being. Vice, however, does not, in fact, cause death. The dissolution of the body is caused by the body's peculiar evils, and these cannot touch the soul.*

*The soul has been described earlier as having several 'parts';
but we are not to think of it as like a material thing made up of
parts into which it can be broken up and so destroyed. Both Plato
and Aristotle hold that the reason* (nous) *is man's true self and
indestructible essence. It seems to be suggested here that conjunction with the body entails the accretion of desires and functions indispensable to mortal life, but that these 'forms' or 'aspects' of soul
disappear with the death of the body, provided that the soul has
been 'purified' by devotion to the pursuit of wisdom.*

AND yet, said I, we have not so far described the chief wages of
virtue or the greatest prize it can hope to win.

It is hard to conceive any greater than those you have already
spoken of.

Can there be anything great in a short span of time? And, as
compared with all time, the whole of this life from childhood to old
age is short enough.

Indeed it is nothing.

Well, ought not an immortal thing to be more seriously concerned with all time than with so brief a span?

No doubt; but what do you mean by that?

Are you not aware that our soul is immortal and never perishes?

Glaucon looked at me in astonishment. Indeed I am not, he replied. Are you prepared to assert that?

I ought to be; and so, I think, ought you. There is no difficulty.

There is for me; but if you find it so easy a matter, I should like
to hear your account.

You shall. When you speak of a certain thing as 'a good,' and
of another as 'an evil,' do you agree with me in thinking of the
evil as always being the thing which corrupts and destroys, and
of the good as that which benefits and preserves?

Yes.

And would you say that everything has its peculiar evil as well
as its good, for instance, ophthalmia for the eyes, disease for the
body in general, mildew for grain, rot for timber, rust for iron
and copper—and, as I say, that almost anything has some special

evil or malady, which impairs the thing it attacks and ends by breaking it up and destroying it altogether?

Yes, no doubt.

Everything, then, is destroyed by its own peculiar evil or corruption; or if that will not destroy it, there is at any rate nothing else that can bring it to an end; for clearly what is good for it will never destroy it, nor yet what is neither good nor evil. Hence if we find that there is a thing whose peculiar evil does indeed deprave it but cannot bring about its utter dissolution, shall we not at once be sure that it is by nature indestructible?

That seems likely.

What of the soul, then? Has it not some special evil which depraves it?

Certainly; there are all the vices we have been speaking of, injustice, intemperance, cowardice, ignorance.

And does any of these vices work its complete destruction? We must be careful here not to be misled into supposing that when a wicked and foolish man is found out, he has been destroyed by his wickedness, which is a depraved condition of his soul. Think of it rather in this way. It is true of the body, is it not? that physical evil, namely disease, wastes and destroys it until it is no longer a body at all, and all the other things we instanced are annihilated by the pervading corruption of the evil which peculiarly besets them. Now is it true in the same way of the soul that injustice and other forms of vice, by besetting and pervading it, waste it away in corruption until they sever it from the body and bring about its death?[1]

No, certainly not.

On the other hand, it would be unreasonable to suppose that a thing which cannot be destroyed by its own vice should be destroyed by the vicious condition of something else. Observe that we should not think it proper to say of the body that it was destroyed simply by the badness of its food, which might be rotten

[1] In the *Phaedo* death is defined as the separation of the soul from the body. The definition is consistent with the indestructibility of soul, which Socrates there tries to prove; but another speaker voices the popular fear that the escaping soul may dissolve into air like smoke. Such would be the death of the soul here contemplated.

or mouldy; only when such food has induced a bad condition of the body itself do we say that the body is destroyed by its own diseased state, occasioned by the bad food. The body is one thing, the food another; and we shall not allow that the evil belonging to that other thing can ever destroy the body, unless it engenders the body's own peculiar evil. By the same reasoning, if bodily evil does not engender in the soul the soul's peculiar evil, we must never allow that the soul is destroyed merely by an evil peculiar to something else.

That is reasonable.

Either, then, we must prove this argument unsound, or, so long as it stands unrefuted, we must deny that fever or any other disease or even slaughtering the body and cutting it to atoms can effect anything towards the destruction of the soul, until it can be shown that the soul itself becomes more wicked and impure because the body suffers in those ways. We shall not allow anyone to say that the soul or anything else perishes merely through the occurrence in another thing of that other thing's peculiar evil.

Well, no one will ever prove that death makes the dying man's soul more wicked.

No; and if anyone does venture to challenge our argument and try to escape the conclusion that souls are immortal by asserting that a dying man does become wickeder, we shall argue that, if what he says is true, wickedness must be a sort of fatal disease with a power of its own to kill those who catch it, quickly or slowly according to the severity of the attack; instead of being merely the occasion of their death, which is in fact caused by other people who punish them for their crimes.

Yes, if that were so, surely there would be nothing very terrible about wickedness, for a fatal attack would be the end of all troubles. But I think we shall find that, on the contrary, it brings about the death of other people to the best of its power, and, far from being deadly to the wicked man himself, it makes him very much alive and fills him with an unsleeping energy.

You are right. For if its own evil and depravity cannot kill the soul, it is hardly likely that an evil designed for the destruction

of a different thing will destroy the soul or anything but its own
proper object. So, since the soul is not destroyed by any evil, either
its own or another's, clearly it must be a thing that exists for ever,
and is consequently immortal.

That follows.

Let us take this, then, as proved. And if it is so, there must
always be the same number of souls in existence. For if none
perishes, their number cannot grow less; nor yet can it be increased, since any increase of the immortal must come from the
mortal, and then all things would end by being immortal.[1]

True.

Well, reason forbids us to imagine that conclusion. And again,
we must not think of the soul, in her truest nature, as full of
diversity and unlikeness and perpetually at variance with herself.

In what way do you mean?

We were thinking just now [2] of the soul as composed of a number of parts not put together in the most satisfactory way; and such
a composite thing could hardly be everlasting.

Probably not.

Well then, that the soul is immortal is established beyond doubt
by our recent argument and the other proofs; [3] but to understand
her real nature, we must look at her, not as we see her now,
marred by association with the body and other evils, but when
she has regained that pure condition which the eye of reason can
discern; you will then find her to be a far lovelier thing and will
distinguish more clearly justice and injustice and all the qualities
we have discussed. Our description of the soul is true of her present appearance; but we have seen her afflicted by countless evils,

---

[1] In the *Phaedo* similar reasoning is employed to support the doctrine of reincarnation: if the soul at death passes into the state of 'being dead,' i.e. existing apart from
the body, and if there is no return journey, the stock of souls must finally be ex-
hausted and life on earth would come to an end. Plato, like any other Greek, would
regard the creation of a new soul out of nothing as impossible. But elsewhere it is
part of the same doctrine that the purified soul *can* escape from the wheel of birth
to dwell with the gods for ever.

[2] At 603 D, p. 337 f., and in the descriptions of injustice (444 B, p. 142) and of the
unjust man (Chap. XXXIV).

[3] Probably a reference to the *Phaedo*.

like the sea-god Glaucus,[1] whose original form can hardly be discerned, because parts of his body have been broken off or crushed and altogether marred by the waves, and the clinging overgrowth of weed and rock and shell has made him more like some monster than his natural self. But we must rather fix our eyes, Glaucon, on her love of wisdom and note how she seeks to apprehend and hold converse with the divine, immortal, and everlasting world to which she is akin, and what she would become if her affections were entirely set on following the impulse that would lift her out of the sea in which she is now sunken, and disencumber her of all that wild profusion of rock and shell, whose earthy substance has encrusted her, because she seeks what men call happiness by making earth her food. Then one might see her true nature, whatever it may be, whether manifold or simple. For the moment we have described—sufficiently, as I think—the aspects shown by the soul in the experiences of human life.

True, he replied.

CHAPTER XXXIX (x. 612 a–613 e)

THE REWARDS OF JUSTICE IN THIS LIFE

Before considering the fate of the soul after death, Socrates expresses a belief in the moral government of the world, which accounts for the sufferings of the righteous as due to offences in a former life. They are not to be attributed to the gods (cf. 379 c, p. 71). He also appeals to experience of life as showing that, on the whole, honesty is good policy. It is not true, as Thrasymachus maintained (343 d, p. 25), that the unjust always has the best of it.

AND now, I continued, we have fulfilled the conditions of the argument; in particular, we have not introduced those rewards

---

[1] Glaucus, it was said, saw a fish which he had caught and laid on a certain herb come to life. He ate the herb became immortal, and sprang into the sea.

which, as you two complained,[1] Homer and Hesiod hold out to men who have acquired a reputation for justice. We have found that, apart from all such consequences, justice is the best thing for the soul, which should do what is right, whether or not it possess the ring of Gyges and the cap of invisibility besides. Accordingly, there can now be no objection to our crediting justice and virtue in general with a full measure of those due rewards which they win for the soul from gods and men, both during life and after death.

I quite agree.

Then you must let me take back the concession I made when you asked me to grant, for the sake of argument, that the just man should have the reputation of being unjust, and the unjust man of being just. It might be impossible, you said, that heaven and mankind should be so deceived, but you wished that justice and injustice simply in themselves should be confronted for judgement. That judgement has now been given; and I must ask you in return to allow justice to enjoy the estimation in which it is actually held among gods and men. We have seen that justice never defrauds its possessor of the blessings that come of being really just. Let us now add the prizes which fall to those whose justice is apparent to all.

That is a fair demand.

You will concede, then, to begin with, that neither of the two characters is hidden from the sight of the gods, who will accordingly, as we agreed at the outset,[2] favour the just and hate the unjust. And the favourite of heaven may expect, in the fullest measure, all the blessings that heaven can give, save perhaps for some suffering entailed by offences in a former life. So we must suppose that, if the righteous man is afflicted with poverty or sickness or any other seeming evil, all this will come to some good for him in the end, either in this life or after death. For the gods, surely, can never be regardless of one who sets his heart on being just and making himself by the practice of virtue as like a god as man may.

[1] In Adeimantus' opening speech, 363 A, p. 48.
[2] In the argument with Thrasymachus at 352 B, p. 36.

No, naturally they would not neglect one who is like themselves.

And must we not think the opposite of the unjust man?

Most certainly.

Such, then, are the prizes which the just man wins from the gods. What may he expect from mankind? If we look at the facts, is it not true that the clever rogue is like the runner who runs well for the first half of the course, but flags before reaching the goal: he is quick off the mark, but ends in disgrace and slinks away crestfallen and uncrowned. The crown is the prize of the really good runner who perseveres to the end. Is it not usually so with the just, that towards the close of any course of action or of their dealings with other people or of life itself they win a good name and bear off the prize from the hands of their fellows?

Yes, that is true.

Will you allow me, then, to say now of the just all that you said yourself of the unjust: that when they are advanced in years they will hold positions of authority in their own country if they so desire, ally themselves in marriage to any family they choose, and so forth? Of the unjust, on the other hand, I will say that most of them, though they may go undetected in their youth, are caught and disgraced at the end of their course; in old age their misery is insulted by citizen and stranger alike; they are beaten and suffer all those torments which you truly called unmentionable: I need not repeat them. May I say all this?

Yes; it is a fair statement.

CHAPTER XL (x. 613 e–end)

THE REWARDS OF JUSTICE AFTER DEATH. THE MYTH OF ER

Several other dialogues (Gorgias, Phaedo, Phaedrus) *describe the fate of the soul before birth and after death in the poetical imagery of myth, since no certain knowledge is attainable, but Plato believed that the indestructible soul must reap the consequences of its deeds, good or bad. Unlike Dante, he leaves the scenery and topography of the other world fluid and vague. Probably some details are borrowed from dramatic representations or* tableaux vivants *shown to initiates in Orphic and other Mysteries.*[1] *Features common to Plato's myths and to Empedocles' religious poem, Pindar's* Dirges, *Orphic amulets found in graves, and Virgil's sixth* Aeneid, *point to a common source, which may have been an Orphic apocalypse, a* Descent of Orpheus to Hades. *They include the divine origin of the soul; its fall to be incarnated in a cycle of births as a penalty for former sins; the guardian genius; the judgement after death; the torments of the unjust and the happiness of the just in the millennial intervals between incarnations; the hope of final deliverance for the purified; and certain topographical features: the Meadow (probably adapted from the* Homeric Meadow of Asphodel*); the two Ways to right and left; the waters of Lethe (or of Unmindfulness, Ameles) and of Memory.*

A new feature, interpolated by Plato, is the vision of the structure of the universe, in which the 'pattern set up in the heavens' (592 B, p. 320) is revealed to the souls before they choose a new life. Plato's universe is spherical. At the circumference the fixed stars revolve in 24 hours from East to West, with a motion which carries with it all the contents of the world. Within the sphere are (1) the seven planets, including Sun and Moon, which all have also a contrary motion from West to East along the Zodiac. Their speeds differ. The Moon finishes its course in a month; the Sun, Venus, and Mercury in a year; while Mars, Jupiter, and Saturn have an additional motion ('counter-revolution,' 617 B) which slows them down so that Mars takes nearly 2 years, Jupiter about 12, and Saturn nearly 30. (2) The Earth at the centre rotates daily on its axis (which is also the axis of the universe) so as exactly to counteract the daily rotation in the opposite sense of the whole universe, with the result that the earth is at rest in absolute space,

[1] Gilbert Murray, 'The Conception of Another Life,' *Edin. Rev.*, 1914, reprinted in *Stoic, Christian and Humanist*, 1940. A learned and sober account of Orphism will be found in W. K. C. Guthrie's *Orpheus and Greek Religion*, 1935. Dieterich's *Nekyia* contains a study of the eschatological myths.

while the heavenly bodies revolve round it. (This interpretation of Plato's astronomy is explained and defended in F. M. Cornford, Plato's Cosmology, 1937.)

What the souls actually see in their vision is not the universe itself, but a model,[1] *a primitive orrery in a form roughly resembling a spindle, with its shaft round which at the lower end is fastened a solid hemispherical whorl. In the orrery the shaft represents the axis of the universe and the whorl consists of 8 hollow concentric hemispheres, fitted into one another 'like a nest of bowls,' and capable of moving separately. It is as if the upper halves of 8 concentric spheres had been cut away so that the internal 'works' might be seen. The rims of the bowls appear as forming a continuous flat surface; they represent the equator of the sphere of fixed stars and, inside that, the orbits of the 7 planets. The souls see the Spindle resting on the knees of Necessity. The whole mechanism is turned by the Fates, Clotho (the Spinner), Lachesis (She who allots), and Atropos (the Inflexible). Sirens sing eight notes at consonant intervals forming the structure of a scale* (harmonia), *which represents the Pythagorean 'music of the spheres.'*

All this imagery is, of course, mythical and symbolic. The underlying doctrine is that in human life there is an element of necessity or chance, but also an element of free choice, which makes us, and not Heaven, responsible for the good and evil in our lives.

SUCH then, I went on, are the prizes, rewards, and gifts that the just man may expect at the hands of gods and men in his lifetime, in addition to those other blessings which come simply from being just.

Yes, the rewards are splendid and sure.

These, however, are as nothing, in number or in greatness, when compared with the recompense awaiting the just and the unjust after death. This must now be told, in order that each may be paid in full what the argument shows to be his due.

---

[1] So J. A. Stewart, *Myths of Plato,* 165: 'a vision within the larger vision of the whole Myth of Er.' It appears that there were no diagrams in Plato's MSS.; so he sometimes helps the reader to imagine a complicated structure by reference to a

Go on; there are not many things I would sooner hear about.

My story will not be like Odysseus' tale to Alcinous; [1] but its hero was a valiant man, Er, the son of Armenius, a native of Pamphylia, who was killed in battle. When the dead were taken up for burial ten days later, his body alone was found undecayed. They carried him home, and two days afterwards were going to bury him, when he came to life again as he lay on the funeral pyre. He then told what he had seen in the other world.

He said that, when the soul had left his body, he journeyed with many others until they came to a marvellous place, where there were two openings side by side in the earth, and opposite them two others in the sky above. Between them sat Judges, [2] who, after each sentence given, bade the just take the way to the right upwards through the sky, first binding on them in front tokens signifying the judgement passed upon them. The unjust were commanded to take the downward road to the left, and these bore evidence of all their deeds fastened on their backs. When Er himself drew near, they told him that he was to carry tidings of the other world to mankind, and he must now listen and observe all that went on in that place. Accordingly he saw the souls which had been judged departing by one of the openings in the sky and one of those in the earth; while at the other two openings souls were coming up out of the earth travel-stained and dusty, or down from the sky clean and bright. Each company, as if they had come on a long journey, seemed glad to turn aside into the Meadow, where they encamped like pilgrims at a festival. Greetings passed between acquaintances, and as either party questioned the other of what had befallen them, some wept as they sorrowfully recounted all that they had seen and suffered on their journey

familiar object, such as the fish-trap in *Timaeus* 78 B. But here, of course, the Spindle is also symbolic.

[1] Odysseus' recital of his adventures to Alcinous, King of Phaeacia, fills four books of the *Odyssey*, including Odysseus' voyage to the realm of the dead, which Plato would reject as a misleading picture of the after-life. It became proverbial for a long story.

[2] In the myth of the Judgement of the Dead in the *Gorgias*, 523 E, Minos, Rhadamanthys, and Aeacus give judgement 'in the Meadow at the parting of the two ways, one to the Islands of the Blest, the other to Tartarus.'

under the earth, which had lasted a thousand years;[1] while others spoke of the joys of heaven and sights of inconceivable beauty. There was much, Glaucon, that would take too long to tell; but the sum, he said, was this. For every wrong done to any man sinners had in due course paid the penalty ten times over, that is to say, once in each hundred years, such being the span of human life, in order that the punishment for every offence might be tenfold. Thus, all who have been guilty of bringing many to death or slavery by betraying their country or their comrades in arms, or have taken part in any other iniquity, suffer tenfold torments for each crime; while deeds of kindness and a just and sinless life are rewarded in the same measure. Concerning infants who die at birth or live but a short time he had more to say, not worthy of mention.[2]

The wages earned by honouring the gods and parents, or by dishonouring them and by doing murder, were even greater. He was standing by when one spirit asked another, 'Where is Ardiaeus the Great?' This Ardiaeus had been despot in some city of Pamphylia just a thousand years before, and, among many other wicked deeds, he was said to have killed his old father and his elder brother. The answer was: 'He has not come back hither, nor will he ever come. This was one of the terrible sights we saw. When our sufferings were ended and we were near the mouth, ready to pass upwards, suddenly we saw Ardiaeus and others with him. Most of them were despots, but there were some private persons who had been great sinners. They thought that at last they were going to mount upwards, but the mouth would not admit them; it bellowed whenever one whose wickedness was incurable or who had not paid the penalty in full tried to go up.[3] Then certain fierce and fiery-looking men, who stood by and knew what

---

[1] This figure, probably taken from some Orphic or Pythagorean source, is repeated by Virgil, *Aeneid,* vi. 748.

[2] This suggests that a limbo for infants was a feature of the Orphic apocalypse. It appears in *Aeneid* vi. 426 ff., discussed by Cumont, *After-Life in Roman Paganism,* 128 ff.

[3] So in Virgil, *Georgic* iv. 493, a roar is heard when Orpheus, returning from Hades with Eurydice, looks back, and Eurydice vanishes.

the sound meant, seized some and carried them away; but Ardiaeus and others they bound hand and foot and neck and flinging them down flayed them. They dragged them along the wayside, carding their flesh like wool with thorns and telling all who passed by why this was done to them and that they were being taken to be cast into Tartarus. We had gone through many terrors of every sort, but none so great as the fear each man felt lest the sound should come as he went up; and when it was not heard, his joy was great.' Such were the judgements and penalties, and the blessings received were in corresponding measure.

Now when each company had spent seven days in the Meadow, on the eighth they had to rise up and journey on. And on the fourth day afterwards they came to a place whence they could see a straight shaft of light, like a pillar, stretching from above throughout heaven and earth, more like the rainbow than anything else, but brighter and purer. To this they came after a day's journey, and there, at the middle of the light, they saw stretching from heaven the extremities of its chains; for this light binds the heavens, holding together all the revolving firmament, like the undergirths of a ship of war.[1]

And from the extremities stretched the Spindle of Necessity, by means of which all the circles revolve. The shaft of the Spindle and the hook were of adamant, and the whorl partly of adamant and partly of other substances. The whorl was of this fashion. In shape it was like an ordinary whorl; but from Er's account we must imagine it as a large whorl with the inside completely scooped out, and within it a second smaller whorl, and a third and a fourth and four more, fitting into one another like a nest of bowls. For there were in all eight whorls, set one within another, with their rims showing above as circles and making up the continuous surface of a single whorl round the shaft, which pierces right through the centre of the eighth. The circle forming the rim of the

---

[1] Undergirths were ropes or braces used, either as fixtures or as temporary expedients, to strengthen a ship's hull. Acts xxvii. 17: 'they used helps, undergirding the ship.' It is disputed whether the bond holding the universe together is simply the straight axial shaft or a circular band of light, suggested by the Milky Way, girdling the heaven of Fixed Stars.

first and outermost whorl (Fixed Stars) is the broadest;[1] next in breadth is the sixth (Venus); then the fourth (Mars); then the eighth (Moon); then the seventh (Sun); then the fifth (Mercury); then the third (Jupiter); and the second (Saturn) is narrowest of all. The rim of the largest whorl (Fixed Stars) was spangled; the seventh (Sun) brightest; the eighth (Moon) coloured by the reflected light of the seventh; the second and fifth (Saturn, Mercury) like each other and yellower; the third (Jupiter) whitest; the fourth (Mars) somewhat ruddy; the sixth (Venus) second in whiteness. The Spindle revolved as a whole with one motion; but, within the whole as it turned, the seven inner circles revolved slowly in the opposite direction; and of these the eighth (Moon) moved most swiftly; second in speed and all moving together, the seventh, sixth, and fifth (Sun, Venus, Mercury); next in speed moved the fourth (Mars) with what appeared to them to be a counter-revolution;[2] next the third (Jupiter), and slowest of all the second (Saturn).

The Spindle turned on the knees of Necessity. Upon each of its circles stood a Siren, who was carried round with its movement, uttering a single sound on one note, so that all the eight made up the concords of a single scale.[3] Round about, at equal distances,

[1] The breadth of the rims is most simply explained as standing for the supposed distances of the orbits from each other. Thus the breadth of the outermost rim would be the distance between the Fixed Stars and Saturn. The names of the planets are given in the *Epinomis,* which was either Plato's latest work or composed by an immediate pupil: Aphrodite (Venus), Hermes (Mercury), Ares (Mars), Zeus (Jupiter), Kronos (Saturn). It is there implied that the Greeks took these names from the Syrians, substituting for Syrian gods the Greek gods identified with them.

[2] I understand this motion to be a self-motion of the three outer planets, Mars, Jupiter, Saturn, slowing down the 'contrary motion' shared by all the planets, so that these three fall farther and farther behind the Sun-Venus-Mercury group and *appear* to be moving in the opposite sense with a 'counter-revolution,' though really moving more slowly in the same sense. See *Plato's Cosmology,* 88.

[3] Aristotle, *de caelo* ii. 9: 'It seems to some thinkers [Pythagoreans] that bodies so great must inevitably produce a sound by their movement: even bodies on the earth do so . . . and as for the sun and the moon, and the stars, so many in number and enormous in size, all moving at a tremendous speed, it is incredible that they should fail to produce a noise of surpassing loudness. Taking this as their hypothesis, and also that the speeds of the stars, judged by their distances, are in the ratios of the musical consonances, they affirm that the sound of the stars as they revolve is concordant. To meet the difficulty that none of us is aware of this

were seated, each on a throne, the three daughters of Necessity, the Fates, robed in white with garlands on their heads, Lachesis, Clotho, and Atropos, chanting to the Sirens' music, Lachesis of things past, Clotho of the present, and Atropos of things to come. And from time to time Clotho lays her right hand on the outer rim of the Spindle and helps to turn it, while Atropos turns the inner circles likewise with her left, and Lachesis with either hand takes hold of inner and outer alternately.

The souls, as soon as they came, were required to go before Lachesis. An Interpreter first marshalled them in order; and then, having taken from the lap of Lachesis a number of lots and samples of lives, he mounted on a high platform and said:

'The word of Lachesis, maiden daughter of Necessity. Souls of a day, here shall begin a new round of earthly life, to end in death. No guardian spirit will cast lots for you,[1] but you shall choose your own destiny. Let him to whom the first lot falls choose first a life to which he will be bound of necessity. But Virtue owns no master: as a man honours or dishonours her, so shall he have more of her or less. The blame is his who chooses; Heaven is blameless.'[2]

With these words the Interpreter scattered the lots among them all. Each took up the lot which fell at his feet and showed what number he had drawn; only Er himself was forbidden to take one. Then the Interpreter laid on the ground before them the sample lives, many more than the persons there. They were of every sort: lives of all living creatures, as well as of all conditions of men. Among them were lives of despots, some continuing in power to the end, others ruined in mid course and ending in pov-

sound, they account for it by saying that the sound is with us right from birth and has thus no contrasting silence to show it up; for voice and silence are perceived by contrast with each other, and so all mankind is undergoing an experience like that of a coppersmith, who becomes by long habit indifferent to the din around him' (trans. W. K. C. Guthrie). Aristotle refutes this theory.

[1] The idea that the *daemon* (guardian spirit, genius, personified destiny) has an individual allotted to it as its portion appears in Lysias, *Epitaphius* 78, Theocritus iv. 40, and Plato's *Phaedo* (myth) 107 D.

[2] These last words 'became a kind of rallying-cry among the champions of the freedom of the will in the early Christian era' (Adam). They are inscribed on a bust of Plato of the first century B.C. found at Tibur.

erty, exile, or beggary. There were lives of men renowned for beauty of form and for strength and prowess, or for distinguished birth and ancestry; also lives of unknown men; and of women likewise. All these qualities were variously combined with one another and with wealth or poverty, health or sickness, or intermediate conditions; but in none of these lives was there anything to determine the condition of the soul, because the soul must needs change its character according as it chooses one life or another.

Here, it seems, my dear Glaucon, a man's whole fortunes are at stake. On this account each one of us should lay aside all other learning, to study only how he may discover one who can give him the knowledge enabling him to distinguish the good life from the evil, and always and everywhere to choose the best within his reach, taking into account all these qualities we have mentioned and how, separately or in combination, they affect the goodness of life. Thus he will seek to understand what is the effect, for good or evil, of beauty combined with wealth or with poverty and with this or that condition of the soul, or of any combination of high or low birth, public or private station, strength or weakness, quickness of wit or slowness, and any other qualities of mind, native or acquired; until, as the outcome of all these calculations, he is able to choose between the worse and the better life with reference to the constitution of the soul, calling a life worse or better according as it leads to the soul becoming more unjust or more just. All else he will leave out of account; for, as we have seen, this is the supreme choice for a man, both while he lives and after death. Accordingly, when he goes into the house of death he should hold this faith like adamant, that there too he may not be dazzled by wealth and such-like evils, or fling himself into the life of a despot or other evil-doer, to work irremediable harm and suffer yet worse things himself, but may know how to choose always the middle course that avoids both extremes, not only in this life, so far as he may, but in every future existence; for there lies the greatest happiness for man.

To return to the report of the messenger from the other world. The Interpreter then said: 'Even for the last comer, if he choose with discretion, there is left in store a life with which, if he will live strenuously, he may be content and not unhappy. Let not the first be heedless in his choice, nor the last be disheartened.'

After these words, he who had drawn the first lot at once seized upon the most absolute despotism he could find. In his thoughtless greed he was not careful to examine the life he chose at every point, and he did not see the many evils it contained and that he was fated to devour his own children; but when he had time to look more closely, he began to beat his breast and bewail his choice, forgetting the warning proclaimed by the Interpreter; for he laid the blame on fortune, the decrees of the gods, anything rather than himself. He was one of those who had come down from heaven, having spent his former life in a well-ordered commonwealth and become virtuous from habit without pursuing wisdom. It might indeed be said that not the least part of those who were caught in this way were of the company which had come from heaven, because they were not disciplined by suffering; whereas most of those who had come up out of the earth, having suffered themselves and seen others suffer, were not hasty in making their choice. For this reason, and also because of the chance of the lot, most of the souls changed from a good life to an evil, or from an evil life to a good. Yet, if upon every return to earthly life a man seeks wisdom with his whole heart, and if the lot so fall that he is not among the last to choose, then this report gives good hope that he will not only be happy here, but will journey to the other world and back again hither, not by the rough road underground, but by the smooth path through the heavens.

It was indeed, said Er, a sight worth seeing, how the souls severally chose their lives—a sight to move pity and laughter and astonishment; for the choice was mostly governed by the habits of their former life. He saw one soul choosing the life of a swan; this had once been the soul of Orpheus, which so hated all womankind because of his death at their hands that it would not consent to be born of woman.[1] And he saw the soul of Thamyras[2]

---

[1] Orpheus was torn in pieces by the Maenads, the women-worshippers of Dionysus.

[2] Another singer, who was deprived of sight and of the gift of song for challenging the Muses to a contest.

take the life of a nightingale, and a swan choose to be changed
into a man, and other musical creatures do the same. The soul
which drew the twentieth lot took a lion's life; this had been Ajax,
the son of Telamon, who shrank from being born as a man, remembering the judgement concerning the arms of Achilles.[1] After
him came the soul of Agamemnon,[2] who also hated mankind because of his sufferings and took in exchange the life of an eagle.
Atalanta's [3] soul drew a lot about half-way through. She took the
life of an athlete, which she could not pass over when she saw the
great honours he would win. After her he saw the soul of Epeius,[4]
son of Panopeus, passing into the form of a craftswoman; and far
off, among the last, the buffoon Thersites' soul clothing itself in
the body of an ape. It so happened that the last choice of all fell to
the soul of Odysseus, whose ambition was so abated by memory
of his former labours that he went about for a long time looking
for a life of quiet obscurity. When at last he found it lying somewhere neglected by all the rest, he chose it gladly, saying that he
would have done the same if his lot had come first. Other souls in
like manner passed from beasts into men and into one another, the
unjust changing into the wild creatures, the just into the tame, in
every sort of combination.

Now when all the souls had chosen their lives, they went in the
order of their lots to Lachesis; and she gave each into the charge of
the guardian genius he had chosen, to escort him through life and
fulfil his choice. The genius led the soul first to Clotho, under her
hand as it turned the whirling Spindle, thus ratifying the portion
which the man had chosen when his lot was cast. And, after touching her, he led it next to the spinning of Atropos, thus making
the thread of destiny irreversible. Thence, without looking back,
he passed under the throne of Necessity. And when he and all the

---

[1] After Achilles' death a contest between Ajax and Odysseus for his arms ended
in the defeat and suicide of Ajax. The first mention is in *Odyssey* xi. 543, where
the soul of Ajax, summoned from Hades, will not speak to Odysseus.

[2] The conqueror of Troy, murdered by his wife Clytemnestra on his return home.

[3] Atalanta's suitors had to race with her for her hand and were killed if defeated. Milanion won by dropping three golden apples given him by Aphrodite,
which Atalanta paused to pick up.

[4] Maker of the wooden horse in which the Greek chieftains entered Troy.

rest had passed beyond the throne, they journeyed together to the Plain of Lethe through terrible stifling heat; for the plain is bare of trees and of all plants that grow on the earth. When evening came, they encamped beside the River of Unmindfulness, whose water no vessel can hold. All are required to drink a certain measure of this water, and some have not the wisdom to save them from drinking more. Every man as he drinks forgets everything. When they had fallen asleep, at midnight there was thunder and an earthquake, and in a moment they were carried up, this way and that, to their birth, like shooting stars. Er himself was not allowed to drink of the water. How and by what means he came back to the body he knew not; but suddenly he opened his eyes and found himself lying on the funeral pyre at dawn.

And so, Glaucon, the tale was saved from perishing; and if we will listen, it may save us, and all will be well when we cross the river of Lethe. Also we shall not defile our souls; but, if you will believe with me that the soul is immortal and able to endure all good and ill, we shall keep always to the upward way and in all things pursue justice with the help of wisdom. Then we shall be at peace with Heaven and with ourselves, both during our sojourn here and when, like victors in the Games collecting gifts from their friends, we receive the prize of justice; and so, not here only, but in the journey of a thousand years of which I have told you, we shall fare well.

εὖ πράττωμεν

INDEX

Academy, xxvi f.; programme of studies at, 211

ADEIMANTUS, xv

ALCIBIADES, xviii, 202

ANAXAGORAS, xxiv

ANYTUS, xvii

Appetite, conflicts with reason, 133 ff.; necessary and unnecessary, 283 f.; unlawful, in dreams, 296; pleasures of, illusory, 307, 312 f.

ARCHYTAS, xxvii, 236, 243, 247

Aristocracy, rule of the best, 145

ARISTOTLE, at Academy, xxvii; on virtue and happiness, 36; on periods of life, 269

Arithmetic, 237 ff., 240 ff.

Art, has no interest but its own perfection, 22 f.; of living, 30; effect of, on character, 88 ff.; censorship of, 90; represents appearances, 321 ff.; twice removed from reality, 327 f., 334 f.; appeals to emotions, not to reason, 335

ASCLEPIUS, 95 ff.

Astronomy, 246 ff.; Plato's system of, 349 f.

Athletes, training of, 93 f.; ferocity of, 100

Auxiliaries, distinguished from Rulers, 102 ff.; manner of life of, 107 f.; have only right belief, 119 ff.; courage of state resides in, 122 f.

Beauty, absolute, 183 f., 201 f.; as aspect of the Good, 221

Belief (*Doxa*), civic virtue based on, 119 ff.; compared to dye, 123; opposed to knowledge, 180 ff.; object of, 184 ff.; fallible, 185 f.; blind without knowledge, 216 f.; second stage of cognition (*pistis*), 222

BENDIS, festival of, 2

BIAS, on friends and enemies, 173

Breeding, eugenic, 158

CALLICLES, xx ff.

CALLIPOLIS, 244

Cave, Allegory of the, 227 ff.; application of, 231 ff., 252 f.; philosopher must return to, 261

CEPHALUS, 2 ff.

CHARMIDES, xvii

Cognition, four stages of, 221 ff., 254

Comedy, effect of, on character, 338 f.

Communism, *see* Private Property *and* Marriage

Constitution, degenerate forms of, 145 f., 264 ff.; results from individual characters, 267

Courage, as virtue of state, 119, 122 ff.; as virtue of individual, 140

CRITIAS, xvii

Currency, as token for exchange, 58

DAMON, 88

Death, not terrible, 76 f.

Delphic Oracle, to regulate religion, 118, 171 f., 262; to approve marriage regulations, 162

Democracy, at Athens, 279; origin of, 280 f.; described, 282 ff.; passes into Despotism, 288; three classes in, 290 f.

Democratic Man, 283 ff.; developed from Oligarch, 297

Desire, diverted to new objects, 191, 301

Despot, as people's champion, 291 f.; human wolf, 292; demands bodyguard, 292; provokes wars, 293; purges the state, 293; robs the people, 295; unhappiness of, 302 ff.; tormented after death, 352 f.

Despotic Man, 296 ff.; origin of, 298; life of, 298 f.; as perfectly unjust man 301; a slave, 303 f.